Reconfiguring the Historical Landscape of Rajasthan

Essays for G.S.L. Devra

Prof. G.S.L. Devra

Reconfiguring the Historical Landscape of Rajasthan
Essays for G.S.L. Devra

Edited by
Mayank Kumar
Suraj Bhan Bharadwaj
Rameshwar Prasad Bahuguna
Sangeeta Sharma

Reconfiguring the Historical Landscape of Rajasthan: Essays for G.S.L. Devra

Edited by Mayank Kumar, Suraj Bhan Bharadwaj, Rameshwar Prasad Bahuguna, Sangeeta Sharma

First Published 2021

ISBN 978-93-5002-693-9

Published by
AAKAR BOOKS
28 E Pocket IV, Mayur Vihar Phase I
Delhi 110 091 India
aakarbooks@gmail.com

Laser Typeset at
Arpit Printographers, Delhi

Printed at
Sapra Brothers, Noida

Contents

Preface

In an era when there was no photocopy machine, no cellphone, no internets and very limited telephonic connectivity, and working with an institution which like most others, had very meagre funds to provide access to academia in general and global in particular, it goes to the credit of Prof. Ghanshyam Lal Devra to transcend these physical barriers and produce historical literature which always remained very contemporary. It is no less than a miracle to witness a historian working at Dungar College, Bikaner, a remote city located on the boundary of great and little Indian Thar Desert to be so contemporary in the selection of themes for historical investigations. He along with his contemporaries like Prof. G.D. Sharma, Prof. S.P. Gupta, Prof. Dilbagh Singh, etc toiled hard in the extremes of summers and winters of the little Indian Desert to unearth the true potential of sources preserved at the archives. His ability to read regional dialects distinguished him from his contemporaries and his quest led him to locate sources at the most unexpected places. Moreover, it was his perseverance to engage with the historical records and gifted ability to appreciate the historical significance of those documents/ sources that helped him explore new dimensions of history of Rajasthan particularly between 16-19th centuries. Highly impressed by the writings of Prof. Satish Chandra, he wanted to pursue doctoral research under his guidance, but soon Prof. Chandra got administrative assignment with University Grants Commission restricting this possibility. However, the impression of Prof. Satish Chandra's writing is quite visible in the historical sensibilities of Prof. Devra. Subsequently he completed his doctoral thesis on 'Administration of the Bikaner State (1574-1818 A.D.)' under the supervision of Prof. Parihar in the year 1976.

Soon after he received the prestigious *Commonwealth Academic Staff Fellowship* in 1982-83 and *Maison des sciences de l home*, Paris, in the year 1983. Subsequently he was awarded the Nehru Memorial Museum and Library Fellowship, 1985-88 and Indian Council of Historical Research fellowship 1992-94. Although, his sources did hint at problems with the contemporary political boundaries, his interactions with scholars made him all the more aware of the limitations of present day political boundaries. He also became aware that contemporary history writing traditions in India, especially pertaining to the medieval period desperately needed to revisit its own orientations. He soon realized that though politico-legal and agrarian-administrative history have their own relevance, historical researches were engaging with new sets of issues with fresh approach towards 'historical sources'.

Prof. Ghanshyam Lal Devra is one such historian who has very eloquently transcended the limitations of modern day geographical boundaries of nation states and linguistic barriers. Along with this he has also challenged the conventional disciplinary boundaries of historical research. If his doctoral research can be classified as agrarian-administrative-economic history then his subsequent writings covered social and cultural history, expanding further to include the emerging field of environmental history. His eagerness to go beyond the so called conventional sources of history has enabled him to explore some of the unexplored dimensions of medieval histories of communities and landscapes. Similarly the expanse of geographical and spatial canvas of his historical sensibilities is visible in his integration of *longue durée* with the structures and events. He remained deeply aware of the social responsibilities of a historian and therefore he regularly contributed articles in the news dailies. At the same time his commitment to organizations of professional historians was evident in his regular participation in the annual sessions of the Indian History Congress, Rajasthan History Congress, and Punjab History Congress, etc.

His doctoral work *Rajasthan ki Prashasnik Vyastha—Bikaner Rajya ke Sandarbha Men* (1574-1818 A.D.) (Administrative System of Rajasthan—with reference to the Bikaner State (1574-1818 A.D.), Dharati Prakashan, Bikaner, 1981 showcases his command over archival sources. *Bureaucracy in Rajasthan, 1745-1829 A.D.*, Dharati Prakashan, Bikaner examines the nuances of early modern bureaucratic setup which was influenced by the Mughal Jagirdari system and the land revenue system. His occasional paper while associated with Nehru Memorial Museum and Library, *A Rethinking on the Politics of Commercial Classes in Pre-colonial India: From Mutassadi to Marwaris*, Occasional Paper, No. XXXVIII, Nehru Memorial Museum and Library, New Delhi, March, 1987 was well received by the academia. Exploring the inter-linkages between trade and commerce on one hand and land revenue system on the other and integrating the commercial potential unleashed by the coming of European trading companies with the new possibilities for investment for the indigenous wealthy sections in more ways than one transcends the artificial boundary of medieval and modern history.

As pointed out earlier Prof. Devra remained committed to his quest for sources which resulted in several research articles: 'Dayaldas as a historian', in *Historians of Rajasthan* (ed. G.N. Sharma), Centre for Rajasthan Studies, University of Rajasthan, Jaipur, 1978; *Kagdo ri Bahis* of the Rampuria Records, Bikaner (Rajasthan State Archives, Bikaner), *Indian History Congress Proceedings* (Summary), 1972; 'Archival Sources of the Panchayat System in Rajasthan—1700-1800 A.D', in *The Sources of Social and Economic History of Rajasthan* (ed. by G.N. Sharma), Centre for Rajasthan Studies, University of Rajasthan, Jaipur, 1977; 'A Study of the Sources Available in the Anoop Sanskrit Library Bikaner,' in *Parampara*, January-March, 1985, Jodhpur, Rajasthan Research Institute, Chopasani; 'Sources on Trade and Trade Routes of Western Rajasthan available in England', in *Sources of Socio-Economic History of Rajasthan and Malwa'* (ed. N.S. Bhati), Jodhpur, 1989, Rajasthani Research Institute, Chopasni; 'Khyat Writing Traditions of the Bikaner State', *Vaichariki*, January-March, 1999, Vidya Shodh Pratishthan, Bikaner. Prof. Devra in his Presidential Address to Rajasthan History Congress in the year 2001, investigated the complex relationship between *Traditional Society and Modern Historical Writings*.

Furthermore, his quest for sources went beyond archival-literary sources and he was very eager to integrate material culture in his analysis of historical processes. Epigraphic sources supplemented his investigations in the historical geography. 'Mehrauli Pillar Inscription of Chandra—One More Study', *Shodh Patrika*, Purnank, 216-17, July-December 2003, Institute of Rajasthan Studies, Rajasthan Vidyapeeth, Udaipur and 'Bhadrakali Temple of Hanumangarh—A Buddhist Archaeological Site of Historical Importance', in *Social and Religious Sources of Rajasthan* (ed. by S.N. Dube), Centre for Rajasthan Studies, University of Rajasthan, Jaipur, 1996; 'Salt Trade Routes of Western India: A Study Based on the Survey Reports of James Tod', Keynote Address at the seminar on *Trade Routes and Urbanization in India with Special Reference to Rajasthan*, Department of History, J.N. Vyas University of Jodhpur, Jodhpur, 21-22 February 2009, published in *Trade Routes, Trade Centres and Urbanization in Western India* (ed. S.P. Vyas), Rajasthani Granthagar, Jodhpur, 2014.

Following set of papers are testimony to his historical sensibility which made him question the limitation of present day political boundaries in the historical investigations of medieval societies. His Presidential Address: 'Political Zone vs. Historical Zone', at the Punjab History, Punjabi University, Patiala in March, 2001 captures his dilemmas and responses to the above mentioned question. Captured 'Trade Relations Between Rajasthan and Sindh/Multan (1650-1800 A.D.)'. Cutting across modern day national boundaries, his paper published in the Indian History Congress Proceedings, 1978,

Moving beyond the immediate neighbourhood of Rajasthan, he went on to examine the 'Ethnicity of Shansabānis of Ghūr (Central Asia): A Study Based on Rajasthani (Indian) Sources', presented at the 19th Conference of International Association of Asian Historians, held at Manila (Philippines), 2006. Paper was published as part of conference proceedings. Another one titled, 'Mongols and Rajputs: A study of the Historical Ethnicity of Martial Races of Rajasthan and Central Asia', was published in *Culture, Polity and Economy* (ed. by Varsha Joshi and Surjit Singh), Rawat, Jaipur 2009. He continued with his investigation: 'Evolution of Antagonistic Rituals in Pre-modern Societies of Asia: A Case Study of Śaka' in '*Ritual Dynamics and Science of Rituals (State, Power and Violence)*', Vol. III, Section IV, *'State and Ritual in India'* (ed. Hermann Kulke and Uwe Skoda), Horrassowitz Verlag, Wiesbaden, 2010. The tradition continued: कुछ अफगान कबीलों की नस्लों की उत्पत्ति का आलोचनात्मक अध्ययन–राजस्थानी स्रोतों के आधार पर (Descent of Some Afghan Races of Afghanistan: A Study Based on Rajasthani Sources), *Jignasa*, Vol. XXI-XXII, 2014-15, Department of History and Indian Culture, University of Rajasthan, Jaipur.

As is evident from the above writings, Prof. Devra was immensely interested in the ethno-history of communities. A cursory glimpse of the following articles captures his grasp over the historical evolution of various communities of the region. It is interesting to note that his quest for historical evolution often encouraged him to transcend the present day political boundaries as pointed out above. To begin with, 'The Internal Expansion of Society and Formation of Medieval Polity,' Presidential Address, Medieval Indian Section, 59th Session, Indian History Congress Proceedings, Patiala, 1998; it was followed by 'Formation and Settlement of Jat Societies in the Northwest Regions of the Indian Sub-continent During the Early Medieval Period', Keynote Address published in the proceedings of the seminar, *The Jats: Their Role and Contribution in the Socio-Economic Llife and Polity of North and Northwest India* (ed. Veer Singh), Maharaja Surajmal Research Centre and Institute, New Delhi, 2007. It is not surprising that a historian interested in historical geography would soon examine the ecological context to explain the historical evolution of communities in a very harsh ecology of western Rajasthan. Thus we have, 'Environmental Crisis and Social Dismemberment in Northwest India During the Pre-colonial Period', Occasional Paper, New Series 3, Nehru Memorial Museum and Library, New Delhi, 2012.

His voyages highlighting the significance of ecological factors has a long list of publications to his credit but his paper 'Desertification and Problem of Delimitation of Rajputana Desert During the Medieval Period,' in *Rajasthan (Ecology, Culture and Society)* (eds. M.K. Bhasin and Veena Bhasin), Raj Publication, Delhi, 1999, (also published in Hindi by J.S. Gehlot Research Institute, Jodhpur) stands out in terms of historical understanding. 'Dust Storms Over Citadels of Northwest India and Afghanistan (A Study of Environmental Disturbances Occurred During the Early Medieval Period)', in *History and Changing Horizon: Science, Environment and Social Systems* (eds. Amit Bhattacharyya and Mahua Sarkar), Kolkata, Setu Prakashani, 2014 and 'A Study of Climatic Disorder and Environmental Challenges in India, Pakistan and Afghanistan During the Medieval Period', Inaugural Address, Second South Asian History Conference, Department of History, Punjabi University, Patiala. Another important contribution has been: 'Forgotten Lakhi Jungle of Punjab: An Epic Contest Between Man and Nature', Shaheed Nanak Singh Memorial Lecture, Guru Teg Bahadur National Integration Chair, Punjabi University, Patiala.

There is a lot to be mentioned about his academic contributions, details of which can be accessed at *www.gsldevra.com* which carries complete bibliographic details. We would like to conclude by a lament that even today larger academia finds it difficult to engage with grassroots level excellent researches in regional languages, and scholars often do not get the kind of recognition they deserve. Prof. Ghanshyam Lal Devra is surely one of them. An exceptional attribute of Prof. Devra is his willingness to share his in-depth knowledge and historical insights with young researchers and scholars. Hundreds of history scholars will vouch for the fact that he has been a towering inspiration and guide par excellence. As it is said that 'Success is not what you accomplish in your life, its' about what you inspire others to do.' This volume is a humble tribute not only to his excellent research and insight but also his ability to inspire and educate at least two generations of young scholars of history.

Introduction

It is ironical that medieval Indian history has most of the time been condemned to abide by the geographical boundaries of the modern-day nation state. Medieval states, especially those bordering north-west or north-east India, cannot be reduced or condemned to follow the present-day national boundaries. If on one hand national boundaries are to be blamed then we cannot also ignore the fact that there are very few historians who can transcend the limitation of multilingual sources of the times. Moreover, there are very few historians who have made concerted efforts to defy the limitations of nations and national boundaries in their examination of the medieval past of Indian history. Prof. Ghanshyam Lal Devra is one such historian who has very eloquently transcended the limitations of modern-day geographical boundaries of nation states and linguistic barriers. Along with this, Prof. Devra has also challenged the conventional disciplinary boundaries of historical research, traversing in his academic journey a wide variety of themes that were largely virgin areas as far as the discipline of history was concerned. If his doctoral research can be classified as agrarian-administrative-economic history then his subsequent writings travelled to social and cultural history and to the emerging field of environmental history. His eagerness to go beyond the so-called conventional sources of history has enabled him to explore some of the unexplored dimensions of medieval histories of communities and landscapes. Similarly, the expanse of geographical and spatial canvas of his historical sensibilities is visible in his integration of *longue duree* of structures and events. He is also aware of the social responsibilities of a historian and therefore he regularly contributed articles in the news dailies. At the same time his commitment to organizations of professional historians can be seen in the regular participation in the annual sessions of the Indian History Congress, Rajasthan History Congress, Punjab History Congress, etc.

The pre-British era history of Rajasthan to a great extent was influenced by the narrative set by Colonel James Tod in his *Annals and Antiquities of Rajasthan.* For more than a century and a half the writings of Colonel James Tod remained the reference point for any researcher interested in the history of Rajputana. A narrative which in the opinion of Thomas Metcalf is a classic representative of *Ideologies of the Raj*, thus perpetuated an image of feudatory character of pre-British era Rajputana. The most effective and sustained critical assessment of this narrative was offered by Prof. Satish Chandra and researchers influenced by his engagement with archival documents, namely, G.D. Sharma, Dilbagh Singh, S.P. Gupta, Ghanshyam Lal Devra, etc. It was under his initiative that we witness a serious challenge to the domination of Persian court chronicle-based history writing tradition and gradual but very effective use of sources available in vernaculars of the Indian subcontinent, especially the domain of princely states of Rajasthan. Intense engagement with the unpublished archival records maintained by the princely states of Rajasthan and now available at the Rajasthan State Archives, Bikaner began in right earnest in the late 1970s.[1]

As happens most of the time the challenge to the stereotypes themselves become another stereotype. This is what happened gradually with the historians who took pains to uncover the worth of rich archival documents of the princely states of Rajasthan. The archives have such a rich repository of administrative documents that most of these first generation historians could not go beyond the initial research. Ghanshyam Lal Devra, with the advantage of being local and based in Rajasthan, gradually moved beyond the confines of the archives and focused extensively on the rich literary documents available for the study of the early modern times. His roots in the region exposed him to parallel narratives prevalent in the society. Historical geography further enabled him to transcend the boundaries of archival sources and such an engagement ultimately reflected in his pioneering research in the environmental history. The potential of field investigation also helped him in reflecting on the ethnographic history of the communities. It is this interest which ultimately led him to go beyond the geographical confines of the present-day nation state.

Although none of the contributors to this volume was ever a student of Prof. Devra in the formal-official meaning of the term, but his historical sensibilities have influenced our academic endeavours. Given the diversity of themes addressed by contributors, papers in the present volume have been arranged in chronological order. J.S. Kharakwal offers a survey of archaeological sites in the Godwar region, i.e. modern-day Sirohi region. Continuity of settlements since pre-historic times makes this region very significant for historical investigations. He focuses on the Chandravati Excavation, with which he has been personally associated. Thus this volume carries the first detailed examination of this site. Kharakwal says that Chandravati was chosen for excavation for three important reasons. The first one was to understand the planning of the settlement, the second reason was to understand the function of the site and the third was to develop better understanding of the late historical and medieval archaeology of southern Rajasthan as the late historical and medieval archaeology has been consistently ignored by the archaeological community. Kharakwal affirms that between 700 and 1300 CE, a diversification in crop-assemblage and associated weeds suggest that the region was under a warm and humid climate, corresponding to the Medieval Warm Period (MWP), known between AD 740 and 1150 worldwide, attributed to increased monsoon precipitation. It is an interesting finding as established scholarship, on the basis of archaeological.

epigraphic and literary sources differ substantially from this formulation.[2] Examining the significance of metallurgical activities in the region of south-eastern Rajasthan, Lalit Pandey argues that initially it was copper-zinc production and later on iron production that places this region in a unique position. He is also trying to explore the role of Bhils in the metallurgical activities of the region. Detailed analysis of the excavation sites help us understand the historical evolution of the associated technology and the kind of objects being produced at these sites.

The third paper of the volume offers a survey of literary and archival sources available in Persian to understand the functioning of *Madad-i-Ma'ash* grants in medieval India. Yakub Ali brings out the changing character of *Madad-i-Ma'ash* grants and for the purpose he does not confine his survey to the Rajasthan region. His survey offers us insights into the changes in the nature of relationships between political authorities and ecclesiastical order. He suggests that it is important to examine the character of *Madad-i-Ma'ash* grants in the larger historical context. The next paper of the volume in the chronological order showcases the history of Rajasthan through the prism of Guru Nanak's travels. This paper discusses the salient features of the historical geography of the Indian subcontinent of medieval times. Guru Nanak's travels also hint at the existence of a diaspora of different communities all across the Asian continent.

Suraj Bhan Bhardwaj through his paper, '*Raja, Praja* and *Rajyadharma:* Popular Imaginations of Kingship in Late Medieval North India' draws attention to the immensely rich tradition of literary and archival repositories located in Rajasthan to carry out historical investigations for the late medieval period. His paper examines the interplay between dominant normative imagination of kingship and popular perceptions. He suggests that there were layers of interactions between *Raja, Praja* and *Rajyadharma*. More importantly, he challenges the colonial narrative of 'oriental despotism' and the unchanging character of medieval Indian social formations.

R.P. Bahuguna's paper on 'Santic Communities in Seventeenth Century Rajasthan' brings out the limitations of modern-day monolithic imagination of 'Santic communities' and homogeneous 'Santic ideology'. He suggests that it is not only Dadupanth but even the Kabirpanth as an organized Santic community that did not emerge before the end of the 17th century. He also emphatically argues that definitely till the end of the 17th century, one finds tremendous fluidity among the followers of different Sants; their sayings were shared and widely circulated across Santic communities. Another very important point he hints at is the growing possibilities of documentation in the 18th century which helps in consolidation of the Santic community as a well organized structure. Abha Singh makes a very pertinent point regarding the history of Mughal India. Examining the writings of W.H. Moreland, she suggests that although Moreland went beyond the dynastic history and was a pioneer in the economic history of Medieval India, but he was deeply imbued in the tradition of Elliot and Dowson who were proponents of dividing Indian history in two parts: Hindu India and Muslim India. In the opinion of Abha Singh though Moreland recognizes the difference between the Indian and British context yet he could not resist the temptation of portraying Mughal economy as merely exploitative and detrimental to the growth of the peasantry.

Regarding the interactions between *longue duree* and structures, Mayank Kumar examines the genealogy/ies of geographies and in what ways canonical geographical imaginations have shaped the administrative and historical rendering of the geographies of Rajasthan. He suggests that geographies to a great extent are social constructions and are shaped by socio-economic-political-cultural-ritual-administrative concerns. Social constructions of geographies are thus manifestations of interplay of multiple narratives of geographies. Although immediate utilitarian concerns constitute the core of social construction but larger hegemonic description play a pivotal role. Thus one can trace genealogies of geographies. Mayurakshi Kumar documents the process of political legitimatization through the construction of the city of Jaipur. He argues that it is important to investigate the relationship between conceptual imaginations of a city and its physical actualization. Mayurakshi Kumar suggests that a city is not merely a building and spatial arrangement. The author not only examines the ideological orientations but has also addressed the political considerations behind the construction of Jaipur. Continuing with the study of urban settlement the next paper by Rajender Kumar examines the importance of the city of Nagaur as a trading centre in the late 18th century. His dexterity to sail through archival sources is manifested in the rich archival references. He relies on extensive documentation available for the period to showcase the very complex character of trading activity in the region. Rajender Kumar stresses that Naguar also emerged as an important centre of production. He argues that the military requirements of the Marwar states played a key role in the emergence of Nagaur as a major production centre of cannons and related products. Moreover, he also documents numerous fairs held in the near vicinity of Nagaur which feeds into the larger economy of the region. Last but not the least, he suggests that it is important to realize that political upheavals in Marwar also played a prominent role in the emergence of Naguar as the most significant trading city of the region.

The next set of papers gradually shifts focus from medieval Rajasthan to the colonial period and subsequent era. Sangeeta Sharma's paper examines the idea of honour and status as it was symbolically constructed, expressed and contested in the political domain in the erstwhile state of Mewar in the region of Rajputana. Significantly, different symbols and rituals were employed in varying political contexts to create legitimacy and to mould people's understanding of the changed political universe. The symbol system undergoes a change when Mewar comes under the sway of British Paramountcy in 1818. The new political dynamics that resulted in the subordination of princely states to the paramount power of the British can be grasped through the prism of symbols and rituals in the political realm. The paper suggests that the new symbol system reflected the superimposition and superiority of imperial symbolism of the British over the traditional symbolism of the Mewar state as also the obsession of the rulers with symbols and rituals of power to camouflage the real loss of power and sovereignty to the British. The paraphernalia of authority, if on one hand, was borrowed from the normative canonical traditions then at the same time princely regimes eagerly imitated British imperial symbolism. Her paper very subtly problematizes the dominant narrative of the 'warrior' principalities of Rajput lineages. Continuing the examination of aspirations and objectives of the princely states of Rajputna, Nidhi Sharma argues how the idea of the federation was being negotiated with princely states of Rajputana. It is interesting to notice the changing position of British colonial power with respect to their idea of federation. Changing fortunes of British control over British India was an important consideration while offering political participation to the native states the global political scenario and nationalist resistance to British domination often compelled them to soft pedal the princely states.

Subsequent papers focus on historical-anthropological investigations of the Raibari community, Bishnois and tribal social formation. Sarita Sarasar examines the changing roles and significance of the Rebaris. Sarita documents the historical process through which an important community like the Rebaris was gradually scuttled to social margins. She argues the ways in which introduction of new technologies influences the fate of the profession-based community; how historical processes pan out the new set of contexts that impact the social relevance of communities. Neekee Chaturvedi traces the historical evolution of the Bishnoi community. She argues that attributing present-day environmental consciousness to the Bishnois is difficult to sustain. However, one cannot discard a certain level of nature consciousness. Religious philosophy of the Bishnois gradually captured the environmental imaginations of the natives in the last decade of the previous century. The author also examines the complex relationship between Bishnoi philosophy imbibed in the ecology of the region and the political compulsions of the state. The last paper of the volume by Netrapal offers a survey of anthropological writings on the tribes and tribal formations. Netrapal documents the process which gradually culminated in the segregation of non-agriculturalists and/or forest dwellers as inferior social formations and ultimately equating tribes and tribal formations as lesser social entities.

It is earnestly hoped that this ensemble of articles is a fitting tribute to the extraordinary genius and robust historical scholarship of Prof. Ghanshyam Lal Devra. Additionally, it is also expected to be a fine addition to the existing readings on Rajasthan which will be of interest to scholars of history as well as for lay readers.

NOTES

1. Suraj Bhan Bhardwaj, R.P. Bahuguna and Mayank Kumar, 'Introduction' in Suraj Bhan Bhardwaj, R.P. Bahuguna and Mayank Kumar, eds., *Revisiting the History of Rajasthan: Essays for Prof. Dilbagh Singh*, Primus, New Delhi: 2017.
2. A. Ghosh, 'The Rajputana Desert—Its Archaeological Aspects', in S.P. Gupta, ed., *A Stein: An Archaeological Tour Along the Ghaggar-Hakra River*, Kusumanjali Prakashan, Meerut: 1989, pp. 98-106; G.S.L. Devra, 'Desertification and Problem of Delimitation of Rajputana Desert During the Medieval Period', *Human Ecology*, Special Issue, No. 7, 1999, pp. 97-107; M.K. Dhavalikar, 'Green Imperialism: Monsoon in Antiquity and Human Response', in *Man and Environment*, Vol. 26, No. 2, 2001, pp. 17–28; Mayank Kumar, 'Adaptations to Climatic Variability: Irrigation, and Settlements Patterns in Early Medieval Rajasthan', *The Medieval History Journal*, Vol. 17, No. 1, 2014, pp. 57-86.

1

Archaeology of the West Banas Area with Special Reference to Chandravati, Sirohi, Rajasthan

J.S. Kharakwal

Introduction

Southern Rajasthan has two rivers of the same name called Banas. The East Banas originates in the hills around Kumbhalgarh and initially flows towards north and eventually joins the Chambal to be part of the Ganga system. Scores of Ahar culture sites are located in the valley of Banas or in its catchment area. The West Banas originates in the remote hills near Sirohi and flows towards south and arrives in north Gujarat via Abu Road. It has been life line for district Sirohi and north Gujarat region as Banaskantha, the name of a district is also named after the river. The area of Sirohi is largely composed of low hills and ridges of Pre-cambrian rocks and drained by the Banas and its tributaries. The area is well known due to a tourist place called Mt. Abu and Guru Sikhar, the highest peak of the Aravalli is located near Mt. Abu.[1]

Geologically this region is south western part of Delhi Syncilnoium. In the central and eastern part of Sirohi are rocks of Delhi super-group represented by variety of granites such as Ambaji, Erinpura, Malani and others. Besides Gabro Chandravati, we have a variety of rocks available in this region like sand stone, quartzite, and some scilicious ones like chert and agate, rhyolite. Also are found evidence of some igneous rocks like metaquartz. The Banas, Sipu, Khari, Krishnavati and Kapalganga are some of the important rivers of this region. Among these Banas is the main one as many important modern settlements like Pindwara, Abu Road and others are situated on its banks.

Stone Age Sites

The Archaeology Department of M.S. University of Baroda carried out an intensive survey of Chandravati in the late seventies of the last century and reported a Mesolithic site at the confluence of Sevarni and Banas near Abu Road, in the foothills of Mount Abu.[2] Artifacts like flakes, blade tools, fluted cores and an engraved core were discovered. The evidence of such early engraved core has made the site and area well known to the Prehistorians of South Asia (Fig. 1: Chandravati Core). While conducting excavation at Chandravati[3] we carried out several round of explorations in Sirohi district to located older, contemporary and later sites. It was done primarily to understand the function and chrono-stratigraphy of Chandravati. We discovered two more sites one each at Syava[4], located 3 km up stream of Sevarnai from Chandravati and another at Arasuri near Pindwara. Besides, we also had information from the local knowledgeable villagers about rock paintings at Viroli, Arasuri, Revdhar and near Ambaji located about 20 km north, 40 km to the west and about 20 km to the east of Chandravati respectively (Fig. 2: Medieval painting

Fig. 1: *Chandravati Core, Photo Courtesy M S University, Vadodara*

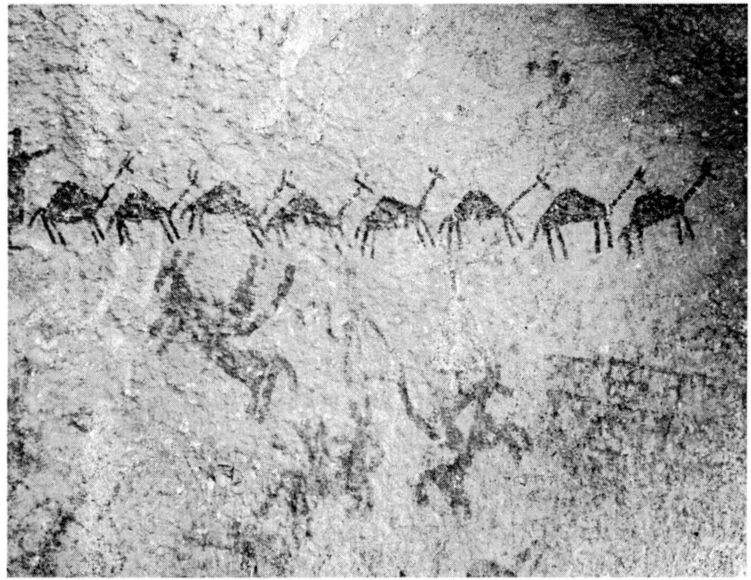

Fig. 2: *Medieval painting in a rock shelter near Revdhar, Sirohi, Photo Courtesy O.P. Sharma Kukki*

in a rock shelter near Revdhar, Sirohi). Considering the subject matter and style, all these paintings appear to belong to medieval period. As recently several Stone Age sites have been discovered by Chintan Thakar and Puna Ram[5] from this area, it is likely that there may be prehistoric painting sites too. The newly discovered Stone Age sites in Sirohi are Kashindra, Viroli, Jabkeshwar Mahadev Fali, Paraga Fali, Gopi dhani, Sanwada R., Udwaria, Churli Khera (Isra), Arasuri (Arasana), Varki Khera (Mandvada Khalsa), Sartaneswar Mahadev (Lotana), Bhadrada Kakar (Nandia), Richheshwar Mahadev (Nadia), Silwani 1, Silwani 2 in Pindwara tehsil, Jod Fali Danvav, Talwar Naka, Bujra Fali Ganka, Khadra Fali, Siyava and Gujari Fali (Nitora) in Abu Road Tehsil, Naradara, Mandwaria, Ummedgarh1, Ummedgarh 2, and Lotiwada in Shivganj tehsil, Gupteshwar Mahadev (Angor), Paladi (Rampura) and Satapura in Sirohi teshil and Lunol in Revdhar Tehsil. Most of these sites have been found on the prominent locations on the hill slopes, particularly near the granite exposures, providing long view, in the alluvial deposit, and away from the river terraces but close to the water source. What is interesting is that most of the sites have yielded small fluted cores, generally not more than 5 cm long, blade lets, strong evidence of parallel sided blades, cores and at one site blade with crested guided ridge (Fig. 3: Centripital Cores from the Banas Valley). However in several cases the character of Mesolithic culture is absent e.g., some sites have large flake tools like end or side scrapers, burins, borers and so on indicating older cultural stages like the Upper and Middle Palaeolilthic ones. Even in one case a small beautifully dressed, though a bit rolled and patinated handaxe was also discovered the length of which is hardly 15 cm. Perhaps it was dressed with soft hammer as size of flake would indicate. A variety of chert, cherty quartzite and agate has been used for making tools. Looking at the evidence we sincerely think that early man was present in this region right from lower palaeolithic times and therefore it is likely that many more prehistoric sites may be discovered in the near future.

Fig. 3: *Centripital cores from the Banas Valley, Photo Courtsey Chintan Thakar*

Bronze Age

The evidence of Bronze Age site has not been discovered so far in the catchment area of the Banas. A few years ago Randell Law has confirmed with his analysis that the Harappans of

Kachchh were obtaining copper from the Aravallis perhaps from Ambaji where we have evidence of smelting and mining (Fig. 4: Copper smelting site at Ambaji near Vasantgarh). There are a few other ancient copper mines near Rohida, Ambaji (Vasantgarh) and at Samoli all located further north of Ambaji in the Aravallis. Local people may have been mining and supplying copper to the Harappans in north Gujarat. It is also likely that the Anart people/Harappans of North Gujarat may have been receiving copper from Ambaji and supplying it further to their relatives in Kachchh and main land Gujarat.[6] It is therefore likely that there may be some Bronze sites around Ambaji.

Fig. 4: *Copper smelting site at Ambaji near Vasantgarh*

Iron Age/Historic Settlements

So far no evidence of early Iron Age and early historic remains has been discovered in the study area. Though a few radio carbon dates from Chandravati indicate that the site was first occupied during the 4th century, there is not enough archaeological material to justify such early occupation at the site. The modern settlement at Rohida is located right on top of an ancient mound, which is spread in an area around 4 hectares. Several temples with epigraphic evidence and dozens of step wells exist in the village belonging to the Parmar phase of Chandravati.[7] A large number of houses in the village are made out of bricks robbed from ancient buried structures. The villagers recollect that several structural phases perhaps belonging to different generations are buried underneath their houses. Very often such brick structures get exposed partially due to modern construction work. A well known epigraphic evidence known as Samoli inscription reported in the late twenties of the last century by Halder[8] is a good evidence to presume that there were some late Historic settlements in this region as the epigraph was inscribed in the year 647. Besides, an inscription from Vasantgarh fort has been claimed dating back to 6th century, which has yet to be examined. The Delhi Group of rocks, superimposing the early formation of the Aravallis Granites, are highly mineralized as number of ancient old workings and smelting sites like Deri Ambaji, Rohida, Samoli, Ambaji near Vasantgarh and others are known.

Medieval Settlements

It is interesting to note that a very large number of medieval settlements and forts are located in the study area. Very large ancient settlements are located at Chandravati and Rohida and forts at Achalgarh[9], Bandhiyagarh, Vasantgarh, Sirohi and other places in this region. Among these Bandhiyagarh has recently been surveyed.[10] According to the report, Bandhiyagarh is perhaps one the largest stronghold in this region which is located in highly inaccessible area of the Aravallis. The researchers have reported remains of ancient temple, several architectural members, icons, plan of the fort enclosing several hillocks and spread in a very large area, besides an inscription belonging to Parmar Phase. It reads the date of VS 1252 (1197 CE).

Chandravati

Chandravati (24°26′17.8″N, 72°44′32.2″E) was reported by James Tod as early as 1822.[11] It is located about 6 km south of Abu Road and about 3 km north of Mawal in Sirohi district of Rajasthan. The ancient site is in fact located on the foothill zone of Mount Abu. A meticulous surface survey of the site was carried out jointly by the Department of Archaeology, M.S. University, Baroda and Rajasthan State Archaeology Department, Jaipur[12] and remains of a fort, remains of more than two dozen temples, *baowris* (step well), and so on.[13] Besides, this team also discovered a Mesolithic site on the confluence of Sevarni and Banas. An engraved core from this site was perhaps the most significant discovery of this site.

The main line of the Western Railway from Marwar junction to Ahmedabad passes through Chandravati and divides the ancient settlement in two parts. Besides, the Abu Road Palanpur highway, running parallel to the railway line, has also been prepared by destroying a major part of the settlement. In fact the railway line as well as the metalled road has severely damaged a major part of the ancient settlement. Besides, a gas pipe line has also severely damaged the ancient settlement. Unfortunately, there has been tremendous loss of innocence to protect this heritage site at governmental as well as local or private or non-governmental levels.

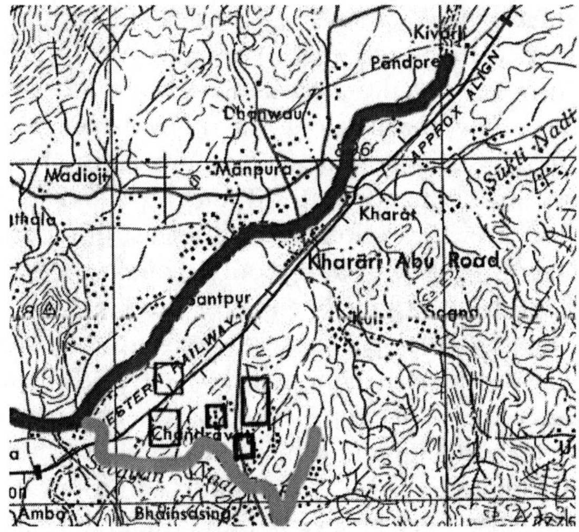

Fig. 5: *Location map of Chandravati*

According to the local tradition the ancient township of

Chandravati was ruled by the Parmar kings of Abu branch and it was spread in a large area. There are number of part-contemporary sites such as Kumbharia and Ambaji about 18 km east of Chandravati, Bandhyagarh about 10 km towards east, Rishikesh about 9 km towards north- west and so on. The entire ancient settlement of Chandravati was spread in almost 50 hectare area in the valleys of Sevarni and Banas. The former is tributary of the latter.

There are a large number of mounds in the entire settlement, the height of which varies from one to ten meters. The entire settlement is supporting dense jungle of *Prosopis,* which was a major hurdle for surface survey. Our careful examination revealed that there are as many as five high and over a dozen low mounds in the entire settlement. Besides these, three dozen circular mounds have remains of temples made of bricks and stones. Among these, the biggest mound A is located to the west of Abu Road Palanpur state highway, which yielded remains of a massive fort. All other mounds are located to the east of the aforesaid highway. In fact, the highway is made by destroying two large mounds, one of which yielded remains of an ancient temple. Mound B is located to the south east of mound A which has been largely destroyed by the aforesaid highway. Local villagers have raised a few houses along the highway on this mound. One has to scale this mound while approaching the museum and mound C at Chandravati. Mound C, squarish on plan, is located about half a kilometer to the east of mound B and close to the modern museum. Mound D is located about 100 m to the south of mound C and mound E is located about 70 m east of mound C. Besides, there are several circular mounds across the settlement, which we strongly suspect that they represent remains of ancient temples. There are remains of a few step wells, one of which was found to the north of mound E and another one to the south and a few across the Sevarni. The discovery of several bunds, a large reservoir and several step wells perhaps indicate that the Sevarni and Banas were not always perennial and hence they may not have been irrigating the ancient settlement round the year between 9th and 14th century when these water bodies were raised.

Remains of a Fort

In mound C, located close to the museum building, were discovered remains of a fort, which is roughly squarish. It is made of bricks and width of surviving wall on top was measured 90 cm. Its southern arm was measured 55 m, northern one 53 m and the eastern and western arms each about 60 m long. The southern arm was partially exposed and it was found strengthened with rectangular and squarish bastions varying in size such as 15.25x3.75 m, 8.25x4.75 m, and 3.25x3.25 m. There were circular bastions on all four corners of the fort, the diameter of which measured 6m. To prepare circular bastions sometimes wedge shaped bricks were also used. In the south western corner the fort wall has survived up to a height of 2 m with 25 courses.

Fig. 6: *Circular and squarish bastion of fort*

The entrance to the fort was given from the north-western corner of the fort. It was discovered about 9 m to the east of north western corner. The width of the gate was measured 2.90 m and it was made of very large dressed stone slabs. It was located at a depth of about 1.10 m from surface. At a distance of 2.80 m north of the entrance was found base of a beautifully dressed octagonal pillar. It appears to be part of a *torana (pillar)*. It is likely that such *torana* may have made the entrance very impressive. It was found that the northern arm of the fort wall has survived up to a height of about 1.50 m (with 27 courses of bricks) from the surface as it was underlined by an earlier structural phase. The fort wall was raised on the foundation with an appearance of flight or offset.

As many as three large structural complexes were partially exposed in this fortified enclosure. One of the complexes or the first one (St. com. 1) was discovered in the south eastern corner of the fort and was oriented north south along the eastern arm. The second complex (St. com. 2) was discovered to the north of the first one with a gap of about 5m and was located in the north eastern area of the enclosure. Both these structures were separated by a street or lane which leads to St. com. 1 and also provide a passage in the eastern arm to approach perhaps to the baori (water structure) and other contemporary settlements.

The third structural complex (St. com 3) was discovered in the south central part of the enclosure. It was in fact located just in front of the main entrance. This complex, though composed of several rooms, was connected with the first structural complex located in the south eastern area.

Structural complex (St. com. 1) composed of 6 rooms, discovered in the south eastern corner of the mound, was partially exposed. And this complex had four small rear rooms and two large rectangular one in the frontal part (Fig. 7). In the first rear room located in the south eastern corner of this complex was found a circular feature of clay with an opening. According to local knowledgeable villagers, this circular feature is part of flour grinding mill. Near this feature were found fragments of medium sized Red and Grey jars and large quantity of charred grains. The charred grains have been identified and the result has been mentioned in the following pages.

Fig. 7: *Structural complex in mound C*

Another complex (St. com. 2) was discovered in the north eastern corner of the fort and it was oriented north-south and spread in an area 30x15.70 m. There was an open space (10x5 m) between these two structural complexes. This open space is protected on the east by the eastern arm of the fort, in which a passage is also provided to approach outside. This complex, spread in an area about 30x17 m, has about half a dozen rooms around an open space in the center. A few rooms located on the western and southern part of this complex were partially exposed. The floor of these rooms was also prepared by laying down squarish bricks (28x28 cm). The floor in an open area was initially prepared by bricks and then a thick plaster of terracotta fragments mixed with lime was applied.

The third complex (St. com. 3) was discovered in the central western part of the mound. As many as four rooms and very large roughly L shaped hall connecting this complex with the first one located in the south western part was discovered. This complex was located about 20 meters south of the northern arm and the main entrance was located in front of this complex.

The highest mound (numbered as mound E) of this

settlement was discovered to the east of mound C and to the west of a hillock, located on the right bank of Sevarni and the oval shaped mound is roughly oriented north-south. On top of this hillock was discovered a watch tower, which not only provides commanding view of the entire settlement but also protects the entire site on the east. It is about 10 m high mound from the surrounding plain. On the western slope of this main mound are two terraces 20 m and 40 m wide respectively which distinguish these three successive cultural levels and give appearance of a flight. Thus the main mound has three successive elevations, the lowest one is hardly 1.5 m to 2 m higher from the ground level, which suddenly rises perhaps due to the remains of a very strong structure buried. A sharp termination of the mound on the western slope marked the remains of western arm of a fort, which turned out to be outer defence wall. It has survived up to a height of 2 m with 20 coarses of bricks. Its width was measured 2 m.

Fig. 8: *High mound (E) and watch tower in the background*

The fort was found oriented NNE-SSW and its outer wall's dimensions were noticed 200x100 m. At the surviving height the width was measured 2 m. The entrance to the fort was given in the southern margin of the western arm, the width of which was measured 2.50 m. On the left side of the entrance was discovered an inscribed slab which read the date of 1325 VS (1268 CE). The inscribed slab has depiction of a cow and a calf, which is known as *surabhi lekh.*

This western arm was strengthened by rectangular bastions whereas the southern one with circular ones. The southern arm was found surviving up to a height of 3.30 m and its length was measured 102 m. In the north western corner of the enclosure were found remains of a step well. It might have used by the royal people living in the fort. The dimension of inner fort was found 94x55 m and the entrance was given in the northern arm.

Structures

The distance between inner and outer arms is about 40m (except for the eastern one) and remains of residential structures were found between these arms as many of them are also visible on the surface. All these structures may be contemporary to the fort walls. Both these defence walls, as explained above, were underlined by older cultural deposit, which may safely be stated as belonging to pre-Parmar phase or older than 9th century CE. The thickness of this older cultural horizon was measure about two meter, which strongly indicate that the pre-Parmar phase settlement at Chandravati begun way back from the Historic phase!

Fig. 9: *Structures on top of mound E*

The high mound was finally flanked by an oval shaped terrace, representing the post Parmar phase deposit (Fig. 9: Structures on top of mound E). It was located about 8 m above from the ground level. After thinning down the dense jungle of *Prosopis* and removing the surface soil, several brick structures were partially exposed right on the surface, the width of which varied from 40 to 55 cm. In the central part of the mound on top were found two squarish (4.10x3.55 m; 3.55x3.45 m) rooms with opening towards north. As many as half a dozen rooms were partially exposed around these two rooms.

Most of the structures on top of the mound were found surviving up to a height of about one meter from their floor level. The floors were prepared by squarish and rectangular bricks 30x20x6 cm, 20x20x5 cm. Some of the room also had a partition wall. On both faces of the entrance small offsets 7x5 cm were found on either side (inner and outer). Such offsets may have been given to fix the wooden doors. Does it mean that they were they holding double doors? In case of the aforesaid main rooms were found prominent circular depressions (diameter 30 cm) on the inner face of the walls close to the entrance. Perhaps long wooden poles may have been placed in such depressions to hold the roof. It is also likely that these depressions may be indicating the thickness of the wooden beams. Sometimes a very layer of lime stone or *kankary* material was laid on the brick floors, which looks rammed and plastered. While making the walls both header and stretcher and English bond system has been used for construction.

Several other structures were partially exposed on the slopes of the mound. Based on superimposition of structures, stratigraphy as many as three different structural phases and a few sub phases were indentified. The average dimension of rooms was found 4x3 m. In fact the settlement of this last phase on top had a rectangular enclosure with an entrance on the western arm. The eastern, western and southern arms of this enclosure were exposed up to a length of 15.40, 23 and

7 m respectively. Though considerable amount of pottery was discovered from this complex, it was extremely poor as far as other minor objects are concerned. A few grey ware potsherds were treated with painted decorations.

Earthquake Resistance House!

There was a very large unfortified open area (about 100m wide) between mound C and E. To understand the cultural deposit two locations were chosen for cutting. The first trench was located to the east of the mound C where as the second one about 100 meters south. In case of the first trench it was found that the house was raised on a 30 cm thick bed of coarse sand. The sand was found resting on a properly arranged bed of boulders perhaps brought from the nearby river. It seems that this kind of tradition may have existed at Chandravati for quite long time as it was noticed in three successive structural phases. Our ethno-archaeological survey revealed that this kind of floor is very useful in many ways. For example, rats and other rodents cannot make their houses in the sand, it prevents moisture in the floor. Hence, the grains on the floor are preserved. Perhaps the most important function of such thick filling of sand is that it may, according to the villagers, work as shock observer when there is an earthquake. This is an excellent example of traditional wisdom that has survived for last few thousands of years. In fact the site of Chandravati is located on a fault zone of geological setting which often receives earthquakes.

Beneath the floor level was discovered a large jar (with 1.40 m height and maximum body diameter 75 cm) in a squarish chamber, the height of which was found surviving up to 1.10m with 16 courses of bricks. The empty space between the jar and chamber was filled with coarse sand. It is a grey ware jar, which has about 2 cm thick wall. It may have been used for storage purpose. Considering the narrow opening of the jar, one may guess that it may have been used for storage of some kind of liquid material. It is because taking out liquid from the base or lower half of the jar is easier than the solid. This chamber as well as the jar was found underlined by an older cultural horizon, identified as pre Parmar (or cultural phase I).

A low mound, representing the lower contours of the site, located about 100 m south of mound C was chosen for controlled excavation (trench P 35) in order to understand the older cultural horizons/stage(s). This low mound was located close to the south western corner of the outer fort wall of mound E. A few residential structures and a retaining wall was found very close to the surface. Soon it was identified that the retaining wall was raised against the street deposit. This street deposit was found resting on an older floor, fire place and hearth belonging to cultural phase I or Pre Parmar phase.

Craft Area

On the southern slope of the mound evidence of certain craft activities were discovered such as as copper-melting, lime-kilns, and so on. Since water of Sevarni was easily approachable from the southern fringe of the site it might have been easier raising crafts in the southern area of the settlements. Small quantity of copper slag was discovered on the south-eastern area of the mound. Of course we did not find any crusible in this area despite which we presume that it was a melting area rather than smelting. Had it been smelting area there may have been considerable quantity of slag and fragments of furnace. Besides, lime kiln was discovered in the southern slope of the mound. The diameter of the kiln was noticed about 2m and it was 78cm deep.

Watch Towers

On a hillock, located to the east of mound E, a circular brick structure was discovered, the diameter of which was found 7.50m (N-S) and 6m (E-W). It is actually an oblong feature partially exposed on the surface, it seems that the surface available on the hill top has dictated the plan of the structure. Besides, several alignments of bricks and fragments of tiles are visible near the aforesaid feature. It is about 100m higher from mound E. In fact this location provides panoramic view of entire Chandravati in general and a commanding view of Mounds C, D, E and other nearby areas. It is therefore this location was identified as a watch tower. There is a flight of bricks from the south eastern corner of mound E leading to the watch tower. The width of the flight was measured 2m (southern one). As many as three more somewhat similar features were discovered on hillocks to the south east and south of mound E. Two of them were located on hillocks across the Sevarni. The discovery of watch towers indicate that the township may be a very important settlement both for economic and administrative reasons.

Cultural Stages

Based on stratigraphy and cultural remains, we could identify three successive cultural stages rather than periods (Fig. 10). Since we did not find any cultural break or natural horizon in the entire deposit at Chandravati we preferred to define the stratigraphy in different cultural stages rather than periods. The entire deposit belongs to the late historic (Pre-Parmar), medieval (Parmar phase) and late medieval (Post Parmar phase) periods without any break. Moreover, the radio carbon dates indicate that the settlement continued until 20th century.

Fig. 10: *Cultural Stages I, II and III are visible in trench DD 19*

In addition to this we seriously suspect that the settlement was perhaps abandoned in the early 20th century due to terrible jolts of earthquake as many surviving walls would indicate.

Stage I

Cultural stage I of Chandravati is represented by the first settlement that was raised on dark grayish or brownish clayey sand perhaps originated due to weathering of the local bed rock. The culture stage I deposit is quite thick as it measured about 2m in mound E whereas in mound C and other places it was represented with a thin layer varying in thickness from 20 to 40 cm. Except for U shaped hearths, fire place and two small brick alignments not much is known about cultural stage I. As far as pottery is concerned, it is represented by Red and Grey wares besides a few pieces of black slipped and bright red slipped pottery was also noticed. A variety of iron objects including nails, arrowheads, rods, sheet fragment and some copper objects, bead of lapis lazuli and a variety of terracotta objects were found. Based on ceramic fossils we suspect that this cultural horizon may be bracketed between 6th and 9th century and it has been leveled as Pre Parmar Phase at Chandravati.

Stage II

This cultural stage was represented by a very large scale construction. It appears that rural settlement of Chandravati turned into a township. As many as three forts, about three dozen temples, several water structures including baowries, bunds and a reservoir, besides a variety of craft activity was raised during this phase. It is bracketed between 10th to 14th centuries and can be equated with the Parmars rule at Chandravati.

Stage III

This cultural stage is represented by an oval shaped mound E. The authors of this phase either reused the older structures or raised new one right on the older ones. The structural activity during this phase was mainly noticed in mound C and E when a large number of residential structures were raised on these mounds right on the older structural complexes. In certain area e.g., in mound C the plain Grey ware was also treated with beautiful painted decorations. A glazed pottery fragment was also discovered. In fact the ceramic assemblage of the earlier stages continued with some change in shapes and surface treatment.

Minor Objects

Several types of minor objects like beads and bangles of terracotta, semi precious stones, metal objects (iron and copper), fragments of glass utensils, and a few terracotta human and animal figurines were discovered. Also were found a large number of terracotta objects perhaps used for entertainment.

Pottery

The pottery assemblage was represented by Red and Grey Ware in all the three cultural stages. Of course, in stage I and II some fragments of both wares were having beautiful surface treatment with somewhat glazing effect. The assemblage was mainly represented by a variety of jars, pots, basins, bowls and lids. All these shapes continue throughout the deposit but with some change, besides some new shapes also appear in every stage. In several trenches grey ware was out numbered by the red ware. In fact most of the pottery shapes with some change also continue in the subsequent phases.

Subsistence

To understand the subsistence, contemporary vegetation and environment studies and analysis of floral remains was carried out by Anil K. Pokharia and his team from Birbal Sahni Institute of Paleobotany, Lucknow. They found that during cultural phase one the following cereals and other edible items were being cultivated at Chandravati: *Hordeum vulgare* (barley), *Paspalum scrobiculatum* (kodon), *Vigna sp.*, *Macrotyloma uniflorum* (horsegram), *Ziziphus sp., Setaria sp.*(foxtail millet), *Ipomoea sp., Medicago sp.* (alfalfa), *Vicia sp., Oryza sativa* (Rice), *Cicer arietinum* (chick pea), *Brachiaria sp., Acacia sp., Indigofera sp., Solanum sp., Pulse sp., Linum usitatissimum* (linseed), and *Sida sp.*

In cultural phase II most of the cereals or other items continued and new introduction of the following cereals and other edible items were found and cultivated: *Panicum miliaceum* (proso millet), *Echinochloa sp., Solanum sp., Polygonum sp., Trigonella occulta*. However in cultural phase III a variety of millets and draught resistant crops came into existence, which have been identified as *Setaria italica* (Italian millet), *Triticum sp.* (wheat), *Triticum aestivum* (bread wheat), *Sorghum bicolor* (jowar), *Panicum miliaceum* (proso millet), *Pennisetum typhoides* (bajra), *Vigna radiata* (green gram), *Vigna mungo* (black gram), *Sesamum indicum* (Sesame), *Cannabis sativa, Lens culinaris* (lentil), *Emblica officinalis, Trianthema triquetra, Trianthema portulacastrum, Pisum sativum, Trianthema sp., Chenopodium sp., Scleria sp. Chenopodium sp., Indigofera sp., Abutilon sp., Gossypium sp., Lathyrus sp. Abutilon sp., Andropogon sp., Trifolium sp, Desmodium sp.*

Based on the above discoveries and his study of lacustral deposit at Chandravati, Pokharia[14] concludes that between 700 and 1300 CE, a diversification in crop-assemblage and associated weeds suggest that the region was under warm and humid climate, corresponding to the Medieval Warm Period (MWP), known between AD 740 and 1150 worldwide, attributed to increased monsoon precipitation. His findings challenges the conventional classification of this period as of greater aridity.[15] In the following stage, between 1300 and 1850, was dominance of drought-resistant millets along with meager large grained cereals and pulses indicate the region probably experienced weak SW monsoon. It was eventually a warm but cool and dry phase.

Nearly a dozen radio carbon dates have been received from Birbal Sahni Institute for Palaeobotany, Lucknow, which range from 3rd century to 19th century CE.[16] Since there is no cultural gap in the entire deposit at the site, it is likely that the site was occupied regularly for last 1700 years. The site has evidence of gradual development from rural to a large township and finally registered decline. Perhaps the site lost its political importance once the Devra rulers shifted their capital to Sirohi in the 15th century due to constant Muslim attacks. But the cultural deposit at Chandravati has shown that the site was not abandoned until the early twentieth century when it was possibly devasted by the earthquake of Allaband. Many structures of this last settlement were found collapsed in a unusual manner.

Conclusion

Thus the human occupation begins in the catchment area of the West Banas form Palaeolithic period. The finding of an Acheulian handaxe, Middle Palaeolithic srapers, variety of centripetal and fluted cores, evidence of levallois and discoidal cores, blades, notches, flake tools clearly indicate long sequence. The surface collection of most of the stone age sites reported in this paper have thus clear signature of existence of Lower, Middle and Upper Palaeolithic phases. These discoveries will spearhead further studies on Stone Age in this region.

Though there is poor evidence of Bronze and Iron Age in the study area, future researches will bring out exciting data. The radio carbon dates have confirmed our presumption that cultural stage I can be safely placed between 5th and 9th century. The radio carbon dates and epigraphic evidence clearly supports the date of Parmar township between 10th and 13th century. We have termed this phase as cultural stage II. Following the Parmars, the Devra Rajputs occupied the township and ruled at Chandravati for another 100 years before they shifted to Sirohi due to constant Muslim invasions. During the Parmar's rule the area of Chandrvati may have been an important center of commercial, cultural and political activity as remains of scores of temples, three forts, watch towers, step wells, mining and smelting areas in the surrounding region besides rock paintings would indicate. It is generally held in the regional history that the township was deserted after the decline of the Parmars. However, the archaeological discoveries and radio carbon dates indicate that the sites remained occupied till the nineteenth century. Thus it seems that Chandravati was a very important late historical and medieval township which may have been controlling commercial activities between Western Rajasthan and north Gujarat and Central India!

Acknowledgement

The Chandravati excavation was a joint venture of State Archaeology Department of Government of Rajasthan and Sahitya Sansthan, JRN Rajasthan Vidyapeeth, Udaipur under the general direction of the author between 2013 and 2016. I express sincere thanks to Archaeological Survey of India, New Delhi for granting us permission for excavation for three seasons at Chandravati. I am grateful to Prof. S.S. Saragdevot, VC, JRN Rajastahn Vidyapeeth Udaipur, I am also grateful to Sri Hrideshji Sharma, RAS, the then director of Department of Archaeology, officers of the Department like Drs Krishnakanta Sharma, Vineet Godhal, Mubarik Hussain, and my students Rohit Menaria, Dr. K.P. Singh, Narayan Paliwal, and Dr. Hansmukh Seth for providing me unflinching support. In fact without Dr. Anil Pokharia work at the site on palaeovegetation we would not have been able to utter a single word about subsistence of people at the site. I therefore sincerely thank Dr. Pokharia and his team.

NOTES

1. B.N. Dhoundiyal, *Sirohi–Rajasthan District Gazetteer*. Government Central Press. Jaipur, 1967.
2. V.H. Sonawane, 'Symbolism of the engraved design on the Mesolithic core of Chandravati', *Pragdhara*, Vol. 6, 1995-96, pp. 33-39.
3. J.S. Kharakwal, 'Preliminary Observation of Excavation at Chandravati, Sirohi, Rajasthan', *Sodh Patrika*, Vol. 67, No. 1-4, 2016, pp. 20-54.

4. Nupur Tewari, 'Syava: A Mesolithic Site in Sirohi, Rajasthan', *Sodh Patrika* Vol. 67, No. 1-4, 2016, pp. 55-58.
5. Chintan Thakar, Puna Ram and J.S. Kharakwal, 'Discovery of Stone Age Sites in the Western Banas,' *Sodh Patrika*, Vol. 70, No. 1-4, 2019 (forthcoming).
6. Rendall William Law, *Inter-Regional Interaction and Urbanisation in the Ancient Indus Valley*, Manohar, Delhi, 2011, pp. 413, and 456.
7. Pratipal Bhatia, *The Parmaras*, Munshiram Manoharlal Publishers, Delhi, 1967; G.H.S. Ojha, *Sirohi Rajya ka Itihas* (2nd ed. Reprinted 1999), Granthagar, Jodhpur, 1911; Puna Ram Patel, 'Rohida ke Aprakashit Tamrapatra', *Sodh Patrika,* Vol. 70, No. 1-4, 2019 (forthcoming).
8. R.R. Halder, 'Samoli Inscription of the Time of Siladitya (VS703)', *Epigraphia Indica,* Vol. 20, 1929, pp. 97-99.
9. Rima Hooja, *A History of Rajasthan*, Rupa and Co., Delhi, 2006, p. 784.
10. Chintan Thakar, Priyank Talesara, K.P. Singh, Deora and Altaf Khan, 'An Archaeological Exploration of Godwad (Sirohi)', *Proceedings First Meeting of Rajasthan Archaeology and Epigraphy Congress*, 2019, pp. 55-64.
11. R.N. Mehta, R.C. Agrawala, V.H. Sonawane and V.S. Parekh, *Chandravati*, M.S. University of Baroda Press, Baroda, 1980; Colonel James Tod, *Travels in Western India, embracing a visit to the sacred mounts of the Jains, and the most celebrated shrines of Hindu faith between Rajpootana and Indus; with an account of the ancient city of Nehrwalla*, W.H. Allen and Co., London, 1839, p. 127.
12. Ibid.
13. Ibid.
14. A. Pokharia, J.S. Kharakwal, Shalini Sharma, Michael Spate, Dipika Tripathi, Ashok Priyadarshan Dimri, Xinyi Liu, Biswas Thakur, Sadan Kumar Basumatary, Alka Srivastava, Kamlesh S. Mahar, Krishna Pal Singh, 'Variable monsoons and human adaptations; archaeological and palaeoenvironmental records during the past millennia in north western India,' *The Holocene* (forthcoming).
15. A. Ghosh, 'The Rajputana Desert—Its Archaeological Aspects', in S.P. Gupta, ed., *A Stein: An Archaeological Tour Along the Ghaggar-Hakra River*, Kusumanjali Prakashan, Meerut, 1989, pp. 98-106; G.S.L. Devra, 'Desertification and Problem of Delimitation of

Rajputana Desert During the Medieval Period', *Human Ecology*, Special Issue, No. 7, 1999, pp. 97-107; M.K. Dhavalikar, 'Green Imperialism: Monsoon in Antiquity and Human Response', in *Man and Environment*, Vol. 26, No. 2, 2001, pp. 17–28; Mayank Kumar, 'Adaptations to Climatic Variability: Irrigation, and Settlements Patterns in Early Medieval Rajasthan', *The Medieval History Journal*, Vol. 17, No. 1, 2014, pp. 57-86.

16. J.S. Kharakwal, 'Preliminary Observation of Excavation at Chandravati, Sirohi, Rajasthan', *Sodh Patrika*, Vol. 67, No. 1-4, 2016, pp. 20-54.

2

Metallurgical Activities in Historic Southeast Rajasthan

Lalit Pandey

Rajasthan is very rich in mineral resources and these minerals have been exploited by man from ancient times. Beginning with mining of copper we get evidences of production of copper, bronze, iron, etc in the regions. At times production was for local consumption but at times the pan Indian network can be located. The present paper makes an attempt to highlight the significance of southeastern Rajasthan as the production centre of different minerals especially copper-zinc and iron. The paper also proposes that the Bhils played an important role in the production of these minerals. Last but not the least, the paper tries to integrate mineral production in southeastern Rajasthan within the larger context of the Indian subcontinent.

Geographically, Rajasthan is located in northwestern India, a triangle between Delhi, the Gulf of Cambay and Bengal. This triangle is an area of physical complexity and transitional between the Indo-Ganges plains and the Deccan plateau on the peninsular landmass.[1] Broadly Rajasthan has been divided into the Thar and Aravalli Range. The Thar is known as Marwar/Thali and the Aravalli Range segregates the major part of eastern Rajasthan. Southeast Rajasthan is known as Mewar—a significant erstwhile princely state.

Geologists divide Rajasthan into four physiographic divisions of these three that appear in southeast Rajasthan. The physiographic features of southeast Rajasthan have determined its drainage system, vegetation and the human settlements and thus it became a centre of human activities from the pre-historic times. Though, the region does not have any perennial river, it always attracted the movement of human beings of various cultures because of its geology. This region consists of minerals in abundance and these minerals have been exploited by man from the ancient times. The Aravalli formations have a major role in it because the Aravalli formations are rich in metallic as well as non-metallic minerals.

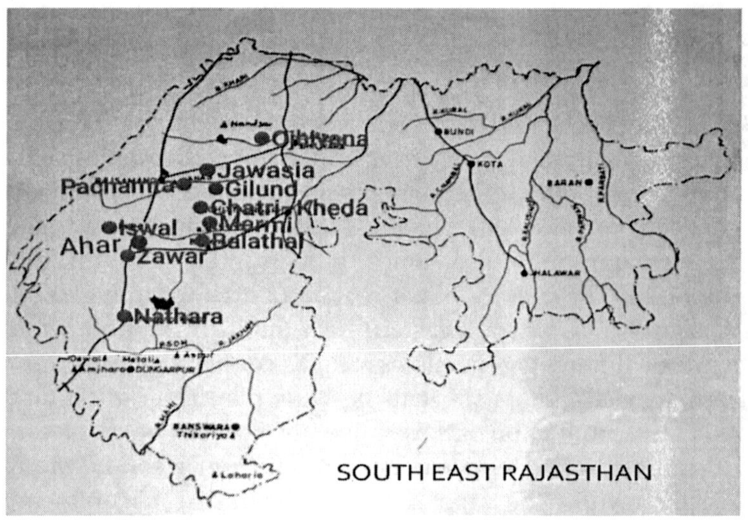

Fig. 1: *Map of Southeast Rajasthan*

The schist, which has been found in the region, contains fine crystals of garnet, mica, copper, lead, zinc, silver, iron, manganese and beryl. Out of these copper and iron attracted men of the Copper and Iron Age cultures respectively.[2] As it is universally known copper is the mother of metallurgy and during the proto-historic times, Chalcolithic cultures of the second half of the third millennium BC, the inhabitants exploited it as utilitarian metal. Therefore, geo-archeologists initiated the exploration to identify the possibilities of old working sites in southeast Rajasthan region and their results are quite rewarding. During the course of their exploration, they collected the evidence of forty-two sites in Delwara- Karoli area (See Figs. 2 and 3). After the investigation they expressed their opinion that most of the copper working activities had ceased towards the beginning of the 19th century CE.

Fig. 2-3 *Large Heap of Slag – Delwara-Karoli*

However, the results of their studies are quite curious and interesting. The conclusions are as follows:

(i) The slag pieces, which were collected and studied are heavy and a massive type. They contain more iron and possibly copper and other silicates.

(ii) The lighter type of slag pieces are with less iron and more of silica and other silicates; and

The evidence of mining and smelting activities at the same site indicates that the habitants have used the locally available copper ore for the extraction of copper metal for further fabrication into useful shapes and sizes.[3]

Copper and Zinc

It is clear from the above cited studies that the ancient people of southeast Rajasthan have developed a skill to get the copper from the available local ore.[4] The Ahar (located in the vicinity of Udaipur) is the first site of southeast Rajasthan which provides the evidence of copper mining and metallurgy. During the course of excavation at Ahar in 1961-62, the excavator H.D. Sankalia recovered some copper tools and heaps of slag-like material. After the scientific analysis of the recovered material K.T.M. Hegde confirmed that the slag is certainly of metallurgical waste. The presence of the remains of copper-melting industry in the form of metallurgical slag along with copper artifacts shows that Ahar was probably a copper-smelting centre around 2000. In addition to this, Hegde expresses the opinion that the high percentage of silica in the composition of the metallurgical slag is quite interesting. According to him it may be due to a deliberate addition of silica during the smelting process as a fluxing agent.[5] In the continuation of the analysis of the Ahar material, Hedge carried out the spectrometric studies of copper ore samples obtained from the Harappan and Chalcolithic sites of Rajasthan, Haryana, Gujarat and Madhya Pradesh. The results of the analysis showed that the artifacts and the ore samples have an agreement of over 92 per cent impurity pattern. This study confirmed that Chalcolithic copper objects were made indigenously, and the metal was extracted from the Chalcopyrite ore deposits in the Aravalli Hills.[6]

After the Ahar excavation, V.N. Misra conducted excavations at Bagor and five copper objects were recovered. Since there is no evidence to suggest that the people of Bagor themselves practised metallurgy, a further exploration was conducted the results of which were quite encouraging.[7] During the excavation, they identified Kotri Dariba which is located at a distance of 22 kilometres. from east of Bagor as a very potential source of copper. The hillsides of Rajpur-Dariba are extensively pockmarked by old shafts.[8] After the excavation at Ahar a limited survey was conducted and around nineteen places of old working sites were recognized. The finding of these old working sites confirms the locally popular name 'Tambavati' of Ahar.[9]

The further excavations at Gilund, Balathal, Ojhiyana, Chatrikheda and Pachmata (all belong to the Ahar culture) also provide the evidence of copper objects. It clearly indicates that southeast Rajasthan was a major centre of copper tool production in the third millennium BC. (See Fig. 4)

The evidence of explorations and excavations provide the information that at most of the places where copper ore occur, one observes old pits, heaps of slag and some crucibles.

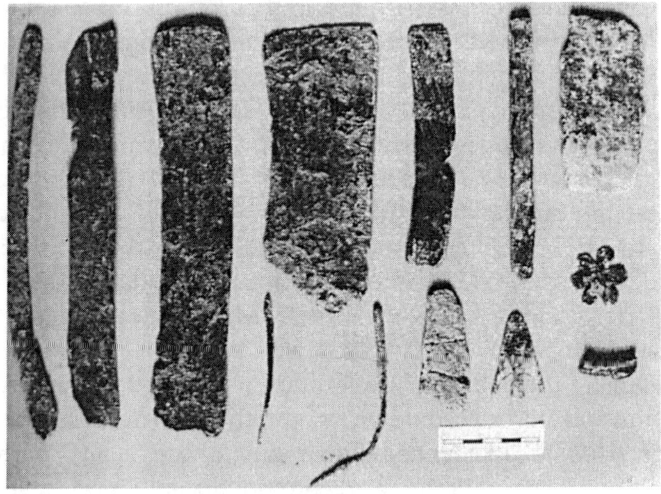

Fig. 4: *Copper implements - Balathal*

It also establishes that copper ore was mined, extracted and processed for long in Rajasthan. But the evidence of numerous deep shafts and large slag heaps indicate that the area of Rajasthan, particularly Aravalli hills was a centre of ancient mining and metallurgical activities. It is obvious from the significant observations that during the late third millennium or early second millennium BC, the people of the region had reached an advanced stage in copper metallurgy in Rajasthan.

It is almost confirmed that copper miming and metallurgy continued even during the early historic period. An important site Nagri (about 15 kilometres to the north of Chittorgarh) was a flourishing town from the fourth century BC to almost the sixth century AD. Besides the inscriptions and architectural activities many copper coins have also been recovered from the site, which indicates the continuity of copper metallurgy.[10] In addition to the evidence of copper metallurgical activities in ancient times, other attractions for the early habitants of the region were zinc and lead. The major centres of these two were Rampura-Dariba, Zawar, Rikhabdeo, Debari, Ghughra, Mando and Wardalia. Among them, the largest deposits of zinc-lead have been discovered in the Rajpura-Dariba mines. As it is confirmed that zinc has a long antiquity in India because the ancient Indians were aware of brass and brass cannot be produced without Zinc.[11] The earliest evidence of brass, which has been recovered in India, is from Taxila (now in Pakistan). Its date is about the fourth century BC. Therefore, to seek an answer to identify the antiquity of zinc in India, a team of archaeologists from the M.S. University of Baroda in collaboration with Hindustan Zinc Ltd., Udaipur and the Research Laboratory of the British Museum carried out an exploration and excavation at Zawar.[12]

During the course of exploration it revealed that many of the mines were worked down to a depth of 120 metres or more. Their deep shafts opened into many galleries and narrow tunnels. All the galleries were provided ventilation holes of 1½ to 2m in diameter at regular intervals. The C^{14} dates of these mine activities, which are available, are 2120+-60 and 1920+-50 years before the present.[13] It is interesting to note that zinc was produced at Zawar even earlier than 765 BC.

Even subsequently during the early medieval and medieval period, Zawar mines remained active as we have evidence of mining and metallurgy of zinc at least till the beginning of colonial era.

It is very interesting to note that during the ancient and medieval times the human settlements have been found in southeast Rajasthan at Nagda, Ahar and Zawar and all these sites were inhabited predominantly by the Bhils. An inscription of King Siladitya (646 AD) of Samoli records opening a mine at a place called Arnyakoopgiri and a temple of Arnyakvasini was also built there for the worship of the local population. Both these terms indicate that the region was a hilly and forest terrain and in context of Mewar the hills and forests are the abode of Bhils. Thus, it can be inferred that the Bhils, the local inhabitants, provided the human resources in mining activities.[14] Furthermore, let me point out that old world Archaeometry provides a very impressive picture of the mining at Zawar. '…By the 12th century, production was on a considerable scale, and perhaps it is not surprising that the first documented historical reference to Zawar occurs in 1380 when Rana Lakshasimha was credited with founding of the mines, production continued on a major scale for about four centuries before ending during the wars and famine which plagued Rajasthan in the early 19th century, and in the face of Western competition. Ironically the Western technology was almost certainly derived from Zawar".[15] It is very difficult not to take cognizance of the fact that a local deity Zawarmata has been very popular among the Bhils of the region. It shows their long association with Zawar. The various Bhil songs testify to it.[16] Equally important is the discovery of charcoal retort dumps at Zawar which are to a great extent a marker of the local Bhils' presence in the region.[17] Thus, can it be suggested that either the Bhils were producers and suppliers of the zinc in the initial phase of mining activities or the Bhils were hired by the regional political formations in the mining activities might have been mobilized as miners. Nandini Sinha Kapoor has highlighted the active role of Bhils in the emergence and consolidation of Sisodia rule in the region. To the extent that the coronation of the king of Mewar is carried out by the Bhil Chieftain.[18] Similarly, for the Khandesh area Sumit Guha has pointed out close associations between Bhils and regional political formations.[19] Bhils have traditionally been engaged in non-agricultural economic activities.[20]

Iron

Besides copper and zinc, southeast Rajasthan also played an important role in the mining and metallurgy of iron. As such geologically, iron ore is distributed throughout the state of Rajasthan with noteworthy deposits in Alwar, Jaipur, Udaipur and Ajmer districts. For example, in 1873 AD there was a report of about 30 pre-industrial furnaces working in the Alwar area which also has old mines.[21] In the region, under discussion, i.e. southeast Rajasthan, the explorations and excavations of various archaeologists including the author provide the information that Ahar, Gilund, Balathal, Purani Marmi, Aguncha, Bhoion-Ki-Pancholi and Nathara-Ki-Pal were the major centres of iron smelting in the past out of which Bhoion-Ki-Pancholi, Iswal and Nathara-Ki-Pal were spread in an area of more than 75 hectares and it can be presumed that these were the industrial towns for iron working.

In Rajasthan, Noh is considered to be the oldest settlement of iron working. The C^{14} date for this site goes back to 950 BC[22] but southeast Rajasthan does not provide any date parallel to it. Apparently, Ahar (Udaipur) appears to be the first site which provides the evidence of old iron working. However, there is no consensus on this issue. Archaeologists have divergent opinions about the presence of iron smelting in the Chalcolithic context.[23] Probably, Balathal (Udaipur) is the first site which provides the C14 dates of iron working in this region of Rajasthan. These C14 dates confirm that during the fourth century BC iron working had begun in this region of Rajasthan.

The excavations at Balathal provide the remains of two furnaces which were heavily damaged. Two roughly cylindrical or barrel-shaped clay rolls were also found close to the furnaces. The surface of these clay rolls were embedded with quartz crystals of varying sizes, a device developed by the Iron Age people in order to increase the temperature and retain the heat for a longer time. Though the settlement of the Iron Age is smaller in size but it provides a substantial amount of iron implements. The implements, which have been recovered from the site, are more than five hundred and those are of domestic use. (See Fig. 5)

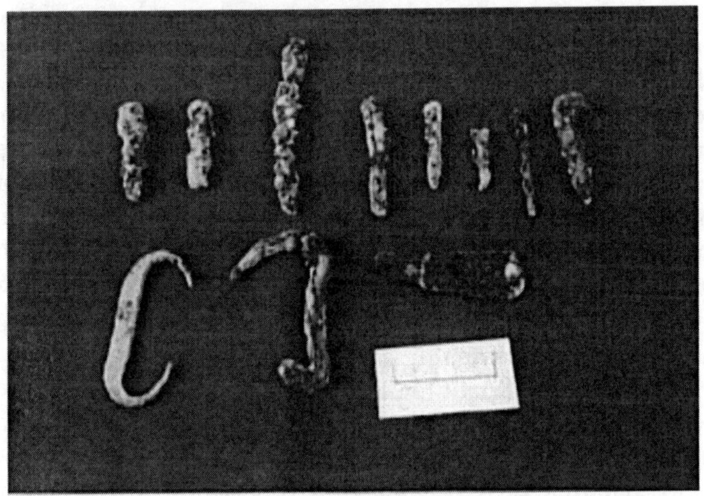

Fig. 5: *Iron Objects - Iswal*

Thus, it can be presumed that Balathal was an important industrial centre during the early historic period. Thereafter, extensive surveys were undertaken around the site to locate the source of iron. After extensive surveys three sites Iswal, Bhoion-ki-Pancholi and Nathara-ki-Pal have been identified as the major source of iron within a periphery of 50 to 75 kilometres from Balathal. It appears that Bhoion-ki-Pancholi was a very promising centre of iron ore. During the course of exploration it is revealed that there are three mounds located and all of them have thick iron deposits in the central part which perhaps contain a high percentage of iron ore as production from this site continued till 50 years ago.

After a continuous excavation for seven years at Iswal, the site has provided very interesting and useful information with regard to the smelting and melting of iron. The ancient site at Iswal covers approximately 75 hectares, with an area of approximately 130x130 m of concentrated production debris primarily in the form of slag. The site, on the basis of the available evidence, is divided into a production area and a habitation zone. The excavations, which concentrated on the iron working area during the last four seasons, provide the evidence of a sizeable amount of slag, ash, a series of furnaces, pottery associated floors and a fair amount of lime. The presence of lime, suggests that the metallurgists of the period have used lime as influx. The site also reveals a very important and unique feature of a large domestic settlement which was separated from the working area at a considerable distance. It appears that it was for the workers and we may call it a commercial colony. As far as the existing knowledge is concerned there is only one site Khairadih[24] in Uttar Pradesh which also provides the evidence of a working area as well as an area for the artisans.

It is very important to discuss in detail the nature of these two sites, Balathal and Iswal because they provide the evidence of iron working into two very different contexts. On the one hand, Balathal is associated with production of iron goods primarily for domestic purposes and on the other hand, Iswal is associated with intensive production of iron that might have been used for commercial/industrial purposes. Unfortunately, we have almost no information about the politico-economic authority managing and controlling this site. Iswal is the only site which offers evidence of continued occupation since the early historic times to the early medieval period. Dates are between 2973 BP to 950 BP and four dates are between 950 to 1580 BP. It shows that from the fourth to the twelfth century. Iswal was a very active centre of human activities. The inscriptional and architectural evidence certifies it.

After continuous excavations the remains of three furnaces along with a number of working levels, were recorded. A close examination of the section has revealed that there were a number of working levels, characterized by the presence of mainly circular or roughly square furnaces. Each level was separated by a well-plastered and rammed layer of soil.[25]

Fig. 6: *Furnace, Iron Smelting - Iswal*

Furnace No. 1: It was pear-shaped and it was sealed by a well plastered and rammed layer on the top and the base. The height of the surviving lateral wall was 75 cm from the outer surface and 65 cm from the inner surface. The base of the furnace measured 83 cm in width and was 12 cm thick (See Fig. 6).

Fig. 7: Twin Furnaces-Iswal: Alternative Levels of Slag

Besides the furnace No. 1, two more furnaces were noticed in the cut section. This indicates that there were a number of furnaces of different kinds used by the inhabitants. Furnaces noticed in the lower levels are well made and large in size. They were built in situ over a stone foundation. The walls of these furnaces were made of clay and had become red burnt due to their constant use. Furnace 2 and 3: These two furnaces were at a distance of 70 cm to each other. Furnace No. 2 was measured 80 cm long (N-S) with a width of 60 (EW) It was roughly triangular. A total of three broken tuyeres were also noticed at the upper part of the furnace. Their average measurement was 12 cm in length with 8 cm width. All these had a hole of one centimetre at the centre (See Fig. 7). Furnace No. 3 was 90 cm (EW) in length with a width of 70 cm (NS). The lateral walls of the furnace were 24 cm thick. It was full of ash and slag. The colour of the lateral walls was red and it was roughly oval in shape.

Fig. 8: *Tuyeres-Iswal*

It is significant to note that during the course of excavations a cluster of broken tuyeres was encountered and the 32 broken retorts. The average length of these tuyeres was 15 to 22 cm. (See Fig. 8) In addition to this, the section of the furnace had alternative slag levels which were separated by a rammed clay floor. The total number of slag levels was nine. Their average thickness was 10 cm and the colour was dark greenish-yellow.

All this evidence suggests a long duration fire activities at the place. A single piece of broken tuyeres of about 40 cm is also recovered during the course of excavations. It suggests that the quite large tuyeres were used for the proper supply of air. The evidence of these long tuyeres can be seen even today at Iswal and Losing village. Besides the evidence of smelting activities, a substantial amount of ore was also recorded at the site (See Fig. 9).

Fig. 9: *Iron Ore - Iswal*

A few samples from this site were examined by Ritesh Purohit of the Department of Geology, MLSU University, Udaipur. The results are as follows.

(i) The ore sample is identified as Goethite ore which is mainly a hydroxide of iron. The mineral is brown to dark-brown blackish in appearance. It is opaque to translucent in the section with earth lustre. It is similar to limonite, another hydroxide of iron, but distinctly distinguished on the basis of two properties, it is crystalline with parallel extinction, but limonite is not. Goethite occurring in the Iswal area is mainly a withered product of Hematite ore. A vast and open iron mining site, which is now abandoned, can be seen in close proximity of the site.

(ii) It appears that the slag samples, which were collected from the site, were used for smelting of the iron by the erstwhile natives. The presence of an immense quantity of slag also signifies that the art of smelting the iron ore was well developed in the area.

(iii) A sample of a rusted knife like object was also analysed. It indicates that it was made at the same place where it was smelted.

Therefore, it can be summarized that Iswal was a major centre of iron smelting in southeast Rajasthan between 2973 to 1540 years before the present. The C14 dates verify it. The erstwhile natives at Iswal were basically engaged in smelting activity because very few iron implements have been recovered from the site during the course of excavation. After continuous excavations for seven years almost fifty iron implements were recovered from the site. The scientific examination of these implements was performed with the collaboration of Jang-Sik –Park, Department of Metallurgy, Hogink University, Korea. The results of the scientific analysis are amazing and the findings throw new light on the history of southeast Rajasthan.

During the excavation one Bi-metallic object was recovered, the finding of this Bi-metallic antiquity is very rare in the Indian context for this time period. It is 131.05 mm in length and 58.68 mm in breadth with a thickness of 5.8 mm. The base and handle of the antiquity are made of copper-zinc alloy (bronze) which was made by the lost wax technique. The top handle is divided into two sections into which an iron blade is inserted. It is highly polished and its base displays artistic work. Ethnographic studies suggest that in Rajasthan also similar kinds of tools are being currently used as 'Goads' for camel. Locally it is popular as 'Ankush' or elephant 'Goad' which is very well documented in ancient and medieval sculptures and paintings.

The results of scientific analysis are also noteworthy in the context of iron implements. It is revealed that four objects were made of 'Steel' containing a substantial amount of carbon.

Thus, it can be said the inhabitants of southeast Rajasthan also followed the same trajectory and they had been using the similar technology which was prevalent in other parts of India like Vidarbha and Junnar in Maharashtra. Probably in the subsequent era this improved sophisticated skill of implements making which helped the Ravals and Maharanas of Mewar in wars; perhaps because of the better quality of arms they could win against their rivals.[26]

Another important feature of the site is the recovery of glass bangles which have been found in a large quantity. They vary from monochrome to polychrome. Some of them are translucent and some are completely transparent. Thus, it can be said that the site was a major centre of pyrotechnological industries for about seven hundred years.[27]

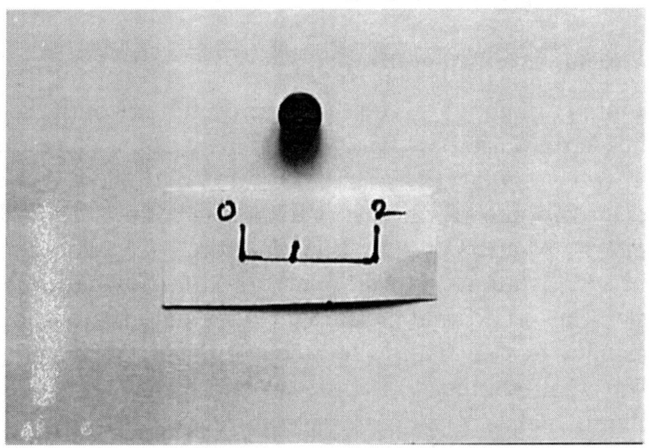

Fig. 10: *Beryl Bead - Iswal*

Besides the iron and glass working a single piece of bead, which is of semi-precious gemstone variety of beryl, is also found at Iswal (See Fig. 10). It is a rare material found in granite rocks and was used as gems. Its specific gravity is determined as 3.6 (approximately) and it is translucent in character.

In addition to it, one pendant of lapis lazuli inlaid with gold is also recovered from the site during the course of excavation (See Fig. 11).

Fig. 11: *Lapis Lazuli Gold Inlaid – Iswal*

Case for Further Integration

As pointed out above, given the geomorphology of the region, southeastern Rajasthan was very rich in mineral resources which were regularly exploited by humans since the ancient past. The combined testimony of the recovered material culture of Nagari[28], Ahar[29], Gilund[30], Bhagvanpura[31], Chosal[32], Bagor[33], Aguncha[34], Balathal[35], Iswal[36], Nathara-ki-Pal[37], Chatrikheda[38], Javasia[39] and Pachmata[40] along with the epigraphic and numismatic evidence and the archaeo-metallurgical activities confirm that southeast Rajasthan had been very actively supplying metals to numerous cultures located in different parts of the Indian subcontinent.

Archaeologically these sites may appear stand alone but we are well aware that each site has been part of a larger network which cut often across traditional timelines. It will not be incorrect to state that the unique geographical location of southeast Rajasthan played a significant role in sustaining and nourishing these networks. To begin with, let me draw your attention to the sufficient number of shards of Grey Ware with straight sides and incurved rims found at Balathal are identical to the shards found at Hastinapur.[41] According to the excavator the date of these shards is around the sixth century BC. Pottery of the same era found in the Ganges region popularly known as Painted Grey Ware has its extension up to the Bhilwara. Likewise there is evidence which confirms the contact between southeast Rajasthan and the Deccan. An inscription of the second century BC of Pratapgarh refers to the term 'Aparanta'. Historically, Kathiwad, Kutch and Sindh besides Konkan forms the 'Aparanta' region.[42] An undated inscription of Nahapan which has been found at Nasik Caves narrates that on the command of Bhattarak, Rishabhadatta (Ushavadatta), the son of Dinika and the son-in-law of Nahapana went to rescue the chief of the Uttambhadra tribe who was besieged by the Malavas. "Pay the order of my Lord", he records, "I went in the rainy season to relieve the Uttambhadras". Furthermore, inscriptions record that after the crushing defeat of the Malavas, Rishabhadatta went to Pushkar Lake for ceremonial consecration.[43] Thus, it can be concluded that southeast Rajasthan was a very prominent centre of natural resources including the mining and metallurgical activities in the past and was closely integrated with the economy of the Ganges plains as well as to the northwestern part of India. It seems, the erstwhile natives of this region had developed a certain kind of guilds of smiths and mine workers who were successfully running it on an industrial scale.

NOTES

1. Praveena, Gullapalli, 'Smelting and Smithing: The Organization of Iron Production in Early Historic Rajasthan', an unpublished thesis, University of Pennsylvania, USA, 2005. *Dissertations available from ProQuest*. AAI3179742. https://repository.upenn.edu/dissertations/AAI3179742, pp. 56-57.
2. V.C. Misra, *Geography of Rajasthan*, National Book Trust, Delhi: 1967, pp. 110-11.
3. G.G. Majumdar and S.N. Rajaguru, 'Early Mining and Metallurgy in Rajasthan', Part I, Copper Around Udaipur, *Bulletin of Deccan College*, Pune: 1962-63, pp. 31-33.
4. The various literary sources also bring to light the fact that copper was considered sacred in various religious functions.

Even today, most of the Hindus perform their rituals only on copper objects.

5. H.D. Sankalia, *Archaeology of Rajasthan*, Sahitya Sansthan, Rajasthan Vidyapeeth, Udaipur: 1988, p. 111-28.
6. K.T.M. Hegde, 'Scientific Basis and Technology of Ancient Indian Copper and Iron Metallurgy,' *Indian Journal of History of Science*, Vol. 16, No. 2, 1981, 189-201.
7. A. Ghosh, *Encyclopaedia of Indian Archaeology*, Munshiram Manoharlal, New Delhi: 2013, pp. 35-37.
8. R. Shrivastava, 'Mining of Copper in Ancient India,' *Indian Journal of History of Science*, Vol. 34, No. 3, 1999, pp. 175-76.
9. Ibid., p. 177.
10. A.C.L. Carllyl, ed., *Archaeological Survey of India Report of a Tour in Eastern Rajputana 1871-72 and 1872-73*, Superintendent of Government Printing, Calcutta: 1878, p. 197.
11. Misra, *Geography of Rajasthan*, pp. 110-11.
12. Willies Lynn, P.T. Craddock, L.J. Gujjar and K.T.M. Hegde, 'Ancient Zinc and Lead Mining', *World Archaeology*, Vol. 16, No. 2, 1984, pp. 222-24.
13. Sankalia, *Archaeology of Rajasthan*, p. 102.
14. 'Samoli Abhilekh' *Nagri Pracharini Patrika*, Vol. I, pp. 311-24.
15. Paul T. Craddock et al., 'Zinc Production in Medieval India', *World Archaeology*, Vol. 15, No. 2, 1983, p. 62.
16. Sharma, G.L. *Bheeli Geet*, Sahitya Sansthan, Rajasthan Vidyapeeth, Udaipur: 1956, pp. 31-33.
17. N.S. Kapoor, *State Formation in Rajasthan: Mewar During the Seventh-Fifteenth Centuries*, Manohar, New Delhi: 2002, p. 130.
18. Ibid., p. 167.
19. Sumit Guha, 'Claims on the Commons: Political Power and Natural Resources in Pre-Colonial India', *The Indian Economic and Social History Review*, 39, 2&3, 2002, pp. 181-96.
20. S.S. Gahlot, and B. Dhar, *Caste and Tribes of Rajasthan*, Jain Brothers, Jodhpur: 1989, p. 221.
21. Chakrabati, Dilip, *India: An Archarological History*, Oxford University Press, New Delhi: 1992, pp. 26-28.
22. A. Ghosh, *An Encyclopaedia of Indian Archaeology*, Munshiram Manoharlal, New Delhi: pp. 318-19.
23. V.K. Thakur, 'Implications of Technology: A Study of Iron in Pre C. 200 BC India', in *Archeometallurgy of India*, ed. Vibha Tripathi,

Sharada Publishing House, Delhi: 1998, p. 363.

24. Chakravarti, *An Archaeological History*, p. 250.
25. L.A. Pandey, 'Report on Excavations at Iswal', *Shodh-Patrika*, Vol. 57, Nos. 1-4, 2005-06, pp. 122-23.
26. L. Pandey, 'Recent Archaeometallurgical Discoveries in South-east Rajasthan, Iswal', in *The World of Iron*, eds. Jane Humphris and Thilo Rehrn, London: 2013, pp. 91-96.
27. Another site Nathara-Ki-Pal, which is very close to Chavand, capital of Maharana Pratap, is a more promising site and it can reveal certain new dimensions regarding the pyrotechnological industries of the region for about seven hundred years.
28. A. Ghosh, *An Encyclopaedia of Indian Archaeology*, Vol. II, Munshiram Manoharlal, New Delhi: 2013, p. 299.
29. Sankalia, *Excavations At Ahar*, pp. 1-6.
30. *Indian Archaeology: A Review*, Archaeological Survey of India, New Delhi: 1959-60, p. 41.
31. Ibid., 1957-58.
32. Ibid., 1958-59.
33. Ghosh, *An Encyclopaedia*, Vol. II, pp. 34-37.
34. *Indian Archaeology: Ä Review*, Archaeological Survey of India, New Delhi: 1980-81.
35. Ibid., 1962-63; V.N. Mishra, V.S. Shinde, R.K. Mohanty, Kurush Dalal, Lalit Pandey, J. Kharakwal, 'Excavations at Balathal, Udaipur, District, Rajasthan', *Man and Environment*, Vol. XXII, No. 2, 1997, pp. 1-12.
36. Lalit Pandey, V.S. Shinde, Jagdeesh Meena, Kulshekhar Vyas, Lal Chand Patel, Hemendra Choudhary, 'Preliminary Report on Excavations at Iswal', *Shodh Patrika*, Vol. 56, Nos. 1-4, 2004-05, pp. 1-7.
37. Lalit Pandey, V.S. Shinde, Jagdeesh Meena, Kulshekhar Vyas, Lal Chand Patel, Hemendra Choudhary, 'A Preliminary Report of Excavation at Nthara-ki-Pal', *Shodh-Patrika*, Vol. 59, Nos. 3-4, 2007-2008, pp. 99-104.
38. Lalit Pandey, P. Teresa, P. Shivalkar, N. Sugandhi, 'Excavations at Chatrikheda', 2009-2011, Unpublished Report.
39. Lalit Pandey, P. Teresa, P. Shivalkar, 'Excavations at Javasia', 2010-11 (Unpublished Report).
40. Lalit Pandey, P. Teresa, P. Shivalkar, 'Excavations at Pachmata', 2015-2017 (Unpublished Report).

41. B.B. Lal., 'Excavations at Hastinapur and Other Explorations in the Upper Ganga and Sutlej Basin 1950-52', *Ancient India-Bulletin of the Archaeological Survey of India,* Vols. 10 & 11, 1954-55, pp. 5-151.
42. Richard Solomon, 'Pratapgarh Pillar Inscription', *Epigraphia Indica,* Vol. XXXIX, Part 3, 1998, pp. 79-80.
43. F. Kielhorn, 'Junagarh Rock Inscription of Rudradaman: The Year 72', *Epigraphia Indica,* Vol. VIII, 1905-06, pp. 36-49.

3

Farmans, Sanads, Parwanas, Hukumnamas: A Survey of Endowment Documents

Yaqub Ali Khan

Historical understanding of the nature and character of state since the Turkish invasion of India has been at the centre of historical debate since long. Image of the state either as theocratic or mere appropriator of agrarian surplus has been modified. British colonial depiction of state as distant entity which was least bothered about its subjects, has been demolished comprehensively. Rather state intervention in the daily affairs of its subject is now well documented usually on the basis of revenue records. The present paper showcases several official documents dealing with various forms of endowments, usually written in the language of the court; Persian. These documents offer us a glimpse of the significant role played by the state not in extending support to the religious establishments and institutions but also to the men and women of piety. Analysis of the content of these documents will help us examine the complex relationships between Kings, administrative apparatus and beneficiaries. This paper is divided into three parts. The first part of the paper deals with the introduction, meaning, different terms, their origin, institutions and individuals which were granted waqf and its offices and officials. The second part deals with the *farmans, sanads, parwanas* and *hukumnamas* issued time to time by the various authorities of the government and the third part of this paper contains the inscriptional evidence of the grants of the *waqf* (*madad-i-ma'ash*) or endowments to the Muslim religious institutions or the individuals.

I

Waqf or *Auqaf,* (plural of waqf) or religious endowments meaning the land grants made for the maintenance of a religious shrine or a mosque, establishing religious, cultural and welfare institutions. These grants were made for the upkeep of institutions. The revenues of a certain village or villages were assigned permanently in auqaf for the maintenance of religious shrines, tombs and madarsas.[1] Any given waqf tried to meet a number of religious and cultural expectations: that the rich must support the poor as a duty to God.[2]

There are hundreds of references which supply abundant information about the *waqf* endowments or *madad-i-ma'ash*. Though not mentioned in the Quran, it derives its legitimacy primarily from a number of *hadiths*. The first one is related to the authority of Ibn Umar and is included in various versions, in the main *hadith* collections: Once the second Caliph, Hazrat Umar-al-Khattab acquired a piece of land in Khayber and came to the Prophet to consult in the matter saying: "O Messenger of God I have acquired land in Khayber which is more precious to me than any property, I have never acquired." The Prophet answered, "If you want make the land itself unalienable and give the yield away as alms." Thereupon, 'Umar gave it away as alms in the sense that the land itself was not to be sold, inherited and donated. He gave it as alms for the poor, the relatives, slaves, the *jihad,* the travellers and the guests'.[3] Another *hadith* often quoted in favour of the legitimacy of the waqf is included in the *sahih* of Muslim: "The messenger of God said, 'when a man dies, only three deeds will survive him: continuing alms, profitable knowledge and child praying for him'."[4]

It is not surprising to note that the practice of assignment of religious endowments originated in ancient times. References of such grants are available from the first century AD. Throughout ancient India it was a regular process. In the last decade of the twelfth century the Turks established their suzerainty in India after defeating Prithviraj Chauhan in the second battle of Tarain in 1192. They also adopted this policy of land grants and other types of subsistence allowances to the needy and the poor, the ascetics and hermits, the scholars, men of noble birth and religious institutions such as *madarsas, khanqahs* and *mosques*. As the *mashaikh* and *ulama* commanded great respect among the common masses, the ruling class sought their blessings to receive their support. Jahangir used to call these peoples as *lashkar-i-doagoan* (army of the prayers) and he is alleged to have said that the prayers of this army were more effective than the efforts of the army of soldiers in winning victories.[5] The sultans and their nobles approached them for blessings, gave them money, made land grants and employed them as highly venerated officers of the state. For this reason the ruling classes assigned cash and land grants to them.

Varieties of terms have been used for this type of financial assistance and land grants. During ancient times these grants were known as *brahmdeya*[6], *agraharas*[7] (grants for religious and educational purposes) and *devdanas*.[8] After the establishment of Muslim rule in India, these terms changed and they were known as *milk,*[9] *inam*[10], *wazifa*[11], and *auqaf* land in the later period these were known as *wajih-i-ma'ash* and *wajih-i-milk*[12]. The *waqf* or *auqaf* grants were made for the maintenance of the religious shrines and tombs while the *inam* grant was conferred upon the poets, artists attached to the royal court. The earliest reference to the *wajih-i-ma'ash* grant in the Indian subcontinent is found in the official documents of Sultan Firozshah Tughlaq's period.[13] *Wajih-i-ma'ash* was a grant in the form of land assigned to the *mashaikhs, Syeds*, the *Ulama*, poets and other deserving persons such as widows for their maintenance in recognition of their piety, need, learning or any service rendered by them to the state. These land grants were given to the aforesaid persons for a lifetime as well as perpetuity to the family.

All such type of grants was known as *madad-i-ma'ash* or

revenue free land grants. But in some documents of Babur and his grandson Akbar, we come across the term *suyurghal*[14] but after the consolidation of their empire they preferred to use the term *madad-i-ma'ash* in place of *suyurghal*. Abul Fazl further mentions that two types of subsistence allowance were given to grantees; allowance in cash known as *wazifa* and land assignmeents known as *milk* or *madad-i-ma'ash* grants.[15] Moreland writes that *sayurghal* was an allowance paid in cash or granted in the form of land assignments,[16] whereas Noman Ahmad Siddiqi suggests that the subsistence allowance in land was known as *madad-i-ma'ash*.[17] The state usually supported individuals with land/cash grants to carry out their endeavours in different branches of knowledge. The recipients were the members of existing religious and literary elites, men of noble lineage, and other similar notables. *Madad-i-ma'ash* was thus a grant of land made in recognition of the need, piety, learning or family of *Shaikhs* and *Syeds* or the religious personalities. The land revenues and other taxes on this land were not realized by the revenue officials of the state.

According to Abul Fazl, the following four classes of people were considered worthy and in need of financial support for subsistence: First category consisted of those who had withdrawn from all worldly occupations and were involved in the search for true knowledge, which became the sole purpose of their life. The second category consisted of the ascetics and hermits who had left the worldly affairs to get rid of selfish desires and human passions. The third category consisted of those who were poor and the needy and did not even have the strength to make arrangements for their subsistence and thus could not engage in search of knowledge and fourth category consisted of persons of noble birth, who needed state support for their subsistence.[18]

The *Sadr* or *Sadr-us-sudur* was responsible for the administration of the *madad-i ma'ash* grants. In each province, the *sadr* undertook the function of supervising the grants; and in the pargana *s* the *mutawalli* was responsible. The *mutawalli* was appointed by the emperor[19] but usually he was also one of the descendants of the saint. The management of the *waqf* property and the *nazr* (offerings) was in the hands of the *mutawalli*. The *mutawalli* was solely responsible for the management of the *waqf* lands, their income and expenditure on the items authorized by the emperor. Sometime a *mutawalli* used to hold two offices at the same time. Mir Saadullah who was *Sadr* (In charge of *madad-i-ma'ash*) of the Ajmer *suba* and at the same time he was also serving as *mutawalli* of the shrine of Khwaja Moinuddin Chishti of Ajmer.[20] *Madad-i-ma'ash* grants were not necessarily hereditary, but Aurangzeb made the land grants completely hereditary.[21]

Akbar had made another class of people eligible for *madad-i-ma'ash* which comprised those villagers who offered hospitality to emperor while on his expeditions and Jahangir to those *zamindars* who assisted him in the revolt raised by prince Khurram against the emperor.[22] One of the most important developments in the history of *waqf*, was the evolution of two distinct forms—the public *waqf* (*waqf-i-khayri*) and the family *waqf* (*waqf-ahli* or *waqf-dhurri*). From a strictly legal standpoint the two forms of *waqf* are identical. Public *waqf* typically, had as their first purpose, support of a public institution such as fountain, a mosque, a hostel, a cemetery, a hospital, *khanqah* or a school while private *waqf* were established to aid the founder's kin and descendants.[23] Sometimes emperors used to examine the validity and continuation of the land grant and renewed it only after its proper enquiry was up to this satisfaction. The *jagirdars* and other authorities were not allowed to interfere in the land given in *madad-i ma'ash*.[24]

II

There are hundreds of documents regarding the endowments of Muslim religious institutions and the sufi shrines by the various authorities. In medieval India these institutions and shrines were offered financial support by the government authorities in the form of land revenue assignments or cash. The shrine of Khwaja Moinuddin Chishti was famous not only among the masses but it was worshipped by the ruling elite also, including the sultans/emperors of the period. The first sultan of Delhi, who came to Ajmer and paid homage to the shrine of Khwaja Muinuddin Chishti, was Sultan Muhammad bin Tughlaq.[25] In fact, it had become an established custom for the sultans of the time to visit the *dargah* of an eminent sufi if he happened to be in its vicinity.[26] The spatial distribution of such grants across the realm as discussed below is testimony to this practice. We will begin with details of endowments made to the famous shrine of Khwaja Moinuddin Chishti followed by grants by Mughal emperors in other parts of their realm.

Emperor Akbar was the first Mughal ruler who captured Ajmer in 1556-57. After conquering Chittor, the capital of Mewar in 1567, he paid his visit to the shrine of the Khwaja and presented a brazen cauldron of a gigantic size to the shrine.[27] He made his pilgrimages to Khwaja on foot every year[28] and continued his visits until 1580. After that, he stopped going to Ajmer and instead deputed his son Daniyal to visit on his behalf.[29] Jahangir and Shahjahan also visited the shrine many times.[30] After defeating Dara Shukoh, Aurangzeb too visited the *dargah*. Again in I680 he paid a visit to the *dargah*.[31] The repeated imperial visits and devotion of the dignitaries resulted not only in the transformation of the complex of the shrine but also in the creation of a considerable number of documents related to *waqf* which are available in public and private possessions.

The *dargah* of Khwaja Moinuddin Chishti had been granted a number of villages in *waqf*. The *gumashta* (agents) of the *mutawalli* used to collect revenue and distribute it among the servants of the *dargah,* and the legitimate claimants. The autonomous chiefs were free in their territories to make revenue-free grants. The earliest reference is found during the life time of the great Chishti saint, Khwaja Moinuddin Chishti of Ajmer itself. Khwaja's eldest son, Khwaja Fakhruddin Abul Khair who was settled in a village named Mandal, few miles away from Ajmer, earned his livelihood by the cultivation of land. The *muqta* of Ajmer urged him to obtain a royal *farman* for the land. He approached his father who went to the royal court.

The ruling Sultan, Iltutmish was having cordial relations with the Khwaja and his disciple, Shaikh Qutubuddin Bakhtiyar Kaki. Knowing the reason of Khwaja's arrival at Delhi, his disciple and vice-regent Khwaja Qutubuddin Bakhtiyar Kaki requested his spiritual master not to go to the court of the Sultan because it was not a practice of the Chishti saints to see the rulers. But breaking the tradition of the *silsilah* he himself went to the court and obtained a *muqarrar dast* from the Sultan Iltutmish.[32]

After the conquest of Ajmer emperor Akbar paid several visits to the shrine of Khwaja Moinuddin Chishti. Akbar granted the village named as Deorai and Sumelpur of pargana Ajmer to the dargah of Saiyid Hussain Khang Sawar as *madad-i-ma'ash* to the *mujawirs* (attendants of the shrine) and for the expenditure on *Urs* festival, illuminations, etc. In 1574-75, he ordered the Shiqdar and Karori of the village Sambhar to supply to Syed Mumtazullah Alam, a Khadim, one man (unit of weight, in Akbar's time a man was equal to about 51.63lbs or about 40 kg.) oil per month for lighting at the *maqbara* (tomb) of Khwaja Moinuddin Chishti. He further instructed the officials of the place not to insist on obtaining a new *farman* in this regard.[33] According to a *farman* dated 28 May, 1576 to the officials of pargana Haveli, Ajmer intimating that village Nadla or Nandila had been granted to Shaikh Fatahullah and his brothers as *madad-i-ma'ash* as they had no means of livelihood and to meet the expenses of the 'urs ceremony of the great Khwaja'.[34]

Emperor Jahangir issued a *farman* on 17 August, 1610, addressed to the '*amils, karkunan* and *karoriyan* of pargana Ajmer informing them that 4,200 *bighas* of land under cultivation and 2,690 *bighas* of fallow land located in *mauza* Nandila, continuing and confirming the royal *farman* of Akbar granted in the name of Shaikh Hashim, son of Shaikh Fatahullah, Shaikh Ismaeel son of Taj Muhammad and other twenty four *mujawirs* and further added that out of the said grant 1,000 *bighas* of land had been kept aside for the expenditure on 'Urs ceremony and the remaining is reserved as *madad-i-ma'ash* for the twenty six grantees.[35]

In I616, Jahangir resumed one hundred *bighas* of land out of two hundred thirty *bighas* which was given to Bibi Jan and other widows of saintly persons and khadims related to the *dargah* of Khwaja Moinuddin Chishti in *madad-i-ma'ash*. It is not clear from this document that how this recovered land was distributed among them? Some of the land was recovered by Jahangir as the recipients failed to appear before him.

During the reign of Emperor Akbar a *sanad* dated 27 August, 1586 from Pahar Singh, son of Man Datta Rai for the grant of ten *koru* (bighas) of rent-free land, worth cultivation, in the village Bhusahi Buzurg in the pargana Saraisa, Hajipur, Bihar was issued in the name of Shah Hazrat Kabir Muhammad, for his livelihood, expenses of the mosque, *khanqah* and the needy and *nazr* (offering) to Hazrat Pir Dastgir Shaikh Abdul Qadir Jilani.[36]

In the year 1616 Emperor Jahangir granted 560 *bighas* of land to Syed Shah Muhammad who was the son of Syed Mansoor as the *madad-i-ma'ash*. In the 12th year of his reign, Jahangir (1617) issued a *farman* for the grant of 20 *bighas* of rent free land, worth cultivation in the same pargana (Hajipur), Bihar with exemption from payment of taxes and other demands in the name of Shaikh Bhikan son of Shaikh Adam, and his sons. In the same year a *farman* was issued by the emperor that about 145 *bighas* of land, uncultivated but liable to cultivation, measured in *Ilahi gaz* situated in the pargana of Gopa Mau, *sarkar* Khairabad had been fixed and confirmed for the *wajh-i-madad ma'ash* of Syed Ahamad Bukhari and his sons. Enjoying their revenue season after season and year after year, for their livelihood, the beneficiaries would pray for the perpetuity of the everlasting dominion. The *hakims*, the *amils*, the *jagirdars*, the present and the future *karories* would work for the perpetuation and confirmation of this *farman*. They would not create trouble to the assignees in connection with the *mal-o-jihat*, the *ikhrajat* and the *awaridat* etc. In this connection they would not ask for the yearly *farman* or a new *parvanchah*.[37]

During the reign of Shahjahan, his most trusted and

honoured noble, Wazir Khan's endowment for the congregational mosque in Lahore which was completed in 1634-35, is worth being mentioned here. For the maintenance of this pious edifice, he had endowed for its expenses all the shops situated on both sides of the road, together with the upper stories, habitable quarters, the large *sarai, hammam,* two wells worked with Persian wheels and several scattered plots of land. Further he mentioned that this endowment was valid, binding, certain and imperative, not subject to be sold, mortgaged or dowered. Further, that *Imam*-preacher attached to the mosque should be highly skilled, the upper storey shops shall be for the use of booksellers of books on Islamic subjects and for bookbinders free of rent. The *Imam*-preacher would receive the remuneration Re 1 to Rs. 10 per diem and *muezzin* four *annas* per day and each teacher Re 1 for each day. The remaining amount will be given to the servants of the mosque and for other necessary expenses, such as providing for the overseer, the carrier of fire wood, the carpet-spreader and other rightful persons attached to the mosque as well as in maintaining guests.[38]

Emperor Aurangzeb issued an order on 9th year of his reign (1676) recognizing Shaikh Pir Muhammad of Salon directly as a grantee for the same piece of land of 200 bighas in the village of Mirzapur Bakhtiyar, pargana Nasirabad, Sarkar Manikpur, suba Allahabad which was earlier granted by a local *jagirdar* under his delegated powers by way of *nazr-i-khadiman-i-haqiq-wa-ma'arif-i-agah* (an offering for the servants of one knowing the mystic truth).[39]

In the forty-third year of Aurangzeb Alamgir (25 February, 1699), a *farman* was issued to the effect that 40 *bighas* of rent-free land, worth cultivation, in the village Rampur, pargana Haveli Hajipur, suba Bihar, which was granted previously under the *farman* of Jahangir in the name of Shaikh Abdus Samad and Shaikh Muhammad and were in possession of their heirs—Bibi Sharifa and others—were being subjected to undue interference and illegal money was exacted from them. The emperor therefore issued a *farman* to all officers of government with the instruction to leave the land in their possession without any sort of interference.[40]

Emperor Bahadur Shah through his *farman* dated 7th Zi'l-hij 2nd RY/1708 recognized and confirmed as *madad-i-ma'ash* all the land grants spread over eight parganas in *suba* of Allahabad and four parganas in *suba* of Awadh, which was assigned either through imperial favour or through local officials and *zamindars* to Shaikh Muhammad Ashraf, the spiritual successor of Shaikh Pir Muhammad of Salon, d.1754. On the *zimn* of this *farman*, a citation was made to the effect that the grantee with a large number of mendicants engaged in propagating the tenets of *sharia'* and *tariqat* in the area and that in some of these villages he had established mosques and *musafir-khanas* (rest houses) in the barren land, had caused habitations to emerge which have been named after his sons.[41]

In the 5th year of Farrukhsiyar's reign a *sanad* was issued on 2 and 12 January, 1716 with the seal of Nawab Sarbuland Khan and others for the grant of one hundred *bighas* of rent-free land in the village Chak Bhikam, in the Bihar *suba* in the name of Khwaja Shah Moinuddin, *Khadim-i-dargah* as *madad-i-ma'ash* and the other, was issued in favour of Bibi Aulia and others for the release of 200 bighas of rent-free land in the village of Chak Yusuf and Chak Jina in pargana of Panwara as *madad-i-ma'ash*.[42]

Another *sanad* was issued in the 8th year of emperor Farrukhsiyar's reign (30 January, 1718) with the seal of Syed Abdullah Khan, Commander-in-Chief renewing the grant of the village Islampur in pargana Arrah of *suba* Bihar in the name of Shaikh Amanullah, as *madad-i-maash* and for the expenses of the mosque, *khanqah* and the students etc.[43]

During the reign of Muhammad Shah, a *sanad* was issued on 27 August, 1723 for revival of previous *sanad* and release of sixty five *bighas* of rent free land in the village of Pir Kokam, in pargana Dharampur, Bihar in the name of Syed Muhammad Waris as *madad-i-ma'ash* and for the expenses connected with the visitors to the *dargah* of Qidwatul Arifin.[44] Another *parwana* was issued during the reign of Muhammad Shah (11 May, 1733) reviving the previous *sanad* for the grant of the village Parshadi in pargana Makair, *suba* Bihar with the exemption from payment of revenue and other demands in the name of Mulla Syed Haider, a dervish, as a gift for the expenses of the *khanqah*, tomb, mosque etc. and also for the heirs of Hazrat Makhdoom Syed Shah Saifuddin Ahmad Mazindrani.[45]

We came across some *farmans* of the Mughal Emperors which were issued in favour of the women also.[46] In this 22nd RY, Jahangir assigned the whole revenue of Rs. 750 of village Gelota, pargana Naraina, of Ajmer Suba to Shaikh Ilmuddin, a cousin of Khwaja Hussain for his livelihood and blessing for the emperor. All the officials including *amils, jagirdars* and *karoris* of the place were ordered to implement the royal order and instructed not interferet in the matter. Also they were not required to obtain fresh or new *farman* in this regard.[47]

Cash Endowments

Besides the land given in *madad-i-ma'ash* there are some references of cash allowances, which were also termed as the *madad-i-ma'ash*. For example, Jahangir has mentioned in his memoirs, *Tuzuk-i-Jahangiri*, that when he went to the monastery of Shaikh Wajihuddin, a disciple of Shaikh Muhammad Ghaus Shattari, which was situated near the palace, the *fatiha* was read by him as the head of his shrine. As it was the occasion of annual anniversary festival of Shaikh Wajihuddin, Rs. 1,500 rupees were given to Shaikh Haider, *Sajjadnashin* of the shrine, for the expenses of the anniversary (urs) and other celebrations. The emperor further bestowed with his own hand Rs. 1,500 more in charity, on the band of *faqirs* who were present in the monastery and made a present of Rs. 500 to Shaikh Haider. In the same way he gave some amount of money for the expenses and some land grants to each of his relatives and adherents according to their merits. The emperor asked Shaikh Haider to bring before him the body of dervishes and deserving people who were associated with him in order that they might ask for money for expenses and for the land.[48]

In later days, besides lands and *jagirs*, daily stipends were also enjoyed by the descendants of Shaikh Wajihuddin.[49]

In 1615, Jahangir sanctioned Rs. 6,000 to the shrine for the maintenance of the *dargah*.[50] In 1628, Shahjahan distributed Rs. 10,000 among the poor and the Khadims of Ajmer. Shahjahan constructed a huge and elegant marble mosque in the khanqah of Khwaja Moinuddin Chishti.[51]

Shahjahan also granted two *tankas* daily for the offerings of flowers on the *mazar* of Bibi Hafiza Jamal, daughter of Khwaja Moinuddin Chishti whose grave is situated in front of the Khwaja's tomb.[52] In 1680 emperor Aurangzeb presented Rs. 5,000 and he made a *nazr* of Rs. 2,000 for the Khadims of the *dargah*. Meanwhile the emperor offered ten *tolas* (equalling to 144 grams) *Itr* (rose scent) at the *dargah* of Khwaja Moinuddin of Ajmer.[53] Prince Azam, visited the *dargah* and gave a *nazr* of Rs. 3,000 to the *Sajjadanashin* or the spiritual head of the shrine.[54] The office of *Sajjadanashin* was held by the descendants of the Khwaja. He may be regarded as the spiritual head of the *dargah*[55] and he was responsible for the expenditure on *langar*, prayer carpets, construction of new buildings, illumination of the buildings and '*urs*' or annual anniversary of the Khwaja. *Nazr* was divided as follows—during the time of Akbar it was divided into five shares, half of it was taken by the *Sajjadanashin* and rest was divided among the other khadims. But during Jahangir's 9th RY (1613-14) some changes took place; now the *nazr* was divided into six shares, and of these, according the previous tradition, *Sajjadanashin* took half.[56]

We have also some information regarding the cash grants made to Muhammad Saleh son of Muhammad Daulat during the reign of Emperor Farrukhsiyar. This document directs the concerned officials that from the treasury of *awqaf* of *dargah* Re 1 should be released daily without any deduction for his livelihood and this sanction was made in response to his prayers and blessings for the emperor's prosperity and it would be continued without any interference with no need for reissue of orders.[57]

III

Apart from these Persian literary records, we have some historical sources in the form of inscriptions providing the evidences regarding *waqf* or *madad-i-ma'ash*. To reconstruct the history of *waqf* in India, the inscriptions supply some very important information. Though there are many inscriptions some important ones have been used for this study.

It is mentioned in an inscription dated 1649-50 that Mughal emperor Shahjahan constructed a huge mosque in the region of Jodhpur. This inscription furnishes important information about the mosque and six shops attached to the mosque which were given in *waqf* for its maintenance. The inscription further warns the future rajas and other officials against interference and also against misappropriation of the rent of the shops attached to the mosque.[58] A Persian inscription of 1694-95 during the reign of Emperor Aurangzeb states that the servant of the royal court, Iradat Khan has endowed the revenues (*mahsul*) of the village Chawkiya for the expenses of annual *Urs* celebrations of Hazarat Shaikh Hamiduddin Mitha Shah of Gagraun (Kota, Rajasthan). It enjoins the future officials not to interfere with it as the maintenance of grant carries great reward with Allah. Iradat Khan (Mir Mubarakullah) was a *manasabdar* under Aurangzeb and was the *subadar* of Malwa.[59]

A Persian inscription is found at the same place, the fort of Gagraun seems to have been placed in charge of Shaikh Firoz when Nawab Iradat Khan who was a grandson of Nawab Azam Khan was the governor of the Malwa. The epigraph assigns the construction of a Jami mosque to Iradat Khan and registers the grant in cash sanctioned by him from the total revenue (*mal-wa-sayir*) of Gagraun for the maintenance of the mosque. It further gives the daily rate of expenditure, viz. Five *bahlolis*, of which three *bahlolis* were meant for the *Imam*, one for the *muezzin*, who would also be responsible for the daily cleaning of the mosque and half each towards the expenses on water arrangements and illumination. It also expresses the belief that whoever from the officials appointed to Gagraun, pay obeisance to Shah Mitha will get his desires fulfilled.[60]

Conclusion

The institution of the *waqf* or *auqaf* has its origin very much in Islam as we have seen during the time of the Prophet Muhammad (PBUH). The Quran itself speaks about the *sadaqat*, *khairat* and *zakat* which were to be used for the needy and the poor and for those who do not have any source of income or livelihood. During the Muslim rule in India, the importance of *waqf* was recognized by the rulers and their nobles. From the very inception we have references regarding it. They endowed with large land grants and cash grants as *madad-i-ma'ash* to Muslim shrines, mosques, khanqahs, renowned *sufi* saints and their relatives who were not having any source of income for their livelihood and maintenance The income from these grants was used to spread mystic ideology as well as to give financial support to theological studies and facilitate those who were visiting these centres.

As a conclusion I may say that I have cited only selected documents related to *madad-i-ma'ash* grants. It does not mean that these rulers granted *madad-i-ma'ash* grants to Muslims only. There are hundreds of documents related to these grants which provide information about the other religious communities also. In India during the Muslim period we have come across hundreds of such type of documents or inscriptions which supply a flood of information. Though the *auqqf* system very much had its roots in the Delhi Sultanate, during the Mughal period it became a regular feature and almost each and every religious institution was endowed with land grants or cash grants by the rulers and their nobles and bureaucrats irrespective of caste, creed, religion and stature. As we have seen in the above pages that such types of documents were only in the form of *farmans, sanads, parwanas* but information is also available in the form of inscriptions which we have discussed above. The above discussion further leads us to conclude that the source material pertaining to *waqf* in India particularly medieval India is not confined only to *farmans, sanads* and *parwanas* etc. but also spread over in large numbers in the shape of inscriptions as archival evidences throughout the country.

NOTES

1. These grants usually also served as a legal means to keep family property intact through generations.
2. Gregory C. Kozlowaski, 'Imperial authority, benefactions and endowments (awqaf) in Mughal India, *Journal of Economic and Social History of the Orient*, Vol. XXXVIII, 1995, p. 360.
3. *The Encyclopedia of Islam*, New Edition, Brill, Leiden: 2002, Vol. xi, p.59.
4. Ibid.
5. Sir Syed Ahmad Khan (ed.), *Tuzuk-i-Jahangiri*, Aligarh: 1864, p.5.
6. R.S. Sharma, *Aspects of Political Ideas and Institutions in Ancient India*, Motilal Banarsidas, Delhi: 1959, p. 255.
7. Ibid., pp. 245, 256, 258.
8. D.N. Jha, 'Temples as Landed Magnates in Early Medieval South India (AD 700-1300)', in R.S. Sharma (ed.), *Indian Society Historical Probings*, People's Publishing House, Delhi: 1993, p. 202. This type of land was granted to the temples.
9. Land grants exempted from the revenue and other taxes.
10. Subsistence allowance in cash.
11. Land given in *Inam* or as gift.
12. *The Encyclopaedia of Islam*, Vol. XI, p. 96
13. *Medieval India: A Miscellany*, Vol. II, Asia Publishing House, Bombay: 1972; Reprinted by Aakar Books, Delhi: 2020, p. 19n.
14. Abul Fazl, *Ain-i-Akbari*, Vol. I, English translation by Blochmann, Oriental Books Reprint Corporation, Delhi: 1977, pp. 278-85.
15. Ibid., p. 278.
16. W.H. Moreland, *Agrarian System of Moslem India: A Historical Essay with Appendices*, Oriental Books Reprint Corporation, Delhi: [1929] 1968, p. 277.
17. Noman Ahmad Siddiqi, *Land Revenue Administration under the Mughals (1700-1750)*, Asia Publishing House, Bombay: 1970, p. 123.
18. Abul Fazl, *Ain*, Vol. I, pp.198-99.
19. Ibid., Vol. 2, Tr. Col. H.S. Jarrett, Oriental Books Reprint Corporation, New Delhi: 3rd Edition, 1978, pp. 350-51; Bashiruddin, *Faramin-i-Salatin*, Delhi Printing Press, Delhi: 1946, pp. 3-4.
20. *Waqai Sarkar Ranthambhorwa Ajmer, 1678-80* (transcript in the

Department of History, AMU, Aligarh: 2 Vols.), p. 436.

21. Rafat M. Bilgrami, *Religious and Quasi Religious Departments of the Mughal Period (1556-1707)*, Munshiram Manoharlal, Delhi: 1984, p. 60.
22. Ibid.
23. R.D. Mechesney, *Waqf in Central Asia*, Princeton University Press, Princeton: 1991, p. 9.
24. Abdul Bari Maani, *Asnad –us-Sanadid, A Collection of, Sanads*, Ajmer: 1954, pp. 5-6.
25. Abdul Malik Isami, *Futuh-us-Salatin* (ed.), M. Usha, University of Madres, Madras: 1946, p. 466.
26. Ibn Battuta, *The travels of Ibn Battuta*, Vol III, ed. and translated by Sir Hemilton Gibb, The Cambridge University Press, Cambridge: 1971.
27. S.A.I. Tirmizi, *Ajmer Through Inscriptions (1532-1852)*, Institute of Islamic Studies, Delhi: 1968, p. 19; Abdul Qadir Badayuni, *Muntkhab-ut-Tawarikh*, Vol. II, (Trans.) Wolseley Haig, Asiatic Society, Calcutta: 1925, p. 105.
28. Abul-Fazl, *Ain-i-Akbari*, Vol. 3, Tr. Col. H.S. Jarrett, Oriental Books Reprint Corporation, New Delhi: 3rd Edition, 1978, p. 399; Nizamuddin Ahmad, *Tabaqat-i-Akbari* (ed.) Brajendra Nath De, Royal Asiatic Society of Bengal, Calcutta: 1927-40, pp. 355-59.
29. Abul Fazl, *Ain*, Vol. III, p. 316 & 402.
30. Khan, *Tuzuk-i-Jahangiri*, p. 146.
31. Saqi Musta'id Khan, *Ma'asir–i-Alamgiri*, (trans.) J.N. Sarkar, Royal Asiatic Society of Bengal.Calcutta: 1947, p. 111.
32. Abdul Haq Muhaddith Didlavi, *Akhbar-ul-Akhyarfi-Asrar-ulAbrar*, Delhi: 1283 AH, p. 51.
33. *Asnad-us-Sanadid*, p. .3
34. Ibid., pp. 5-6.
35. Christian W. Troll (ed.), *Muslim Shrines, Their Character, History and Significance*, Oxford University Press, Delhi: 1989, pp. 54-55.
36. K.K. Datta (ed.), *Some Farmans, Sanads and Parwanas (1578-1802)*, Published under the authority of State Central Record Office, Political Department, Patna: 1962, Basta No. 815, p. 126.
37. M.A. Ansari, *Administrative Documents of Mughal India*, B.R. Publishing Corporation, Delhi: 1984, pp. 49, 51, 55, 57, etc.
38. W.E. Begley and Z.A. Desai (compiled and translated), *Taj Mahal:*

The illumined Tomb, University of Washington Press, Seattle: 1989, pp. 183-84.

39. Syed Z.H. Jafri, 'The Mughal–Nawabi legacy under "Siege" in the age of Empire (1860-1880): Familial grants and the Waqf of Khanqah-i-Karimia, Salon, India,' in Miura Toru (ed.), *Comparative Study of Waqf from the East: Dynamism of Norm and Practices in Religious and Familial Donations*, Toyo Bunko, Tokyo: 2018, pp. 200.
40. Datta, *Some Farmans, Sanads*, Basta No. 242, p. 11.
41. Jafri, 'The Mughal, pp. 201-02.
42. Datta, *Some Farmans, Sanads*, Basta No. 865, p. 74.
43. Ibid., Basta No. 163, p. 62.
44. Ibid., Basta No. 424, p. 84.
45. Ibid., Basta No. 591, p. 43.
46. Ibid., p. 47.
47. Ahmad, *Farameen-i-Salatin*, Dilli Printing Works, Delhi: 1926, p. 11-12.
48. Khan, *Tuzuk-i-Jahangiri*, Vol. I, pp. 425-26.
49. Muhammad Ali Khan, *Mirat-i-Ahmadi* (ed.) by Syed Nawab Ali, Oriental Institute, Baroda: 1927-28, p.70; *Medieval India Quarterly*, Vol. 1, No. 2, Aakar Books, Delhi: 2020, pp. 68-69.
50. Khan, *Tuzuk-i-Jahangiri*, pp. 146, 256.
51. Abdul Hamid Lahori, *Padshahnama*, Vol. II, (ed.) Maulvi Kabiruddin and Maulvi Abdur Rahim, Biblotica Indica, Calcutta: 1867-68, p. 346; Shyamaldas, *VirVinod*, Vol. II, Motilal Banarsidas, Delhi: 1886, pp. 324, 330-31.
52. *Asnad–us-Sanadid*, p. 204.
53. *Descriptive List of Vakil Reports addressed to the Rulers of Jaipur*, 2 Vols., Rajasthan State Archives, Bikaner: 1972, Nos. 172, 184, etc.
54. *Waqai Sarkar Ranthambhorwa Ajmer*, p. 376.
55. H.B. Wilson, *A Glossary of Judicial and Revenue Terms of British India*, W.H. Allen and Co, London: 1875, p. 455.
56. *Asnad-us-Sanadid*, pp. 68-9, 110-111.
57. Asfaque Ali, *Tarikh-i-Awqaf*, Aga Khan Program for Islamic Architecture and University of Washington, Cambridge and Seattle: 1984, p. 286.
58. *Annual Report on Indian Epigraphy*, Archaeological Survey of India, Delhi: 1955-56, D-153.

59. *Epigraphia Indica: Arabic and Persian Supplement*, Archaeological Survey of India, Delhi: 1968, pp. 77-78.
60. *Annual Report on Indian Epigraphy (1965-66)*, Archaeological Survey of India, Delhi: 1968, p. 161; Yaqub Ali Khan, *Muslim Monuments of Rajasthan*, B.R. Publishing Corp., Delhi: 2011, pp. 172-73.

4

Travels of Guru Nanak in Rajasthan

Jaspal Kaur Dhanju

Guru Nanak's life, travels and teachings raise many historical and philosophical problems and offer a wide scope for conflicting interpretations.[1] Guru Nanak was born in 1469 AD when the Lodis had firmly established themselves in Punjab. His father Mehta Kalu, a Khatri of the sub-caste Bedi was the patwari of Rai Bhoi di Talwandi (presently Nankana Sahib in Pakistan). He was a precocious child and easily learnt whatever was taught to him. And there was something in his genius that he sought the company of religious men to deepen his understanding about the knowledge of truth. As a married man he moved to Sultanpur where his sister lived. He was dissatisfied with the existing forms of religious lives and practices because too much of ritualism which had entered into society and made them formalistic and devoid of meaning and truth. At the age of about 30, he left Sultanpur to spend nearly twenty years visiting numerous places in and outside the Indian subcontinent and met all shades of religious people—*sadhus, jogis, sufis, naths, maulvis, pandits, siddhs* and held long discussions with them. In the early 1520s, he settled at Kartarpur (now in Pakistan).

The way he responded to the existing social milieu brings out the uniqueness in message and teachings of Guru Nanak. The best and authentic source for his message or teachings are his own compositions enshrined in the bani of Sri Guru Granth Sahib. These teachings have a universal appeal and hold good for all ages. He travelled far and wide in order to enlighten humanity as a whole and deliver to them his message of love, peace, devotion to God, social justice, religious tolerance and universal brotherhood of man. When we study his travels, we can discern his message which he desired to propagate and spread amongst the people with whom he came into contact. However, it is problematic to reconstruct the itinerary of Guru Nanak due to scarcity of contemporary sources. Undoubtedly he is one of the most widely travelled amongst the saints and gurus of the world. Apart from the *Wars* of Bhai Gurdas and *janamsakhis* we may depend upon local traditions available in the form of the earlier works of Pandit Tara Singh Narotam[2] and Giani Gian Singh[3] and later works like those of Kirpal Singh and Fauja Singh.[4] Contemporary sources on the life and travels of Guru Nanak are scant except brief verses known as *Babarvani* in which the Guru refers to the invasions of Babar. Therefore the evidence given in the later accounts is generally used by historians to construct the 'history of Nanak.'

The *Wars* of Bhai Gurdas refer to the travels of Guru Nanak to the east, west and north without any hints of his journey to the south, and most of the time do not name the places where he travelled. It is not easy to analyse the nature and content of the *janamsakhi* literature whether they are hagiographies or biographies or merely a collection of anecdotes about the life of Guru Nanak or anthologies of the stories told of his life. However one fact is accepted by the exponents as well as critics of the *janamsakhis* that without them it is not possible to have any knowledge about the life and travels of the Guru. W.H. Mcleod has worked on this piece of Sikh literature and his oft quoted statement brings out the real significance of the *janamsakhis*, "In spite of their manifest shortcomings we are bound to rely on the *janamsakhis* for almost all of our information concerning these events for there is nothing to replace them and little to supplement them."[5] So in spite of the fact that they are inadequate and unreliable, they are still useful to construct the history of Guru Nanak. Further, as the *janamsakhis* contain much of the oral tradition, we cannot ignore them as they are an expression of the beliefs and practises of those people amongst whom they were prevalent. They are a testimony to the impact made by Guru Nanak's personality; also they reflect the ideals and values of those among whom they were popular.

An attempt has been made in this paper to reconstruct the itinerary of Guru Nanak in the region of Rajasthan or Rajputana as it was called during the medieval period. It is generally accepted that he visited this region during the second *udasi*. The account given in the *Meharban Janamsakhi*[6] and Giani Gian Singh's *Tawarikh Guru Khalsa* have been used for the purpose. Sodhi Meharban is credited to have given a more detailed and systematic account of the Guru's travels, co-ordinating his sacred writings with events of his life and giving his own exposition on the hymns of Guru Nanak. In fact the wide gaps left in Bhai Gurdas's account may be filled up with the help of Meharban's account.

The first pothi of the Meharban tradition known as *Pothi Sachkhand* was compiled between 1640 and 1650. It is divided into *goshthis* or discourses which give lengthy interpretations of Guru Nanak's compositions. In one of the *goshthis* titled as 'Interaction of Guru Baba Nanak with a Vaishnav', it is stated that after visiting regions of the south, Baba came into the land of the Rajputs.[7] In the Bikaner region he came across a Vaishnav seeker of Name of God. He wished Ram Ram to Baba Nanak, which was reciprocated by Baba. Vaishnav sat close to Babaji after paying obeisance when baba was in meditation. After a pause, he asked, very humbly, permission of Baba to say some thing, which was granted affectionately and he was asked to talk frankly. Then the Vaishnav told him that he heard a lot about the fame of Baba but that God was very kind, and the same famous Baba was in front of him to be seen with his own eyes. He further, more humbly, made a prayer to Baba to reveal something related to God so that his soul gets satiated. Then Baba Nanak uttered in *Rag Parbhati*, following *hymn*, 'Listen Thy slaves of God what one can say in praise of His beauty, one can't explain his colour, which is most beautiful, best of all. The praise of sight can't be described. Only He knows his depth and secrets, no one else can comprehend that.'[8]

Then those present there said again that the God is beautiful, no doubt. But the beauty which has come upon you Baba, is also beyond description. They asked if there was someone else, who could decide the order in this world. Then Baba Nanak uttered the following: 'That I have considered this issue with my inner conscience and my mind has agreed according to the *gurshabad* that none else is companion of the creatures, O dear, believers, only God takes their care day and night. All that happens is as per his divine order. O, brothers, say waheguru.'[9]

The persons from the gathering kept on sharing and discussing more and more with Baba Nanak with utter humbleness and devotion. In the end they touched the feet of Guru Nanak, became his disciples, started worshiping the Guru, became *Nanakpanthis* and were satisfied.

The next *goshthi* is entitled 'Guruji in Bikaner Town Interaction with Govind Lok'.[10] Guru Baba Nanak entered Bikaner town. There a pure and pious, self practising person met Baba Nanak very respectfully and Guruji also welcomed him and offered a seat to him calling him with titles such as Govind Lok, Bhagat. Those people sat down after paying respectful obeisance to Baba Nanak and after a pause, respectfully asked for his permission to say something. Baba asked them to talk from their heart, without any hesitation. They asked if there was any remedy to ensure that the life remains in the body and body remains as it is forever. They requested him to tell them about any practice to do so as to ensure it. Then Baba uttered the following, 'Listen O Ram's servants, this is quite difficult, the matter is not limited to preaching only but to adopt. You have asked and I/have myself told you. It is not of any worth if you do not adopt or practise this. If I say and you practise after listening, then it benefits both you and me. You will get what you sought.'[11] Then the devotees and the religious people said they were humbled and if there were some fortunates amongst them, the

Guru will preach them. And further on whom Baba's kindness, is bestowed he will practise with your blessings. Then Guru Nanak further interacted with them on various spiritual issues, which they listened to with utter patience, devotion and respect. They touched the feet of the Guru, uttered "guru guru" became disciples of Guru Nanak, *Nanakpanthis,* and returned fully contented.

The next *goshthi* is titled 'Travel to desert area and interaction of Baba Nanak with one Patel'.[12] Beyond Bikaner, Baba Nanak moved through uninhabited lands to a distant place which was completely deserted and totally devoid of any population, the population if any was scattered over long distances where it was quite difficult to reach, and another problem was also of looters and killers in the place region. If one escaped the thieves, one may die of thirst. But Baba did not show any sign of hunger or thirst. Then he reached a habitation in that desert. Mardana was also accompanying him. The inhabitants asked which way they reached here? When they were told the way they came here, then they again asked this way one may come across mounted dacoits and if one escapes them then one may die of thirst. Why did you chose this way? Then Baba said that his journey was facilitated by the same from whom the people were afraid of. People were astonished on listening such reply that how Baba and Mardana were protected through this dangerous journey.

The headman of that place, Patel, came to see Baba along with 15-20 people, he being a knowledgeable and religious person, wished Baba and sat close by. He was also astonished when Baba told him the way they came here, as he was aware of the dangers of that way. He said that no human being could survive the difficulties of this way, which power has helped to reach here? Then Baba elaborated: "If one kills his self pride with *shabad,* then he fears not death. If he desires to live, then death catches up with him, he gets no chance to run away from it. One who is capable of causing death, his name is elixir, to escape death one should worship name of God. He alone is saviour and destroyer. These is none else. Those who remember God, live in discipline of religion, remain gentle, pious and pure." But Baba Nanak in his true humility referred to himself as to kucheel, with perishable body, with low intellect. He told them that with the grace of complete Guru he had learnt that without meditation all else was false. "One who remembers and meditates God's name he is blessed. Say brothers, Ram Ram, Waheguru Waheguru."[13]

Thereafter, with utter devotion and humility, Patel continuously kept interacting with Baba Nanak on various philosophical and spiritual issues which baba answered through hymns with ease and made him comfortable. Fully satisfied and contented he bowed at the feet of Baba Nanak and called him his Guru. All the persons accompanying him also became disciples of Baba Nanak, became *Nanakpanthis* and repeated Nanak is great, with whose grace better sense prevailed.

The next *goshthi* is titled 'Guruji in Rajputana—Interaction of Guru Baba Nanak ji (with God fearing people).'[14] From that town while coming back Guru Baba Nanak, reached another town in the land of Rajputs beyond Bikaner. The inhabitants used to practise Vaishnavism and were good religious people. While Guru Nanak stayed there, word spread that Nanak Bhagat, Bedi Khatri who was famous for squandering Modi Khana of Daulatkhan had come over there. Many people came to visit Baba Nanak. A good natured knowledgeable person also came and wished Ram Ram to Babaji which was reciprocated as such. Then Baba Nanak started a dialogue with the Vaishnavs by inquiring about their well-being. They also responded respectfully by saying that we are quite well and had been blessed further after having a glimpse of him. After a pause they asked Babaji to elaborate about which was the best creation of God, out of all creations by him. The Baba said, 'Of all the virtues deeds, worships and creations, the best and the most beautiful is God himself and the most beautiful and best is Gurbani which facilitates union with Him and by listening singing, reading and practising all the sins get washed from the mind. But the true guru and his bani can be possessed only if one has good fortune earned as a result of good deeds of the previous birth, thereby one could achieve salvation. This the best thing, O, brother, servants of Ram.'[15]

They bowed and said that he was great who had all this enlightenment and remained engaged in a long discussion on various spiritual issues to get their doubts removed. They touched the feet of Baba, became his disciples, *Nanakpanthis* and said Dhan Baba Nanak Satguru Baba Nanak and Waheguru Baba Nanak. Thereafter Baba Nanak came across more Vaishnavas on the land of Bikaner, again in the town of Bikaner where he had similar discourses and the inhabitants paid obeisance and became his disciples.

Tawarikh Guru Khalsa of Giani Gian Singh refers to a discourse which the Guru had with the Dhundia sect of the Jains in Bikaner.[16] Starting from Sultanpur along with Mardana the Guru travelled through Jaito, Bhatinda, Bhatnair, Sirsa he reached Kolayat and Bikaner where he seems to have had a discourse with the Jains of the Dhundia sect. The Priest enquired whether he ate old or new corn. He affirmed that he who ate new and full grain, drank cold and unstamped water and shook the trees of the forest to eat their fruit destroyed life and would never attain pardon. The Guru in reply said, all these things were mere superstitions and as far as forgiveness was concerned it was in the hands of the Almighty.[17]

The Dhundhias thought that by keeping their faces covered and by not bathing, they would not kill organisms. However Guru Nanak guided them by saying that life and death was in the hands of the Almighty. They should recite the true name of God and remain happy by good thoughts and good actions. The Guru said, 'The lord alone kills and restores life; no one else can protect anyone from him. They who go without giving alms or any cleansing baths; their shaven heads become covered with dust. After bathing, the Muslims recite their prayers, and after bathing the Hindus perform their worship services. The wise always take the cleansing bath.'[18]

From Bikaner Guru Nanak and Mardana proceeded through Marwar, Jaisalmer and Jodhpur to Ajmer where he visited the dargah of Khwaja Moinuddin Chisti. He had a religious discourse with the Pir of the dargah where he is said to have guided them to be true Muslims and explained the real meaning of Namaz. He also seems to have travelled to Pushkar, Udaipur, Chittorgarh, Thalawar, Nathdwara and the Jain shrine at Mount Abu.

In the end we may say that, the *udasis* of Guru Nanak 'become a spiritual conquest of the four quarters of the world'. In this paper the Vaishnavas and the Jains of the Dhundia sect in Bikaner and the Muslims at the Dargah of Chisti at Ajmer acknowledged the superiority of the message of Guru Nanak, fell at his feet and many became his disciples. It has been pointed out that verification of *janamsakhis'* information is a useful technique to determine their authenticity. This can be done by comparison with external sources or relics if exploratory studies are undertaken in regions supposed to have been visited by Guru Nanak. Oral tradition can also be used to corroborate the evidence given in the *janamsakhis.*

NOTES

1. A.C. Banerjee, *Guru Nanak and His Times,* Publication Bureau, Punjabi University, Patiala: 2003, Preface.
2. Tara Singh Narotam, *Sri Guru Tirath Swangray,* Nirmal Panchayati Akhara, Haridwar: 1975.
3. Giani Gian Singh, *Tawarikh Guru Khalsa*, Langauge Depatment, Punjabi University, Patiala: 2011, 5th Edition.
4. Fauja Singh and Kirpal Singh, *Atlas: Travels of Guru Nanak,* Publication Bureau, Punjabi University, Patiala: 1976.
5. W.H. Mcleod, *Guru Nanak and the Sikh Religion,* Oxford University Press, Delhi: 2001, p. 9.
6. *Janamsakhi Shri Guru Nanak Dev ji Shri Meharbanji Sodhi,* Dr. Kirpal Singh (ed.), Sikh History Research Department, Khalsa College, Amritsar: 1962.
7. Ibid., p. 331.
8. Ibid.
9. Ibid., p. 332.
10. Ibid., p. 336
11. Ibid., p. 337

12. Ibid., p. 339.
13. Ibid., p. 340.
14. Ibid., p. 345.
15. Ibid.
16. Giani Gian Singh, *Tawarikh Guru Khalsa,* Langauge Depatment, Punjabi University, Patiala: 1970, pp. 52-53.
17. Harbans Singh, *Guru Nanak and Origins of the Sikh Faith,* Punjabi University, Patiala: 1969, p. 143.
18. *Sri Guru Granth Sahib,* Shiromani Gurudwara Prabandhak Committee, Amritsar, Ang. 150.

5

Raja, Praja and *Rajyadharma*: Popular Imaginations of Kingship in Late Medieval North India

Suraj Bhan Bhardwaj

The idea of kingship in pre-colonial India has received a good deal of attention from scholars for a long time. Textual sources of varied genres have been conventionally used to reconstruct the conceptions of kingship in ancient and medieval times. Usually, sources of the ancient period used for the purpose are in Sanskrit and present a largely brahmanical perspective on state and society, while those of the medieval period are Persian court chronicles that ingeniously mould Islamic precepts to construct unique theories of Indo-Islamic kingship for the Delhi Sultanate and the Mughal state. Such texts and textual traditions were evidently produced by members of the intellectual and social elite who held certain socio-religious dispensations and were or may have been part of their contemporary power structures. Thus, these sources can be considered, in varying degrees, as having a largely classicist and/or statist perspective in so far as the protection of the material interests and social pre-eminence of certain classes and/or the overarching authority of monarchy is/are privileged by them. Conceptions of kingship in them have been privileged as constituting the dominant pre-colonial discourse on statecraft and kingship.

In the modern scholarly literature on pre-modern idea of kingship heavily based on such sources, what has so far eluded and thus merits a systematic study, is the possibility of locating alternative perceptions/conceptions of kingship. Seeking to fill this vacuum, this essay argues that such perceptions can be traced in the folk tales and folksongs of pre-colonial rural society in late medieval north India. Folklore has its obvious problems of chronology, spatial provenance and authorship, which have deterred scholars from using it as a source for history-writing in general and explains their excessive reliance on written records. Nevertheless, folklore can be imaginatively and fruitfully used for understanding what can be considered a subaltern perspective on kingship, among other things a perspective often emanating from lower sections of the society and hence different from that of the elite. At the same time, considering the fluid and oral nature of folksongs and folk tales, they need to be read with caution with regard to possible changes in content and perspectives in the course of their multiple renditions across time and space.

Beginning with a brief overview of the perceptions of kingship in textual sources, this essay focuses on the perceptions of kingship in select popular folk tales of north and north-western India (more precisely, eastern Rajasthan, parts of Haryana, western Uttar Pradesh) that were recorded by colonial ethnographers in the late nineteenth century and/or fashioned into musical performative narratives (*swang*) by rural bards in the late nineteenth and early twentieth centuries and still widely narrated and enacted before rural audiences. The essay demonstrates that the perceptions of kingship in these stories, while converging and diverging with those in literary sources on several points, constitute a unique discourse on ideal kingship and its ingredients (such as sense of justice, honour and duty, righteousness, honesty, humility, tolerance, forgiveness) prevalent in the politically disempowered and socio-economically under/non-privileged class/es. This subaltern discourse can be seen as a counterpoint to the dominant elite discourse of ancient brahmanical normative texts and medieval Indo-Persian court chronicles. For the peasant communities grappling with various forms of inequity and oppression arising out of the state and society through the ages, constructing this discourse and thereby valorizing a simple ethical ideal of kingship were a way of envisioning an alternative socio-political utopia. In times of acute distress such as during disturbed political conditions following the decline of Mughal imperial authority in the late seventeenth and early eighteenth centuries, engaging in such discourse through remembrance, narration and performance was arguably an inspired way of enduring and even resisting oppression by the political elite. Thus, reconstructing subaltern conceptions of kingship in peasant society is an important and hitherto unexplored area in the study of medieval Indian history. As is evident from the paragraph, above, oral tradition that is constituted by folk tales and their musical renditions can be construed as representing a subaltern perspective on kingship, emanating from the rural society.

In the ancient sources,[1] the king (*raja*) is often seen as a divine/semi-divine and superhuman figure,[2] but not as one exercising absolute, unbridled authority. Rather, his position, though supreme, is sought to be hemmed by moral, customary and institutional constraints or checks.[3] Further, his duties towards his subjects (*praja*) that constituted *rajadharma* are elaborated and emphasized, his foremost duty being that of protecting his subjects, as also performing acts of public welfare.[4] His deviation from duties, pleasure-seeking and acts of cruelty and oppression are condemned and thought to have fatal outcomes for him; even overthrow and killing of unjust, tyrannical, wayward and evil rulers are justified.[5] Moreover, kingship is occasionally conceived as acquired through the approval and consent of nobles, high functionaries and common people;[6] in some instances, it is even thought to be produced by a sort of social contract between the ruler and the subjects.[7] Corresponding to the idea of *rajadharma* is that of *prajadharma* that chiefly consists of the duty of subjects to pay taxes to the king in respect of the protection given by him,[8] but at the same time the king's power to tax his subjects is sought to be regulated by certain principles to prevent arbitrary taxation and ruthless exploitation.[9] Hence, the relation between the two is envisaged as reciprocal, if not explicitly contractual. This reciprocity lies in their discharge of moral obligations towards each other: the king is to provide protection and efficient grievance-redressal mechanism and promote public welfare, and, in turn, the subjects are to pay him taxes.

Notable among the medieval texts that offer theoretical expositions on kingship is Abul-Fazl's *Ain-i-Akbari.* In this work, kingship is conceived dually, i.e. as originating in divine appointment, and in a social contract between the ruler and his subjects.[10] Divine and contractual nature of a ruler's office, thus, constitute the two pillars in Abul-Fazl's theory of sovereignty.[11] Placing his political patron, Akbar, at the centre of his discussion on the divinity, of the sovereign, Abul-Fazl regards him as *farr-i izadi* or 'divine light' and *zil allah* or 'shadow of god', suggesting that he was a representative of god on earth. The divinity of the ruler, emphasized by Fazl, was impressed upon the people through court rituals adopted by Akbar such as *jharokha darshan,* i.e. the practice of giving a glimpse of himself (*darshan*) from a window (*jharokha*) to his admirers every morning a ritual adapted from the Hindu practice of having a glimpse of the deity. Expounding the idea of social contract between the ruler and his subjects, Abul-Fazl regards taxes as a reward of sovereignty, as an entitlement of the king for treating and protecting his subjects without discrimination on the basis of faith.[12]Abul-Fazl, thus, credits Akbar for creating, through his policy of religious tolerance and non discrimination, *sulh kul* (lit. 'absolute peace'), i.e. a state of universal peace and social harmony. But at the same time, in Abul-Fazl's view, the king is the protector of the subject's life and honour, and hence no moral limits could be set to the fiscal obligations (i.e. taxes) owed by the latter to the former; the subject should be thankful even if he were made to part with all his possessions by the protector for his life and honour.[13] Overall, in Abul-Fazl's works, it appears that the idea of a ruler's divine origin and absolute power assumes overriding importance in comparison to his contractual relation with the subjects. Both brahmanical texts and Abul-Fazl's chronicle, belonging to different temporal, political and cultural contexts, emphasize the divine nature of kingship. But while the former tempers royal power with a strong element of obligation and duty, the latter shows greater accent on the absolute paternal authority of the divine emperor Akbar who is envisioned as *insan-i kamil* or the 'complete man', endowed with all desirable qualities or virtues and hence irreproachable and unsurpassable. Thus, while the brahmanical theory of kingship was general and not modeled on the conduct of any specific ruler, Abul-Fazl's was largely an Akbarid notion of kingship.

Marking a departure from these theories in many ways are folk tales. Folk musical-cum-theatrical performances such as *swang/svang* and *tamasha* played an important role in shaping the peasant's world view which consisted of, among other things, a clear and simple conception of ideal kingship. This conception was articulated in the form of narratives about the lives of legendary rulers, known for their many virtues, and it was these virtues such as justice, morality, duty, sacrifice, struggle, forbearance and truthfulness that constituted their notion of kingship. It may be reasonably presumed that popular notions of kingship are as old as the very institution of kingship. They have co-existed with elaborate elite theories of kingship and state in religious, semi and non-religious texts, without gaining visibility in the written records. Thus, although credible information on the history of folk tales in the peasant society of medieval north India is inadequate and fragmentary because of their fluid, oral character, there must have been a well-established, long-standing tradition of recounting them in one form or the other since at least the medieval period, considering their survival in the nineteenth century (and even to this day).

In as early as sixteenth century, Narsingh Meo of Kajhota village composed a ballad 'Hasan Khan ki Katha'[14] on Hasan Khan Mewati, a Khanzada ruler of Mewat. This work may be considered the earliest extant example of local perception of historical events in the region preserved through the medium of folk poetry. But it was in the late nineteenth and early twentieth centuries that a large number of folk tales in various parts of north and north-west India were collected and recorded by British officials who donned the mantle of amateur ethnographers and folklorists. Notable among such collections are the three-volume *The Legends of the Panjab* by Capt. R.C. Temple;[15] *The Giant Crab and Other Tales of Old India* by W.H.D. Rouse;[16] *Indian Fairy Tales* by Maive Stokes;[17] *Tales of the Punjab Told by the People* by Flora Annie Steel;[18] and *Romantic Tales from the Punjab with Indian Nights' Entertainment* by Charles Swynnerton.[19] Besides, in the late nineteenth century, Alexander Cunningham had also reported stories of Badgujar Rajput chiefs from the Alwar region of eastern Rajasthan.[20]

These folk tales had been orally preserved and narrated for generations by bards or minstrels (*charans, bhats, mirasis*), wandering mendicants (*jogis, sannyasis*) and brahmins at least since the medieval period. By the eighteenth century this long tradition of storytelling gradually developed into a rich performative art of *swang/svang* characterized by music, dance and dramatics. Kishanlal Bhat is regarded as the father of the *swang* tradition and placed in the first half of the eighteenth century, more precisely between 1730 and 1750. In the eighteenth century, Saadulla Khan of Aakeda village in the Nuh district of Mewat composed 'Pandun Ko Karo',[21] a Mewati rendition of the sanskrit epic *Mahabharata*, sung by wandering bards / minstrels (*mirasis*) in the region. By the early nineteenth century, the *swang* art form had further developed so that the number of actors playing different roles increased. In the second half of the century, there emerged two famous exponents of this folk tradition, Ali Baksh and Pandit Deepchand. The former is credited with the composition 'Nal-Daman',[22] a tale of the trials and tribulations of a mythical king Nal and his wife Damayanti, drawn from the *Mahabharata* and popular in the Mewat region. Deepchand is said to have wandered in the villages of Haryana, popularizing his *swangs*, the most notable of which are those on Raja Bhoj and Sarande, Nal-Damayanti, Gopichand Maharaj and Raja Harishchandra.[23] By the early twentieth century several practitioners had played a crucial role in enriching and developing this art form in parts of Haryana, eastern Rajasthan and western Uttar Pradesh. But the credit for taking it to new heights can justifiably be given to Pandit Lakhmichand (CE 1902–48). Prior to his time, performances were staged on open grounds by a small number of actors before a standing audience that gathered around them. But Lakhmichand carried out fundamental changes in the performative aspects of *swang* tradition: *swangs* began to be staged on a raised platform, the physical distance between actors and audience increased as the actors performed on the stage while the seated audience watched them from a certain distance, actors and musicians became separate entities, and the success of the show depended as much on the performance of the actors as on the music and lyrics.

In the nineteenth and twentieth centuries, in Haryana, eastern Rajasthan and western Uttar Pradesh, performances based on such folk tales attracted thousands of peasants from many villages, near and far. Many of the stories and their protagonists were largely drawn from epic and Puranic legends, but they were re-interpreted or re-fashioned by the narrators/performers in terms of the peasants' own life experiences and rendered in forms, dialects, idioms and styles familiar and appealing to them. They themselves emerged out of peasant societies, the bards and artistes could hence act as key players and spokesmen in shaping and voicing the peasant world view. While the historicity of the protagonists remains dubious at best, what is of primary importance is that they are often projected as embodiments of such ideals as justice, integrity, duty, sacrifice, forbearance, compassion and truthfulness, and often pitted against trying or difficult circumstances and/or characters who represent counter-ideals such as injustice, deceit, immorality, greed, lust, hubris and ruthlessness. Through the motif of struggle between the key protagonists and adversarial situations and/or people, these tales unambiguously convey simple binaries of right and wrong, just and unjust, moral and immoral, virtue and sin, sacrifice and greed. These stories when recounted through enlivening musical-cum-theatrical performances before a rural audience helped the peasants perceive an affinity between their everyday struggles, sorrows and miseries and those of the mythical characters and thereby empathize with them. The stories also gave expression to their struggle against injustice at the hands of the oppressive ruling class. The simple ethical ideas, contained in the stories, came to be imbibed by them as essential components of their culture and value system. Understandably, such stories and performances must have left a deep imprint on the minds of the rural audience, as they still do.

More importantly, for the purpose of this essay, the ethical content of these stories or songs also shaped the peasant's perception of an ideal ruler and his ideal relation with the state (personified by the ruler). Hence, stories celebrating some rulers for their proverbial justice and benevolence, such as Rama, Vikaramaditya, Mordhvaj, Puranmal and Bhoj, underscore these desirable qualities of a ruler, while other stories of rulers such as Harishchandra, Bhakt Prahlad, Dhruv and Nal presented them as victims of injustice by the state who emerged victorious through their trials and tribulations. It was through these stories—whether of benevolent, just rulers or dispossessed, suffering ones—that the peasants would have conceptualized the duties of the ruler and the subjects and the relation between them. This made the medieval Indian peasant mentally beholden to his *prajadharam/prajadharma*, i.e. his moral duty (*dharam*), as a subject (*praja*), to pay a share of his produce as revenue to his ruler (*raja*)—a duty that he had inherited and imbibed from his ancestors. At the same, he held the ruler beholden to its *rajdharam/rajadharma*, i.e. its duty to govern the subjects 'justly'.[24] In the peasant's world view, his ideal relation with the ruler was thus based on the reciprocal adherence to their respective customary duties (*rajdharam, prajadharam*). In times of good harvest, the peasant paid the land revenue to the ruler provided it was based on customary rates. However, it was the imposition of non-customary levies, along with crop failures and other natural disasters that roused his ire: he considered such levies unjust, illegitimate and a transgression of *rajdharam*, and resorted to protests or revolts. Thus, historically, a tradition of rebellion/protest against the perceived injustice of the ruling class had always been present in the peasant society and was constantly underpinned by the oral tradition that projected such injustice as a violation of *rajdharam*. Interestingly, stress on the king's moral duty to administer justice and the peasant's to pay customary taxes as well as the oppressed peasants' recourse to rebellions—all echo dharmashastric prescripts on principles of taxation and justifications for the deposal and killing of tyrant kings, as discussed before. These parallels point to a wider, long-standing perception of kingship shared by the folk tales and brahmanical normative texts, notwithstanding differences in forms and some ideas (such as the divinity of the king or the pivotal role of brahmins stressed in the normative texts but absent in the folk tales).

Against this backdrop of the peasant's world view articulated through folk tales and folk songs, the essay will discuss at length certain folk tales that encapsulate the popular perceptions of kingship. As mentioned earlier, Narsingh Meo's sixteenth century ballad 'Hasan Khan ki Katha' is perhaps the earliest extant specimen of folk poetry[25] that embeds a popular idea of kingship in its account of the historic battles of Panipat (1526) and Khanwa (1527), their key players, viz., Babur; Ibrahim Lodi, the Sultan of Delhi; Rana Swanga, the Rajput ruler of Mewar; and Hasan Khan Mewati, the Khanzada chief of Mewat. Introducing himself as a resident of Kajhauta village in pargana Maujpur of Alwar sarkar, i.e. in the region of Mewat, the bard Narsingh Meo prefaces his narration of the historic battles with a discussion of both ideal and counter-ideal kingship. On the one hand, he praises King Vikaramaditya for his benevolence and justice that made him popular among his subjects and a memorable figure for successive generations. On the other hand, he condemns Ravana, the king of Lanka in the epic *Ramayana*, for his misdeeds and his propensity to cause pain to others.[26] Representing both Ibrahim Lodi and Hasan Khan Mewati as the counter-ideal of kingship, he blames Ibrahim Lodi for his injustice, arrogance and apathy which resulted in his defeat and death at the hands of Babur in the Battle of Panipat (1526),[27] and Hasan Khan Mewati for his foolhardiness which led to his unwarranted involvement in the Battle of Khanwa (1527), and eventually his defeat and death, again, at the hands of Babur. The fateful outcomes of their follies were bloody massacres on the battlefield, extinction of Lodi and Khanzada dynasties and devastation of their kingdoms. In Narsingh Meo's perception, both had failed to discharge their *rajdharam*: Lodi remained indifferent to the threat of Babur's impending invasion despite having a huge army at his command and several chieftains on his side, while Hasan Khan out of sheer hubris and foolishness incurred Babur's enmity by seeking to bring Lodis back to power, despite his son's good counsel and Babur's offer of friendship. One's apathy towards the duty of protecting his kingdom from external invasion and the other's injudicious decision to endanger his kingdom's safety both constituted acts of injustice to their subjects and hence a violation of *rajdharam*. Thus, two aspects of ideal kingship are discernible in Narsingh Meo's analysis of the battles: one, the king should be just and justice-loving; two, he should protect his subjects (and conversely, not jeopardize their security). While this conception of ideal kingship, used by a rural bard to explain the tragic fate of Ibrahim Lodi and Hasan Khan, is situated in the context of specific historic events in the sixteenth-century north India, it emanated from the peasant society and has a certain degree of universality in reflecting the peasant's perception of state. It could, then, be invoked across time and space in situations where the state or its personification, i.e. the ruler, was seen as committing excesses, particularly in case of fiscal exactions, an area of perennial conflict between the state and the peasant. In such situations, this conception may well have served to inspire even incite the peasants' resistance to what they perceived as undue and unjust revenue demands of the state. This explains why this conception is recurrently found woven into folk tales of just and unjust rulers that have been recounted across generations. It is these folk tales that the essay will turn to in explaining the nuances of the conception of kingship.

The *swang* 'Jyani Chor', composed by Haryanvi bard Pandit Lakhmichand,[28] is centred on the heroic exploits of Jyani Chor, son of a poor Meo peasant Bhura from Chorgarhi village in pargana Tijara in eastern Rajasthan. Bhura was often imprisoned for non-payment of revenue to the state. Jyani's family's dire economic circumstances and his father's mistreatment at the hands of the oppressive state officials forced him to become a bandit in his youth. Hence his name Jyani Chor ('thief' or 'dacoit'). A Robin Hood-like character, Jyani used to rob rich landlords and redistribute the wealth so acquired, among the peasants. In the tale, he and his close friend Nar Sultan were on their way to their *dharam-behen* (foster sister) Maravan's home in Narvargarh when they found, while bathing in a river, a wooden plaque drifting in the waters. Inscribed on the plaque was a plea for help by a woman named Mahakade. Identifying herself as a Hindu kshatriya[29]woman, Mahakade claimed to be in the captivity of a Muslim ruler, Adali Khan, and entreated any brave Hindu man to rescue her. Jyani Chor took upon himself this daunting task and asked Nar Sultan to continue his journey to Narvargarh. He entered Adali Khan's capital in disguise, but at the same time had the news of his arrival sent to Adali, thereby daring him to catch Jyani. Adali, too, took up the gauntlet and summoned an assembly in his court where he announced that anyone who caught Jyani would be handsomely rewarded. A *sunar* (goldsmith) named Dhammal rose to accept this challenge and assured Adali that he would have Jyani behind bars soon enough. When Jyani came to know of Dhammal's pledge, he decided to teach him a lesson. He reached his home in the guise of his son-in-law whom his daughter had not seen for the last 12 years. Failing to recognize Jyani, Dhammal's daughter was overjoyed at the return of her long-lost husband. So were her mother and Dhammal when he returned in the evening. Thus establishing his identity as Dhammal's son-in-law, Jyani ensconced himself at his house where he was pampered with care and attention, while Dhammal spent days looking hard for Jyani in the city. Finally, one day Jyani tricked his daughter into giving him all her gold jewellery on the pretext of getting them polished, and fled. At this Dhammal realized how clever Jyani had duped him and his family, and humbly accepted his defeat before Adali. Next, the city's *daroga* (inspector-in-chief of police) took the charge of apprehending Jyani. The latter, too, set about entrapping him in his net of deception. Disguised as a woman, he roamed around the *chauki* (police station), seeking to draw the *daroga's* attention even as he was busy contriving ways to catch Jyani. Expectedly, the *daroga* fell for what he saw as a young woman in blooming health. When Jyani asked him what was keeping him busy, he revealed that he had been entrusted with the task of caging a dangerous and cunning bandit Jyani and showed the cage specially made for him. When asked to demonstrate how he would put such a notorious bandit in the cage, the *daroga* foolishly entered it, and Jyani locked it from outside. As Jyani disclosed his true identity, the *daroga* realized how he had been charmed into incarcerating himself. Adali was infuriated at the *daroga's* humiliation and himself set out on horseback to catch Jyani. Even as the day of frenetic search turned into an exhausting evening, Jyani Chor was nowhere to be found. Adali came across an old woman whom he asked whether she had seen Jyani. Responding in the affirmative, she said that he had indeed come to her in a tired and worried state, and would later return for an overnight stay at her place, but would flee if he saw Adali. She suggested that he put on her clothes so that Jyani would not recognize him in the old woman's guise. He did so and lay in wait for Jyani through the night. On the other hand, Jyani, who had actually deceived Adali as the old woman, rescued Mahakade from Adali's prison and fled. Adali was outsmarted and left astounded.

That the tale was probably set in the medieval period can be gleaned from the social background of Jyani Chor. Excessive burden of land revenue often forced peasants to desert villages in the Mewat region, as evinced by the Rajasthani archival sources of late seventeenth and early eighteenth centuries.[30] Some may even have taken to banditry in desperation. They can be considered 'social bandits' who lived on the margins of the rural society by robbing and plundering the rich, but remained within the bounds of the moral order of the peasant community. Though regarded by the state as common criminals, they were robbers of a special kind who were hailed by the peasants as heroes, champions, avengers, fighters for justice since they were seen as righting wrongs when they defied the state or its representatives. Social banditry was a widespread phenomenon throughout recorded history in many agricultural societies characterized by the oppression of poor and/or landless peasants by the representatives of state. It embodies a rather primitive and crude form of organized social protest of peasants against such oppression, but the actions of social bandits do not go beyond the restoration of the traditional order which leaves the oppression and exploitation of the weak and poor within certain limits.[31] Driven to banditry by the state's excesses, rising to avenge the injustice committed by the 'evil' ruler and defeating the ruler through sheer force of wit, Jyani Chor conforms to the idea of social bandit and appears to be a folk hero forged by rural bards out of the actual historical incidence of social banditry in medieval north India.

The ruler Adali, the antagonist of Jyani Chor, may be connected to the historical Adil Shah Suri (1555–56) of the Afghan Sur dynasty. His rule was overthrown when the Afghan forces led by his minister and general Hemu were defeated by the Mughal forces led by Bairam Khan in the Second Battle of Panipat (1556). While the tale of Jyani Chor may have originated in the Sur period, the historical context linking the two characters is difficult to determine. First, while the story concerns a Meo bandit, the historical Adil Shah is not known to have ruled the Mewat region directly, and his commander Hemu's attempts to establish his rule there, too, was defeated. Second, the story must have undergone many imperceptible changes in the course of its long oral transmission and multiple renditions till the early twentieth century when it was given its present form by Lakhmichand. However, one change that is discernible in the narrative is the religious colour given to the conflict between Jyani Chor and Adali Shah. In the *swang*, the inscription on the wooden plaque found by Jyani and Nar Sultan in the river expresses the anxiety of Mahakade, who identifies herself as a Hindu kshatriya woman, at the prospect of being forcibly married to a Muslim ruler and her earnest plea for rescue addressed to a brave Hindu man. Jyani eloquently expresses his deep anguish not so much at the plight of the woman but at the possibility of Hinduism being destroyed (presumably by the dishonouring of a Hindu woman being forced into marriage with the Muslim ruler). This communal dimension may not have been part of the medieval tale, since there is ample evidence of politically motivated matrimonial alliances between Rajput and other Hindu rulers/chiefs and Muslim ones which did not apparently attract any censure in the contemporary sources. Lakhmichand who rendered this medieval tale into a *swang* is also less likely to have deliberately and consciously introduced this communal tension. Living in the early-twentieth-century north India, he is more likely to have inherited a world view wherein identities were getting more sharply drawn along communal lines and communities were becoming culturally polarized. Such a cultural world view that posits relations between communities as irreconcilably antagonistic, when widely held in the society at large and transmitted across generations to individuals, groups and communities, also leaves its imprint in artistic and literary works, as it did in Lakhmichand's rendition of the tale. Thus, the religious colour that the conflict between Jyani Chor and Adali Khan acquired, however briefly, in the story reflects the cultural ethos of the composer's own time period rather than that of the period in which the story originated. However,

Lakhmichand seems oblivious to the fact that Jyani, a Meo, belonged to a region where a long process of Islamization since at least sixteenth century had still not given Meos a strong and distinctly Islamic religio-cultural identity even as late as the mid-nineteenth century, leaving them as avid followers of both Muslim and Hindu cultural practices.[32] But it is quite plausible that the story belonged to a period when the Islamic identity of Meos was beginning to be shaped, and hence the fluidity of this inchoate identity perhaps facilitated the projection of Jyani as a Hindu saviour of a Hindu Rajput woman from the clutches of an oppressive, lustful, Muslim ruler.

In the *swang* 'Virat Parva' composed by Pandit Lakhmichand[33] and based on an episode from the epic *Mahabharata*, Pandava brothers after losing in a dice game with their collateral cousins, the Kauravas, were forced to spend 12 years in exile and another year incognito. In the final year, they and their common wife Draupadi took service in the royal household of Virat Nagar under false names. One day the king's evil brother-in-law Kichak lusted after Draupadi who served the queen as a maid under the name Sairandhri. As he tried to force himself upon her, she reprimanded and instructed him in *rajdharam*. She reminded him that he was the ruler (*raja*) and she his subject (*praja*), and spoke at length on the ideal relation between the two. In the perception of his subjects, the king stands only second to god who is the creator and master of all; his right to rule entitles him to this near-divine stature. But the king earns this right through great efforts and struggles and should not take it for granted. He should look upon his subjects as his children just as the latter look up to him as father. He should consider such paternalistic relations with his subjects sacred and inviolable. Every king should rule as did the legendary Rama of the epic *Ramayana*—*ramarajya* being the popular metaphor for an ideal state and Rama being the model for an ideal king in the popular conception of kingship in pre-modern (north) India (as also contemporary India). This conception enjoins upon the king to adhere to the *rajdharam*: refrain from doing injustice to innocent subjects and punish those who do so. This *swang* makes Kichak and Draupadi the personifications of the ruler and the people, showing how the people could resist when the ruler seeks to violate his *rajdharam* and remind him of his moral duties and obligations.

The *swangs* 'Jyani Chor' and 'Virat Parva' define the ideal of kingship (*rajdharam*) in terms of its anti-thesis embodied by unethical and unjust rulers (viz., Adali and Kichak) and justify popular resistance to such rulers, whether by way of subterfuge (as in the case of Jyani) or verbal remonstrance (as in the case of Sairandhri). On the other hand, there are *swangs* that define this ideal of kingship in terms of the exemplary conduct of ethical and just rulers, but at the same time emphasize the role of common people as the keepers of royal conscience who admonish such rulers for their faults and/or instruct them on ideal rulership. Both kinds of tales ascribe agency to people as moral arbiters of the ruler's conduct and, therefore, the source of his legitimacy and authority. In doing so, these tales privilege the popular idea of kingship over the statist one as articulated in texts produced by the ruling elite.

Notable among the tales of just rulers is that of Vikramaditya's justice[34], which was and still is popular in the rural society of north and central India. In this tale, Vikramaditya is shown as a ruler who used to move about the kingdom in disguise in order to find out subjects in distress. The king's nocturnal peregrinations in disguise are a common trope in folk tales that reinforces the popular conception of a 'just' king's commitment to his subjects' welfare through direct involvement in information-gathering. In one such solitary nocturnal trip on horseback, the exhausted King Vikramaditya dozed off while his horse moved into a nearby field and began to eat the standing crops. After a short while, the peasant who had cultivated the field turned up. Seeing the horse eating his crops, he thought that the horseman had deliberately led his horse into the field in order to feed it. He became furious, railed at him and demanded compensation for the damage to his crops. The king proposed to settle the matter with some money, but the peasant refused. Thinking him to be some herdsman or trader, he insisted on taking the case to the royal courthouse and tied both him and his horse to a tree to prevent their escape. Next morning the peasant took them to the courthouse where the judge, upon hearing his plea, decided that the horseman be punished with fifty lashes. But before the punishment could be carried out, a minister present in the courthouse identified the king in disguise and immediately fell at his feet in apology for not accompanying him on his trip. Shocked at finding out that the horseman he was about to punish was none other than King Vikramaditya, the peasant, too, furiously pleaded at his feet for forgiveness. But further shocking everyone, the king solemnly declared that the essence of his justice lay in the inevitable punishment of the guilty and he himself being guilty was not above the law and deserved punishment; he, thus, asked the peasant to whip him and serve the cause of justice.

The ideal of impartial punitive justice as an integral component of the pre-colonial popular conception of kingship is arguably taken to its peak in this tale: justice while being personal, i.e. stemming from and subject to royal will and dispensation, becomes so impersonal and absolute at the hands of a proverbially just king that he himself, when guilty, is subject to its principle of retribution. In the moral universe of peasants living in a hierarchical society, privileging this sort of retributive justice as a key constituent of ideal kingship democratizes justice in an essentially non-democratic milieu and becomes an ingenious reaction to what were perceived as unjust laws and interventions of the state or ruling class. In doing so, this idea of justice (and by extension kingship) indirectly gives agency and voice to the oppressed underclass of peasants, otherwise denied to them in reality.

Similar in essence to King Vikramaditya's tale are those of Badgujar Rajput chiefs popular in the Alwar region of eastern Rajasthan since the early sultanate period, i.e. the thirteenth century. These stories that laud the legendary justice of

Badgujar chiefs were recorded by Alexander Cunningham in the late nineteenth century.[35] In one such story, King Neen had a pond dug for his subjects, but as its water turned red and undrinkable he asked the brahmin priests for an explanation of this unusual phenomenon. They explained that the water turned red because he had the pond dug by people of different castes, thereby causing an intermixing of castes. They suggested that he bury his son and daughter-in-law alive in the pond in order to purify the water. Accordingly, he performed a *yajña* (grand sacrifice) and interred his son and daughter-in-law alive within a tomb erected under water. Thereafter, the water miraculously became drinkable again. According to Cunningham, the local people still believed that the spirits of the king's son and his wife roamed around the pond on horseback at night, and that it was their sacrifice that had cleansed the water forever, and hence they still worshipped them. Like Vikramaditya who had himself punished for the sake of justice, King Neen, his son and daughter-in-law made the supreme sacrifice for the welfare of their subjects. In both tales, the conduct of royal personages is modelled on the popular ideal of kingship wherein heightened concern for administering justice and ensuring people's welfare characterize the king's governance.

Somewhat different from the tales of just rulers Vikramaditya and Neen who apparently needed no stimulus or persuasion from their subjects to act justly, are the tales of just rulers who occasionally needed a lesson in ethical governance from people. It is in these tales that people are given far greater visibility, voice and agency vis-à-vis the kings, and social hierarchies (of caste, class, gender) are temporarily jettisoned: not only the people score higher over the kings in wit, practical wisdom and worldly experience, but the kings too accept their failings and eventually live up to the popular expectations from an ideal ruler. The first among these tales is the *swang* of Raja Bhoj and Sarande, attributed to Pandit Lakhmichand[36] and immensely popular in the rural society of Haryana. In this tale, Bhoj, the ruler of Ujjain, was a paragon of *rajdharam*. He scouted around the city in disguise with his sidekick, a *bhand* (court jester) named Manva, seeking information about the grievances and miseries of his subjects. One day, Manva *bhand* informed him of a barber who was worried to death over the marriage of his young and beautiful daughter, Sarande. That no suitable boy could be found from within the barber's community for Saranade, who was of marriageable age, gave sleepless nights to the family. As Sarande confided in her friends her parents' worry, one of them told her in jest to marry King Bhoj who was well-known for alleviating the miseries of his subjects and would surely end her woes. Besides, he was young and handsome a reason enough for her to marry him. But Sarande retorted in mock pride that she would not even deign to have her feet washed by him, much less marry him. In other words, she suggested in jest that she did not find even a king suitable for her. As Manva told Bhoj of this friendly banter, the latter mistook Sarande's words of jest for those of insult and summoned the barber to his court where he asked for his daughter's hand in marriage. Even as the barber initially refused the offer on the ground that the king did not belong to his community, his wife's intervention eventually led to Sarande's marriage to the king. However, soon the king made his motive for marriage clear. He told Sarande that he did not marry her to make her his queen but to avenge his insult. He banished her from the palace and forced her to live a lonely miserable life outside the city walls. But Sarande did not lose courage in the face of this adversity; she assiduously learned to play *been* (flute) and soon became an expert and widely acclaimed flutist. As the renown of her music spread far and wide, she went to the court in disguise for playing flute. Suddenly, in the course of her enthralling performance, she fell on the floor. When asked the reason, she explained that the floor felt burning hot, and asked the king to pour cold water on her feet to cool them off. Captivated by her music, the king fell for her ruse: he got up and unsuspectingly did as asked. At this Sarande broke into peals of laughter and revealed her face. By fulfilling her vow of making the king wash her feet, she outwitted him. But her ingenuity won his admiration, and he happily accepted her back.

The musical rendition of this tale, especially the lively and witty dialogues of King Bhoj and Sarande, in a language and form familiar to peasants have held great appeal for them. This was more so because of its embedded conceptions of kingship and of the socio-political relation between the ruler and the ruled. The king who is projected as possessing divine or semi-divine attributes in the ancient and medieval texts that emphasize on supramundane sources of political legitimation is a far cry from the king cast in this folk tale as one who is not superior to his subjects in intellect and wisdom, nor too socially distant from them. Bhoj, a mighty king, is not averse to marrying the daughter of a barber, traditionally ranked quite low in the caste hierarchy, to avenge his perceived dishonour. Moreover, he ends up losing to her in a veritable battle of wits and happily accepts his defeat. The king's proverbial might is no match for a poor low-caste girl's cleverness. If the barber girl Sarande is construed as representing the common people, her diligence in learning music and her intelligence in outsmarting the king suggest the power of people's will and wit that could on occasion even humble a king. The king's close relationship with a jester, belonging, again, to the 'lowly' caste of minstrels, is also quite at odds with the divine conception of kingship. It is the jester, as the king's constant companion and confidante, who serves as a link between the ruler and the ruled by apprising the king of his subjects' conditions and grievances, as well as perceptions about and expectations from him. The jester, therefore, is not merely the king's entertainer but doubles up as his conscience-keeper, representing the people's voice. Here, the jester replaces the high-caste brahmin priest whose advisory role and legitimizing and corrective powers over the king are so expatiated upon in the brahmanical texts. Both Sarande's and Manva's relations with the king represent the ways in which people could successfully wield moral power over the king and thereby make his rule 'just' and in consonance with the popular idea of *rajdharam.* Neither the jester's proximity to the king nor the barber girl's symbolic triumph over the king erases or disrupts the actual socio-political hierarchies, but they do serve to notionally reduce the distance between the ruler and the ruled by bringing the two closer. In the process, a popular notion of ideal kingship is articulated in a relatively more inclusive and less hierarchical way that radically departs from the divine conception of kingship wherein the king derives his authority from divinity, is hemmed by a stratified ensemble of socially privileged and politically powerful elite, and remains distanced from the common masses. In the popular notion of kingship, as embedded in this tale, the king is not only powerful, justice-loving and a true follower of *rajdharam*, but is also not above his ordinary subjects in thought and intellect. Moreover, members of lower castes such as minstrels and barbers are very much part of the king's political life. Interestingly, such a notion of kingship dispenses with the role of high-born State functionaries intervening between the king and the people. More importantly, internalizing this ethical ideal of kingship through repeated musico-dramatic enactment of such tales made the medieval peasant believe in a customary reciprocal relationship between the ruler and his subjects.

Similar in content and essence to the tale of King Bhoj and Sarande is another *swang*, 'Four Girls and a King', that may have been composed sometime in the late eighteenth century and received its present form at the hands of Pandit Lakhmichand.[37]Like the afore-discussed *swang*, this one too encapsulates the popular idea of kingship. In the tale, like King Bhoj, an unnamed king moved about the city in disguise in order to gather information about his subjects' conditions, troubles and grievances. In one such trip, the king in the tale overheard four girls conversing in a garden. They were discussing what had the best taste in the world. Curious to know more, the king summoned the girls to his court the next day and asked them separately on what they were discussing. The first girl when asked about what she was telling her friends the day before disclosed that she was telling her friends that meat tasted the best. When asked about her caste, she conveyed that she belonged to the *bhand* (minstrel caste). The king countered by saying that the people of her caste did not even touch meat much less eat it and hence it would not be possible for her to know its taste. She admitted that she had never tasted it but assumed that it was the best, since she used to see from her rooftop that in an eatery at the back of her house where meat was served no part of the animal carcass was wasted. After the people had eaten, the left-over bones were devoured by dogs, those discarded by the dogs were carried away by crows, and those still left by the crows crawled with ants. Pleased with her reasoning, the king sent her back with rewards. The second girl when asked the same question said that she thought alcohol tasted the best. But she claimed to belong to the brahmin caste, and the king questioned how would she know the taste of alcohol if the brahmins did not consume it. She explained that every evening she watched from her roof people buying and drinking liquor from a liquor shop, and found that the same people who struggled their way back home in a heavily inebriated state would keep coming day after day to consume liquor. This made her conclude that alcohol must taste good enough to draw people every day. Again pleased with her answer, the king rewarded her. The third girl of the *bhat* (bardic caste) said that she thought sexual intercourse to be the most pleasurable act. She admitted that she was too young to experience sexual gratification, but claimed that she could sense it, since she found that her mother who had almost died giving birth to her younger brother was overjoyed at delivering another baby after a few months. This proved wrong her earlier idea that her mother would not risk suffering the pain of childbirth again. She thus reasoned that sexual pleasure must be great enough for people to put their lives at stake. Satisfied with her argument, the king rewarded her as well. Finally, the king summoned the fourth girl and asked her the same questions. The girl belonging to the jat caste said that lying was the most enjoyable act in the world, and that everyone, including the king, lied. Surprised at her answer, the king asked her to rethink her response, but the girl insisted that she had expressed her considered opinion, and that she could prove her statement if she got six months' time and a sum of six lakh rupees. The king agreed to her conditions and sent her back with the said sum. After six months, the girl returned and asked the king to accompany her to a new beautiful palace she had built. She claimed that the palace had a beautiful 'spiritual' hall where if a person completely devoted his mind to the thought of god, god would appear in person before him. Upon arriving at the palace, the king sent in his minister to test if her claims were true. The girl told the minister that god would surely appear to him if he single-mindedly prayed to him, but would not do so to one who was of illegitimate birth. The minister went inside and sat there with his thoughts fixed on god, but after some time looked around and found nobody. He reasoned with himself that if he admitted that he did not see god, he would face the shame and dishonour of being considered a misbegotten child. Hence, after coming out, he lied to the king that he had seen god. When the king asked him about what god said to him, he again lied that god had forbade him to reveal. Not satisfied with his response, the king sent in another minister who, too, thought the same as did the first one when he saw no one inside and lied about seeing god for the fear of public ridicule. Next, the king went inside and had the same dilemma when he saw no god: he thought to himself that if he, unlike his ministers who had claimed to have seen god, admitted that he did not, he would risk not only losing his honour but also facing a revolt by his subjects. He, too, thus ended up lying that he had seen god. When the girl asked him thrice to confirm whether he had seen god, he lied every time and that too unhesitatingly. Finally, as the girl refuted his claim by saying that no one, not even the king, could see god, the king remembered the girl's claim that everyone, including the king, lied. Realizing that the girl had devised an elaborate ploy to make him lie and thereby prove her point, the king admitted lying and so did his ministers. The girl explained that while the poor would lie out of compulsion, the king had no compelling reason to do so, thereby proving that lying was enjoyable in its own way. Impressed at her intelligence and self-confidence, the king asked for her hand in marriage.

In this tale, as in the previous one, a just king in accordance with his *rajdharam* seeks to find out his subjects' woes, aspirations and expectations, and comes across the four girls who 'enlighten' him on some important truths of the socio-cultural lives of common people. The girls who represent the common people's voice impress upon the king that meat-eating, drinking, sexual intercourse and lying are not condemnable moral vices but everyday practices in the lives of people, and that kingship is not a sacred, divine institution untouched by such worldly practices. In particular, lying was a means of survival and resistance in the medieval rural society: the peasant would try to 'misappropriate' the share of crop yield payable to the state or its landed intermediaries (zamindars, jagirdars) and, in turn, reduce his own fiscal burden by willfully misinforming the revenue officials about or concealing from them, certain standing crops or the area of land under cultivation of certain crops. Such acts when detected by the state officials were deemed as 'theft of revenue' and punished by way of levying fines, as amply attested in the Rajasthani sources, particularly the *hasil farohi* columns of *arsattas*.[38] Yet the peasants persisted with such acts of deception that actually became 'weapons of the weak', a covert form of peasant's resistance to the state's oppressive revenue demands. In emphasizing the universality of lying, the Jat girl also drove home the fact that for the poor in general, lying was a way of surviving against all odds, and for the peasant in particular, a way of ensuring his subsistence in the face of crushing revenue demands of the state and its landed intermediaries. In this sense, the jat girl embodying the peasant's voice highlighted his miseries and compulsions before the king who personified the state. Significantly, the fact that the four young girls made the king understand the fundamental existential reality of people's lives suggests that the king was no wiser than his subjects and needed a dose of popular experiential wisdom for 'just' governance. This, in turn, again implies that in popular wisdom, ideal kingship and proper discharge of *rajdharam* rested on a close cooperation between the ruler and the ruled. Equally significant is the gendered nature of the class relations between the state and its subjects in the three tales. The personified metaphor for the state is masculine, i.e. a king or a prince, while that for the subjects is feminine, i.e. Draupadi, Sarande and the four girls. In each tale, the wisdom and/or conduct of the dominant is challenged by the subaltern on the grounds of certain common shared socio-ethical values that were supposed to govern and circumscribe the functions of both, but the hierarchical nature of the relationship itself is not questioned. This suggests that class hierarchies, like gender hierarchies, are not considered open to subversion, though the violation of ethical norms of conduct in these hierarchical relationships by the dominant is subject to censure and condemnation.

From the foregoing discussion of the folk tales one can discern certain common features of the peasant's conception of ideal kingship and of the ideal relation between the king and his subjects. First, ideal rulers are just, benevolent and caring towards their subjects; they abide by the rule of law and the principles of justice and altruism. Second, just rulers do not carry a divine or semi-divine stature, nor can claim any social or intellectual superiority over their subjects; rather, they are accessible to and seek access to people. Third, they may occasionally and unwittingly commit acts of injustice or may become oblivious to their fallibility as human beings. At such crucial junctures, they are reminded of their duties by one of their subjects who voices the concerns of the common masses. In such situations, the due performance of *rajdharam* or ethical governance is premised on the reciprocity between the ruler and the ruled, whereby the ruler is receptive to popular wisdom and advice and not averse to acknowledging his faults and making amends. Legitimacy of a ruler is thus derived from his proximity to the people, from his living up to the ideal constructed by them, not from claims to pre-eminence over them. Fourth, rulers who abandon or deviate from their *rajdharam* face remonstrance, rebuke and humiliation at the hands of the people. It is the people who adjudge the ethicality of a ruler's conduct or otherwise and respond accordingly. The arbitrary exercise of power by the ruler and/or his officialdom to the detriment of peasants' interests was a strong possibility within the only available political institution in pre modern India, i.e. monarchy, and was indeed a harsh reality in many cases, as peasant protests and rebellions throughout the medieval period show.

But despite, or probably because of such despotic tendencies of the monarchical set-up, the popular idea of benevolent and just kingship thrives in the peasant societies, fortifying their resilience, optimism and capacity for resistance.

The preceding discussion of the idea of kinship embedded in the folk tales brings one to the problem of historicizing these stories. In other words, what are the possibilities of locating these stories in specific temporal and spatial contexts? Admittedly, as mentioned before, the provenance of these stories remains uncertain, and can broadly be pinned down to medieval north India. Since they have been part of a long-standing, regionally variegated oral tradition of rural societies in north India and appeared in the recorded history only from late nineteenth century (i.e. in the accounts of colonial ethnographers), they can be justifiably presumed to have existed in the medieval times, or perhaps even earlier. Their survival and popularity owes to their function and relevance in the societies where they have been narrated, sung or enacted. Their function, as discussed before, was to provide the peasant communities a vision of an ideal mythic past when people lived in peace under benevolent and just kings without suffering injustice and oppression. This function of the folk tales assumed greater relevance in hard times when burden of fiscal exactions weighed heavily on them. Conjuring up and collectively invoking and remembering this past through repeated performances infused in them the strength to confront, resist and demand justice from oppressive rulers.

The exaltation of a just and benevolent kingship in the afore-discussed folk tales may well have gained greater currency in the increasingly conflictual relationship between the state and peasantry of north India in the late medieval period. From the Rajasthani archival sources such as *arzdashts, arsattas* and *chithis* of the late seventeenth and early eighteenth centuries, it appears that Mughal mansabdars, unable to realize revenue from their jagirs in the wake of uncertainties in collection, were forced to farm out their jagirs to various bidders for revenue collection rights (ijara). In particular, the mansabdars who held jagirs in Mewat resorted to assigning their ijara to the Rajput rulers of Amber and the jat chieftain Churaman. The latter, in turn, fiercely competed with each other to acquire the right to collect revenue from the areas under the jurisdiction of mansabdars. By deriving this right from the Mughal state (or its direct representatives, the mansabdars) through ijara or revenue-farming, they interposed themselves as a new stratum of authority between the mansabdars and the peasants, imposing numerous non-customary levies on them and constantly contesting the legitimacy of each other's claims to agricultural surplus. At the same time, the traditional claims of the Mughal state to land revenue, as also its politico-administrative control, was progressively eroded. On the one hand, this led to the impairment of traditional mechanisms of grievance-redressal for the peasantry who bore the brunt of increased revenue demand. On the other hand, the absence of well-defined legitimate claims of the state on surplus made it impossible for the peasantry to satisfy the multiple claimants who ruthlessly exploited them.

The peasants with their faith in an ideal reciprocal relation with the state based on certain customary rights and duties accepted the standard land revenue demand of the state and considered fulfilling it as their duty (*prajadharam*) provided the state was just and caring towards them, i.e. it abided by the ethics of good governance (*rajdharam*). At the same time, the peasants opposed the state's revenue demand if it flouted the customary practices and led to their exploitation and immiseration. As is evident from numerous instances of peasant petitions recorded in the Rajasthani sources, the Meo peasants were well aware of the fact that their villages were part of jagirs assigned to imperial mansabdars by the Mughal emperor, not that of the Amber Raja's watan jagir (patrimonial estate), and that the mansabdars had, in turn, assigned the ijara of their villages to the Amber Raja. They viewed the emperor as their highest appellate authority and knew that neither the mansabdars nor the Amber Raja had any legitimate right to respectively transfer revenue-collection rights and collect non-customary taxes. That is why they retained faith in the justice administered by the Mughal state and repeatedly petitioned the emperor, seeking his intervention against the 'illegitimate' levies imposed and forcibly collected by the Amber Raja. They clearly perceived Amber Raja as a disruptor of their customary relationship with the Mughal state, and the imposition of non-customary taxes by him as a violation of *rajdharam* so exalted in their oral traditions. In other words, the peasants understood the behaviour of the ruling class and expected the state to perform its *rajdharam*, its duty of administering justice to its subjects. But failure to get relief in most cases would have, on the one hand, heavily dented the image of the Mughal rulers and, on the other, provoked rebellions throughout the region.

It was in this context that tales celebrating just rulers and condemning unjust ones assumed greater popularity among the peasants. Such tales articulating the peasant's perception of ideal kingship became the means of eloquently expressing their rejection of and protests against an exploitative state that sharply deviated from the ideal of *rajdharam*. Invoking a mythic idyllic past when rulers were just, caring and self-sacrificing also helped them grapple with a fraught politico-economic situation that led to their increased impoverishment and degradation.

The political turmoil of the late medieval period may not have been the only factor lending currency to such folk tales valourizing the conceptions of ideal kingship, since such inspirational tales would have been deployed time and again in all situations of state repression that provoked peasant rebellions, but the intensity of exploitation and the frequency of peasant complaints and uprisings in this period certainly would have added considerable vigour and life to these tales. Hence, the recurrent contestations between the state and the peasantry in the medieval period made these tales an enduring integral part of the peasant culture.

The medieval context of these tales perhaps also explains why they do not exalt historical rulers, much less the Muslim rulers. While the long-known and widely-circulated epico-Puranic stories of Hindu rulers may well have provided the template for the folk tales, the oppressive revenue system of medieval states in north India often headed by Muslim rulers may not have been conducive to idealizing any historical ruler. As far as it is evident, the burden of taxes in medieval India was not necessarily heavier than that in early India, nor were the Muslim rulers any more oppressive than their Hindu counterparts in early India. But the choice of glorifying Hindu rulers of dubious historicity and situating them in a remote mythic past was a conscious one, for doing so would help to ideologically contest and undermine the legitimacy of any actual ruler/state when the peasants perceived him/it as oppressive to the extent of breaching the idealized customary relationship between the ruler and his subjects. That the rulers of these folk tales such as Vikramaditya or Bhoj were archetypes of ideal rulers and not compared to or even comparable to any actual historical ruler facilitated the construction of the desired conception of kingship in the peasant communities. On the other hand, since the Mughal emperors, as also many of their officials holding jagirs/mansabs, in large parts of medieval north India were incidentally Muslim and the revenue demands of Mughal mansabdars/jagirdars and, later, ijaradars were becoming increasingly onerous for the peasantry particularly in the late medieval period with bleak prospects of justice or relief from exploitation, the peasant communities had no reason to extol the Mughal emperors as exemplary kings in their folk tales (not even Akbar, projected as a tolerant and just emperor by Abul-Fazl and other chroniclers, found space in them).[39] At the same time, Muslim rulers are not vilified in these tales either (except in the story of Adali and Jyani Chor whose communal overtones are arguably the handiwork of Lakhmichand in early twentieth century). This suggests that the folk conception of kingship, while explicitly laudatory of mythical Hindu rulers, was not an overt, summary rejection of Muslim rulers on grounds of religious affiliation.[40]

Another notable feature of the conception of kingship in these tales is its contrast with that of Rajasthan. This is linked to the differences in the behaviour of the ruling class vis-à-vis the people and to the presence or absence of political patronage to bards in different areas. In Rajasthan, which witnessed the evolution of Rajput states from the early medieval period, the people's attitude towards the Rajput rulers in general has been one of respect and honour even to this day. A sizeable class of bards (*charans, bhats*) and brahmins, receiving patronage for generations from these rulers, has over a long time inculcated mass's obedience to and respect for the ruling elite through their songs, tales and genealogical records that valourize Rajput dynasties and rulers. The Rajput rulers, on their part, have registered their presence and participation on numerous public occasions, particularly festive and ritual ones. Their visibility and accessibility has helped sustain their power and influence as well as a notion of benevolent kingship in the public mind.[41] Such an exalted image of kingship cannot be seen in Mewat, Haryana, western Uttar Pradesh or parts of Punjab. In these areas, no oral tradition of glorifying real dynasties or rulers took roots, as there were no long-established dynasties, like those of the Rajputs, to patronize a class of bards and/or priests who could compose eulogistic tales and genealogies. On the other hand, as discussed before, these areas witnessed recurrent rural unrest, particularly so in the wake of the breakdown of Mughal administrative machinery, the rise of competing claimants to power, territory and revenue, and the intensification of exploitation of peasantry in the late medieval period. In this context, the notion of kingship articulated through a long-developing tradition of *swang* could only be shaped by the peasant society's perception of an ideal ruler, i.e., one who is righteous, justice-loving and caring. In other words, this notion encapsulated the peasant's vision of a non-oppressive and just political system, and did not cater to the ruling elite's need for political legitimacy and power.

The conception of kingship in the folklore of rural societies does not constitute an elaborate, systematic and coherent theory such as those found in the ancient brahmanical texts or medieval court chronicles. Yet, it has several ingredients of such a theory: the position, qualities and duties of a king; the relation between the king and his subjects; the customary and moral checks on the king's power; and the avenues of addressing the problem of monarchical despotism. In this sense, the discourse on kingship in the folk tales, if closely seen in their socio-political and geographical contexts, reveals not a mere wishful longing for some unattainable political utopia of a mythical past, but an embedded, heightened political consciousness of an otherwise unlettered, powerless peasantry grappling with the harsh political reality of their times (growing revenue demand, abuse of power by revenue officials, landed intermediaries and armies of state, collapse of grievance-redressal mechanisms, depredations of contenders for politico-economic control of territories). It was this consciousness that helped to shape a conception of kingship that was composed of sharp binaries of rulers who are little more than symbols of justice and injustice, benevolence and malevolence, morality and immorality. And it is this ethically charged conception that acted as a mode of protest against oppression by real kings and posed a challenge to their legitimacy. This conception, born of the peasant's life-experiences and world view and autonomous of any political patronage or control by the ruling elite, was, therefore, a driving force for struggle, resistance and survival in the peasant's lives more powerful than the alternative folk conceptions in other areas (such as northern and western Rajasthan) that extolled the ruling dynasties, legitimized their political authority and cultivated deference and obedience to it.

NOTES

1. These are vedic ritual texts, epic poetry (e.g. *Mahabharata* and *Ramayana*), prescriptive treatises on socio-religious norms (e.g. *Dharmasutras* and *Dharmashastras*), *Puranas*, and treatises on statecraft (e.g. *Arthashastra, Shukranitisara, Rajanitiprakasha, Kamandakiya-nitisara*). Relevant portions of these texts have been collated and compiled by P.V. Kane in Vol. 3 of his monumental five-volume *History of Dharmaśāstra,* Bhandarkar Oriental Research Institute, Pune, 1973.
2. For instance, several texts such as *Manusmriti, Naradasmriti, Markandeya, Agni* and *Bhagavata Puranas, Arthashastra, Rajanitiprakasha,* etc., tend to project the king (*raja*) as associated with various deities (as made from or having in his person their parts,as their human incarnation or as performing their functions on earth). Even outside the realm of brahmanical texts, this tendency of glorification of the king's office can be seen in the attempts of court panegyrists and poets to trace the descent of various dynasties to the sun, moon or, later, fire; in the practice of addressing kings as *deva* ('god') in the sanskrit dramas, in the use of epithets *devanampiya/devanampriya* ('beloved of the gods') and *devaputra* ('son of god') for the Mauryan emperor Ashoka and the Kushana rulers, respectively (Ibid., pp. 23-24).
3. The ancient texts address various exhortations to the king in order to exercise a restraining and corrective influence. These exhortations repeatedly emphasize the observance of *dharma,* a broad, multi-interpretable, sacred and inviolable socio-political ideal or principle that encompasses norms, laws, duties and obligations for individuals and social groups. Besides impressing upon the king the importance of performing his *dharma,* these exhortations also enjoin the king to seek counsel of ministers, the *purohita*(royal priest) and learned brahmins, and respect the dictates of *shastras*; they even prophesize and justify the ruination, destruction or deposal of whimsical, cruel, tyrannical, misguided and incompetent kings. The *Ramayana*'s account of Rama abandoning his wife Sita despite knowing her to be chaste, because the people suspected her chastity after her long stay in Ravana's captivity, suggests that the pressure of public opinion

also could force the king to take certain decisions against his will. Thus, the texts bind the royal power with many checks and limitations (ibid., pp. 96–98).

4. For instance, the *Santi Parvan* of the *Mahabharata* and *Manusmriti* extol protection as the highest *dharma* of the king. The protection, according to Brihaspati cited in *Rajanitiprakasha,* consists in punishing internal aggression (such as by thieves, robbers and trespassers) and meeting external aggression. The *Gautama Dharamsutra* assigns to the king the special responsibility to award just punishment and protect the *varnas* and *ashramas* according to the shastric rules and bring them back to the path of their proper duties if they swerve from it (ibid., p. 56). Kamandaka's *Nitisara* clarifies that the subjects need protection from the king's officers, favourites and enemies, as also from thieves and even the greed of the king himself (ibid., pp. 58–59). The *Manusmriti* enjoins upon the king, when protecting his subjects against invasion, not to run away from battle and promises heaven as a reward for kings who die fighting in battles (ibid., p. 57). Besides protection, public welfare constituted another major set of duties. The *Arthashastra* calls upon the king to support the helpless and aged people; the cripple, blind and diseased; lunatics, widows, orphans and pregnant women; and the victims of calamities by providing them medicines, food, lodging and clothing according to their requirements. The *Rajanitiprakasha* prescribes relief of unemployed men of various castes as the king's duty. Medhatithi, a commentator on the *Manusmriti,* advises that the king support his subjects during famine by distributing food from his treasury (ibid., p. 59). Indeed, equating the people's welfare with the king's welfare, the *Arthashastra* states: 'In the happiness of the subjects lies the happiness of the king, in their welfare lies his welfare; ...what is pleasing to the subject(s) constitutes his good' (ibid., p. 61). In a similar vein, the *Santi Parvan* and *Nitiprakashika* declare that the king, like a pregnant woman, should not do what is pleasing to him, but what would conduce to the good of the people. Privileging secular acts of welfare over religious ones, the *Santi Parvan* dismisses the utility of *tapas* (austerities) and *yajña* (sacrifice) for a king who looks after his subjects well (ibid., pp. 61–62). Linked to the idea of welfare-oriented kingship is that of paternalistic kingship: texts such as *Arthashastra, Yajnavalkyasmriti* and *Santi Parvan* advise the king to act as a father to his subjects, while the *Ramayana* highly praises Rama for doing so. This idea is also reflected in

an edict of the Mauryan emperor Ashoka where he calls all men his children (ibid., pp. 62–63).

5. For instance, the *Shukranitisara* considers a king who oppresses his subjects and causes the loss of *dharma* as made up of the parts of demons (*rakshasas*). The *Manusmriti* states at one place that a king who harasses his subjects loses his life, family and members, and at another that the *danda* (the royal sceptre symbolizing the king's punitive authority) when wielded by a voluptuous and unjust king recoils on its head and destroys him together with his relations.Further, there are instances of and prescripts for killing and deposing tyrannical kings in ancient literature. The *Santi Parvan* and *Bhagvata Purana* mention the story of King Vena killed by the brahmins because he was jealous of the gods, wanted sacrificial offerings to be made to himself and violated *dharma*. The *Arthashastra*, when dealing with the evil results of the lack of discipline in kings, points to hot-tempered kings falling victim to popular fury or the fury of ministers. The *Shatapatha Brahmana* refers to the expulsion of Dushtaritu Paumsayana. The *Anusasanaparvan* of the *Mahabharata* sanctions the killing of a cruel king by the people, while the *Santi Parvan*, *Manusmriti*, *Yajnavalkyasmriti* and *Shukranitisara* permit deposing such a king (ibid., pp. 25–27, 97).
6. For instance, the *Ayodhya-kanda* of the *Ramayana* refers to king Dasharatha summoning an assembly of vassal kings, citizens and rural inhabitants to seek their approval for his choice of crown prince, viz., his eldest son Rama. The *Adiparvan* of the *Mahabharata* mentions the unanimous selection of Parikshita as king by the citizens of the capital at the death of his father, Janamejaya. There is also some inscriptional evidence for the popular election of historical kings, such as the Shaka KshatrapaRudradaman in Saurashtra and the Pala ruler Gopala in Bengal. Further, the Chinese Buddhist pilgrim Hiouen Thswang refers to Harshavardhana being made a king by an assembly of ministers summoned by the chief minister Bhandin after the death of Rajyavardhana. The *Rajatarangini* narrates the story of a poor man Yashaskara being chosen as king by the brahmins (ibid., pp. 29–31).
7. For instance, in the legend of Manu Vaivasvata narrated in the *Arthashastra*, he was made a king by the people who agreed to assign one-sixth of their produce as the royal share in respect of the protection accorded by him (ibid., p. 31). However, this does

not suggest that the king was projected as a democrat in social terms; rather he was exhorted to defend the hierarchical four-fold caste system, confer and protect various privileges due to the brahmins and rule in concord with them and in accordance with their advice (ibid., p. 25).

8. The texts cite several reasons for the people to pay taxes. The *Gautama Dharmasutra* states that they should do so because the king protects them (ibid., p. 189). Protection being the rationale for taxation, the *Manusmriti* condemns to hell a king who levies them without affording protection (ibid., p. 191). The *Santi Parvan, Manusmriti, Baudhayana Dharmasutra, Naradasmriti* and *Arthashastra* consider taxes as the *vetana* (wages) of the king the result of a contract between the people and the first human king, Manu. The *Katyayanasmriti* justifies the king's entitlement to one-sixth of the produce of land on the ground that he is the real owner of the earth, while those residing on the land have only a qualified ownership (ibid., p. 189). The *Santi Parvan* and *Shukranitisara,* while enumerating three principals and perennial sources of royal income, viz., land revenue, tolls and custom duties, and fines levied on wrongdoers and defeated litigants, implicitly regard peasants, traders, manual workers and artisans as the principal tax payers (ibid., pp. 190–91).

9. The *Dharmashastras* or *Smritis,* prescribe several principles for taxation. First, they ordain that the king could not levy taxes at his sweet will pleasure but only at rates fixed by the *Smritis* or varying according to the value of the taxed commodity or the situation (whether normal or perilous/calamitous). The *Dharmasutras* of Gautama and Vishnu and the *Manusmriti* sanction the king's entitlement to one-sixth of the produce in normal times, while the *Arthashastra, Manusmriti, Santi Parvan* and *Shukranitisara* prescribe one-third as the royal share in times of distress. Even while recommending heavy taxation, the texts advise the king to temper this extreme step in various ways: the *Arthashastra*, for instance, requires that the king beg/request people for heavy taxes, not impose such taxes more than once in the same distress, nor do so on inferior lands; the *Santi Parvan* gives a specimen of a long address to be given by the king to the people wherein heavy taxation is demanded and justified on the ground of countering enemy invasion, which, if successful, would lead to the loss of their lives and property. Second, the texts prescribe that the taxes be imposed in such a way that they are felt to be light and not excessive by those taxed. Explaining

this principle through analogy in a poetical language, the *Udyogaparvan* of the *Mahabharata* states that just as a bee draws honey from flowers without injuring them, so too should a king take wealth from men without harming them. Describing this principle somewhat differently but with as much flourish, the Buddhist text *Dhammapada* states that the king should act like a gardener who prepares garlands without harming trees or their leaves and not act like one who prepares coals from trees (i.e. by burning them). The *Manusmriti* advises the king not to tax the subjects heavily out of greed, and thereby cut off the roots (of prosperity, contentment, etc.) of the people, nor to levy no taxes at all and thereby cut off his own roots (i.e. reduce himself to bankruptcy). Third, as the *Santi Parva* recommends, the taxes, if and when raised, should be increased gradually (ibid., pp. 184–86). Further, the texts complement the principles of taxation with those of expenditure, suggesting that the royal income be earned, preserved and spent judiciously. For instance, the *Manasollasa* advises the king to spend three-fourths of the yearly revenue and save one-fourth, while the *Shukranitisara* prescribes that the king save one-sixth of his total income and spend half of it on the upkeep of the army, one-twelfth each on charity, ministers, inferior officials and his private expenses, and also that king have as much stock of grains as required for three years' consumption in his kingdom (ibid., pp. 187–88). While states historically have been instrumental in maintaining a patriarchal social order, as is reflected in the brahmanical discourse, the issue is beyond the scope of this article.

10. Iqtidar Alam Khan, 'Akbar's Personality and Traits and World Outlook: A Critical Appraisal', in *Akbar and His India*, ed. Irfan Habib, Oxford University Press, New Delhi, 1997, p. 90.
11. Irfan Habib, *Bharatiya Itihas me Madhyakaal*, tr. and ed. Ramesh Rawat, Granthshilpi, Delhi, 1999, pp. 162–63.
12. Ibid.
13. Abul-Fazl, *Ain-i-Akbari*, Vol. 1, 3rd edn, Royal Asiatic Society, Calcutta, 1977, p. 291; Irfan Habib, *The Agrarian System of Mughal India 1556-1707*, 2nd rev. ed., Oxford University Press, New Delhi, 1999, p. 230.
14. Narsingh Meo, 'Hasan Khan ki Katha', *Shodh Patrika*, Vol. 4, October–December, Rajasthan Vidyapeeth, Udaipur, 1970.
15. R.C. Temple, *The Legends of the Panjab*, 3 Vols., Bombay Education Society, Bombay, 1884.

16. W.H.D. Rouse, *The Giant Crab and Other Tales of Old India*, David Nutt, London, 1897.
17. Maive Stokes, *Indian Fairy Tales*, Calcutta, 1879; repr. Ellis & White, London, 1880.
18. Flora Annie Steel, *Tales of the Punjab Told by the People*, Macmillan & Co. Ltd., London, 1917.
19. Charles Swynnerton, *Romantic Tales from the Punjab with Indian Nights' Entertainment*, Archibald Constable, London, 1908.
20. Alexander Cunningham, *Report of a Tour in Eastern Rajputana in 1882-83*, Vol. XX, Archaeological Survey of India Reports, 1885; repr. Indological Book House, Varanasi, 1969, pp. 122–24.
21. Munshi Ram, 'Mewati Lok Sahitya evam Mewat ka Arthik Vishleshan', in *Shreejan*, ed. Chhangaram Meena, Babu Shobharam Rajkiya Mahavidyalaya, Alwar, 2006, pp. 99–102.
22. Jeevan Singh Manvi, 'Ali Baksh ki Krishanlila evam anya Khyal', in *Shreejan*, ed. Chhangaram Meena, Babu Shobharam Rajkiya Mahavidyalaya, Alwar: 2006, pp. 81–89.
23. Puranchand Sharma, *Pandit Lakhmichand Granthavali*, Haryana Sahitya Academy, Chandigarh, 1996, p. 17.
24. *Rajadharam* and *prajadharam* are the colloquial variants of the Sanskrit terms *rajadharma* and *prajadharma*, respectively. Hereafter, these colloquial forms are used in the essay as they are in the folk tales.
25. This work was found transcribed in *gutka* No. 213, kept in the Digambar Jain temple of Neminath Swami in Tonk district, Rajasthan. The year of composition is *posh vadi* 14, VS 1639/ CE 1582. Its untranslated original version was published in Devanagari script by Mahavir Prasad Sharma in October–December issue of *Shodh Patrika* (Sahitya Sansthan, Rajasthan Vidyapith, Udaipur) in 1970. The work is in verse and has a mix of words from old mewati dialect and persian. For a transcription of the entire work in Roman script and a summary of its content, see Suraj Bhan Bhardwaj, *Contestations and Accommodations: Mewat and Meos in Mughal India*, Oxford University Press, New Delhi, pp. 242–55.
26. More specifically, Narsingh Meo blames Ravana for making many enemies with his misdemeanour and undue interference in others' affairs. He abducted Sita and did not even heed his wife Mandodari's good counsel. He thus incurred the enmity of Rama (Sita's husband). As a result, Rama's army (of

monkeys) wreaked havoc on his prosperous city of Lanka. The consequences of his misdeeds destroyed his wealth and well-being.

27. According to Narsingh Meo, Ibrahim Lodi, in the heat of youth, had his opponents killed or buried alive in the walls of his fort and thus had made many enemies in his 'home'. Further, while Babur was marching from Kabul to attack Hindustan, he was busy playing dice (*chaupar*) in his palace all the time. Hasan Khan rejected Babur's offer of 100 parganas in and around Bayana and his own granddaughter in marriage to Nahar Khan, Hasan Khan's son, and, instead, was bent upon fighting Babur for no reason except that he wanted to put Muhammad Lodi, the dim-witted minor son of Ibrahim Lodi, on the throne of Delhi.
28. Puranchand Sharma, *Pandit Lakhmichand Granthavali*, Haryana Sahitya Academy, Chandigarh, 1996, pp. 44–73.
29. Kshatriya is the warrior caste and second to the priestly caste of brahmins in traditional Hindu caste hierarchy.
30. For details, see Suraj Bhan Bhardwaj, 'Peasant–State Relation in Late Medieval North India (Mewat): A Study in Class Consciousness and Class Conflict', *Medieval History Journal*, Vol. 20, No. 1, 2017, pp. 111-54.
31. E.J. Hobsbawm, *Primitive Rebels: Studies in Archaic Forms of Social Movement in the Nineteenth and Twentieth Centuries*, Manchester University Press, Manchester, 1959; E.J. Hobsbawm, *Bandits*, Weidenfield & Nicolson, London, 1969; Anton Blok, 'The Peasant and the Brigand: Social Banditry Reconsidered', *Comparative Studies in Society and Economy*, Vol. 14, No. 4, 1972, pp. 494–503.
32. For details, see Bhardwaj, *Contestations and Accommodations*, Chapter 3.
33. Sharma, *Pandit Lakhmichand Granthavali*, pp. 267–312.
34. This story was narrated to me in 1988 by Mr Banwari Lal, son of Bakhtawar Mal, Dhareru village, district Bhiwani, Haryana.
35. Cunningam, *Report of a Tour in Eastern Rajputana in 1882-83*, pp. 122–24.
36. Sharma, *Pandit Lakhmichand Granthavali*, pp. 170–90.
37. A.K. Ramanujam, ed. and coll., *Bharat ki Lokkathaye*, tr. Kailash Kabir, NBT, Delhi: 2001, pp. 93–97.
38. For details, see Bhardwaj, 'Peasant–State Relation', pp. 111-54.
39. However, Akbar and his favourite companion Birbal have been the subject of many anonymously composed popular humorous

stories and jokes that had been circulating in north India since at least the early eighteenth century. These stories that often end in Birbal outwitting Akbar can be read in contrary ways: as signifying 'Hindu' subversion of 'Muslim' power, or as signifying a form of apotheosis of Akbar. Indeed, the stories have a subversive aim in establishing a clever brahmin jester's victory over a mighty Muslim emperor in the battle of wits, but, through the agency of humour, they seek to humanize implicitly, even glorify Akbar who inspired in the masses reverence, not to direct some suppressed communal antagonism towards him and dehumanize him into a demon. By integrating Akbar into the popular culture of north India, the stories enormously add to his stature as a humane ruler and, hence, are as much a visible and valuable indicator of his impact on Indian history as his forts, chronicles written by his court historians and paintings painted by his artists are (see C.M. Naim, 'Popular Jokes and Popular History: The Case of Akbar, Birbal and Mulla Do-Piyaza', *Economic and Political Weekly*, Vol. 30, No. 24, 1995, pp. 1456–64). At the same time, it must be noted that these amusing stories cannot be seen as commentaries on contemporary political situation, as the folk tales, as discussed in the essay, but have a decidedly political subtext.

40. It is quite possible that the folk tales celebrating the just rule of mythical Hindu kings helped buttress the colonial historians' interpretation of medieval period as that of Muslim tyranny and their depiction of Muslim rulers as oppressive and anti-Hindu, in contrast to their projection of British rule as based on the rule of law and justice.

41. Marzia Balzani in her historico-anthropological study of the survival of kingship in the modern city of Jodhpur in northern Rajasthan shows how a form of kingship persists in this area though legally kings do not exist (see Marzia Balzani, *Modern Indian Kingship: Tradition, Legitimacy and Power in Jodhpur*, James Currey, Oxford, 2003). Through a set of ritual practices and appeals to a fluid notion of tradition, the royal power and the notion of divine/semi-divine kingship is legitimized and consolidated and the Rathore rulers continue to command deference from people.

6

Formation of Santic Communities in Seventeenth Century Rajasthan: The Case of Dadupanth

Rameshwar Prasad Bahuguna

Dadupanthis and various modern scholars working on the history of Dadupanth have always assumed the existence of a full-fledged, hierarchically organized and well established sect of Dadupanthis in Rajasthan during the 17th century. It is believed that Dadu himself founded the organization which was carried forward by various groups of his disciples. Modern scholars such as W.M. Callewaert and David N. Lorenzen have argued that sectarian organizations such as Dadupanth and Kabirpanth flourished from the time of their founders, namely Dadu and Kabir. Another scholar, Daniel Gold is of the opinion that it was not before the end of the 17th century that Dadupanth developed into a well-established organization. However, far from being a well demarcated and structured panthic organization, Dadupanth in the 17th century was a loose community of various groups of *sants* (truth example) who accepted Dadu as their religious leader but who at the same time were also the followers of other great sants of the medieval period such as Kabir .and Raidas. It was an amorphous gathering which attracted a large number of sants in Rajasthan and outside. Even bairagis, Kabirpanthis and Raidasis joined the fold of Dadupanth in Rajasthan. Naraina in Rajasthan had not yet emerged into the monastic centre of the Dadupanthis and it was a multi-centered community.

Recent Western writings on the medieval north Indian bhakti movement underline the process of gradual 'sanscritization' and 'Hinduization' of the communities formed by the followers of Kabir and Dadu. Charlotte Vaudeville[1], Daniel Gold[2], Winand M. Callewaert[3] and David N. Lorenzen[4] have, in different ways, have attempted to show the process by which sant-based formations such as Kabir panths and Dadupanths have been absorbed into conventional Hinduism. An attempt has been made in this paper to show that these panthic communities retained most of their radical anti-brahmanism until the late medieval period, although they may have changed their symbolic and cultural strategies in the changing milieu of the 18th century.

Most of the scholars have suggested the existence of well organised and well demarcated sects in the names of the major sants such as Kabir and Dadu right from the beginning. However, there is very little evidence to show that non-brahmanical sects such as Kabirpanth and Dadupanth existed in institutionalized form till the end of the seventeenth century. To be sure, the term 'Dadupanth' was used by some followers of Dadu and we find the evidence of its use in the *Dabistan-i-Mazahib* also[5]. But for most part of the 17th century Dadupanth existed more in the form of a loose association of non-brahmanical sants who used it as a platform for religious propaganda. From various references in the seventeenth century texts such as Jan Gopal's *Dadu Janma Lila* and the *Bhaktamals* of Jagga and Chain, it is clear that many vairagis, Raidasvamshis, Dhannavamshis, Pipavamshis and Namavamshis were among the active followers of Dadu.[6] It would not be correct to assume that they left their original sects to join the Dadupanth.[7] There were no organized sant-based *panthas* during most part of the seventeenth century. It is quite possible that the names of great sants such as Kabir, Raidas, Dhanna, Pipa, etc. were used by their latter-day followers to emphasize their affiliation with one of them. The prevalence of such a practice did not, however, imply the creation of organized and well structured *panths* (sects).

Dadupanth served as a nucleus of non-brahmanical santic gatherings during the seventeenth century. These gatherings were open to the followers of various sants and there is little evidence to show that the followers of Dadu subordinated the spiritual authority of other great sants to that of Dadu. From the testimony of Jan Gopal himself, it is evident that Kabir occupied a high place among Dadu's followers and Dadu himself is represented as an incarnation of Kabir and depicted as constantly singing Kabir's verses.[8]

The 17th century saw many generations of Dadu's followers but they were all scattered in various parts of Rajasthan. They swang the verses of Dadu along with those of other leading sants such as Kabir. Dadupanth had not yet developed into a hierarchic, sectarian organization. It is clear from such texts as *Dadu Janma Lila Parchi,*[9] the *Sarvangi of Dadupanthi Rajab*[10], and the *Sarvangi of Gopaldas*[11] that the supporters and followers of Dadu were not part of any particular organization and moved from one santic community into another. They gave most important place to Dadu in their songs and compositions but also were equally attached to the memory of Kabir and other great sants of the early sixteenth century. Jan Gopal informs us that Dadu did not make any particular place the centre of his activities and he constantly travelled from one place to the other. Disciples were not organized under a single hierarchical organization. Naraina near Jaipur had come to be seen as a sacred centre by the followers of Dadu but there is no evidence for the existence of ritualized worship of Dadu during most of the seventeenth century. All this is clear from Jan Gopal's *Dadu Janma Lila* which was written about two decades after the death of Dadu in 1603. This work, which is the first important, full-fledged santic hagiographic account, underwent many interpolations later. The legendary episodes of Dadu's life, particularly his meeting with Akbar, are important for throwing light on the political perceptions of the ordinary followers of the sants.

Sant religious poetry of the later medieval period is replete with reference to the notion of sant as *shoorma*. Adopting the imagery of Rajput notions of chivalry and heroism but rejecting the Rajput political culture of fighting for territory and rank, the santic perception of sant was that of a hero who suffered at the hands of religious authorities, officials and rulers and yet ultimately emerged triumphant due to his superior spiritual and moral values. A kind of anti-brahmanical charisma came to be associated with the sant figures of the past. They came to be looked upon as objects of religious exaltation and glorification.

Jan Gopal's *Dadu Janma Lila*—the earliest legendary account of Dadu's life, written a few years after his death, gives a similar description of the sant's encounter with the Qazi and *faujdar* of Sambhar[12]. The work also contains a legendary account of the acceptance of Dadu's spiritual greatness by emperor Akbar, his courtiers and various chiefs of Rajasthan. Dadu as a sant is shown superior to all of them. When he is persuaded to visit Fatehpur Sikari and enlighten Akbar on spiritual matters, he establishes complete spiritual dominance over the Emperor, his courtiers and Brahman ideologues. When a brahman advisor of Akbar named Tulsi (different from Tulasidas, the author of *Ramacharitmanas*) said "Hail to the King", Dadu ignored his greeting and instead said "Hail to God". He made it clear that he would bow only before God and none else. He also refused to accept the theory that the Emperor was an incarnation of God[13]. Jan Gopal writes that in his discussions with Akbar which lasted for forty days, Dadu "spoke with the firmness of Prahlad and with the wisdom of Kabir"[14].

Needless to say, the entire account is legendary and there is no documentary evidence to show that Dadu ever visited Fatehpur Sikri and met Akbar. This fact, however, does not detract from the value of this account as it and other hagiographic accounts on the lives of sants reveal the non-brahmanical perception of the qualities of a *sant*. The hagiographers often use the phrase "victory, victory" whenever the brahmans and rulers are made to bite the dust and surrender before the sant. Clearly, in symbolic terms at least, the sant-hero becomes the new authority figure. What is significant about such a perception of 'santhood' is that it reveals the political expectations of the ordinary people who by imputing certain qualities to the sants imagined the overturning of existing hierarchies. The harsh reality that the relations of domination and subordination remained intact did not prevent the lower-caste groups to at least culturally and symbolically offer resistance to the dominant groups. Marc Bloch, the famous French historian, noted long ago in his study of 'royal touch' that the tendency to believe something which never happened in reality or was contradicted by experience is an essential feature of the so-called "primitive" mentality.[15] There is a legend about the literary encounter between the famous bard Durasa Adha, who had been patronized by both Rana Pratap and Akbar and who composed poems in praise of his royal patrons, and sant Rajjab. The legend, as narrated by Raghodas in his Bhaktamal, depicts how Durasa Adha had become arrogant due to his literary achievements and due to his links with the rulers and how he was ultimately vanquished in a literary duel by an ordinary follower of Dadu[16]. At a time when the bards and Brahman courtiers were presenting their Rajput patrons as heroic figures, unorthodox religious communities developed a different perception of valour and heroism. The leading sants were being regarded as sant-shoormas and sant-sipahis. Along with the cult of local and folk deities, the culture of sant-heroes formed an important part of the socio-religious life of the common people in many parts of northern India.

From the hagiographic sources such as Jan Gopal's *Dadu Janma Lila Parchi,* it becomes evident that Dadupanth did not exist as an organized panthic community in the decades following the death of Dadu in 1604. Jan Gopal frequently alludes to large number of sant-followers of Dadu who were also the followers of Kabir, Raidas, Pipa and other sants. He also mentions of many followers of Dadu who were bairagis. One of the important dimensions of the medieval Bhakti movements—both santic and vaishnava—is the rise, growth and transformation of the religious community of bairagis (or vairagis) during the Mughal period. The dominant trend in modern scholarship and historiography is to treat the bairagis as a vaishnava sect and link them to the conservative stream of Saguni Rama-bhakti, usually associated with the upper-caste followers of the fifteenth century Bhakti preacher, Ramanand. A close examination of evidence contained in both Indo-Persian and vernacular sources, however, reveals an altogether different picture of the bairagis and their position in the Bhakti-based religious communities of the Mughal period. The bairagis drew upon the elements of both santic and vaishnava bhakti and in the process subverted the hegemony of dominant religions during the sixteenth and seventeenth centuries. Many of these bairagis travelled across different parts of northern India, particularly western Rajasthan, where they were active among the followers of Dadu.

Shahabuddin Iraqi is of the opinion that Satnamis of Narnaul, who rebelled against the Mughal state in1672, were different from the Sadh sect founded by Bir Bhan in 1643. He also believes that although the Indo-Persian chroniclers have used the terms 'bairagis' and 'mundiyas' for the satnamis, the latter were neither part of the sect of the mundiyas as described in the *Dabistan-i Mazahib* nor should they be called bairagis. Iraqi assumes that the bairagis were wandering ascetics while the satnamis were householders.[17]

However, it would be wrong to assume that the term 'bairagi' was used exclusively for the ascetic Ramanandis in the seventeenth century. Undoubtedly, the ascetic followers of Ramanand were called bairagis rather than Ramanandis in the seventeenth century. Rarely does one come across the use of the term ' Ramanandis' in the seventeenth century sources, one exception being the *Dabistan-i Mazahib* where its author classifies the vaishnavas of a particular sect as 'Ramanandis'.[18] A mid-seventeenth century author of a sufi narrative calls Ramanand himself a bairagi[19]. But the term was used frequently for many sants and their followers many of whom were householders. Kabir, who had come to be seen as a disciple of Ramanand by the end of the sixteenth century but who rejected ascetic way of life, is represented as a bairagi (or vairagi) in the *Dabistan*. It is important to note here that while the author of the *Dabistan* observes that renunciation, worship of Vishnu and his incarnations, pilgrimage to vaishnava religious centres and use of certain vaishnava symbols are features of the bairagis, he soon moves to a description of other attributes that create a radically different image of the bairagis and their community. Here, the focus is not on asceticism and is no longer the defining characteristic of a bairagi. Bairagis are neither Hindus nor Musalmans, and their community is open to everybody: "Whoever among the Hindus, Musalmans, or others, wishes, is received into their religion; none are rejected, but, on the contrary, all are invited."[20]

Daniel Gold has suggested that the mid seventeenth century image of Dadu was that of a Darvesh (sufi saint) and not of a mythical figure who ultimately became an object of ceremonial worship. According to Gold, Dadu's tomb at Naraina was treated in the manner of a sufi shrine. The emergence of Dadupanth as a "distinct sectarian institution" was only a late seventeenth century phenomenon. At the end of the seventeenth century a charismatic figure Jaitram emerged on the scene and began to exercise authority over Dadu's followers. He remained in control of Dadu's *gaddi* at Naraina for about four decades and it was during this period of early eighteenth century that he organized Dadu's followers into a well-knit sect.[21]

The early history of Kabirpanth is shrouded in mystery. Some modern scholars and Kabirpanthis of various hues believe that the *panth* was founded by Kabir himself. There is, however, no evidence to trace the history of Kabirpanth to a date before the end of the seventeenth century. The term 'Kabirpanth' or 'Kabirpanthi' in the pre-eighteenth century sources is hardly used. The author of the *Dabistan-i-Mazahib* in the mid seventeenth century gives a detailed account of Kabir and attributes large following to him, yet he also does not refer to the existence of Kabirpanth.[22] In the *Bhaktamal* of Raghodas, there is a reference to 'Kabir Sahib Kau Panth' but the work was written in the second decade of the eighteenth century and not around 1660, as is believed by some scholars.[23] Linda Hess, who has carried out detailed research on the *Bijak of Kabir* is of the opinion that the assertion that Kabirpanth emerged in Eastern Uttar Pradesh and Bihar between 1600-50 is based on "rough guess work".[24] She makes the important point that most of the manuscripts of the *Bijak* belong to the post 1800 period.[25] Dharmadas, who is considered to be the founder of the Chhatisgarhi branch of Kabirpanth, is a mysterious figure about whom very little is known. His followers believe that he was initiated into Kabirpanth directly by Kabir himself and chosen as his successor by the sant. Most of the scholars however are of the opinion that there is a long chronological gap between their periods. Raghodas in his *Bhaktamal* has mentioned large number of Kabir's disciples including 'Guru Dharamdas'.[26] But since this *Bhaktamal* was written in the second decade of the eighteenth century it is quite possible that by that time Dharmadas had came to be regarded as the founder of the Chhatisgarh branch of the Kabirpanth. The names of some of Dharmadas's successors in this branch are also mentioned by Raghodas.

From the above discussion, it becomes evident that the claim of the official histories[27] of the Dadupanth and Kabirpanth that the sects were founded by the original sants themselves cannot be taken seriously. Each of these *panths* has viewed its history as a linear development from the lifetime of the original sant. The long hiatus between the lifetime of the great sant and the period when well-organized, well-demarcated panth began to emerge in his name is generally overlooked. Before the final stage of 'routinization' or 'crystallization' set in into the sant movement, there was a long period of transitional broad-based, fluid religious culture.

The followers of the sants travelled from one place to another in various parts of northern India during the 17th century and swang the verses of their religious heroes. They did not hierarchically privilege the verses of one particular sant over those of others. As is clear from the *Panchvani* anthological tradition, Kabir was immensely popular among Dadu's followers during the seventeenth century and was given equal respect, if not more. If the verses of Dadu are found in larger number then those of Kabir in the *Panchvani* anthologies complied by various followers of Dadu during the seventeenth century, the explanation should be found not in the existence of sectarian tendencies among them but in the ultimate limitations of oral transmission in the later medieval period. Dadu was, after all, historically and spatially closer to them than Kabir was. But still the popularity of sant-based religious culture spread in various parts of northern India and Kabir's sayings were included in large number in most of the anthological traditions. However, neither the sant-anthologies nor the *vanis* of the great sants of the early period acquired the status of sectarian texts during the 17th century. Moreover the verses in the anthologies were still subject to changes and interpolations and were not yet fixed. There did not yet emerge a "textual community" of believers of one particular sant during most of the seventeenth century. The utterances of Kabir and other sants were immensely popular during the seventeenth century. They, however, lacked the scriptural status that came to be associated with Nanak's *Vanis* and the Adi Granth during the same period.

Since there is considerable evidence for the evolution of many Kabirpanthi and Dadupanthi establishments and monasteries during the 18th and 19th centuries but relatively little evidence for the existence of organized Kabirpanth and Dadupanth during the pre-18th century period, one may venture to suggest that when Kabirpanth and Dadupanth did emerge during the late medieval period, each one of them emerged not as one single *panth* but as many mutually competing organized entities in different geographical settings. In the case of Dadupanth, Naraina near Ajmer gradually emerged into the most important centre of Dadupanthi activities but it was one among many such centres during the course of the 17th century. As the non-brahmanical panths such as Dadupanth and Kabirpanth developed their ritual, hierarchical, monastic and mythological apparatus, sants such as Kabir and Dadu lost their santhood and came to be seen as divine incarnations.[28]

While 17th century in northern India is largely characterized by a non-brahmanical sant-based broad religious culture which glorified the great sant-collective and which regarded Kabir as the greatest religious hero, eighteenth century is marked by the emergence of myriads of low-caste divisive sects evolving their own systems of rituals and placing their own sant in a position of dominance over others. Thus, apart from Kabirpanth and Dadupanth, various other sects such as Dariyapanth, Bawripanth, Shivanarayani panth and many others emerged in various regions of northern India. The panths faced external and internal constraints from the very beginning.

NOTES

1. Charlotte Vaudeville, *Kabir*, Oxford University Press, Oxford: 1974, later published in a revised form under a new title, *A Weaver Named Kabir*, Oxford University Press, Delhi: 1993 pp. 40-47.
2. Daniel Gold, *The Lord as Guru: Hindi Sants in the North Indian Tradition*, Oxford University Press, Delhi: 1987, pp. 3-6, and 'The Dadu-Panth: A Religious Order in Rajasthan Context' in Karine Schomer et al., eds., *The Idea of Rajasthan: Explorations in Regional Identity*, Vol. II, Manohar, Delhi: 1994, pp. 242-64.
3. Winand M. Callewaert, 'Dadu and Dadu-Panth: The Sources', in Karine Schomer and W.H. McLeod, eds., *The Saints: Studies in Devotional Tradition of India*, Motilal Banarasidas, Delhi: 1987, p. 189
4. David N. Lorenzen, "The Kabirpanth and Social Protest", in Karine Schomer and W.H. McLeod, eds., *The Saints: Studies in Devotional Tradition of India*, Motilal Banarasidas, Delhi: 1987, pp. 284-96. Also see his *Who Invented Hinduism? Essays on Religion in History*, Yoda Press, New Delhi: 2006
5. *Dabistan -i-Mazahib*, written c. 1658, ed. by Nazar Ashraf, English tr. by Anthony Troyer and David Shea as *Schools of Religions* in three vols. Details. The sections dealing with the religious system of the Hindus have been reproduced as *Hinduism During the*

Mughal India of the 17th Century, Khuda Bakhsh Oriental Public Library, Patna: p. 255.

6. For references to *vairagi* followers of Dadu, see Jan Gopal, *Dadu Janma Lila,* edited and translated by Winand M. Callewaert, as *The Hindu Biography of Dadu Dayal,* Motilal Banarsidass, Delhi: 1988, pp. 9: 24, 9: 25 and 13, 10, and Jagga, *Bhaktamal* in Agarchand Nahata, ed., *Raghavadaskrit Bhaktamal* with a commentary (Tika) by Chaturdas (Chaturdas Krit Tika), Granthank 78, Rajasthan Oriental Research Institute, Jodhpur: 1965. Verse 51, p. 278. For reference to Mohan 'Dhannavamshi', see Jagga, *Bhaktamal,* verse 59, p. 279. For 'Raidasvamshi' devotees, see Jagga, *Bhaktamal,* verse 62, p. 279 and Chain, *Bhaktamal,* verse 76, p. 285. For references to 'Pipavamshi' *sants,* see Chain, *Bhaktamal,* verse 63 and 67, p. 284. For 'Namavamshi' Teeku, see Chain, *Bhaktamal,* verse 76, p. 285. The Bhaktamals of Jagga and Chain have been included in the form of appendices in Agarchand Nahata, ed., *Ragavadaskrit Bhaktamal.*
7. See, for instance, the comment of Shahabuddin Iraqi that Jagannathdas was previously a Kabirpanthi and later became a disciple of Dadu, 'Historical and Religious Dimensions of Dadupanthi Sources', *Islamic Culture,* Vol. LXXI, No. 3, 1997, p. 44.
8. Jan Gopal, *Dadu Janma Lila,* 1: 17, 2: 4.
9. This work contains details of Dadu's birth in a cotton carder's family at Ahmedabad, his initiation by Baba Budhan, his decision to leave his family and home, and his travels in various towns of Rajasthan. Sambhar and Amer figure prominently in his clashes with both Hindus and Muslims and in his persecution by the Qazis and brahmins. Long story of an encounter between him and the Qazi of Sambhar along with his encounter with Bhagwant Das and Man Singh is also mentioned. Forty days spent by Dadu at Sikri and his discussion with Akbar finds a prominent place in Jan Gopal's account. Last few years were spent by Dadu in preaching in various parts of Rajsthan. Jan Gopal mentions about forty places visited by Dadu in Rajsthan in the course of his travels which spanned twelve years.
10. See Winand M. Callewaert, ed. *The Sarvangi of the Dadupanthi Rajab,* Department Orientalistiek Katholieke Universiteit Leuven, Belgium: 1978.
11. See Winand M. Callewaert, ed., *The Sarvangi of Gopaldas: A 17th Century Anthology of Bhakti Literature,* Manohar, Delhi: 1993
12. Jan Gopal, *Dadu Janma Lila,* ch. 3: 1-17. The account can also be

found in later hagiographies such as Raghodas's *Bhaktamal.*

13. Ibid., chs. 5 and 6.
14. Ibid., ch. 7: 1.
15. Marc Bloch, *The Royal Touch*, Eng. trans., Translator & Publisher, London: 1973 (originally published in French in 1924).
16. Raghodas, *Bhaktamal*, Rajjab ji Kau Barnan, pp. 381-82, 188. See also Vrajlal Varma, *Sant Kavi Rajjab*, Rajasthan Oriental Research Institute, Jodhpur: 1965.
17. Shahabuddin Iraqi, *Bhakti Movement in Medieval India: Social and Political Perspectives*, Manohar, New Delhi: 2009, pp. 229-30, 235 n.10.
18. *Dabistan-i Mazahib*, Eng. trans. by Anthony Troyer and David Shea as *School of Religions*, originally published in three volumes, Publisher, London: 1843, reprint, Khalil & Co., Lahore: 1973, p. 262.
19. See 'Mirat ul Asrar' of Shaikh Abdul Rahman Chishti cited in S.A.A. Rizvi, *History of Sufism in India*, Vol. 2, Munshiram Manoharlal, Delhi: 2002, p. 412.
20. *Dabistan*, p. 263.
21. Gold, 'The Dadu-*panth*: A Religious Order in its Rajasthan Context' in..., pp. 249-50.
22. For the account of Kabir, see *Dabistan-i-Mazahib*, op. cit. pp. 184-91.
23. Winand M. Callewaert, an eminent authority on the Dadupanthi sources, has given 1720 A.D. as the date of the composition of Raghodas's *Bhaktamal*, see his 'Dadu and the Dadu-*panth*: The Sources..., p. 186. The description of Kabirpanth in Raghodas's *Bhaktamal* appears under the heading of "Chaturpanth Vigat Barnan" (Account of Four Sects). These four sects are Nanakpanth, Kabirpanth, Dadupanth and Niranjanipanth. After narrating various episodes in Kabir's life in *Mool Chhappayas* 349-52 (pp. 177-78), Raghodas turns to a description of various disciples of Kabir in *Mool Chhappayas* 353-358 (pp. 178-179). From Raghodas's description, it is clear that Dharmadasi branch of Kabirpanth was already in existence in the beginning of the eighteenth century.
24. Linda Hess, Preface to English trans. of the *Bijak of Kabir*. translated by Linda Hess and Shukdev Singh, Essays and Notes by Linda Hess, Motilal Banarasidas, Delhi: 1986.
25. Ibid., appendix C, p. 165.

26. Raghodas, *Bhaktamal*, pp. 178-79.
27. See, for instance, the official Kabirpanthi biography of Kabir written by Gangasharan Shastri, *Kabir Jivan Charitra* (Hindi), first edn., 1976, Kabir Vani Prakashan Kendra, Varanasi: 1991. See also Narayandas, *Sri Dadu Panth Parichay*, 3 Vols., Shri Dadudayalu Mahasabha, Jaipur: 1978-79.
28. First important Kabirpanthi hagiographic work which regards Kabir as an incarnation of the Supreme Being and subordinates various deities of the Hindu pantheon to Kabir's authority is *Anurag Sagar*. The work is associated with the Chhattisgarhi Kabirpanth and is in the form of a dialogue between Kabir and his 'chosen successor' Dharmadas. See the Lucknow edition printed in 1989.

7

Colonial Construction of the Precolonial Economic History of India: A Reappraisal of W.H. Moreland's Writings

Abha Singh

Colonial regimes often tried to legitimize their rule by re-writing the pasts of the subjugated peoples and by denigrating their cultures and civilizational achievements. The twin purpose behind the design was to promote the colonial aspect and also to discourage them from demanding any share in the power. The classic example of such an attempt was H.M. Elliot and John Dowson's *The History of India as Told by its Own Historians*, a project which started some time after the 1840s just to tell the bombastic Bengali *Babus* about India's past history of Hindu-Muslim conflict. It was only due to the British rule that peace was established for the Hindus. In the same way, W.H. Moreland articulated that during the Mughal times there was minimal development in terms of economic activity. The development has taken place only under the colonial administration.

History writing during the colonial period was largely commissioned by British Indian civil servants-cum-administrators. They principally concentrated on dynastic history and attempted to highlight the despotic and tyrannical conduct of Indian rulers. Their underlining intention was to present a contrast to the 'benevolent' British rule. They viewed Indian society as stagnant, Indian institutions static and the Indian attitude towards life fatalistic, 'other worldly'. Against this backdrop I wish to analyse where Moreland and his works fit in.

William Harrison Moreland (b. Belfast, July 13, 1868; d. Gerrad's Cross, Buckinghamshire, September 28, 1938) joined the British Indian Civil Service in 1889. His very first appointment was as Settlement Officer (1889), North-Western Provinces (later known as United Provinces of Agra and Oudh); served as Assistant Commissioner in 1894; then he worked as Joint-Magistrate (1897) and then Magistrate and Collector (1899) and the very same year became the Director of Land Records and Agriculture in the United Provinces. Almost throughout his career he served in the United Provinces and remained there for twenty-five years before retiring in 1914 at the age of 46. His long stay in Northern India focused largely on serving the revenue department as he enjoyed the highest office of Director of Land Records and Agriculture of the United Provinces for fourteen years (1899-1912). His knowledge, passion and experience in revenue matters is well reflected in his effort to establish the Agricultural College (1905) by upgrading the existing agricultural school at Cawnpore (Kanpur) now known as Chandra Shekhar Azad University of Agriculture and Technology. Even after his retirement he served as Agricultural Advisor for two years to the Princely State of Indore.

A brilliant eulogy on W.H. Moreland is written by Margaret H. Case in 1965.[1] She has meticulously pieced together the life history and works of Moreland. Therefore, here, I do not intend to present the same. The focus here is to look at Moreland's idea of history, particularly economic history, and how he articulated it.

Before critically examining Moreland's work, let me first chronologically analyse the extensive work done by Moreland in various fields. His published works can broadly be divided into three major categories: i) on society and economy particularly on revenue and agrarian structure, etc., ii) translations of Dutch records, and iii) a few treatises on polity.

It is extremely interesting that so long as he served as a civil servant he brought out *four* treatises one on *The Agriculture of the United Provinces: An Introduction for the Use of Landholders and Officials* (1904)[2] and *The Revenue Administration of the United Provinces* (1911)[3], *An Introduction to Economics for Indian Students* (1913)[4] and *General Note on the Agricultural Conditions and Problems of the United Provinces* [*Provincial and District Notes on the Agricultural Conditions and Problems of the United Provinces*] (1914)[5]. These were mainly intended to highlight a) the state of affairs of agriculture in India and more so b) the intention was to bring out a sort of handbook for the ICS trainees working in the Land Record office to enhance their understanding of the working of the Indian rural economy, particularly agriculture and revenue, which he rightly believed was quite indigenous and unique to India. Moreland himself acknowledged the purpose that, 'Government laid down the rule that all junior officers of the Indian Civil Service should undergo training in the methods of survey and soil-classification…As time went on the value of these classes diminished…In 1904, therefore, it was decided at my suggestion to abandon the separate survey classes and to utilize part of the time so saved by placing junior officers under the orders of the Directors of Land Records and agriculture for training in the elements of survey…I have therefore included in the classes of the last few years a course of informal lectures on the principles and the development of the revenue administration of the provinces, and these lectures form the basis of the present work.'[6]

However, whatever Moreland wrote before 1914 was largely generic in nature and his real work based on concrete notes on medieval economy in general and Mughal economy in particular appeared out only after his retirement. Once he was back in Britain, the sheer quantum of his writings multiplied in spite of his health issues particularly his increasing deafness. The first preliminary survey of the Mughal economy was brought out by Moreland in 1916 on the *Ain*[7] followed by a series of articles almost every year[8], till his major publication came out in 1920, *India at the Death of Akbar* followed by *From Akbar to Aurangzeb* (1923) and *The Agrarian System of Moslem India* (1929) in which he crystallized his ideas on Mughal Indian economy. His last monograph was *A Short History of India* with A. Chatterjee (1936); while his articles on 'The Pargana Headman (Chaudhuri) in the Mogul Empire'[9] and 'The Ships of the Arabian Sea About A.D. 1500'[10] were his last publications, published posthumously.

Moreland's early writings and what he produced and crystallized in the form of three major *Essays on Medieval Economy* suggest little contrast; in his later essays he modified his own understanding of the pre-colonial economy. Moreland examined the complexities of land relations with regard to peasants, *zamindars*, assignees (*jagirdars*) and revenue farmers (*ijaradars*). His constant refrain was 'remember that diversity is more probable than uniformity in the conditions that prevailed, and it would be unsafe to conclude that institutions which flourished in the Upper Duab were equally common in Benaras.'[11] Irfan Habib in his *Preface* to the *Cambridge Economic History of India* recognizes Moreland's concerns that 'relate to the structure and dynamics of economic life under a system of relations of production'.[12]

Moreland believed 'the dynastic and military history of the period is now tolerably accessible to students', but it is impossible 'to obtain the... connected view of the position of the peasants in their relations with the state'.[13] Moreland's writings begin with stress on the high morals of 'peasant welfare' which, according to him, pre-colonial states failed and the *British Indian state aimed to fulfil*. Nonetheless, in spite of his distinct biases he, with admiration commends that Sher Shah's practices and reforms further 'developed and extended under Akbar into a remarkably complete and effective organisation' and 'Akbar's statement of the revenue then... resembles the later settlements effected under British rule. In some details, too, it was 'curiously modern'.[14] He applauds that, 'he distinctly enjoined his officials to deal directly with the cultivators...'[15]

Peasant Ownership

Moreland was greatly influenced by the writings of Bernier and he largely agrees with Francois Bernier's observations. Bernier remarks, 'the land throughout the whole empire is considered the property of the sovereign…'[16] Though Moreland does not cite Bernier for his understanding of the peasant ownership issue nonetheless shared Bernier's same idea on the ownership issue. Writing in 1911 in his monograph for revenue officials he commented, 'the originally complex land tenures of England had so far developed that the conception of individual ownership was definitely established: every bit of English land must have a definite owner…; and the first English revenue officers in India set to work to find out who was the owner of each portion of land…'[17] He begins his work with the basic assumption that, 'The prominence of question of *right* [enjoyed and claimed by landholders and their tenants] is, however, a *recent* development in Indian agrarian history, and *belongs almost entirely to the British period…*'[18] According to him, 'in Moslem India, as in the India of the Hindus, the agrarian system was a matter of *duties* rather than rights'. We know conclusively how utterly confused the British Indian civil servants were to even think that Indian peasants enjoyed ownership rights from the very beginning. Thus, in spite of Moreland's brilliant understanding of medieval economy he continued to call Mughal land revenue 'rent' and not 'tax' implying thereby that the state possessed ownership rights[19] like in medieval Europe which is conclusively questioned by Irfan Habib. Habib finally settled the issue in his seminal work on the *Agrarian System of Mughal India* saying that in the Mughal period it was the peasant who possessed the property rights.[20]

However, on account of this basic wrong premise of the ownership issue, Moreland found it difficult to understand the complexities of land tenures, particularly the *zamindari* rights.

Zamindars

From the very beginning, Moreland was anxious to understand

the complexity of *zamindari* rights. Somewhere he was not convinced with the British understanding of the *zamindar* being the 'landlord', or 'owner of the land'. He addressed his revenue officials clarifying, 'One fact that emerged was that the persons who paid revenue were known as *zamindars*, and it was natural for English officers to conclude that the *zamindars* were the land owners, and in fact they were treated as such. But the term had really a different meaning, and indicated primarily the person who undertook to pay the revenue...'[21] Therefore, 'it is necessary to get some idea of how they came into existence and gradually gained their present position'.[22] Thus Moreland acknowledged the glaring mistake that 'the early English officers found zamindars and left landowners.'[23] He boldly accepted the fault and declared, 'that *zamindars* were not necessarily owners of the land on which they paid revenue...'[24] His understanding on the class of *zamindars* seems of extreme clarity. He believed from the very beginning that *zamindars* were an 'intermediate' class between the state and the cultivators and it did not 'exist' from the very beginning, rather 'evolved'.[25] A fact that Moreland himself had openly acknowledged, 'There is little or no evidence to show that intermediaries of other classes came into existence during the earlier period...'[26] He had the clarity that, 'among other conditions—their influence depends on the origin of their tenures.'[27] And how did they evolve as an 'intermediary'? He argues that there was 'temporary conversion of rajas into zamindars: the raja continued to collect revenue from the cultivators and paid a portion of it to the Maharaja or Emperor who had imposed his domination...Stubborn rajas had of course to be extirpated, but apparently those who accepted the new order of things...found a place within the empire and remained in positions varying from that of feudatory chief to that of zamindar.'[28] Moreland believes following the 'chaos' the Mughal decline created these hereditary chiefs who were earlier subdued but continued to have a clan base and enjoyed local authority got the opportunity so they resumed 'local authority'. 'Thus, instead of the original polity in which the produce of the land was shared between two parties only, we now find usually the three sharers (and sometimes more) the state, the cultivators, and the intermediaries or zamindars.'[29] He also acknowledged, 'occasionally, too, the headmen [muqaddams] seem to have become a zamindar of his own village'.[30] However, he could not systematically trace the process of this transformation which Nurul Hasan and Irfan Habib could finally find.

Nurul Hasan in his pioneer study on *zamindars* which is considered to be seminal in the sense that for the first time he highlighted categories of *zamindars*—primary, secondary and autonomous chieftains.[31] The category of autonomous chieftains constituted of *rajas, rais* and *ranakas* which Moreland had also recognized but as the 'only' category of the *zamindars*. The category of 'intermediary' *zamindars* was those of the *chaudhuries, khots* and *muqaddams*; while primary *zamindars* were often peasant-proprietors who held the proprietorship of one or more villages and used to get their land tilled with the help of hired-labour. However, these categories were not *exclusive,* instead they often overlapped. As for the category of *zamindars* of autonomous chieftains long before Nurul Hasan, Moreland had arrived at the same understanding, though vaguely and shakily. Moreland was quite convinced as for the conversion of the 'subjugated' rajas turning into *zamindars*. But he was hesitant to see the presence of *muqaddams* as *zamindars* which he could only explain as a phenomenon developed following the chaos, resulting in the Mughal decline. Even he noticed commercial classes turning into *zamindars* which he terms 'perplexing tenures where there are now two sets of proprietors, superior and inferior, both entitled to maintenance from the land.'[32] In fact, Moreland's fault lies in the fact that he could not see the presence of layers within the broad category of the *zamindars* and saw them as a singular category. Though he rightly identified 'subdued chiefs' as *zamindars,* he failed to see the presence of primary *zamindars*. Later, Irfan Habib in his scholarly seminal empirical research concluded and traced the origin of the term *zamindar* as a distinct category. Habib looks into the origin of the term *zamindar* as a conscious attempt on the part of Firuz Shah Tughluq to accommodate the old (subdued chieftains; *khots, muqaddams, maliks*) as well as newly created Muslim aristocracy (*mafrozis*; the state created rural aristocracy).[33]

There are any number of issues pertaining to *zamindari* rights that Moreland failed to comprehend: For him during Akbar's period there was a direct relationship between the state and the cultivators. For Moreland only the autonomous chieftains/rajas were the *zamindars*. According to him they were not present in the 'Regulation tracts' (i.e. *zabti* provinces) instead existed in the peripheral/borderland areas—Rajputana, Gondwana, 'in the mountainous country south of Allahabad and Benaras'.[34] Thus Moreland believed that there were no *zamindars* in the directly governed territories of the Mughals. The confusion arose on two counts: a) Moreland could identify only 'one' category of *zamindars*, i.e. the chiefs/rajas which had a stronghold in the borderland areas; b) More importantly confusion arose on account of Moreland's erroneous understanding of the *Ain's* statistics on account of Blochmann's major slip in printing *Ain*'s statistics in which he dropped the column headings which mentioned *zamindar* castes and *zamindars'* retainers provided by Abul Fazl for the directly administered territory (*zabti* provinces) for every pargana of the Mughal Empire. The statistics conclusively confirms the presence of *zamindars* in almost every pargana of the Mughal Empire.[35]

Nonetheless, in spite of all the misjudgments what is important is Moreland did recognize that *zamindars* under the Mughals were not the *proprietors* of those lands over which they were collecting revenue. He believed that accepting them as owners by early British administrators was an 'error'. He was therefore constantly trying to locate the origin of the *zamindars* and to some extent he succeeded. He was able to identify at least two such categories of *zamindars*, one from the chiefs (autonomous), and the other those who were subdued and assimilated; though he could not clarify, and probably was not aware of, that during the Sultanate period the 'subdued chiefs' (*rais, ranas* and *ranakas*) got subsumed into the class of superior right holders in the rural hierarchy along with *khots and muqaddams* who later, along with Muslim *mafrozis*, by the proclamation of 1353 of Firuz Shah Tughluq got integrated into one single class, that of the *zamindars*. Thus, though Moreland rejected the idea of *zamindars* being the owners of land, it never occurred to him that throughout the medieval period it was the peasants who were the proprietors of land.

Jagir

Another land tenure which Moreland talks about is *jagir* (land assignments; paid to the *mansabdars* in lieu of salary). 'For another', comments Moreland, 'the practice of assigning the revenue for specific purposes, which is one of the outstanding causes of the financial collapse of successive empires, was already well established. The superior officers of the state all held military commands and were remunerated for their services not by cash salaries but by the grant of lands (*jagirs*) from which they were entitled to collect the revenue; similar grants were made for other purposes, such as religious endowments [*madad-i ma'ash/suyurghal*]; and it is easy to understand that in a court of oriental profusion a large share of the revenue of the empire would eventually be dissipated in this way.'[36] In 1929 Moreland brought out another write up entitled 'The Peasant in History' as part of 'An Introduction to the Linlithgow Report' in which he talked about the exploitation of peasants at the hands of revenue assignees (*jagirdars*). Moreland again relying on Bernier's analysis that *jagirdars* often on account of their temporary interests were hardly interested in the welfare of the peasants or attempted to invest in for the extension or improvement of agriculture:

> The Timariots [*jagirdars*], Governors, and Revenue contractors [revenue farmers; *ijaradars*] , on their part reason in this manner: 'Why should the neglected state of this land create uneasiness in our minds? Why should we expend our own money and time to render it fruitful? We may be deprived of it in a single

> moment, and our exertions would benefit neither ourselves nor our children...'

As a result of their tyranny:

> That drives the cultivator of the soil from his wretched home to some neighbouring state, in hopes of finding milder treatment...[37]

Moreland based on Bernier argues that the burden of taxation was comparatively less and there was comparatively less burden on peasants in the territories of the rajas: 'There are signs that in the north and centre of India things were sometimes rather better in the Hindu States, because peasants sometimes sought a refuge there when oppression became intolerable.'[38] However, new research on Eastern Rajasthan done by S.P. Gupta shows conclusively that as far as exploitation of peasants and burden of taxation on peasants is concerned it was no less in the territories of the *rajas* (Amber). According to S.P. Gupta incidence of taxation in Eastern Rajasthan varied between 44 to 46 per cent of the total produce.[39]

Ijara

Further, Moreland did see *thekadars* (what Moreland calls them rent collectors; subletting of *zamindaris;* Mughal *ijara* revenue-farming) as a major cause of exploitation of the peasants. 'The thekadars', recalls Moreland, 'default in their payments: fresh thekas are given for lower payments..., and gradually the income of the estate becomes insufficient to maintain the proprietor, while the cultivators are being "squeezed" by irresponsible thekadars...'[40] A tendency (*ijara*) which Mughal emperors, particularly, Aurangzeb was constantly discouraging (in 1676 CE Aurangzeb forbade the practice of revenue-farming in Gujarat) and rightly emphasized by Irfan Habib as the cause of the oppression of the peasants.[41]

To conclude, Moreland can be described as the father of economic history writing in India and we cannot take away from him the credit of leading from the front the study of economic history as a 'distinct' discipline. Instead of relying on dynastic or socio-religious and cultural history he chose to compare the economic development of the pre-colonial regimes to construct the superiority and pre-eminence of British administration by putting forth the vast economic data and analysis. This is more markedly apparent in his monographs which he published after his retirement than in his early writings when he actually served as an Indian civil servant. Before him no one studied exclusively and so extensively land revenue related aspects of the pre-colonial societies. Moreland's writings begin with stress on high morals of 'peasant welfare' which, according to him, the 'British Indian state aimed to fulfil'. His early writings, however, suggest a comparatively positive approach to Mughal rule; he appears less harsh compared to his later works. Moreland began his writings to justify the niceties of British rule. However, as he dug deeper into the subject his data started betraying his own presuppositions, his very idea of the 'superiority' of the race which teaded to dominate Moreland's thought. There are very many problems in accepting Moreland's judgments on pre-colonial economy. Nonetheless his insights are exceptionally scholarly and erudite. Undoubtedly he worked within the colonial framework, with a colonial mindset. However he did understand the complexities of medieval economy and its diversities. At times he found it difficult to criticize the Mughal economy and Mughal policies, so appreciated their efforts, particularly that of Akbar, as an aberration. With all shortcomings, no doubt he truly pioneered the understanding of the pre-colonial Mughal economy. Rather he set the pace for the economic historians to think unearthing the Mughal economic history on new lines. However, till the end, Moreland operated within the broad framework of studying the Indian economy with the colonial mindset and the binary of 'Hindu' and 'Moslem' India.

NOTES

1. Margaret, H. Case, 'The Historical Craftmanship of W.H, Moreland (1868-1938)', *Indian Economic and Social History Review*, Vol. 2, No. 3, 1956, pp. 245-58.
2. W.H. Moreland, *The Agriculture of the United Provinces: An*

Introduction for the Use of Landholders and Officials, Pioneer Press, Allahabad: 1904.

3. W.H. Moreland, *The Revenue Administration of the United Provinces*, Pioneer Press, Allahabad: 1911.
4. W.H. Moreland, *An Introduction to Economics for Indian Students*, Macmillan and Co., London: 1913 (within Moreland's lifetime between 1913-1938 eight editions of the book got published).
5. W.H. Moreland, *General Note on the Agricultural Conditions and Problems of the United Provinces*, Government Press, Allahabad: 1914.
6. Moreland, *The Revenue Administration*, pp. i-ii.
7. W.H. Moreland, 'The *Ain-i-Akbari* – A Possible Base-Line for the Economic History of Modern India', *Indian Journal of Economics*, Vol. I, 1916, pp. 44-53.
8. W.H. Moreland, 'Prices and Wages Under Akbar', *Journal of Royal Asiatic Society of Great Britain and Ireland*, October 1917, pp. 815-825; W.H. Moreland, and A. Yusuf Ali, 'Akbar's Land Revenue System as Described in the *Ain-i-Akbari*', *Journal of Royal Asiatic Society of Great Britain and Ireland*, January 1918, pp. 1-42; W.H. Moreland, 'Value of Money at the Court of Akbar' *Journal of Royal Asiatic Society of Great Britain and Ireland*, July 1918, pp. 375-385; W.H. Moreland, 'The Agricultural Statistics of Akbar's Empire', *The Journal of the United Provinces Historical Society*, June 1919, pp. 1-39; W.H. Moreland, 'Some Thoughts About the "Drain" in India', *Asiatic Review*, NS, Vol. XVI (October 1920), pp. 33-40; W.H. Moreland, 'The Shahbandar in the Eastern Seas' *Journal of Royal Asiatic Society of Great Britain and Ireland*, No. 4, October 1920, pp. 517-533; W.H. Moreland, 'The Study of Indian Poverty' *Asiatic Review*, NS, Vol. 16, October 1920, pp. 616-630; – Discussion, pp. 631-639; W.H. Moreland, 'The Development of the Land Revenue System Under the Mughal Empire', *Journal of Royal Aciatic Society of Great Britain and Ireland*, January 1922, pp. 19-55; W.H. Moreland, 'Indian Peasants and His Critics' *Edinburgh Review*, Vol. CCXXXV, April 1922, pp. 246-262; W.H., Moreland, '*The Journal of the United Provinces Historical Society*, Vol. III, December 1923, pp. 146-161; W.H. Moreland, 'Some Side-Lights on Life in Agra, 1637-39', *The Journal of the United Provinces Historical Society*, Vol. III, December 1923, pp. 146-161; W.H. Moreland, 'Indian Export of Cotton Goods in the Seventeenth Century', *Indian Journal of Economics*, January 1925, pp. 225-245; W.H. Moreland, 'A Dutch Account of Mogul Administrative

Methods', *Journal of Indian History*, April 1925, pp. 69-83; W.H. Moreland, 'Village Surveys', *Indian Journal of Economics*, Vol. VI, 1925-1926, pp. 69-81; W.H., Moreland, 'Akbar's Land Revenue Arrangements in Bengal', *Journal of Royal Asiatic Society of Great Britain and Ireland*, January 1926, pp. 43-56; W.H. Moreland, 'Sher Shah's Revenue System', *Journal of Royal Asiatic Society of Great Britain and Ireland*, No. 3, July 1926, pp. 447-459; W.H. Moreland, 'Coinage of Mahmudis', *Journal of Royal Asiatic Society of Great Britain and Ireland*, 1927, p. 101; W.H. Moreland, 'The Mogul Unit of Measurement', *Journal of Royal Asiatic Society of Great Britain and Ireland*, 1927, pp. 102-103; W.H., Moreland, 'The Kingdoms and Provinces Subject to the Great Mogol', *Journal of Indian History*, Vol. VI, August 1927, pp. 149-162; W.H. Moreland, 'The Indian Peasant and His Future', *Edinburgh Review*, CCXLVIII, October 1928, pp. 262-275; W.H. Moreland, 'The Indian Peasant in History', *Near East and India*, XXXV, March 14, 21, 28, 1929, pp. 330-331, 365, 394. A paper read before the Indian Section of the Royal Society of Arts, March 8, 1929.

9. *Journal of Royal Asiatic Society of Great Britain and Ireland*, October 1938.
10. Ibid., January and April 1939.
11. W.H. Moreland, *The Revenue Administration*, p. 28.
12. Tapan Raychaudhuri and Irfan Habib (eds.), *The Cambridge Economic History of India*, Vol. I: *c.1200-c. 1750*, Orient Longman in Association with Cambridge University Press, Delhi: 1982, p. xi.
13. W.H. Moreland, *The Agrarian System of Moslem India: A Historical Essay with Appendices*, Oriental Books Reprint Corporation, Delhi: [1929] 1968, p. xi.
14. Moreland, *The Revenue Administration*, pp. 16-17.
15. Ibid., p. 28.
16. Francois Bernier, *Travels in the Mogul Empire, AD 1656-1668*, Second edition revised by Vincent A. Smith, Oxford University Press, London: 1916, p. 5 (and many more 204, 226, 232, 238).
17. W.H. Moreland, *The Revenue Administration*, p. 4.
18. Ibid.
19. Ibid., p. 220
20. Irfan Habib, *Agrarian System of Mughal India*, [1963] 2000, Oxford University Press, Delhi: pp. 123-35.
21. Moreland, *The Revenue Administration*, pp. 5-6.

22. Ibid., p. 5.
23. Ibid.
24. Ibid., p. 6.
25. Ibid., p. 9.
26. Ibid., p. 10.
27. Ibid., p. 26.
28. Ibid., pp. 10-12.
29. Ibid., p. 18.
30. W.H. Moreland, *The Revenue Administration*, p. 24.
31. S. Nurul Hasan, '*Zamindars* Under the Mughals' in *Religion, State and Society in Medieval India*, edited and Introduced by Satish Chandra, Oxford University Press, New Delhi: 2005, pp. 135-50. First published under the title, 'The Position of the *Zamindars* in the Mughal Empire', *Indian Economic and Social History Review*, Vol. I, No. 4, 1964, pp. 107-19.
32. W.H. Moreland, *The Revenue Administration*, p. 23.
33. For details see Irfan Habib, *Economic History of Medieval India, 1200-1500*, D.P. Chattopadhyaya Series, *History of Science, Philosophy and Culture in Indian Civilization*, Vol. VIII (1), Longman Pearson, Delhi: 2011, p. 68.
34. W.H. Moreland, *India at the Death of Akbar*, pp. 3-4; Moreland, *The Agrarian System of Moslem India*, pp. 122-23, 279.
35. This is for the first time brought to the notice by Prof. Irfan Habib in his article 'The Zamindars in the Ain', *Proceedings of the Indian History Congress*, XXI Session, Trivandrum: 1958, pp. 320-23. Also see *Agrarian System* (2000), pp. 170-71.
36. W.H. Moreland, *The Revenue Administration*, p. 12.
37. Bernier, *Travels in the Mogul Empire*, pp. 226-27.
38. W.H. Moreland, 'The Indian Peasant in History: An Introduction to the Linlithgow Report', *Journal of the Royal Society of Arts*, No. 3988 (April 26, 1929), p. 611.
39. S.P. Gupta, *The Agrarian System of Eastern Rajasthan*, Manohar, Delhi: 1986, pp. 144-55.
40. W.H. Moreland, *The Revenue Administration*, pp. 22-23.
41. Irfan Habib, *Agrarian System*, pp. 274-76, 328-29.

8

Genealogy/ies of Geographies: Cultural-Hegemonic to Counter/ Complimentary Narratives

Mayank Kumar

> ..."imagination is a capitalist literary criterion developed through certain institutionalized processes of socializing, while memory is a criterion developed by communities that have not lost ability for realism."[1]

Although, in the very next sentence G.N. Devy stated that, 'These, ...were untenable premises if put to the test of fact, history or reason'. Nevertheless, his statement offers a tool to understand the interplay between imaginations and realism in the depictions of geographies. Most of the times, it is the register of 'utilitarian' concerns which are closer to realism, however, anxieties of geo-political considerations result in reliance over 'imaginations' which, even if we do not consider to be capitalistic literary criterion, are creation of 'canonical' literary traditions. Larger social context, which include ever so present concern for legitimacy of one's 'regime' or one's 'literary creativity demonstrated in the depiction of geographies', results in push towards institutionalized social archetypes. Be it imaginations or memories, both need a medium to be expressed, which is most of the times offered by language. 'There is well established view that culture has no other expression but language'. For example even 'the origin of dreams is in the ability to remember, in memory. In other words we are made to believe that memory cannot exist entirely in the absence of language.'[2] It must be pointed out at the outset that the language as medium of expression can be script based or visual. In the oral tradition dominated societies of India, especially till the early modern times, considering only the written manuscripts as medium of expression of linguistic creativity will be problematic.

According to Devy, who says, 'In our literary past, most of the linguistic creativity has been in the oral tradition. Though people knew how to write, writing was not used as a means of educating the next generation in remembering these compositions. ...we had ...tremendous era of literary productivity in ancient Tamil and post Vedic Sanskrit; but by and large, knowledge, literature and memory were handed down not through writing but through speech and oral media. What developed in India as oral tradition was not just 'writing' on walls and boards, but also compositions of texts, documents, or what one describes as "manuscripts". They follow the logic of speech and not the logic of orthography. The aim here is not in any way to establish writing as redundant but only to indicate that considering what is non-written as non-manuscript would be inadequate in accounting for India's linguistic and imaginative traditions.'[3]

The debate over the 'literary creativity' expressed in oral/vernaculars which in the process of documentation is to a great extent influenced by well established canonical literary traditions. To substantiate the arguments let me place a comparison between following two compositions; the first is an eulogy of *Med-Pat*, i.e., Mewar region written by a Jain poet, Hem:

मेद पाट वर्णन प्रशास्ति
स्वस्ति श्री अवनि तिलक, मेद पाट विख्यात।
देश सबे सिर सेहरौ, रोग नहीं तिलमात।1।
देबां में सुरपति बड़ो, तारां में जिम चन्द।
सरिता में गंगा बड़ी, गिर में मेरु गिरन्द।2।
सबल देश में दीपतो, मोटो देश मेवाड़।

सरबर तरवर अति घणा, प्रोढ़ा अनल पहाड़।3।
पग–पग पाणी पंथ सिर, पग पग अम्बा रूंख।
पग पग दीसै सेलढी, चखीयां जावै भूख।4।
देश देशना मानवी, आबै जुगतै जात।
च्चाबो चिहुँ (दिस) देशां मई, चतुर्भुज विख्यात।5।[4]

[With the pronouncement of auspicious word, I begin to describe the glory of Med-Pat-Mewar. It is crown of all the lands, without a single fault. The way Indra is king of gods; moon among stars, Ganga among rivers, Meru among mountains, similarly Mewar shines away among countries. It has got numerous ponds, tanks and a good forest cover, along with it beautiful and most ancient mountain series. The availability of water and trees in this land is immense. Sugar cane is produced in such a good amount that it is easily available and it is so sweet that one is sufficient to satisfy the thirst. These are very famous. The ladies of the region are very beautiful.]

And the second is a contemporary literary representation of Thar region locally known as Thal or Thali.:

थली वर्णन

थली सिरदार वर्णन

दसे दिस चावउ भोल्हो देस।
ऊंडा जल पीवइ बुरि असेस।।
कहइ जे बोल मिलई सुखकार।
सहु सिरि देस थली सिरदार।।
जिहां नहीं कूड़ कलेस बजार।
गिणहीं नहिं किणसूँ द्रोह लिगार।।
धान थोड़े धार करइ साधार।
सहु सिरि देस थली सिरदार।।[5]

[It is the best country in the world. The water is available at great depth, but is very good for mind. It is very famous, and everybody knows, that Thali is the king of land. There is no trouble on this land. Nobody fights. Prosperity is limited, however people are religious. Thali is the king of land.]

Rooted more firmly in the canonical literary tradition of geographical knowledge, Jain poet Hem locates *Med-Pat* in the wider context of mountain Meru and river Ganga. The significance can be better comprehended if we consider the salient feature of *puranic* geographies as enunciated in various *puranas*.

S.M. Ali, on closer examination of *puranic* geography suggests that, 'Meru or the abode of the Brahma is the pivot of and the key to the puranic geography of the world. It is the point of reference round which are symmetrically arranged mountain systems of the puranic world. The mountains delimit and are closely associated with the regions and the countries, which collectively from the puranic continents. ... The Vedas do not mention Meru. It is referred to as Mahameru or the 'Great Meru' in the Taittiriya Aranyaka, but there is no indication of its location or size. The epics, the Budddhist and the Jain scriptures and the *puranas* contain practically identical notions regarding the size and extent of Meru and its central location in relation to the continents or major regions of the world.'[6]

Furthermore, with reference to rivers, it is suggested that, 'Corresponding to the patterns of the major mountain ranges of Jambu Dwipa, the *puranas* give an account of its drainage pattern which too, is arranged symmetrically round the central pivot, the Meru. The *puranas*, first of all, give an account of the origin of the main rivers which rise in Meru and flow towards four cardinal points. Then they deal with the course of each of these rivers mentioning the various topographical features which occur in the river's basin from its source to its mouth.' And, 'Ganga has the same relationship to the river-systems of the world as Meru has to its mountain ranges. ...Ganga is a celestial river which has been very picturesquely compared in the *puranas* with Milky Way'.[7]

On the other hand geographical descriptions in vernacular literary traditions are devoid of such references to *puranic* geography. Depictions in such traditions appears to be based on observation and thereby closer to realism as suggested by

Devy. In other words, along with literary depictions imbibed in the canonical traditions, such vernacular imagery of geographies offer an alternative or counter narrative. In the same vein it is interesting to note that vernacular depiction of geography of a region provide simultaneous delineation of 'vices' and 'virtues' of the region. Thus, unlike 'conventional' imageries of geographies we get a glimpse of human comforts and discomfort with the various feature of the landscape of the region. For example let me quote vices of Thali whose virtues have already been cited.

थली दोस वर्णन

उड़ई जिहां खेह न थंभि रहइ।
वज्जई जिहां पवन न किउही सहइ।।
जल खारउ सोइ पावेइ वली।
फिट देस कुदेस कुखंड थली।।
पट मासे नीर निवाण लहइं।
जिहां चउपद जीवति स्याइ रहइ।।
जिहां त्रस जलइ नर आस फली।
फिट देस कुदेस कुखंड थली।।
जिहां सूरख लोग पिसाच जिसा।
काला अति भूछ कि भूत जिसा।।
भरी रीवड छाछि पिवंति रली।
फिट देस कुदेस कुखंड थली।।[8]

[It is a place where sand blows without any restriction. Here wind blows at great speed. Water is brackish, so it is not potable hence Thali is such a bad land to live in. Ponds retain water only for six months, and livestock suffers due to limited availability of water. Thali is such a bad land to live in. Here people are like *pichas*—ghost and black as ghost. People drink lot of *chhachh.* Thali is such a bad land to live in. People keep beard and moustache and their face is full of dust, which blows here continuously. It is like *yamraj*—god of death accompanies the peasants who work in these conditions. Thali is such a bad land to live in.]

A closer examination of geographical depictions offers

insights to the inherent genealogies, literary as well as other administrative concerns or at times complex layers of overlap. For example, the Revenue Minister of Marwar in the second half of seventeenth century, Diwan Munhto Nainsi visualizes Mewar as a political unit and describes it accordingly. He has provided a detailed description of mountains of this region. He describes the rivers of the region which emerge from these mountains as well as agrarian potential of the territory.

रूपजी-वासरोड़ देस रै फाळसे छै। रूपजी सूं कोस 3 जीलवाळो दिखणनूं छै। जीलवाळाथी कोस 3 रीछेर बीच अमजमाळरो बडो भाखर छै। लाँबो कोस 5 छै। उलै-कांनी कैलबो छै। वाघोर रै आगै घाटो गांव छै। तठा आगै घाटो गांव छै। तठा आगे भोरड़ारो पहाड़ लांबो कोस 5 उतर-दिखण छै। तठै भोरड़ नै मठावळा बीच समीचो गांव कूंभावतां सीसोदियारो उतन छै। उदैपुर से समीचो कोस 17, रूपजीथी कोस 12 छै। कूंभळमेर सूं कोस 10 समीचो छै। तठा आगे मछावळो पहाड़ कौस 7 लांबो छै। गांव 9 मठावळा दोळा। मछावळा उपर पांणी घणो। झाड़ घणा। वेरणी नावै। तठा आगै वरवाडो। तठासूं वर नदी नीसरी छै। बनास नीसरी छै। तठा आगै घांसेररो मगरो कोस 1 लांबी छै। तठा आगै पीडरझांपरो मगरो छै। घांसरे ने पीडरझांप बीच झांसनाळो कोनरो कोस 2 छै। तठा आगे खमणरी मगरो छै। तठै लोहसींग गांव छै। तठै एक छोटी-सी नदी नीसरी छै। तठा आगै ईसवाळरो मगरो छै। गिरवारा भाखरांसूं जाय लागो छै। ईसवाळ उदैपुरसूं कोस 5 उतर पछिमनूं छै। जीलवाड़ा थी कोस 5 देसूरी। देसरूी थी कोस 1 घांणेरो, कुभळमेर री तळेठी तठै। आगै कोस 2 कुंभळमेर रो पहाड़ कोस 15 री गिरदवाय में छै। सादड़ी, राणपुर, सेवाडी तांई कुंभळमेर रो मगरो छै। सेवाड़ी कुंभळमेर सूं कोस 7 छै। तठा आगै राहगरो मगरो छै। निपट वडी ऐदी ठोड़ छै। पांणी पहाड़ मांहे निपट घणो छै।[9]

[Ropji-Vas road is located at the entrance of Mewar. Jeelwaro is located three *kos* away from Ropji-Vas road.Three *kos* east of Jeelwaro is Reechher. Reechher is located in the cut of the mountain Vaghor. There is Amjamal Mountain in between Reechher and Jeelwaro. It is five *kos* long. Beyond it lies the Kailvo. There are villages in the valley of Vaghor. There is five *kos* long mountain Bhoraràro lying north-south beyond Vaghor. All the villages between Bhorad and Machhawla in this region are part of *watan* of Kumbhawat Sisodias. The region is 17 *kos* from Udaipur and 12 *kos* from Roopji. From

Kumbhalmer it is 10 *kos*. There is 7 *kos* long Machhavalo Mountain beyond it. There are 9 villages around Machhavalo. There is plenty of water available on this mountain. It is full of vegetation and beauty which cannot be described. Beyond it there is Varvano Mountain and river Var and Banas originate. Beyond it lies the 1 *kos* long hill of Ghanser. It is followed by hill of Peeparjhhanp. Between these two, at an angle lies the Jhhansnalo. Beyond it lies the hill of Khaman. There is located a village known as Lohseeng. A small seasonal river originates from this place. Beyond it lies the hill of Eesval. Hill of Khaman culminates with the beginning of Girvara. Eesval is five *kos* north-west of Udaipur. Desoori is 5 *kos* from Jeelvaro. One *kos* from Desoori is Ghanerao in the valley of Kumbhalmer. The mountain of Kumbhalmer is stretched in 15 *kos*. The mountain of Kumbhalmer is extended till Sadri, Ranpur, and Sewani. Sewani is 7 kos from Kumbhalmer. Beyond it lies the hill of Rahgaro. It is very difficult terrain. The hill is full of water.]

In the above narrative of geography we can discern amalgamation of several traditions. In accordance with the *puranic* traditions, where 'Corresponding to the patterns of the major mountain ranges of Jambu Dwipa, the *puranas* give an account of its drainage pattern...' Furthermore, 'The authors of the *puranas* believed that rivers originate in lakes, so each river has, in their accounts, invariably a lake visible or invisible (underground) as its source. ... rivers with all its tributaries is considered by the authors of the *puranas* as one river.'[10]

A cursory look at the following description of the course of river Banas by Nainsi shows the influence of both puranic tradition as well as administrative concerns, most eloquently depicted by Abul Fazl in his *Ain-i-Akbari*.

जरगारा भाखरथी नीसरी। तिको जरगो उदैपुरसूं कोस 29 छै। उठाथी रोहिड़ै गांव आवै। जको राजा हरचंदरो बसायो छै। उठाथी कोस 2 गांव बरबाड़ो मेवाड़री तठै आवै। आगै कठाड़ गांव ·मदाररै गांव माछ में नै घांसाररै मगरे बीच नीसरै नै कांम-सकराही गांव वसै छै तठै आवै। उठाथी खभणोर आवै, उदैपुर थी कोस 12। उठाथी कोठारिये आवै। तठा आगै गांव मोही तंवराँवले। तठा आगै जावद-नंदराय बीच नीसर नै गाँव छै, उठै चोलेर रो पारसनाथ छै।

उठा आगै पाड़लोळी जाजपुर रो गाँव छै, तठै आय नै जाजपुर आवै। तठाथी सावड़ रै गाँव देवळी आवै। आगै डावर तोडा रै गाँव आवै, तठै खारी वध ानोर वाळी भेळी हुई। आगै तोडा थी कोस गोकर्ण राह छै। बडो तीर्थ छै। मधुकीटभ तपस्या की छै। रावण तपस्या की छै तठै आवै। तठा आगै तोडारा गाँव विसळपुर रावर आवै। तठै सोसादीये रायसिंघ मोहल कराया छै। तठा आगै बणहड़ै हुय टूंक आई। पछे मलीरणै रै गाँव झूंपड़ाखैड़े सोहड़ भगवंतगढ सैसभारिजै मलीरणै रे वीछूंदे नै हुय जीरोत रो गाँव हाडोती रो हुय नै आगै खंडरगढ चावळ भेळी हुई। तठे देबी वरवासण रो थांन छै।[11]

[River Chambal originates from the mountains of Jargara, which is 29 *kos* from Udaipur. It flows to village Rohire, founded by king Harchand. From there it goes to village Barvaro. It flows along the village Kathan and Machh. Then it intersects the hill of Ghansar and reaches the village of Kam- Sakrahi. Then it reaches village of Khabhran, some 12 *kos* from Udaipur. From there it reaches Kotherey and goes to village Mohi of Tunvaras. Then it bypasses villages of Jadav-Nandrav and reaches the village of Choler of Parasnath. it reaches Jajpur after crossing village Parloli. It goes through the village of Devli. Then it reaches village Dabar Toda where river Khari of Badhnor merges in it. Nearby is located the famous pilgrimage place of Gokarn Mahadev. It is said that the infamous demon Madhukeetabh and Ravan meditated here. Afterwards the river crosses village Visalpur where Rai Singh Mohal, a Sisodia, constructed a palace. Then after crossing Banharen it reaches Tonk. In between it crosses village Jhunprakher and Beechhunde and moves on to Harauti by merging in the river Chambal.]

The description of the river from its origins in the mountain till its end point has been a puranic tradition. A region is described along the course of rivers. However, description of habitation is representative of administrative concerns. Abul Fazl describes Subah of Ajmer and its sarkars in terms of revenue possibilities along with a demographic profile. Nainsi's description is also in consonance with the 'traditional styles such as travel accounts'[12] practiced extensively by Persian chronicles. It is important to note that most of the times such descriptions are based on the first hand observations and much closer to realism; based on memory as suggested by Devy.

In his description of Hindustan Babur says, 'The greater part of the country of Hindustan is situated on level land. Many though its towns and cultivated lands are, nowhere has running waters. Rivers and in some places, standing-waters and its 'running-waters' (aqur-sular). Even where, as for towns, it is practicable to convey water by digging channels (ariq), this is not done. For not doing it there may be several reasons, one being that water is not all a necessity in cultivating crops and orchards. Autumn crops grow by the downpour of the rains themselves; and strange it is those spring crops grow even when no rain falls.'[13]

It is interesting to note the way Abul Fazl engages with the geography of the realm. He offers two distinct but complimentary ways of geographical descriptions. While offering a panoramic overview of the Indian subcontinent he relies on the existing traditions which seem to be an amalgamation of Islamic notions of cosmos and brahmanical vision of the cosmos.[14] However his descriptions also carry an insight to his concern as official history writer of the Timurid dynasty. He is the chosen one, His following description seems to be an author who has to write good about the territory controlled by his master:

> Hindustan is described as enclosed on the east, west and south by the ocean, but Ceylon, Achin, the Moluccus, Malacca and a considerable number of islands are accounted within its extent. ...With all its magnitude of extent and the mightiness of its empire it is unequalled in its climate, its rapid succession of harvests and the equable temperament of its people. Notwithstanding of its size, it is cultivated throughout. You cannot accomplish a stage nor indeed travel a *kos* without meeting with populous towns and flourishing villages, not without being gladdened by the sight of sweet waters, delightful verdue and enchanting downs. In the autumn and throughout the depth of winter the plains are green and the trees in foliage....[15]

Before moving to the description of the province of Rajputana by Abul Fazl, let me draw your attention to the description of Emperor Babur cited earlier. It is the same landscape but descriptions are almost diagonally opposite. Nevertheless, let us move to the description of Rajputana by Abul Fazl, which constitute an important province of the empire. It is to be noted that rather than mountains and river being the marker of geographic descriptions one witnesses a transition towards more realistic description, most probably due to administrative concerns. Following description of Subah Ajmer in *Ain-i-Akbari* captures this:

> This territory contains many forts, but the most important are Ajmer, Jodhpur, Bijaner, Amarkot, Abugarh and Jalore. Hadaoti is also called the sarkar of Nagor, It is inhabited by the Hada (Hara) tribe. This Subah comprises 7 sarkars and 197 parganahs. The measured land is 2 Krors, 14 Lakhs and 35, 941 bighas, 7 biswas. The revenue in money is 28 krors 84 lakhs, 1557 dams, (Rs.7,210,308-14-9) of which 23 lakhs, 26336 dams (Rs.51,158-6-5) are *Suyurghul*. The local force is 86,500 cavalry, 347000 infantry.[16]

It is very interesting to compare descriptions of a region in two different sets of writings of Munhta Nainsi. Quite distinct from his description in *Khyat* Nainsi offers politico-administrative description in his *Vigat*.

> आदि सहर मंडोवर थौ सास्त्र माहै नै पदमपुराण माहे बात छै भोगशील परवत मेर रौ बेटौ कहै छै तिण रौ भोगशील महातम घणो कहौ छै माडलस्यूर माहादेव नागाद्रीह नदी सूरजकुंड रो घणो महातम वखाणीयों छै
>
> मंडोवर सहर री आदि थापना मन्दोदर दईत री कीवी छै ईण थोंड़ मन्दोदर री बेटी रावण दईत लंका रै धणी परणी छै[17]
>
> [Old habitation was at Mandavor. This is a very old settlement. Canonical literature, *Padma Purana* mentions this. Bhogishail Mountain of this region is considered to be the son of mountain Sumeru. Temple like Mandaleswar Mahadev, etc are considered to be very sacred. It is believed that Mandor was established by demon Mandodar and it is the place where his daughter Mandodari got married to Ravana, the King of Lanka.........]

Soon after describing the history of the pargana Jodhpur, Nainsi switches the register and geographical descriptions and turn eyes into the state. Here his concern is not the canonical genealogy of geography, rather revenue potential of the region, which includes not only agrarian, animal, forest resources, but also human resources. It can be suggested that information available in this register was a result of greater integration with the Mughal polity. Information provided by Nainsi under following categories: agrarian, waste, forest, river, mountain, which are further divided into ek-sakhi or do sakhi, i.e., single crop a year or double cropping is possible. Nature of irrigation possible in each village, natural inundation, artificial irrigation, whether based on wells or river or monsoon rains has been described. Furthermore, caste wise description of each village, composition of villages, revenue from each village. Various kinds of taxes being levied in the region and their contribution in total revenue of the village has been described, thus, producing something like a map of the region. Such descriptions of geographies carry multiple registers and offer us a window to trace the genealogies of such descriptions.

Last but not the least, let me cite a case study of emergence of a settlement in Jaisalmer region based on epigraphic evidence to argue that none of the traditions; puranic, Persian chronicle, politico-administrative enjoyed undisputed hegemony rather complex layering of norms of these traditions constitute the genealogies of geographies during early modern times. I have argued at another place that during an era of growing aridity in the early medieval times, we witness emergence of settlements in the interiors of the desert quite away from the banks of rivers.[18] This transition was reflected in the epigraphic descriptions where we find growing use of term; *devamatrka* (i.e., rain-fed) along with *nadimatrka* (i.e., river-fed)[19]. Greater appropriation of monsoon rains, as mentioned by Babur, for agricultural production offered colonization of areas not immediately irrigated by rivers, perennial and/or seasonal. Quite distinct from the canonical delineations of geographies, one notices incorporation of such fresh negotiations with geography in the descriptions of geographies. Traditional-conventional-canonical are being gradually supplemented with these new details of geographies. As pointed out earlier Nainsi in his *Vigat* offers village-wise description of land cultivated through *devamatrka* (i.e., rain-fed).

The trend of incorporation of fresh vision of geographies continue when British extended their paramountcy over the region. Without going into the details, let me point out that even a cursory look at the delineations of geographies in the writings of colonial administrators, particularly Alexander Cunningham suggests that genealogies of geographies were being redrawn and defined in terms of religious divisions. He says, 'The geography of India may be conveniently divided into a few distinct sections, each broadly named after the prevailing religious and political character of the period which it embraces, as the *brahmanical*, the *Buddhist*, and the *muhammadan*.'[20] In the very beginning of his magnum opus; *Annals and Antiquities of Rajasthan or The Central and Western Rajpoot States of India*, Colonel James Tod says, 'The basis of this work is the geography of the country, the historical and statistical portion being consequent and subordinate thereto. It was, indeed, originally designed to be essentially geographical; but circumstances have rendered it impossible to execute the intended details, or even to make the map so perfect as the superabundant material at the command of the author might have enabled him to do.'[21] Further while explaining his orientation he says, 'It was also intended to institute a comparison between the map and such remains of ancient geography as can be extracted from the *puranas* and other Hindu authorities;...'[22]

It will not be inappropriate if we shift our glance a bit towards the global scenario. Apart from developments in the cartography there were commercial considerations to extensively document the landscape across the globe. Though different but in a related context Richard Grove and Vinita Damodaran have suggested that, 'The intellectual origins of environmental history as a self-conscious domain of enquiry can be traced to the encounter of 17th and 18th century western Europeans with the startlingly unfamiliar environments of the tropics and the damage inflicted on these environments in the course of resource extraction by European empires....'.[23] This process of documentation was developed primarily in the form of "historical geography". Similar trends can be seen in the writings of Tod, who seems to borrow from historical writings, 'Most of the *Pooranas* contain portions of historical as well as geographical knowledge; but the *Bhagvat*, the *Scanda*, the *Agni*, and the *Bhavishya* are the chief guides'.[24] It is interesting to note that Colonel Tod while examining the geographical descriptions of *Puranas* is on the one hand contextualizing in the contemporary European understanding of geographical locations of different parts of the earth. 'The *genesis* of India commences with an event describe in the history of almost all nations, the deluge, which, though treated with the fancy peculiar to the orientals, is not the less entitled to attention.'[25] Further, he tries to offer explanations on the basis of contemporary European understandings. He writes, 'I am aware of the meaning given to *Soomer*, that thus the Hindus designated the north pole of the earth. ...the sacred mountain (Soomer) is claimed by the Brahmins as the abode of Mahadeva, Adiswar or Baghes, by the Jains as the abode of Adnath, the first Jiniswara or the Jain lord. Here they say he taught mankind the arts of agriculture and civilized life. The Greeks claimed it as the abode of Bacchus; and hence Grecian fable of this god being taken from the thigh of Jupiter, cofounding *meros* (thigh), with the *meru* (hill) of this Indian deity.

...These traditions appear to point to one spot, and to one individual in the early history of mankind, when the Hindus and the Greek approach a common focus; for there is little doubt that Adinath, Adiswara, Osiris, Baghes, Bacchus, Menu, Menes, designate the patriarch of mankind, Noah.'[26]

Along with this we notice extensive documentation of natural resources of India by the British administrators. GSL

Devra has pointed out that Colonel Tod carried out a survey of salt producing areas of western India, from Sambhar to Rinn of Kutch.[27] This trend was further consolidated in the preparation of gazetteers and settlement reports. The paper is trying to understand multiple ways geography was negotiated and in what ways it has been captured in the descriptions.

NOTES

1. G.N. Devy, *The Being of Bhasha: Knowledge, Society and Aphasia*, Orient Blackswan, Hyderabad: 2009, p. 2.
2. Ibid., pp. 7-9.
3. Ibid., p. 9.
4. 'देश वर्णन' [Desh Varnan], *Maru Bharti*, ed., Agarchand Nahata, Vol. 2, No. 2, 1954, p. 49.
5. थली वर्णन [Thali Varnan], *Maru Bharti*, ed. Agarchand Nahata, Year 2, No. 1, 1954, pp. 81-83.
6. S.M. Ali, *The Geography of the Puranas*, People's Publishing House, New Delhi, Third Edition: 1983, p. 47.
7. Ibid., pp. 60 and 63.
8. थली वर्णन.
9. Munhta Nainsi, *Munhta Nainsi ri Khyat* (ed. Badri Prasad Sakariya), Vol. I, Rajasthan Oriental Research Institute, Jodhpur: 1960, pp. 36-37.
10. Ali, *The Geography of the Puranas*, p. 60.
11. Nainsi, *Munhta Nainsi ri Khyat*, Vol. I, 1960, p. 42.
12. Pinar Emiralioglu, *Geographical Knowledge and Imperial Culture in the Early Modern Ottoman Empire*, Ashgate, Surrey: 2014, p. 2.
13. Zahiru'din Muhammad Babur, (Translated by A.S. Beveridge) *Babur Nama*, Low Price Publications, Delhi: 2014 (First Published 1921), p. 486.
14. Abu'L Fazl Allami, *The Ain-i-Akbari*, Vol. III, (Translated by Colonel H.S. Jarrett) (Revised second edition by Jadunath Sarkar), Oriental Books Reprint Corporation, New Delhi: 1978, pp. 11-125.
15. Ibid., p. 7.
16. Ibid., p. 277.
17. Munhta Nainsi, *Marwar ra Pargana ri Vigat* (ed. Narain Singh Bhati), Vol. I, Rajasthan Oriental Research Institute, Jodhpur:

1968, p. 1.

18. Mayank Kumar, *Monsoon Ecologies: Irrigation, Agriculture and Settlement Patterns in Rajasthan during the Pre-Colonial Period,* Manohar, Delhi: 2013.
19. B.D. Chattopadhyaya, 'Irrigation in Early Medieval Rajasthan', *Journal of the Economic and Social History of the Orient,* Vol. 16, Parts II-III, December 1973, p. 298 (298-316).
20. Surendranath Majumdar Sastri, (ed.), *Cunningham's Ancient Geography of India,* Chuckervertty, Chatterjee & Co. Ltd., Calcutta, 1924, (First published in 1871), p. LXI.
21. Colonel James Tod, *Annals and Antiquities of Rajasthan or The Central and Western Rajpoot States of India,* KMN Publishers, New Delhi: 1971 (1821), p. 2.
22. Ibid., p. 2.
23. Richard Grove and Vinita Damodaran, 'Imperialism, Intellectual Networks, and Environmental Change: Origins and Evolution of Global Environmental History, 1676-2000', Part 1 and 2, *Economic and Political Weekly,* 14 and 21 October 2006, pp. 4345-54 and 4497-4505.
24. Tod, *Annals and Atiquities,* p. 17.
25. Ibid.
26. Ibid., p. 18.
27. G.S.L. Devra, 'Salt Trade Routes of Western India: A Study based on the Survey Reports of James Tod', *Trade Routes, Trade Centers and Urbanization in Western India* (ed. S.P. Vyas), Rajasthani Granthagar, Jodhpur: 2012.

9

Eighteenth Century Jaipur City: Imagined and Constructed

Mayurakshi Kumar

Monumental architectural constructions are closely associated with political manoeuvres and mediums to establish political rule. Historically, in India construction of robust but equally decorative edifices of royalty in the form of palaces, temples, idols, *charbaghs* (gardens), mosques, tombs and more importantly cities, was one of the most elaborative tools for stamping political supremacy. Through this paper, an attempt will be made to glance at one of this projection of political articulation i.e. Jaipur city, which became not only a capital city but also expounded social, political, economic cultural experiments of its builder and ruler Sawai Jai Singh.

The study of a city is incomplete without understanding its structural composition and the meanings that it carries. Any exclusive study of a city cannot be undertaken without realizing one basic trajectory that the word 'city' means different things in different historical periods and regional contexts and it is in accordance to this, that one can gauge the true meaning and uses that a city serves.[1] The city of Jaipur, its innate participation in the systematic urbanization of the Kachchwaha domain, made it the focus of two types of urbanism i.e. 'politically charged urbanism' and 'commercially charged urbanism'.[2] The recounting of all these patterns is an essential theme of the present study.

True understanding of the invariant relation between the two domains i.e. the political sovereignty and its representation through edifice of cityscape as it was visible in Jaipur, necessitates the engagement with the previous historiographical studies pertaining to the stated associations as it has been glanced in the context of the Indian set-up.[3] Historians studying the notional projections of royalty, especially under the medieval rulers of sultanate and Mughal era have drawn out a close association between the expansionist zeal, constructional endeavour and the resultant urbanization initiated by the rulers. The medieval and the early modern centuries mark the era of both assimilative as well as expansionist politics. Correspondingly, one notes that 'the changing appearance of the cities, spacious mosques, domes, gateways and arches were added to the temples, tanks and massive buildings of the pre Turkish towns'.[4] Irfan Habib while analysing the growth of urban economy during the Delhi sultanate postulated that the change in political rule was followed by the 'replacement of the Rajput rural nobility by the Turkish urban ruling class, together with a new system of appropriating surplus production from land, which resulted in the consumption of a large part of that surplus in cities and towns'.[5] Apart from basic changes in the administrative ruling machinery, which brought about shifts in the potentials of the urban settlements another major visible pattern of increasing urbanization during the sultanate era, was the shifting of capital base under the rule of different rulers. With almost each ruler laying the foundations of a new capital city, the scope of urbanization and the variants of associated urbanism also widened. Sunil Kumar, while discussing the shifting capitals under the sultanate rulers, states that, 'it is possible to notice how the reproduction of new capitals and courts in Delhi regions was not just a part of the period's cultural expectations, it was a necessity dictated by the ways in which society and politics were structured at this time'.[6] Thus, for rulers the establishment of new cities was not only a representation of economic and political supremacy but it became the need of the hour for the new cities as was the best way out, to bring the ever increasing population of the old cities and new controlled areas under one fold. The cities defined not only economic worth of the ruler but also showcased the political, social and cultural flare of the time. Erection of cities and especially the capital or imperial city, therefore symbolizes the true art of kingship with all its political paraphernalia. Nilanjan Sarkar, while basing himself upon the famous treatise *Fatawa-i-Jahandari*, of renowned writer and reader of politics i.e. Zia-uddin Barani, asserts that 'the connection between kingship and city is evident, no person, how so ever mighty or capable, can hope to assert dominance and sovereignty without the city, they being the principal territorial components of rulership. The capital city is the indisputable political centre, the possession of which (by the ruler), turns it into a theatre for the performance of suzerainty and protection which in turn becomes an essential job of the king'.[7]

In line with the above statement it can be asserted that the Imperial City became a representation of the true personality of the ruler, by not only showcasing the ruler's desire to accomplish successful exercising of political pragmatism, power display, but also helped him in monitoring the slow and steady entry of his unchallenged name in the history books. Amongst the rulers who are remembered to this day, many are recalled more for their architectural contributions than for their political authority. Thus, the city structures have forever remained an essential tool in the route to achieve a perfect principled sovereignty.

The enclosing of the main city with huge walled structures became another tool for expounding the political rule as well as safeguarding frontiers. The construction of walled cities therefore became the characteristic of the town cities in medieval era and represented the cultural way of the royal-popular continuum. The city therefore became an embodiment of different meanings articulated and circulated by its varied makers i.e. the ruler and the ruled. Their divisions into various quarters on grounds of creed, caste, and occupations of the social and political groupings landed it versatile meanings. The cityscape, thus carried economic, cultural and social significances too along with the main political character. The cities became entities of performances, political gamesmanship, social layering, cultural exuberance, and economic temperament. According to K.N. Chaudhari, the urban history of any settlement or society can be written from two different points of view. First, each town or city is treated in terms of its unique history. Even when such urban centres are grouped together and treated collectively the time scale is all-important. Second approach is to consider the totality of the political, economic and social order, which sustains the urban localities as visible entities'.[8] Stephen P. Blake furthers the notion of growing proximity between state formation, city building and urbanization by discussing the construction of Shahjahanabad, by seeing it as an important medium for expounded kingship and its varied paraphernalia. The city according to Blake, deserves special focus as it is the centre for most of the political, bureaucratic, economic enterprises of the ruler. Blake sees the city as an imperial mansion, where 'the patrimonial-bureaucratic emperor dominated the social, economic and cultural life of the city, and he dominated its built form as well'.[9] Thus according to Blake, while fitting in as a true example of patron-client affiliation, 'Shahjahanabad was the urban conclusion to the patrimonial- bureaucratic premise of the city, the city as mansion an inescapable implication of the state as household'.[10]

The Indian buildings across different historical periods especially during the ancient and medieval centuries encompass not only the ideology of its builder but in fact its gridded pattern is closely influenced by the traditional knowledge of *vastu vidya* or *vastu shashtra,* which literally translates to 'science of architecture'. The utilization of this science is not only evident in construction of smaller spaces i.e. houses but also even in monumental buildings like temples, cities, palaces and many others. It is therefore essential to engage with the conceptual frame of *vastu shashtra* and only then one will be able to situate the influence specifically in case of the city i.e. Jaipur. Vastu in simpler terms means dwelling and its locational site. The intricacies of the vastu is defined by the site and its planned articulations in form of units or *mandalams* in the site and where and how they are placed. The prescribed variants of the vastu are squares but they can change in accordance to the availability of the space. Thus dwelling in vastu is ideally a place whose environment is suited for the settlers in that space. In figurative sense buildings under *vastu shashtra* are prepared under the principal of *vastupurusamandala,* where each segment not only has relative association with nature but even bodily representation of the human being and hence the above term.

Michael W. Meister states that one of the earliest Indian texts containing information on *vastupurusamandala* to plan cities and buildings is Varahamihara's *Brihat Samhita* written in 6th century.[11] Reena Patra, through her close study of various historical treatises on vastu (*Mansara, Brihat Sanhita, Vastu Chakra, Vastu Tattava, Purana Manjari* and others), tries to define vaastu-purusha-mandala and postulates it represents metaphorical link between people, buildings and nature all being components of the universe. She further asserts that a building in perfect state or order is viewed as Purusha, the 'man' of the universe representing pure energy or soul. Mandala means astrological chart or diagram. Thus inversely vastupurusa makes the site a microcosmic aspect of the macrocosmic Purusha.[12] Tillotson opines that in the vastupurusa model, the core is represented through representational head i.e. Bhramsthana.[13] Stephen P. Blake, too opines that the construction of the Shahjahanabad along with the selection of the site, was done after working out the true balance between universe and earth. Blake notes that the defining principle behind Shahjahanabad was same as that which was prevalent in India since ancient times i.e. *axis mundi* or centre of the earth or universe.[14] Under the concept the seat of power with its political head becomes sacred axis mundi, where heaven, hell and earth meet. This cosmic union concept advanced right into the Mughal period, and was even taken up during the construction of Jaipur in 1727, even if it origins are traceable to Hindu Vastu concepts.[15] However, the Mughal buildings cannot be merely seen as influenced by the Hindu science of architecture but even showcasing Islamic architectural model too, which also gives significance to relationship between man and universe.[16] Similar to concept of Vastupurusa, the Islamic architecture model talks of a building having human anatomy, having three divisions i.e. body (*jism*), soul (*nafs*) and spirit (*ruh*).[17] Accordingly, in Shahjahanabad, the palace became the head, central market its backbone and Jama masjid (place of worship) as heart.[18] By engaging with this conceptual origin of architectural designing in India, it can be seen that whatever the time or place, the structures especially seats of power or the capital city required extensive planning and blue proofing of designs. These models of architectural designs can have there own specific religious overtones but in reality, their working is understandable only when the implementation stage is successful, which is always influenced by the individual perception of the builder and the erector along with the challenges presented by the space or site.

Based on the above discussed discourse, one can delineate the need for engaging in cityscapes and their historical outpouring throughout the medieval and early modern centuries and thus accordingly the rise of Jaipur city as the political, social, economic and cultural capital in the 18th century will be contemplated in the study ahead.

Establishment of Jaipur City

Jaipur as a city, was established by Sawai Jai Singh an aspect that needs not much contemplation. However, it is essential to learn about the logical motive force, which pushed Sawai Jai Singh to undertake such a lavish architectural endeavour which established his aura as a great builder. True to our knowledge, Kachchwahas of Amber had a good nexus with the Mughal rulers, as not only the domain ruled by them acted as a buffer zone but also provided an entry point to the Mughals into the larger affairs of Rajputana. Correspondingly, all the Kachchwaha rulers owing to their very benevolent ties with the imperial centre successively secured and expanded the frontiers of their *watan* Jagir. However, by the mid 17th century and the turn over of the century, as the fortunes of the Mughal rulers fluctuated, the bonhomie and goodliness of the associated principalities also shifted. This holds true even for the Amber Jagir, as the notional as well as the practical friendly ties with the centre started going downhill, and was no longer situated on a level footing. In this particular background, when Sawai Jai Singh, sat on the throne, he was presented with the challenge of redefining the frontiers of his principality, which he tactically handled with ideological manoeuvring and gamesmanship, of his political goals of expansion, consolidation and centralization of *Ijara* tenure.

He introduced many significant administrative, economic, social and religious changes, which had a lasting impact during and after his tenure. Of all these introductions most effective yet understated change, was the shifting of the capital from Amber, and establishment of a new capital city of Jaipur. For all practical concerns of the time, the shift in capital was validated at the expense of increasing population of Amber city and its not so very expanding territorial boundary, thereby causing a major crunch of space. However, apart from this practical intention, which may have been the need of the hour, certain other concerns dominated the shift and needs to be justly studied by the scholars. The capital city and its evolutionary development under the auspices of Sawai Jai Singh represented a major transition in the philosophical understanding of the political ideologue. The city structure also was a representation of a scared domain, as by establishing close linkages between his political might and religious outlook, Jai Singh managed to provide religious legitimacy to his expansionist endeavours. Thus, accordingly Jai Singh managed to justify the construction of a new capital city of Jaipur by the constant popularizing the notion that it was the 'microcosm of the universe, symbolic of the sacred cosmic order'.[19] The personality traits, political understanding, religious identifications of the ruler played a significant role in the new city space of Jaipur. Evidently Jai Singh, aimed to establish himself as the supreme lord of the Rajputana land and thereby displayed all intentions to get his name recorded in history as a great builder. The naming of the city on his name also marked a step ahead in this direction. Jai Singh's continuous attempts to establish his supremacy were not restricted within the confines of the territorial space of Rajputana, and even flowed out through representational architectural structures especially *vedshalas* (Jantar-Mantar observatories) in regions of Mathura, Delhi, Banaras, Ujjain apart from Jaipur. Through such constructions Sawai Jai Singh was also motivated by the zeal of religious appropriation handed down to him by his predecessor especially Raja Man Singh who also got Man Mandir Ghat constructed in Banaras in the 16th century. Interestingly this very ghat became the attached site of observatory constructed by Sawai Jai Singh in 1710. It can be stated that such constructions having religious and astronomical objectives also served the pragmatic purpose of promoting political control with popular support.

Catherine B. Asher and Cynthia Talbot have studied the patterns of continuation and dis-continuations between the central imperium and regional principalities after the slow process of central decline had ushered in major debacles of a control nexus. They have asserted that the creation of new a city by Jai Singh, was one chapter in the long drawn struggle for independence that was being asserted by the regional powers.[20] The Mughal mansabdars, being good manipulators of situations, understood the conditions of late 17th and early 18th centuries, in all righteous approach and saw it as an opportunity to either declare full or partial independence from the hegemonic control of the state. However, one can question the statement in the context of Sawai Jai Singh, as despite establishing a new city with his own name, he continued his own associations with the centre and in fact his book *Zizmohammadshahi*, was named after the Mughal ruler Mohammad Shah. Thus, even if Jai Singh, aimed to carve out a niche for himself, he never removed himself from the umbrella control exercised by the Mughal superior. It can be therefore, asserted that the city created in 1727, does stand out especially because it added a new chapter in the Indian history of city structuring, planning and the related patterns of urbanization. The city stands out as a uniform architectural structure, with clear-cut indications of planning being carried out in every nook and corner of its layout, an aspect that will be further discussed in the paper.

Having addressed the exponential political, social and ideological matrix which pushed Sawai Jai Singh to shift the capital and also simultaneously lay foundations of the new city, another question which holds currency and needs further elaboration is which ideas stimulated the notional process of planning involved in the structuring of the city. Was it a mere representation of the foresightedness of its creator or was it's planning an embodiment of various nuances of external (foreign) and internal (Indian) influences. It can be rightly asserted that the idea of the new city was the brain child of Sawai Jai Singh's perceptional understanding of power equations, but the real planning was the co-terminus evolution of varied notions and ideas generated by different enchanted yet educated minds of the time.

Some of the travelogues, brought forth by those who visited Jaipur during the 19th and 20th centuries, highlight that the plan and the layout of the city was influenced by European prototypes. This stand of the foreign visitors gets further applicability and support, as the 18th century records from the *pothikhana* [library] of Jaipur, indicate towards the maintenance of continuous correspondence between Jai Singh and European scholars and architects, as the former was extensively interested in European mathematics and astrology. Exploration of pothikhana has further opened the eyes of one and all, to the rich collection of world maps and atlas being maintained there at the behest of the ruler. The richness of the pothikhana is even corroborated by the *Kapad Dwara* documents, which furnish information about a 18th century circular map of the world, painted on cloth with meticulous detailing of longitudes and latitudes. This map was inscribed with *Nagari* characters and was prepared and copied at the behest of Jai Singh, from a European version, which originally dates to 1669.[21] However, the maintenance of such maps and letters of correspondence though do indicate that the ruler was in continuous touch with European developments, but it does not indicate that European architectural heritage and its intricacies were the sole influence behind the making of the city of Jaipur. In fact, true to the context of such records it can be highlighted that the European building tradition may be one of the many, if not the only influence, that may have impacted the styling of Jaipur city. Yadvendra Sahai, has taken a stand in opposition to one represented by the travellers.[22] He argues that the European influence is nowhere visible in Jaipur city. Yadvendra Sahai, further pushes the case for indigenous origin of architectural patterns of building constructions and there styling. He compares the Jaipur city, with the Indra Puri of Indra, discussed in *shilpa shashtra* and opines that like Indra Puri, even Jaipur had nine rivers, seven gates and straight broad avenues crisscrossed by streets at right angles.[23]

He also overlooks even the over-arching role played by the state Diwan Vidyadhar, a Bengali brahman, in the maintenance of strict vigil over the architectural constructions of the time. He in fact sees the city and its various constructions as the whole sole endeavour of Sawai Jai Singh and a brainchild of his architectural prowess. The second level of disagreement highlighted by Sahai, is questionable as all the information relating to layout of buildings, maps and blueprints of the city, material purchased and used for the construction, were supplied to Vidyadhar as chief Diwan and interestingly the *arsatta (roznamcha) imarti*, the archival notings related to building material purchased was stamped by Vidyadhar himself.

Thus unlike, Sahai's perception, Vidyadhar enjoyed supreme powers and was the chief overseer of all the constructional activities taking place in Jaipur city and Jai Singh always sought first hand information from him, in relation to the progress of work. One of the by lanes named after Vidyadhar and leading towards his haveli (and still located in the present day Jaipur), also stands testimony to the status of rank enjoyed by the Diwan.

Ashim Kumar Roy and Giles Tillotson, have opined religious fervour and zeal of the ruler, as the main reason for the construction of the city. Accordingly, they argue that the architectural constructions of the Jaipur city clearly fall in line with the status quo of Hindu kingship and Hindu city models. In their arguments the traditional knowledge base of Indian constructors, evidently on display in the ancient text of '*Shilpa Shashtra*', dominated the understanding of the city.[24]

Tillotson states that, 'surprisingly enough although it seems untypical, Jaipur's grid represents no novelty; indeed it follows a long established tradition. It embodies a conception of a city defined in a series of texts known as *vastu shashtras*, which are canonical treatises, usually in sanskrit, and a guide regarding architecture, design and planning'.[25] He tries to trace the long tradition of existence and compilation of these sources in India, from time immemorial, especially from 5th century onwards. He further mentions the example of Rajavallabh composed by Mandan Sutradhar, during mid 15th century at the bidding of his patron Rana Kumbha of Chittor. The work dealt with the conception of *vastu shashtra* involved in the making of the buildings in Chittor.

However, while talking about the notional existence of science of *vastu shashtra*, in India from traceable historical times, Tillotson, argues that this science form was only randomly used in the laying of foundations and creation of structures in other cities and in fact it was only in Jaipur city that it was consistently used in every erected structure. Tillotson reasons out that scarcity of such extensively planned cities is related to the simple fact that not many other builders were ready to shift their capitals and there by lay the foundations of new cities. Even if they did think in terms of engaging in any building activities they were actually restricted within the confines of older structures. The risk element, (especially the depletion of state revenue owing to diversion of entire treasury for the whole sole purpose) involved in creating of these new structures, further made such constructional activities rare. As a collective impact of these and many other factors, even when opportunities to plan and build an entire city from scratch to completion were abundant, the ideas were soon abandoned even after being initiated. It is within this frame of limited examples of cities being laid out in a planned way, that Jaipur stands testimony to the experimenting zeal, risk taking spirit and political interest of Sawai Jai Singh, who rightly deserves the tag of 'great builder'.[26]

Apart from the above mentioned frames of study relating to the ideological basis behind the architecture of Jaipur city, third level of discussion has focused upon the borrowed elements from the Mughal prototypes. It has been stated by this set of scholars that, the Mughals were forerunners, as far as the building activities were concerned. Also since they were ruling as imperial heads, they had more resources at their disposal and land to be brought under usage and therefore they could undertake huge architectural constructions, including establishment of new cities. With many learned men of pen, wisdom, scientific understanding flocking the Mughal court from regional as well as international frontiers, spirited discussions on varied issues could take place very easily and decorative engagements and sharing of art and architectural knowledge was one them. Thus, it was no small deal, that the Mughals were the creators of three of the most famed and discussed capital cities of the medieval era i.e. Fathepur Sikri, Agra, and Shahjahanabad. Even if we take out the name of Sikri and Agra, from this discussion on planned cities, then even Shahjahanabad alone can justly push the case of these scholars focusing on Mughal architectural worth, and its continuum in regional and sub-regional pockets. Among these scholars, the work of Catherine B. Asher stands out, as she draws the likewise conclusions by highlighting the associations between the Mughals and the Kachchwahas, prevalent at the level of sharing of architectural logistics and interests involved in the erection of buildings. She argues that it was because of the support and protection provided by the Mughal rulers that Kachchwaha rulers namely Man Singh and Sawai Jai Singh were able to carry out their constructional activities peacefully, both within and outside the sphere of their w*atan* Jagir.[27] The outlined patterns of similarities between the architectural heritage of Shahjahanabad and Jaipur stands in opposition with the argument which sees Jaipur as the sovereign turf of kingship postulated by a Hindu ruler, on shastric and vaishnavite principles.

Monica Horstmann and James Hastings emphasize that the building of the city of Jaipur as well as the temples within the city were indicators of self-assertions by the Kachchwaha rulers, Sawai Jai Singh against the Mughals. These authors have overemphasized the importance of the shastric model in their portrayals of presenting Jaipur as a 'Hindu City'. Hindu kingship model was also forwarded by Tillotson along with Sachdev, who focus on the Shastric articulation of statecraft. They opine that the Jaipur rulers, used the shastric norms and modified it to accommodate the existing buildings in the city. They compare Jaipur with other so-called Hindu cities, such as Madurai, Dabhoi, Sikar and Swanganer. They trace the Kachchwaha-Mughal alliance and highlight the career of Sawai Jai Singh, but they do not discuss the extent and exact nature of Mughal sovereignty over the Kachchwaha political environment.[28]

Fatima Imam disagrees with the above mentioned Hindu city model and argues that the availability of the archival data in the private collection of Sawai Jai Singh clearly indicates that he used the architectural example of the Mughal cities.[29] She further adds that Sawai Jai Singh enjoyed power and prestige amongst the Mughal mansabdars and therefore was made a collective *Subedar* of many *subas,* a power enjoyed by only select few *Mansab* holders. In these *subas,* too Jai Singh carried out constructional activities and got many residential quarters known as Jai Singh *Puras* constructed. The term *pura* means town and there are references of maintenance of at least five *puras* by Jai Singh, in areas apart from Jaipur. One reference from Kapad-Dwara, clearly furnishes first hand information about such constructions. The recorded plan talks of a *pura* at Ujjain, which was prepared in the second decade of 18th century. It gives the names of the places, notes about ownership of land, 20 havelis of kayasthas, havelis of Mahajans, Mahvidya Kund, Sita Kund, Maratha Village, Thakur-dwara (temple), house of Trilok Chand, bazar of thatheras (brass merchants), cloth merchants, mosque of Shah Muhammad, haveli of Nihal chand and many other details.[30]

Fatima Imam, further says that Sawai Jai Singh's real achievement lies in the successful incorporation of Mughal patterns by making subtle changes to suit the needs of the environs. The cities in India always mushroomed around the forts and rulers always took residence in a capital with difficult access because of natural or artificial barriers such as deserts, ridges or forts. Jaipur possessed all of these advantages. At the same time, this city was different from the other Rajput cities because it was not built on a ridge or mountain, such as the cities of Jaisalmer, Jodhpur and Bharatpur. Jaipur was very accessible and like Shahjahanabad, there was less emphasis on the fortification around the city. The fact that Jaipur was built on an open plain reflected Sawai Jai Singh's confidence, even though he chose an area in the vicinity of Amber, so as to continue the traditional relationship in the area.

Selection of the Site and Planning

Jaipur lies 5 miles south of Amber, the old capital city on a small plain. It was surrounded by hills on three sides and a dam was built on the northern side. Sawai Jai Singh laid the foundation of his new city in 1727 AD and named it after him. Sawai Jaipur or Sawai Jai Nagar is the earliest recorded reference related to the city in the archival records of the time.

'Kurmvillas' written by poet Virachit furnishes information about the establishment of Jaipur City in 1787 VS, in the month of *sawan* (August). It talks about different palaces like Pritam niwas, Chandra mahal, Badal mahal, Govind mahal (which was compared with heaven). Writer further states that Jainagar (Jaipur) is a representation of Indra puri on earth and it houses the domain of all four varnas.[31]

Planning of the City

It has been indicated in the initial pages of the present study, the pattern of shifting capitals was trending during the medieval and early modern centuries. It holds true even in case of Jai Singh, who shifted the capital of Kachchwahas from Amber to Jaipur. However, the answer to the question as to why this shift was made by Jai Singh, remains elusive and devoid of any historical causations and arguments by the scholars. This question needs real exploration, especially in the light of the power and centrality enjoyed by Amber for some near about 700 years, immediately before 1727, the year the foundation of Jaipur was laid. Also since Sawai Jai Singh, may have used the new city as a tool for power and status enhancement, what calls for a closer study of the notional transitions responsible for the shift in the capital, is the well established fact that even after deciding to shift capital and naming it after him, Sawai Jai Singh never separated himself from imperial control and in fact remained attached to the Mughal head as he sought imperial recognition for his city, an aspect which is well documented in the annals of history. Corroborating information is provided below. Just after the completion of the main wards of the city of Jaipur, Jai Singh applied to the Mughal emperor for the imperial recognition for his newly founded city. In 1733 AD, he sent a 'Parwana', to the emperor Muhammad Shah. Sawai Jai Singh received the following reply from the imperial head, "Maharaja dhiraj Sawai Jai Singh had informed that he has founded a new city under the name of Sawai Jaipur in the imperial territory near Amber and has requested the name of Sawai Jaipur instead of Amber may be written in the imperial records. His request has been accepted and it is ordered that Sawai Jaipur may be written instead of Amber in future".[32]

Ashim Kumar Roy, claimed that as originally planned,

Jaipur was to have only four rectangular blocks, namely those occupied today by the 1. Palace, 2. Purani basti, 3. Top-khana, 4. a block combining Modikhana and Vishesh varji.[33] The city of Jaipur was planned not only to have straight and wide roads but also to achieve the almost uniform height and similarity of architecture of the houses built on the main road.

Jaipur City: Walls and Gates

When we first engage in the study of Jaipur city, its huge walls and gates draw major attention. Sawai Jai Singh not only focused upon the internal beautification and uniformity of his city but was also equally interested in providing his city and its population the necessary protection through walls and entryways through the management of huge gates. The wider expanse of these walls and gates not only effectively provided the necessary barricading, but helped Sawai Jai Singh to draw the attention of one and all towards the over all expanse and scaling of the city achieved by him. The wall is on an average 6 metres high and 3 metres thick and is pierced by a total of seven gates, representative of shastric calculations.[34] The main gates are, Chandra Pol (west side), Suraj Pol (east side), Jorawar Singh Pol/Dhruv Pol (north side), Ajmeri Gate, Naya Pol, Swanganeri Gate and Ghut Darwaza (southern side)

According to Yadvendra Sahai, "a masonry cemented wall built of mud, stone, mortar covered with smooth terracotta plaster, averaging in height about 20 metre and 9 metre in thickness surrounded the whole city. The terracotta colour was chosen because it was the nearest in appearance to the red sandstone of which ideally the walls should have been constructed".[35] The bondage was not perfect and structurally it was not a strong wall. After construction it turned really bad in shape and in the 19th century it was almost ruined. Sawai Ram Singh got them repaired by the State Public Works Department in the year 1872-74 at a cost of Rs. 32,749.[36]

The Chowkries (Wards)

The principal streets of the city define the grid of the mandala and divide the city into chowkries (wards).[37] The names of these Chowkries from west to east are 1. Topkhanadesh, 2. Modikhana, 3. Vishesh varji, 4. Ghat darwaja, 5. Topkhana Hazuri, 6. Purani basti, 7. the Palace and 8. Ramchandarji. Talking of these chowkries, Ashim Kumar Roy says "of these six residential blocks, the development and planning of chowkri Topkhana Hazuri on the extreme east of the city seems to have been neglected. This chowkri did not have and even now does not have straight roads dividing the blocks in a grid iron pattern".[38] The low developmental level of this area may be associated with the assumption that, when the city was created, the area was not of much considerable usage and was therefore developed in a haphazard manner, and later on became the residential space for those who were poor and had always lived on the margins of urban settlements. The nature of planning of this chowkri is also indicative of the deep-set social divisions that existed and exist till this day in the region.

The division of the city into wards and their subdivisions into sub-wards, by different scales of grids, relates to the system of social distribution, the patterns of settlement of people according to the caste or jati, that is defined by the shashtras and now is more commonly known as the 'mohalla system'.[39] Another interesting account is furnished through the document of 1839 VS, wherein an order was passed by the State with reference to a khati (wood-worker), named Koju, living in the Khatiya Mohalla. For his good work, prize money of 38 rupees was to be handed over to him by the Daroga *Imarti*, on behalf of the State and for the same he was asked to present himself in the court, so as to sign on receiving the same amount.

Catherine B. Asher also talks about this feature of Jaipur and also Amber city. She says that on the order of the ruler, 'a huge map of Amber, about 21 square feet was produced'.[40] Inscriptions on the map indicate that members of a single profession occupied neighbourhoods. The similar pattern is evident even in Shahjahanabad, but over there it was not representative of shashtra based *jati* division of cityscape and was done more specifically to prevent chaotic conditions from prevailing in the city. Working upon the same hypothesis, while understanding the mohalla division of Jaipur city, one needs to address the question, whether Jai Singh, based himself upon the shastric nuances of city division in accordance to the jatis and their functions and thereby was engrossed in caste based social understanding, or was he merely dividing the city mohallas in accordance to occupational as well as jati consideration, under the garb of practical political concern of avoiding any rifts between different communities in near future, especially if they were settled together, instead of different mohallas. Thus, keeping in sight the future issues relating to the social disturbances, Sawai Jai Singh may have induced the systematic caste-based division of mohallas. Vibhuti Sachdev and Giles Tillotson, have tried to assess this very division of mohallas, but managed to present the case study of only Brahmapuri, i.e. the brahmin mohalla. Thus, the exercise undertaken by the two, appears significant but only partially as it did not open up the nature of other mohallas.

City Palace

The strongest base of the city was its palace. According to Stephen P. Blake, who studied the city of Shahjahanabad, 'the palace fortress was the centre of not only the city and the empire but also the universe.[41] The sacredness of capital cities as the centre of universe has been discussed in classical Hindu texts also. The centrality of the palace complex, as sacred or the centre of the universe has specific political dimensions as well. The palace complex functions both as a public space as well as a private residence. The administrative headquarters were the focal point of the complex and served multiple functions. The rulers made executive decisions, sent military expeditions, celebrated victories, bestowed honours, convicted criminals, tried traitors, welcomed dignitaries and conducted diplomatic missions from the confines of the palace complex itself. Of many visitors to the Jaipur court, the account of Bishop Heber stands out, as he tried to beautifully note the pomp and decorative displays of the palace. As a catholic missionary he visited Jaipur in 1832 and commented on its open pavilions with marble pillars, richly carved. He further asserted that even though these pavilions were inferior in size, in all other respects they were equal to the hall of audience in the castle of Delhi.[42]

Thus the palace was always buzzing with activities and provided the base for not only the display of regalia of authority, but also stood forth as a place through which Sawai Jai Singh broadcasted his social as well as cultural pluralism.

The Palace Complex

It consists of a series of gates or pols from east Sereh Deorhi, Udaipal, Jaypal, Vijaypal, etc., spacious squares, pleasing structures like the *Diwan-i-am* (Sabha Niwas), *Diwan-i-khas,* but the most impressive building in the royal sector is the Chandramahal, the seven-storied palace.[43] According to Vibhuti and Tillotson, 'the shastric texts specify seven storeys from the palaces of Kshatriya kings and the Chandramahal is one of the few Rajput palaces to achieve this paradigmatic number'.[44]

On the ground floor of this Chandramahal is the Pritam Niwas with a small audience hall in its centre. The next two storeys are occupied by the magnificent Sukh Niwas, above this is Rang Mahal also known as the Sabha Niwas. Apart from that there is Chavi Niwas, Shri Niwas and Mukut Mandir.

Sawai Jai Singh constructed the Jai Niwas bagh and Nichla bagh in the tradition of the Mughal garden.[45] Besides the royal palaces, public halls, courtyards and gardens, this complex also housed the Karkhanas (departments) for various manufacturing and patronage purposes. Over the years, during the 18th century many other buildings were added to this complex. In 1749, Ishwari Singh (1743-50) constructed a victory tower, the Ishwar Lat or Swarga Shuli. The tower is seven storeys high. It is one of the conspicuous landmarks in the city. Ashim Kumar Roy also narrates a romantic tale about love of Ishwari Singh and that he built the tower to see his lover[46] and in 1799 Pratap Singh (1778-1803), built the famous building of Jaipur i.e. Hawa Mahal. The designer of this remarkable structure has been identified as Lal Chand Ustad.[47]

These are some of the features of the palace complex of Jaipur of Jai Niwas, the Royal house of the Kachchwaha rulers of Jaipur.

The planning of the city was governed by geometry and symmetry. The plan divided the city into nine rectangular *nidhis* or sectors. Central axis of the city, which was 3.2 kms in length, was laid from east to west, between the gate of Suraj Pol and Chand Pole, connecting with straight roads. This axis was crossed by three roads at right angle dividing the city into nine blocks, which were further sub-divided by lanes and galleys.

Initially, the main roadside area was reserved for markets at Chand pole, Kishan pole, Gangauri, Tripoli, Chaurarasta, Johari Bazar, Sireh Deorhi, Ram Ganj and Ghat bazar. Since the beginning these are the specialized markets dealing with the business of particular commodities. Kapad-dwara documents also details about the phase devolution of the market centres. Ram Ganj, finds continuous entry in the documents, which indicates that though the designing of the market was done in Sawai Jai Singh's time, it was completed only after his death. The market came to handle a well-organized trade in cotton wool, with the development of a *rui-ki-mandi* (shopping area for cotton wool), in its panorama.[48] *Jama-Kharch Imarti* records furnish details about daily expenditure made for the maintenance of buildings. Specific details are also provided with regards to the salaries distributed to people who helped in proper functioning of public buildings like gardens, water bodies, community houses etc. One of the documents supplies information of distribution of Rs. 18 and 7 to Khiwaram Mahajan and Jagrup Mahajan respectively.[49] More importantly the document also speaks of distribution of Re. 1 to a Kumhar (Potter), Rs. 6 each to Kaslo, Khuspal, Dayapal, and Re. 1 each to Govido and Nandu, who all belonged to mali (Gardner) community.[50]

Virachit in 'Kurmvillas' gives information on the establishment of numerous bazars or markets in Jaipur. Most of these markets were located near chowkries and were flourishing and lots of money exchanged hands as Kuber (Hindu God of wealth) like figures were its owners. The shops had perforated panels, which acted as decorations as well as allowed light and air to pass through.[51]

Over the years instead of being recognized for its architectural heritage, Jaipur came to be renowned for trade and commerce a fact corroborated by the Kapad-Dwara and the *parwanas* secured in the Bikaner state archives. In fact, it is a well-established fact that Sawai Jai Singh had himself invited many traders from across India, to settle down in Jaipur. According to Ashim Kumar Roy, the tax exemption granted to the traders and artisans was the major incentive, which helped to draw into the net these community representatives. In order to support and promote these trading activities, Sawai Jai Singh had very early laid the foundations of all the major markets i.e. Sireh Deorhi, Kishan Pole, Johri Pole, and Gangari.[52] According to the map LS/14 (dated 1725), in the city palace museum collection, which has come to be known as the progress report map, 162 shops were constructed by the State in each of these bazars.[53] All these shops were uniform in shape; size and all these features were also ordered to be in harmony with each other. Almost immediately afterwards similar bazars were constructed along Chandra Pole, Tripolia, Ramganj and were ready before 1734. The shops were constructed in typical architectural style on both sides of the road. They were only single storied and any vertical expansion was disallowed as the first floor of the shops were reserved for the masses of the city, so that they could watch the royal processions from there.[54]

Temples as City Structures

Apart from the palace complexes and the economic zones, temples were also of great significance. They also came to represent the religious outlook of the ruler. The first temple to be built in the new city was that of Shri Govind Dev. This temple is a large rectangular single-storied building. Govind Dev temple closely resembles a Mughal public audience hall. In both the audience hall and the Govind Dev temple there is a flat-roofed temple chamber with a pillar façade behind which the ruler in the audience hall sat down as the deity in the temple is enthroned for *darshan*.[55]

Catherine B. Asher, saw the temple and its construction as a representation of Jai Singh's conceptualization of *Divine right* to rule. In fact a very popular legend circulates in this context that while initially erecting the audience hall, Jai Singh aimed to incorporate his own image in the centre of the hall, but when the deity visited him in his dream, he got the statue of Govind Dev placed inside the hall.[56] The flat roof, small dark dingy chambers and other architectural features indicate that this temple was built in a hurry; possibly it was first used as residential quarters. Some scholars are of the impression that in order to protect that temple from Muslim invasion, it was constructed in this manner. But Catherine Asher, questions this assumption. Tillotson, supports the legend about that dream, and asserts that it was the reason behind the not so impressive style of the temple, as it was devoted to the deity only later on and was not part of the initial plans of Jai Singh. It was devoid of *shikhar*-topped styling and also lacked haveli style temples, the dominant patterns of the Nagara temple architecture of those days.[57] According to Catherine Asher, most of the temples constructed inside the city, were devoid of all such features and only dissimilar structure is that of Kalki, future Vishnu temple. It was provided with a *shikhar*, unlike other temples, which had a plain decoration and therefore Catherine B. Asher, asserts that it appears that the orders may have been passed to erect the temples in such a manner.[58] Going by the plain designs, with common architectural styles of the temples inside the Jaipur city, one can raise the question as to why such a construction took place and what reasons necessitated the evolution of such a evolutionary style of temple. When the idol of Govind Dev, was installed within the final abode i.e. the city palace, Jai Singh ordered his officials to donate from the annually accumulated land revenue, revenue from *khalisa* and non- rural taxes, *peshkash* and other finances, a sum of one rupee for Govind Dev and four aanas for his custodian Ramsaran. The officials and even the common masses followed such orders by the state religiously. Apart from them even the royal ladies contributed in the Govind Dev temple. In one reference the Raj Mata, of Jaipur donated one thousand rupees to the temple of Govind Dev.[59]

After having underlined the trajectories of scholarly understanding, forwarded in the context of the city of Jaipur, it can be postulated that the divergent course of historical causations, leading up to the making and remaking of historical map of Jaipur, were majorly stimulated by the political, social, economic and cultural world view of Sawai Jai Singh, the founder of Jaipur city and its population. The history of Jaipur city, is distinguishable, not only at the level of its planned architectural creation, but also for standing tall during the patterned transition from late medieval to early modern centuries. More than being a political and religious centre as has been understood in the previous readings, Jaipur stands out equally on the social and cultural front. The concentrative evolution of Jaipur city as a prosperous hub bringing together heterogeneous social groupings was a defined political motive force of its ruler.

NOTES

1. Yogesh Sharma and Pius Malekandathil (eds.), *Cities in Medieval India*, Primus Books, Delhi: 2014, p. 1.
2. Ibid., p. 8.
3. The notional frame of political sovereignty i.e. the real process of political control assumes an important place in case of Sawai Jai Singh and Jaipur, his new capital venture because as a ruler Sawai continued to be called as a Mansabdar of Mughals, even though he did present a picture of an independent ruler. In subjective terms, his political domain i.e. the city continued as a part of Mughal subha, but Sawai through his political manoeuvering easily evolved into both political head as well

as custodial hegemonic head of the place.

4. Indu Banga, *The City in Indian History*, Manohar Publishers, Delhi: 2005, p. 70.
5. Ibid., p. 72.
6. Sunil Kumar, 'Court Capital and Kingship: Delhi and its Sultan in Thirteenth and Fourteenth CE', in Albrecht Fuess and Jan Peter Hartury (eds.), *Court Cultures in the Muslim World, Seventh to Nineteenth Century*, Routledge, London & New Delhi: 2011, p. 124.
7. Nilanjan Sarkar, 'An Urban Imaginaire, c.a. 1350: The Capital City in Ziya, Barani's *Fatawa-i-Jahandari*', *The Indian Economic Social History Review*, 2011. pp. 407-24.
8. K.N. Chaudhari, 'Some reflections on the towns and the country in Mughal India', *Modern Asian Studies*, Vol. 12 (1), 1978, pp. 77-96.
9. Stephen Blake, *Shahjahanabad: The Sovereign City in Mughal India 1639-1739*, Cambridge University Press, Cambridge: 2002, p. xii.
10. Ibid., p. 25.
11. Michael W. Meister, "Geometry and Measure in Indian Temple Plans: Rectangular Temples", *Artibus Asiae*, Vol. 44, 1983, pp. 266–96.
12. Reena Patra, 'A Comparative study on Vasstu Shastra and Heidegger's, Building, Dwelling and Thinking', *Asian Philosophy*, Vol. 16, 2006, pp. 199-218.
13. Vibhuti Sachdev and Giles Tillotson, *Building Jaipur: The Making of an Indian City*, Reaktion Books, London: 2002, pp. 155–160.
14. Blake, *Shahjahanabad*, p. 29.
15. Ibid.
16. Ibid., p. 34.
17. Ibid., p. 35.
18. Ibid.
19. Ibid., p. 29.
20. Catherine B. Asher and Cynthia Talbot, *India Before Europe*, Cambridge University Press, New Delhi: 2006.
21. Gopal Narayan Bahura and Chandramani Singh (eds.), *Catalogue of Historical Documents in Kapad-Dwara, Part II: Jaipur Maps and Plans*, Jaipur Printers, Jaipur: 1990, p. 22.
22. Yadvendra Sahai, 'A Patron of Architecture: Some features of the City as built by Jai Singh II', in Rakesh Hooja, Rima Hooja

and Rakshat Hooja (eds.), *Constructing Rajpootana—Rajasthan: Collected Narratives in Remembrance of Bhupendra Hooja,* Rawat Publications, Delhi: 2010, pp. 335-46.

23. Ibid.
24. Ashim Kumar Roy, *History of Jaipur City,* Manohar Publishers, Delhi: 2006.
25. Giles Tillotson, *Jaipur Nama,* Penguin India, New Delhi, 2006, p. 23.
26. Ibid., pp. 25-27.
27. Catherine B. Asher, 'Excavating Communalism: Kachhwaha *Rajdhrama* and Mughal Sovereignty', in Rajat Datta (ed.), *Rethinking A Millennium: Perspectives on Indian History from Eighth to Eighteenth Century,* Aakar Books, Delhi: 2008, pp. 222-48.
28. Sachdev, p. 47.
29. Fatima Imam, 'Indian paradigms of political authority and usage of urban spaces: comparative analysis of Jaipur as an eighteenth century example', *Studies in History,* Vol. 31, No. 2, 2015, pp. 155-77.
30. Bahura, *Catalogue of Historical Documents of Kapad-Dwara,* Document No. 171, Fig No. 49, p. 35.
31. J.K. Jain (ed.), *Kurmvilas: Jaipur Rajyake Kachchwaha Shashkonka Itihas* by Poet Virachit, Rajasthan State Archives, Bikaner: 1991, p. 448.
32. Bahura, *Catalogue of Historical Documents of Kapad-Dwara,* Part 1, p. 639.
33. Roy, *History of Jaipur City.*
34. Sachdev, *Building Jaipur,* p. 47.
35. Jai Narayan Asopa (ed.), *Cultural Heritage of Jaipur,* United Book Traders, Jodhpur: 1982, p. 33.
36. Ibid.
37. Sachdev, *Building Jaipur,* p. 49.
38. Roy, *History of Jaipur City.*
39. Sachdev, *Building Jaipur,* p. 50.
40. Asher, Excavating Communalism, p. 231.
41. Blake, *Shahjahanabad,* 2002.
42. Jadunath Sarkar, *A History of Jaipur,* Orient Blackswan, New Delhi: 2009.

43. Bahura, *Catalogue of Historical Documents of Kapad-Dwara*, Constructional Design of Chandramahal, Document No. 109, Fig. No. 39, p. 29.
44. Sachdev, *Building Jaipur*, p. 65.
45. Imam, 'Indian paradigms of political authority', 2015.
46. Roy, *History of Jaipur City*, p. 54.
47. Sachdev, *Building Jaipur*, p. 11.
48. Bahura, *Catalogue of Historical Documents of Kapad-Dwara*, Document No. 199, 200, and 204, pp. 38-39.
49. *Arhsatta Imarti*, Bag No. 18, Rajasthan State Archives, Bikaner (RSAB).
50. *Jama Kharch Imarti*, Bag No. 5, (RSAB).
51. Jain, *Kurmvilas: Jaipur Rajyake Kachchwaha*, pp. 448-49.
52. Roy, *History of Jaipur City*, pp. 57-58.
53. Asopa, *Cultural Heritage of Jaipur*, p. 34.
54. Asher, *India Before Europe*.
55. Asher, Excavating, p. 235.
56. Hooja, *Constructing Rajpootana Rajasthan*, p. 344.
57. Sachdev, *Building Jaipur*, p. 55.
58. Asher, Excavating, p. 234.
59. *Dastur Komwar*, Vol. No. 8, event of V.S. 1781/A.D. 1724. p. 47, (RSAB).

10

Nagaur: A Trading Mart of Marwar State in the Late Eighteenth Century

Rajender Kumar

The 18th century has an important place in the field of trade-commerce in the history of Marwar. This was the time when Marwar was freed from the influence of Mughal sovereignty and started its independent rule. The grant (*Tankhwah-i-Jagir*) from the Mughals had now ceased to be available to the state. Hence, the rulers of Marwar were in great need of new financial resources for the governance of the state. The Marwar rulers took many important steps to strengthen the economic condition of the state, such as, the business class was given several concessions in trade, inviting merchants from neighbouring states to settle and trade in Marwar and made arrangements for development and protection of trade routes.[1] Nagaur became the main centre of trade and commerce with this view.

The important book *Marwar Ra Pargana Ri Vigat* of the 17th century shows that at that time Nagaur was a major centre of big-scale industry and trade in the vast region.[2] The archival records of Marwar state prove that the commercial importance of this place became increasingly visible in the second half of the eighteenth century. The various series of archival sources such as *sanad parwana bahis, Jama kharch bahis, khajana bahis,* and *karkhana bahis* of Marwar state, preserved in the Rajasthan State Archives, throw light on the trade and commerce of the erstwhile Marwar state. Therefore, an attempt has been made to write this paper in light of these sources. It is known from these sources that during the period of study the woolly blankets of this place were in great demand in Rajputana.[3] Along with this, Nagaur was also famous for ivory toys,[4] copper, brass,[5] iron utensils[6], and tools[7], manufacture of cotton cloth and production of salt, gypsum[8] and red stones.[9]

Archival records related to Nagaur provide information about the erstwhile trading system. During this period, widely traded products had to cross various stages of the market before reaching the customer. There were different levels of market —*Haat, Chohatta* or *Bazaar,* and *Mandi*. Producers or external traders used to send their goods through local traders or on their own to the *mandi,* which was a wholesale centre, where there were many shops of allied products. In these *mandis,* the deal was made in wholesale. These *mandis* used to be under the city administration, which always kept an eye on the activities here. It also levied taxes on the sale of merchandise. Under this, there were check-posts of *sair,* which used to collect tax from merchants. In this work, especially *Daroga, Navisadan, Kanungos, Tabindar, Vatwal, Gumashta Bholavaniya, Kayal,* and *Bhatriyas* were involved.[10] The second level of distribution of merchandise was called *Chohatta* or *Bazaar,* where retail and wholesale merchants had many permanent and temporary shops. Such markets were commonly held in the township. The small producers of the state brought their goods here and the retailers bought goods from this market. The location of the *haat* or shop depended on the demand for goods which were located in many neighbourhoods of towns and in rural areas where the local consumers used to buy goods according to their needs. When the goods of the external traders came to Nagaur city, the goods were checked by the *sair's* staff at the main entrances of the city, after which the *Vatwal* and the *Kayal* or *Vajandar* (weightier) used to measure the goods and determine the tax as per the rules.[11]

Ironwork in Nagaur was practised since the medieval period. The largest numbers of luhars (blacksmiths) in the entire Marwar state were settled in Nagaur. Even a village named Luharpura was established for them near Nagaur[12] where Multani Luhars also lived.[13] These blacksmiths used to make different varieties of iron goods. According to the first page of *Mardumashumari Raj-Marwar*, there were some iron mines in Jodhpur, Sojat and Jalore pargana *s* of Marwar state. Probably from here, there may have been iron supplies to other places in the state. Apart from iron, brass, and bronze utensils, tools were also prepared in good quality. In 1778, iron implements were brought from Nagaur for construction (*Kamathana*) in Jodhpur Fort, which included 200 *Aadu*, 60 *Mandoli*, 40 *Naraja* and 10 *Rambha*.[14] Similarly, five hundred maunds iron was sent from Nagaur to Jodhpur in 1785.[15] *Hande, Chariya, Dabra, Parat, Thal, Thali, Lote, Katori, Kudchi* of brass, *kadao* of iron, and bronze utensils were also made of high quality[16] and exported to various states of Rajputana as well as to the external states.[17]

Nagaur was a trading centre where traders from other countries such as Kashmir, Multan, Kabul, and Sindh used to come to trade. In 1753, one *seer* of saffron was purchased from each merchant as Bhavanigir of Kashmir, and Sami Narharpuri by the State Department, for which Rs. 65 and Rs. 45 were paid respectively.[18]

Apart from this, Nagaur was a major centre for raw wool production after Bikaner but the manufacturing and transaction of woollen goods were in abundance throughout Rajputana. Its brief description is as follows:

Wool Production and Trade Centre

Nagaur pargana was the largest wool-producing region of the state of Jodhpur. Woollen products such as blankets, *lunkar, namde, bhakala, loi,* and *pattu* were traded by local traders at a large level. For example, in October 1778, a thousand blankets were ordered from Nagaur, which cost Rs. 10 per piece.[19]

It was known from the contemporary archival records of Jodhpur state that there was an exuberant production of wool from the nearby villages of Nagaur. The people of *Jat, Bishanoi, Gurjar,* and *Meghwal* communities were involved in the production of wool in the Nagaur paragana. The Jats produced wool and also made and sold wool products.[20] The *Gurjar* was also a major wool-producing community. Among the states of western Rajputana, their number was highest in Marwar.[21] The *Gurjars* came from Ajmer in Marwar and most of their settlements are in the eastern parganas of Marwar.[22] There is another caste *Pinjara* involved in this business. They were named *Pinjara* since their work focused on spinning and cleaning the raw wool. The wool producers used to give the shreds of wool to the *Pinjara* for cleaning, and the *Pinjara* used their tools to clean the raw wool and make it white and soft to complete the product.[23] In addition to the above, there were some other castes whose engagement in this work can be called an important contribution. Among them were mainly *Lava, Chhimpa, Chamar, Oli,*and *Gadaria* castes. The Lava caste business was also associated with wool production. They used to cut wool and were both Hindus and Muslims. Work of wool dyeing was done by the people of the *Chimpa* caste. All the wool merchants gave their wool to the *Chimpas* to dye, but later they started buying and selling their goods.[24]

Many traders of the time purchased wool directly from the villages of Nagaur. For example, the *Mahajans* of Kishangarh bought wool from nearby villages of Nagaur instead of buying wool from the Nagaur *mandi*.[25] Therefore, it is clear that wool was produced in large quantities in the villages of Nagaur pargana.[26] The village of Alai near Nagaur was a big wool centre, from where people bought wool and wool products to sell in the Nagaur *mandi*. According to one source of information, a *bhambhi* (a lower community) of the village of Alai had brought a number of 46 woollen *lunkars* to the city, where a *Mahajan* bought them from him.[27] Similarly, information is derived from many *bahis* of Jodhpur *Bahiyat* section that a large number of woollen goods came from the nearby villages around Nagaur[28] and this city provided them with a large market.

Export

Sheep, wool, and blankets were exported from Nagaur

to Sindh, Multan, and many states of Rajputana including Bikaner and Jaisalmer.[29] Woollen blankets were in great demand there.[30]

Table 1: Exports of Woolen Products from Nagaur[31]

Sr. No.	*Place of Export*	*Products*
1.	Bikaner	Wool
2.	Nohar	Wool
3.	Churu	Wool
4.	Kishangarh	Woollen Clothes
5.	Pali	Wool and Woollen Clothes
6.	Jodhpur	Wool and Woollen Clothes
7.	Kota	Woollen Clothes
8.	Indore	Woollen Clothes
9.	Multan	Woollen Clothes

According to the Jodhpur records in March 1795, the Pathans of Multan had purchased woollen clothes through the local wool broker Bhau, on which deal, the government levied Rs. 17 as *hasal*.[32] Similarly, there is a mention of sending a woollen garment of Rs. 3,000 to Indore through the merchant Sukha.[33]

This description proves that Nagaur emerged as a major trading center of wool in the second phase of the 18th century.

Nagaur has been the oldest city of Marwar and an important centre of national political activities. During the Sultanate and Mughal period, the spread of composite culture and military activities were conducted on a large scale. Consequently, in the 18th century, this city has been the largest pargana of the state and the core centre of its economy. Large factories of military goods manufacturing also developed here, in which the factories of gunpowder and cannon manufacturing were prominent. These factories required iron, coal, lead, sulfur, salt, wood, and hundreds of other items. Some items came from different places of the state and many items had to be imported from outside states through traders. As a result,

Nagaur flourished as a huge trading centre.

This city was the backbone of the Marwar state army during the 18th century. Its main base was the factories located here, which manufactured weapons for the army. Based on the archival sources, it is briefly mentioned as follows:

Weapon Manufacturing Centre

The importance of Nagaur in this period increased even more because here the state had established factories for making cannons, iron balls, guns, and gunpowder.[34]

Nagaur was called the second capital of the state of Marwar during the period of study. The strategic importance of Nagaur was certainly one of the important reasons. Weapons factories were established here to provide excellence to the state from a military perspective. The establishment of Muslim rule in India led to a large settlement of blacksmiths in Nagaur. Large guns were made for the state by these blacksmiths, and various new technological weapons were manufactured. The work of making bows and arrows was done by the *Kabanigars* and the blacksmiths. In the entire Marwar state, this work was done at a high level in Nagaur itself.[35] In the sequence, a large state factory for making cannons was established here. According to a reference, in 1767, after purchasing iron worth Rs. 1,000, the iron balls were made for cannons and *rehkalas* (a type of small cannon) after handing over the ravages of the Nagaur factory.[36] According to another source of information, in the same year, iron worth Rs. 500 was sent from Maroth to make cannonballs in a Nagaur factory.[37]

The factory of making shells in Nagaur was not only limited to making iron balls for cannons, but also for making small and large firearms of artillery, making different sizes of iron balls and their associated weapons and equipment. This is also confirmed by state documents from the latter part of the 18th century. For example, in 1780–81, there was an order to build 5,000 iron balls for cannons for the struggle with the *Talpuriyas* of Sindh and send them to the army.[38] Similarly, another reference gives information that in 1800, a total of

2,000 iron balls were made for the five cannons of Pandit Balwantrai's artillery, i.e. 400 balls for each cannon and it was ordered to have them prepared quickly within a week.[39] Preparing such so many iron balls in 7-8 days implies that a large number of manpower was engaged in this industry.

Gunpowder Factory

Major components of gunpowder such as saltpeter (*Shora*) and wood coal were produced in Nagaur on a large scale. In addition to the state factories, people of the local Sorgara community also produced *Shora* or *Daru* on a large scale and the local traders used to sell it. From an instance dated 1771, it is said that when the need for gunpowder was required in the capital, it was ordered to buy daru from the merchants of Nagaur and the people of the Sorgara community and immediately send it to Jodhpur.[40] According to another reference, 25 maunds of *daru* were sent to Phalodi from Nagaur in 1781.[41]

There were also large-scale ammunition factories in Nagaur and Jodhpur[42], from where the forts, bastions, and military cantonments located in all the pargana *s* of the state were supplied. Thus, to fulfil the military requirements, several trading firms were established in Nagaur, which also contributed to the promotion of trade here.

All kinds of guns, big and small, were manufactured and repaired in Nagaur. The guns of the army battalions of Marwar were repaired from Nagaur itself. For example, in 1791, 30 guns, 4 *Junjayal* and one *Ramchangi* gun from a battalion were sent to Nagaur for repair due to technical defects and physical damage.[43]

In addition to the manufacture of arms and weapons, the purchase and sale of opium and tobacco in Nagaur were also done on a large scale. It is found from a reference that 50 maunds of tobacco were sent from Nagaur to Jodhpur.[44] Similarly, many foreign merchants traded opium in Nagaur. For example, in July 1753, two maunds and eight and a half seers of opium for the army in Nagaur were bought by the merchant Sami Dayalpuri. In November of the same year, opium worth Rs. 279 and 6 annas was purchased from Multani Devi Chand.[45] The transaction of tobacco and opium in large quantities illustrates the commercial importance of Nagaur.

The fair held in Nagaur region also played a pivotal role in the businesses prosperity of Marwar state.[46] Large businesses, religious and animal fairs were organized from time to time in many main towns and cities of the then Bikaner, Jodhpur and Jaisalmer.[47] In these fairs too, there was large-scale trading of merchandise.

Role of Fairs in Nagaur's Business Prosperity

Fairs had an significant place in the then local trade. These fairs were held at different places at different times. In the fairs, along with the sale of merchandise, cattle were also traded. Here goods and animals were brought from distant places to sell. Full arrangements were made by the state government for the organizing and security of the fairs.[48]

Nagaur Fair

In Nagaur, a fair was organized every year for the purchase and sale of sheep, camels and oxen where traders from far areas came to buy animals.[49] Camels of Nagaur were also exported to the Deccan, for example, in 1781, a large number of camels were sent from Nagaur to the Deccan through Harlal Mundhada.[50]

Mundwa Fair

Mundwa was an important trading site of the Nagaur pargana , where a grand fair was held on 5th March each year[51], lasting for a period of one and a half months. In this fair, along with the transaction of trade goods, camels, bulls, horses, sheep, and goats, were widely traded.[52] Woollen cloth was also brought for sale here in large numbers. For example, the Lahiri traders of Nagaur city had brought a cart loaded with woollen cloth to sell at the Mundwa fair.[53] It is clear that woollen clothes were also sold in large quantities in this fair. It is known from the Jodhpur *Bahiyat* that in addition to camel carts and cattle, gold and silver were also sold at the Mundwa fair. This was purchased in the presence of government officials and its information was recorded in the account.[54] Thus, along with the items of daily use in the fair, precious goods were also traded. The Mundwa fair was very famous for the purchase of camels. Apart from the states of Rajputana,[55] other states of India also purchased large numbers of camels. For the Nawab of Awadh Shuja-ud-Daula, camels were purchased[56] from the fair at Mundwa in 1773, through his minister Hayat Khan.[57] Similarly, in 1778, Maratha Ahilyabai's officials also purchased 300 camels from the fair at Mundwa.[58]

The trade goods sold at this fair are estimated from the fact that in 1775, the state received an income of Rs. 85,000 due to the goods coming from Umarkot and its surrounding areas.[59] It is clear from these facts that the state earned a lot from the fair at Mundwa.

Merchant Class of Nagaur

Local traders play a key role in establishing a place as a vast trading centre. The merchants of Marwar were pioneers in this field and made Nagaur famous not only in Rajputana but in distant states. The merchant class of Marwar mainly consisted of *Mahajans, Maheshwaris, Saahs, Bohras* and *Oswals*.[60] Apart from these, people belonging to castes such as *Brahmins, Gusains, Charans, Bhats* and *Banjaras* were also engaged in trade. Many references to trade by *Ramanandi Sadhus* also derive from the then archival documents.[61]

The *Mahajan* class in Marwar was in an economically sound position during the 17th-19th centuries.[62] Large firms of the traders of this business community were located in the state, even their branches were established in the states outside Marwar. These big traders were called *Kothiwal*.[63] In the latter part of the 18th century Vijaychand, Khushalchand, Mohandas, Veerchand and Anupchand, etc. were the chief *Kothiwal* of Nagaur.[64] They also contributed significantly to their respective fields as bankers.[65] These Kothiwal merchants were so prosperous that when the state was faced an economic crisis, they provided assistance to the state. Nandwana Bohras of Nagaur have been the main contributors in this situation. For example, when the city of Nagaur was besieged by the Marathas in 1754, Maharaja Vijay Singh had to take a loan from the local Gudla and Nandwana Bohras for military expenditure.[66] Similarly, Riddheram, Girdhar, Tarachand, Ramdas, Balaram and Sadaram gave loans of Rs. 35,000 to the state in 1767.[67]

Lohia Ramchand-Sahabram was a big iron merchant of Nagaur.[68] Mohta Bharmal was a prominent merchant of Nagaur, who had many firms in Sindh and Bahawalpur, so the exchange of wool and woollen goods with other items was done here.[69] Shahram Nagauri, Akhairam Nagauri, Kasu Karnani, and Mukund Das Parikh were the prestigious wool merchants of Nagaur.[70] Saah Ajba,[71] Lodḥa Bharmal, and Vyas Kaniram[72] were big traders who dealt in camels. Lodha Bramal trade in cotton with Bikaner.[73] Other prominent merchants were Lohia Harlal-Lachhmandas,[74] Muhnot Bharmal[75] and Lohia Bagsiram.[76]

Efforts were made by the state to ensure that most of the traders would come to Nagaur to do their business. For this, merchants were given various types of exemption in taxes and guarantee of the safety of their goods. The merchants of Nagaur, Binechand Bathia, used to trade horses and *Tarameva* between Nagaur and Jaipur. The state was given a tax rebate of Rs. 10 on 100 horses and a quarter tax on *Tarmeva*.[77] Similarly, Mohnot Jogidas, a businessman from Kishangarh, was given half exemption[78] in *hasal* (tax) on selling *khand* (sugar) in the markets of Nagaur so that he could always continue with his business in Nagaur.

Documents from the 18th century reveal that some branches of Brahmins—*Bohras, Paliwals, Joshis, Acharajs,* and *Purohits,* were specially engaged in business activities. In the latter part of the 18th century, the Bohra class became the dominant business class of Marwar. The Bohra traders also provided financial assistance to the state from time to time.[79]

For example, substantial amounts from Bohra Nandwana Deepchand, Nandwana Pokardaas, and Nandwana Daulatram were borrowed by the state.[80] Nandwana Bohras of Nagaur provided financial support to the state several times when needed.[81] In this sequence, Joshi Brahmins of Sanchor were important, who were known as *Sanchora Joshi* and *Sanchora Viraman*. They had many shops in Nagaur town.[82] They mainly traded in cotton, paddy, and grocery goods.

The sages of the Gusain and Ramanandi sects were also associated with the business work. They especially traded clothes, grocery goods, and horses. In the second half of the 18th century, Sami Khushalpuri, Sami Shankaragir, Sami Vasudevagir, etc. were the major clothing merchants.[83] In 1763, a cloth of Rs. 469 was purchased from Sami traders at the house of Thakur Jait Singh of Nagaur Pargana.[84]

The *Charan* and *Bhat* traders were engaged in trade in large numbers in the Marwar and Bikaner states.[85] However, their main task was to transport merchandise from one place to another. They walked with a flock of camels and bulls called *katar* and *balad* respectively. The reason for their marching with large convoys was the responsibility of protecting the goods. Their convoys had an excess of paddy, salt, tobacco, opium, and jaggery.[86] They also carried merchandise of traders outside Rajputana.

The other important trading class of Marwar was the *Banjaras*. They did not engage in the direct transactions of trade, but rather carried the goods of merchants from one place to another. They mainly traded salt and paddy in Marwar.[87]

Trading Routes Passing Through Nagaur and Their Utility

The geographical conditions of Nagaur played an important role in the development of trade and commerce here. In Rajputana, the former medieval rulers established trade contacts and routes with important states like Delhi on one hand and Gujarat and Malwa on the other. During the Mughal period, towns like Ajmer, Nagaur, Merta, Chittor, etc. acted as a link when Nagaur, Umarkot, Jhalrapatan and Ajmer were established as major trade centres for merchandise.

According to Abul Fazl's *Ain-i-Akbari,*[88] we find many references to the trade routes which passed through Rajputana. According to this, a route which connects Agra to Ahmedabad had two ways which passed through Marwar, one had to go via Nagaur and another one via Jalore.[89] These important trade routes were in constant practice even during the 18th century. The most prominent route was towards Sindh, Thatta, and Khairpur. As a result of being situated on these important trade routes, many cities and towns of Marwar later became famous as big trading centres. In this sequence, Nagaur's importance was increased because it was situated on a route that ran from Delhi to Ahmedabad,[90] Sindh, Kabul,[91] and Multan[92] to Patan and from Malwa to Bikaner or Rajgarh.[93] Nagaur also connects northern states such as Punjab and Bikaner to the Deccan.[94] Traders and their convoys used to take short-distance routes to protect their goods from looters. As a result, new routes were also made by the merchants according to their convenience. For example, in 1776, a new route was built by the merchants between Dehu-Madpura near Nagaur, for its security state was ordered to the *daroga* (in-charge of check post) of the *sair* of Nagaur.[95]

This statement proves that the location of Nagaur was located on an important trade route. As a result, the city was established as a major trading centre.

In conclusion, it can be said that in the second phase of the 18th century, Nagaur was the economic capital for the state of Marwar. Its proximity to Ajmer was ideal for Marwar in strategic terms. In order to maintain control over the central province of Ajmer, many Marwar forces were deployed here, due to which the rapid urbanization and industrialization of this town were made. With the encouragement of the state administration, many merchants from outside states settled here and started trading activities at the international level. As a result, Nagaur remained an important trading centre not only for Marwar but also for the far eastern and western states from the medieval period to the early 19th century.

NOTES

1. *Khas Rukka Parwana Bahi,* No. 1, V.S. 1822-1866/1765-1809 AD, *Hath Bahi,* No. 1, V.S. 1824/1868 AD, Jodhpur Records, Rajasthan State Archives, Bikaner. These documents refer to the invitation and concession orders given by the Marwar ruler to the traders.
2. Muhnot Nainsi, *Marwar Ra Paragana Ri Vigat,* ed. Narayan Singh Bhati, Vol. 2, Jodhpur: 1969, pp. 421-24,
3. *Daftar Hajzuri Bahi,* No. 24, V.S. 1881/1824 AD; *Haqiqat Bahi,* No. 1, V.S. 1825/1768 AD, p. 639, Jodhpur Records, R.S.A.B.
4. Fazula and Bula were the first-class artisans of ivory toys, whose toys were also purchased by *Kilikhana* (Dept. of Equipment)- *Sanad Parwana Bahi,* No. 21, V.S. 1835/1778 AD, p. 6F-1, Jodhpur Records.
5. *Sanad Parwana Bahi,* No. 21, V.S. 1835/1778 AD, p. 11F-2, 12F-2, 14F-2.
6. Ibid., p. 49F-2.
7. *Sanad Parwana Bahi,* No.21, V.S. 1835/1778 AD, p. 8F-1.
8. Ibid., p. 14F-1, *Sanad Parwana Bahi,* No. 43, V.S. 1848/1791 AD, p. 29F-1
9. *Sanad Parwana Bahi,* No. 13, V.S. 1830/1773 AD, p. 23-30; *Sanad Parwana Bahi,* No. 20, V.S. 1835/1778 AD, p. 17; *Sanad Parwana Bahi,* No. 30, V.S. 1841/1784 AD, p. 371F-1-2.
10. *Bahi Jagat Aamdani,* No. 83, V.S. 1822/1765 AD; *Sanad Parwana Bahi,* No. 21, V.S. 1835/1778 AD, p. 44F-1-2, 45F-1, 47F-1; *Bahi,* No. 35, V.S. 1843/1786 AD, p. 95F-2, Jodhpur Records.
11. *Sanad Parwana Bahi,* No. 21, V.S. 1835/1778 AD, p. 55F-2.
12. Ibid., p. 53F-2.
13. *Sanad Parwana Bahi,* No. 43, V.S. 1848/1791 AD, p. 83F-1
14. *Sanad Parwana Bahi,* No. 21, V.S. 1835/1778 AD, p. 8F-1.
15. *Sanad Parwana Bahi,* No. 32, V.S. 1842/1785 AD, p. 39F 1.
16. *Sanad Parwana Bahi,* No. 20, V.S. 1835/1778 AD, p. 17F-1-2, *Sanad Parwana Bahi,* No. 53, V.S. 1843/1786 AD, p. 93F-1, 29F-1; *Sanad Parwana Bahi,* No. 43, V.S. 1848/1791 AD, p. 28F-2, 29F-1.
17. *Sanad Parwana Bahi,* No. 32, V.S. 1842/1785 AD, p. 28F-2, 29F-1; *Sanad Parwana Bahi,* No. 21, V.S. 1835/1778 AD, p. 11F-2.
18. *Bahi Khajane Re Jama Kharch Ri (Daftar Hazuri),* No. 1, V.S. 1810/1753 AD, p. 52-53.
19. *Sanad Parwana Bahi,* No. 21, V.S. 1835/1778 AD, p. 47F-2.

20. *Khema ra Karkhana Talke Ri Hath Bahi,* No. 81, V.S. 1849/1792 AD, *margashirsh sudi 7; Sanad Parwana Bahi,* No. 16, V.S. 1833/1776 AD, *miti kartik vadi* 13.
21. The Gurjars settled mostly in Parbatsar, and eastern parganas of Marwar.
22. Munshi Hardayal, *Mardum Shumari Raj-Marwar,* Jodhpur: published by order of the Marwar Darbar, 1894, p. 44; Munshi Hardayal, *The Castes of Marwar,* Jodhpur:, 1994, reprint, p. 37.
23. Munshi Hardayal, *Mardum Shumari Raj-Marwar,* p. 550.
24. *Sanad Parwana Bahi,* No. 17, V.S. 1833, *miti asadh sudi* 5, p. 41F-2.
25. *Sanad Parwana Bahi,* No. 17, V.S. 1833/1776 AD, p. 33F-2.
26. *Sanad Parwana Bahi,* No. 47, V.S. 1852/1795 AD, *miti kartik vadi* 4.
27. *Sanad Parwana Bahi,* No. 52, V.S. 1855/1798 AD, *miti pratham shrawan vadi* 11.
28. *Sanad Parwana Bahi,* No. 37, V.S. 1844/1787 AD, p. 49F-2; *Bahi,* No. 39, V.S. 1845/1788 AD, p. 98F-2; *Bahi,* No. 57, V.S. 1860/1803 AD, p. 52F-2.
29. *Sanad Parwana Bahi,* No. 19, V.S. 1834/1777 AD, *miti asadh sudi* 1; *Bahi,* No. 21, V.S. 1835/1778 A.D., *miti posh vadi* 11, *miti asadh vadi* 13; *Bahi,* No. 39, V.S. 1845/1788 AD, *miti posh vadi 7; Bahi,* No. 45, V.S. 1850/1793 AD *miti shrawan sudi* 2; Jodhpur Records; *Jagat Bahi,* No. 81, V.S. 1807/1750, *miti bhadrapada sudi* 9, Bikaner Records, R.S.A.B.
30. *Daftar Hazuri Bahi,* No. 24, V.S. 1881/1824 AD; *Haqiqat Bahi,* No. 1, V.S. 1825/1768 AD, p. 639.
31. *Jagat Bahi,* No. 81, V.S. 1807/1750 AD, *Sawa Mandi Sadar Bahi,* No. 3, V.S. 1805/1748 AD; *Bahi,* No. 4, V.S. 1807-10; *Bahi,* No. 11, V.S. 1822/1765 AD, Bikaner Records; *Sanad Parwana Bahi* No. 19, V.S. 1834/1777 AD; *Bahi* No. 30, V.S. 1841/1784 AD; *Bahi,* No. 39, V.S. 1845/1798 AD; *Bahi,* No. 47, V.S. 1852/1795 AD.
32. *Sanad Parwana Bahi,* No. 47, V.S. 1852/1795 AD, *miti phalgun vadi* 9.
33. *Sanad Parwana Bahi,* No. 30, V.S. 1841/1784 AD, *miti bhadrapada vadi* 10.
34. *Sanad Parwana Bahi,* No. 30, V.S. 1841/1784 AD, *miti bhadrapada vadi* 10.
35. *Sanad Parwana Bahi,* No. 32, V.S. 1842/1785 AD, p. 50F-1.
36. *Sanad Parwana Bahi,* No. 7, V.S. 1824/1767 AD, p. 43F-1.

37. Ibid., p. 286F-1.
38. *Sanad Parwana Bahi,* No. 25, V.S. 1838/1781 AD, p. 16F-2.
39. *Sanad Parwana Bahi,* No. 58, V.S. 1862/1805 AD, p. 53F-2
40. *Sanad Parwana Bahi,* No. 11, V.S. 1828/1771 AD, p. 80F-2.
41. *Sanad Parwana Bahi,* No. 25, V.S. 1838/1781 AD, p. 56F-2.
42. *Sanad Parwana Bahi,* No. 11, V.S. 1828/1771 AD, *miti posh sudi* 1, *Bahi,* No. 43, V.S. 1848/1791 AD, p. 37F-1,113F-2; *Bahi,* No.52, V.S. 1855/1798 AD,p. 39F- 2.
43. *Sanad Parwana Bahi,* No. 43, V.S. 1848/1791 AD, p. 70F-1.
44. *Sanad Parwana Bahi,* No. 32, V.S. 1842/1785 AD, p. 49F-2.
45. *Bahi Khajane Re Jama Kharch Ri (Daftar Hazuri),* No. 1, V.S. 1810/1753 AD, pp. 2-3.
46. G.N. Sharma, *Social Life in Medieval Rajasthan (1500-1800),* Lakshmi Narain Agarwal, Agra: 1968, p. 317.
47. James Tod, *Annals and Antiquities of Rajasthan,* Vol. II, Penguin, Delhi: 1971, p. 157, 424; K.D. Erskine, *Rajputana Gazetteers: The W.R.S. Residency and Bikaner Agency,* Vol. II, The Pioneer Press, Allahabad: 1909, p. 258.
48. *Sanad Parwana Bahi,* No. 21, V.S. 1835/1778 AD, *miti posh vadi* 7.
49. *Haqiqat Bahi,* No. 1, V.S. 1825/1768 AD, p. 639, Jodhpur Records, R.S.A.B.
50. *Sanad Parwana Bahi,* No. 25, VS. 1838/1781 AD, p. 25F-1.
51. *Sanad Parwana Bahi,* No. 32, V.S. 1842/1785 AD, p. 45F-2; *Bahi,* No. 35, V.S. 1843/1786 AD, p. 98F-1-2; *Bahi,* No. 48, V.S. 1853/1796 AD, p. 90F-1; *Bahi,* No. 49, V.S. 1854/1797 AD, p. 26F-1; *Bahi,* No. 56, V.S. 1859/1802 AD, p. 18F-1.
52. *Khas Rukka Parwana Bahi,* No. 1, V.S. 1824/1767 AD, *miti ashwin sudi* 5; *Sanad Parwana Bahi,* No. 21, V.S. 1835/1778 AD, *miti margashirsh sudi* 12; *Bahi,* No. 35, V.S. 1843/1786 AD, p. 95F-2; *Bahi,* No. 39, V.S. 1845/1788 AD, *miti margashirsh vadi* 9, Jodhpur Records
53. *Sanad Parwana Bahi,* No. 29, V.S. 1840/1783 AD, *miti margashirsh sudi* 13.
54. *Sanad Parwana Bahi,* No. 39, V.S. 1845/1788 AD, p. 48F-2
55. Thirty five camels were purchased from Mundwa fair for Jaisalmer ruler Rao Bakhtawar Singh. *Sanad Parwana Bahi,* No. 56, V.S. 1859/1802 AD *miti posh vadi amavasya,* Jodhpur Records.
56. A large number of camels were purchased by Hayat Khan, whose *Hasil* of Rs. 650 were deposited in the *sair* (A check post,

where taxes were realized by officials) but Jodhpur Maharaja ordered to return Rs. 650 in the form of tax collected from them.

57. *Sanad Parwana Bahi,* No. 13, V.S. 1830/1773 AD, *miti magh vadi* 14, p. 65F-1.
58. *Sanad Parwana Bahi,* No. 21, V.S. 1835/1778 AD, *miti margashirsh sudi* 12, p. 20F-1.
59. *Sanad Parwana Bahi,* No. 15, V.S. 1832/1775 AD, p. 56F-2.
60. *Sanad Parwana Bahi,* No. 1 V.S. 1821/1764 AD, *Bahi,* No. 53 V.S. 1856/1799 AD; *Haqiqat Bahi,* No. 1, V.S. 1821-30/1764-1773 AD, *Bahi,* No. 5, V.S. 1846-50/1789-1793 AD; *Khas Rukka Parwana Bahi,,* No. 1, V.S. 1822-1866/1765-1809 AD, p. 23, 54.
61. *Sanad Parwana Bahi,* No. 10, V.S. 1827/1770 AD *miti ashwin sudi* 4.
62. *Sanad Parwana Bahi,* No. 10, V.S. 1827/1770 AD, p. 271F-2; Tod, *Annals and Antiquities of Rajasthan,* vol. II, p. 127.
63. *Sanad Parwana Bahi,* No. 12, V.S. 1829/1772 AD, p. 27F-2.
64. *Sanad Parwana Bahi,* No. 5, V.S. 1823/1766 AD, p. 82F-1.
65. *Sanad Parwana Bahi,* No. 17, V.S. 1833/1776 AD, p. 33F-2.
66. *Sanad Parwana Bahi,* No. 35, V.S. 1843/1786 AD, p. 92F-2.
67. *Sanad Parwana Bahi,* No. 5, V.S. 1823/1766 AD, p. 46F-2.
68. *Sanad Parwana Bahi,* No. 21, V.S. 1835/1778 AD, p. 55F-2.
69. *Sanad Parwana Bahi,* No. 32, V.S. 1842/1785 AD, *miti ashwin vadi* 1.
70. *Sanad Parwana Bahi,* No. 32, V.S. 1842/1785 AD, *miti ashwin vadi* 1, Jodhpur Records; *Jagat Bahi,* No. 81, V.S. 1807/1750 AD, *miti bhadrapada sudi* 4, 9, 10, Bikaner Records.
71. *Sanad Parwana Bahi,* No. 21, V.S. 1835/1778 AD, p. 46F-1.
72. Ibid., p. 47F-1.
73. *Sanad Parwana Bahi,* No. 43, V.S. 1848/1791 AD, p. 69F-1.
74. *Sanad Parwana Bahi,* No. 21, V.S. 1835/1778 AD, p. 46F-1.
75. He deposited Rs. 700 in the treasury in the month of *Ashwin* in the year 1778 AD, *Sanad Parwana Bahi,* No. 21, V.S. 1835/1778 AD, p. 46F-2.
76. Lohia Bagsimal Deposited Rs. 1,000 in the treasury of state in the month of *Ashwin* of 1784 AD, *Sanad Parwana Bahi,* No. 32, V.S. 1841/1784 AD, p. 39F-1.
77. *Parwana Bahi,* No. 43, V.S. 1848/1791 AD, p. 77F-2.
78. Ibid., p. 78F-2.

79. *Sanad Parwana Bahi*, No. 17, V.S. 1833/1776 AD, p. 7F-1.
80. *Sanad Parwana Bahi*, No. 21, V.S. 1835/1778 AD, p. 44F-2; *Sanad Parwana Bahi*, No. 32, V.S. 1842/1785 AD, p. 34F-2.
81. *Sanad Parwana Bahi*, No. 5, V.S. 1823/1766 AD, p. 46F-2.
82. *Sanad Parwana Bahi*, No. 10, V.S. 1827/1770 AD, p. 59F-2.
83. *Bahi Khajane Re Jama Kharch Ri (Daftar Hazuri)*, No. 1, V.S. 1810/1753 AD, p. 52-53.
84. *Sanad Parwana Bahi*, No. 1, V.S. 1820-21/1763-64 AD, *miti asadh sudi* 5.
85. *Sanad Parwana Bahi*, No. 17, V.S. 1833/1776 AD, p. 182F-1, Jodhpur Records; *Kagad Bahi*, No. 12, V.S. 1859/1802 AD, *Jagat Bahi*, No. 81, V.S. 1807/1750 AD, *Bahi Jagat Aamdani*, No. 83, V.S. 1822/1765 AD, Bikaner Records.
86. *Sanad Parwana Bahi*, No. 17, V.S. 1833/1776 AD, p. 182F-1, Jodhpur Records; *JagatBahi*, No. 81, V.S. 1807/1750 AD, *miti ashwin sudi*, 9, Bikaner Records.
87. A*nad Parwana Bahi*, No. 5, V.S. 1823/1766 AD, p. 82F-1, *Bahi*, No. 10, V.S. 1827/1770 AD, *miti falgun vadi* 5.
88. Abul Fazl, *Ain-i-Akbari* (ed.), H. Blochman, Vol. I, Asiatic Society of Bengal, Calcutta: 1873.
89. G.N. Sharma, *Social Life in Medieval Rajasthan (1500-1800)*, p. 323.
90. *Sanad Parwana Bahi*, No. 10, V.S. 1827/1770 AD, p. 15F-1.
91. Rajender Kumar, 'A Study of Trade Routes of Western Rajputana in Late Eighteenth Century', *Virast*—A Research Magazine, J.R.N. Vidyapeeth, Udaipur, Vol. 2, January 2015, p. 51.
92. *Sanad Parwana Bahi*, No. 10, V.S. 1827/1770 AD, p. 15F-1.
93. *Kagad Bahi*, No. 4, V.S. 1820/1763 AD, *miti bhadrapada sudi* 14; *Sawa Mandi Sadar Bahi*, No. 3, V.S. 1805/1748 AD, *Bahi*, No. 4, V.S. 1807-10/1750-53 AD; *Jagat Bahi*, No. 81, V.S. 1807/1750 AD, Bikaner Records; *Sanad Parwana Bahi*, No. 33, V.S. 1842/1785 AD, p. 81F-1, Jodhpur Records; Munshi Sohanlal, *Tawarikh Rajshree Bikaner: The Government Press*, p. 69; Tod, op. cit, Part 2, pp. 1108-10.
94. *Sanad Parwana Bahi*, No. 25, V.S. 1838/1781, p. 238F-1-2, Jodhpur Records.
95. *Sanad Parwana Bahi*, No. 17, V.S. 1833/1776 AD, *miti posh vadi* 4, Jodhpur Records.

11

Symbolism, Rituals and Political Legitimacy in Mewar: From Sovereignty to Subordination

Sangeeta Sharma

The relationship between culture and nature was expressed through symbolism even in the early stages of human history. In each culture, a set of powerful symbols have evolved over centuries that not only have a high inspirational value but also provide specificity to a particular group. Every nation-state and society communicates its identity through a set of symbols. A social group conveys its aspirations, way of live, behavioural code, familial relationships, fantasies and taboos through symbols. There is hardly a realm, even in modern times, which does not transmit its system of beliefs and values through rituals, often projecting certain symbols. An important realm, which has a strong symbolic dimension, is the political universe. Symbolic apparatus has remained crucial in a range of political systems and movements up to the present times. Commonly, rituals and symbolic devices that communicate authority have been associated with monarchical polities in which rulers were considered divine and distant who radiated supernatural power. Nevertheless, in modern political systems too, whether democratic or communist, which are based on rational principles, symbolism and rituals have a pervasive and profound importance designed to serve multiple purposes.

As the states grew larger in size and the powerholder became distanced from the ruled, the political environment became dependent on symbolism and rituals. "Authority... is an abstraction and people can conceive of who has authority and who does not only through symbols and rituals".[1] Symbolic devices and rituals are impregnated with strong narratives and convey subtle or not-so-subtle messages about the identity of the political actors and assist in their image construction. Ceremonial gestures, rites and symbols express the importance of the office, charisma of the personality and project the authority of the powerholders in the public eyes. In a political culture, performance of rituals has special significance for legitimization of authority. It has been aptly observed that "Ritual is used to constitute power, not just reflect power that already exists."[2] In a monarchical system coronation ceremony adds to the legitimization and continuation of authority. In a democratic polity oath-taking ceremony ensures and legitimizes the position of the powerholder. From tribal to monarchical and democratic polity, change and continuity, enthronement and legitimization are intrinsically linked with performance of specific rituals.

Symbols and rituals play an important role in representing, communicating and reinforcing the ideological beliefs of the political actors and also serve as reminders of group membership or allegiance to a political organization. Symbols are used to reinforce group solidarity and signify the unity of one group in conflict with the other.

Symbolic icons and ritual ceremonies have an important role to play in political conflict and political change. Just as there are symbols of stability and maintenance of an order, there are symbols of struggle and revolution (would like to retain the terms struggle and revolution). The periods of struggle are those historical moments when the established network of symbols and rituals undergo change. The leaders of a political struggle either generate new symbols and ritual forms to delegitimize the existing regimes or they transform the existing and potent classical symbols by infusing them with new meanings and adapt them for their own political purposes. The ritual observances laden with powerful symbolism are often staged to agitate feelings and sentiments, thereby inciting men to action. Just as ingenious symbols are devised to achieve reversal of an established order, inspirational symbols are conceived to prepare men for a new order. For instance the processes of state formation and making of the nation are heavily dependent on symbolism.

Further, an attempt is made to recapitulate the temporal trajectory of the symbols and rituals in the political culture of the erstwhile state of Mewar in the region of Rajputana. It seeks to examine the changing nature of symbolism in differing political contexts. The potent icons and rituals that lent legitimacy, honour and identity to Mewar potentates undergo a change with the imposition of British Paramountcy in the region. It demonstrates the dependence of both the regimes on symbolism to project authority, honour, hierarchy and legitimacy.

I

In the context of symbols, it would be apt to examine the elaborate system associated with different native states of Rajasthan. In the warrior culture of the state, *pagri* or *pag* (turban), *mooch* (moustache), *khadag* (sword), horse etc. assumed inordinate importance as symbols of honour and heroism. The donning of *kesariyabana*[3] (wearing saffron robes) and the scenario of Rajput princesses in their complete adornment marching to commit *jauhar*(collective immolation) persist as poignant yet ultimate examples of Rajput chivalry, sacrifice and courage. Pertinently, both honour and dishonour are significant in political culture. While sharing *thali* (platter), food, opium, *pan* (betel leaves), *pagbadalna* (exchanging turbans) were considered as a highest mark of confidence and friendship, refusal and to do so was perceived as dishonourable to the other person.

Amongst the Rajputana states, the erstwhile state of Mewar, occupie an illustrious place in the history's proverbial 'hall of fame' not only as mark of respect for their ancestry and antiquity but for their persistent armed struggle against the Mughal invaders for preservation of freedom and honour.

Political symbolism associated with its chivalrous saga not only occupies a place of pride in the historical and creative writings, but has captivated the imagination of a people belonging to diverse regions, communities and political contexts over a period of centuries. Mewar, itself, has survived in public memory as a symbol of fierce pride in one's independence and self-respect as well as resistance and suffering.

Founded towards the close of the fifth century, the erstwhile state of Mewar was ruled by the illustrious clan of the Guhilots, also known as the Sisodiyas, till independence. Forced by circumstances, Maharana Bhim Singh had to recognize the sovereignty of the English over Mewar in 1818. British paramountcy over Mewar led to clear and undeniable restrictions on effective sovereignty of the Maharana and despite treaty stipulations and pledges to the contrary, intervention in internal affairs led to the dilution of the internal sovereignty as well. It was a subtle move on the part of the British Raj to preserve and sustain the monarchical rule, its outward symbols of authority and the inviolability of the ruler's person in his state. Meanwhile, the third decade of the twentieth century gave rise to popular agitation in Mewar against British imperialism, aristocratic rulers and the reactionary feudal chiefs. In 1948, the state of Mewar with its capital at Udaipur became a part of the Indian Union. Consequently, the state underwent a transition from a monarchical to a democratic polity. From being the exclusive preserve of the monarchs of a single clan, the State of Mewar adapted to democratic institutions, norms and way of life. Significantly, different symbols and rituals were employed in all these varying political contexts to create legitimacy and to mould peoples' understanding of the changed political universe.

Hierarchical political systems, especially the monarchical polities, often use potent icons or myths of legitimacy, in most cases revolving around the divine origin. One of the earliest symbols that Mewar rulers carefully evolved, as their legitimizing and identifying feature, was the myth of ancestry that bestowed divinity on the ruler. They sought to establish their supernatural antecedents not only by claiming ancestry from Lord Rama, a popular and predominant deity of the Hindu pantheon, but they regarded Lord Shiva, another powerful divinity of the Hindus as the real crowned King of Mewar. These myths were perpetuated in public memory by rituals that were performed by the kings to reinforce their divine nature, e.g. the ruler superseded the brahmin priest as officiant of the ceremonies at the shrine of Eklingji; he reserved the right to distribute symbols of religious authority to the priests of Eklingji; assumption of the title of Diwan of Eklingji; exhibition of this divine connection on official correspondence. In all the royal processions on important occasions, the deity of Lord Shiva preceded the Maharana. The shrine of Eklingji, a small stone emblem, evolved as a symbol that implied the continuity of Guhilot rule over Mewar.[4] The name of Eklingji was invoked in common parlance as well as by the ruling elite, while greeting each other. Swearing in the name of Eklingji ensured a commitment to a promise.

The Ranas regularly re-legitimated their link with Lord Rama through various symbols and rituals. The banner or flag of the Sisodiyas with a gold sun on a crimson field was a symbol that proclaimed their relationship with the *Suryavansh* (Race of the sun). In fact, sun as a symbol of their divine descent, was given universal precedence in Mewar. The main entrance to the city is called *Suryapol* (portal of the sun), chief apartment or hall of the palace was called *Surya Mahal* (hall of the sun) and to the *Surya Gokhra* (balcony where an imposing symbol of the sun was placed) the maharanas paid their obeisance which formed a daily ritual performed before every meal.[5] These served as constant reminders of the maharana's status as the sun's representative.

In addition to this, rituals, forms of worship and art forms were also devised that sought to reinforce the illustrious and divine descent. A popular mode by which the maharana sought to consolidate his identity and distinctness as the supreme and divine authority among his people and nobility was through patronization of religious festivals organized by the state. Religion became a potent political instrument for perpetuation and enhancement of the ruler's legitimacy and status. Dussehra was the most prominent a state festival in almost all Rajput states where rulers claimed descent from Lord Ram since the festival was celebrated as *Vijayadasmi* (victory festival) in commemoration of the victory of Lord Ram over Ravan, the demon king. It sought to refurbish their divine link with the deity. The Maharana worshipped the *khejri* tree on Dussehra since Lord Ram had performed the same ritual while leaving for a life in the forest. The maharana even held his durbar in a canopy fixed on the platform near the tree, known as *Khejrika Durrikhana*.[6] These festivals formed those rare occasions when people had a glimpse of the durbar (Maharana) who was not commonly accessible for public viewing. Hence, they eagerly looked forward to these splendid festivals and participated with great zest and enthusiasm. More significantly, by staging large-scale rites people were able to identify with the power and supremacy of the ruler and the jagirdars' subservience to the central authority.

Durbar, court of the rulers, formed the centre stage of their symbolic apparatus and main theatre where hierarchical relationships were symbolically and ritually defined and acted out. The word durbaris of Persian origin was introduced to India by the Mughals. "It could be used to describe a ruler's court and even the ruler himself, who might be referred to as durbar *saheb*".[7] The ceremonials and grandeur of the durbar served as an open and visual confirmation of the primacy of the ruler and also an opportunity to define the hierarchy of the Jagirdars. A prestigious ritual placement in formal durbar was pertinent to an individual's status and honour. In comparison to other states, the seating arrangement in Mewar durbar was symbolic of their parity with the maharana. In durbar, they ranked above the crown prince, who occupied a lower/ inferior seat, "a custom unprecedented in India" and granted in consequence of the stigma that came to be attached to the heir-apparent after he attended the Mughal Emperor's court.[8]

Ceremonial protocol for each chief comprised of a well choreographed and intricate process that had to be scrupulously observed by the maharana. The maharana honoured his chiefs by issuing royal insignia and marks of honour and through transactions of specified gifts which were considered symbols of honour on important occasions throughout the year e.g. horses, *siropav* (dress of honour), *pag* (head dress), *langar* (wearing gold in the feet), jewels and the privilege of having meals with the Maharana. These symbols and ritual embellishments were in a sense "barometers" or "visual statement" of variable honour and status. The transgression or unauthorized appropriation of royal insignia by any chief invited punishment from the Maharana e.g. Rawat Padam Singh of Salumber was fined Rs. 1,100 because he had worn pearls in his *kalangi (*decoration adorning the *pag*) a royal symbol to which only the maharana was entitled.[9] In fact, distribution and conferment of regalia itself became an arena of conflict and struggle amongst the jagirdars and also between the maharanas and the jagirdars. Originally, the criteria for awarding royal insignia to the chiefs were their unusual valour in the battlefield and loyalty to the Maharana but later these privileges were largely hereditary and based on precedence.

Another symbolic dimension of public recognition about which the princes were deeply sensitive was the titles and the styles of address. The titular designations of the rulers were based on a variety of criteria. Some were hereditary, self-awarded by ancestors to bolster their prestige or at times bestowed by an external power e.g.the Mughals and later on, the British. The Mewar potentates adorned themselves with numerous titles that not only replenished their legitimacy within their dominion but also reinforced the dominance of their clan Sisodiya over other ruling clans in the native states of Rajputana. The title of *Hindua Sooraj* (Sun of the Hindus) was their most coveted honorific. It signified Mewar's place of honour at the head of the Rajput clans not only due to their refusal to marry their daughters to the Mughal emperors and their struggle against the Muslim invaders but also as a mark of respect for the antiquity of their clan. This illustrious title inspired awe and respect for the Sisodiyas even amongst the British who were induced to give a superior rank and placement to the Maharana of Mewar. Due to their legendary association with Chittor and its chivalrous defense, the Mewar rulers were proud of their epithets like *Chittora* or Lord of Chittor, the ornament of the 36 royal races. They were not addressed by the commonly used prefix 'Maharaja'; instead they styled themselves as Maharanas. Within their domain, the Maharanas were, however, popularly addressed as 'Diwan' i.e. representative of Lord Shiva, the presiding deity of Mewar.

While the Mewar potentates duly cherished their own dynastic and ancestral titles, they resisted the imposition of any external symbols and appellations that were bestowed upon by superior powers or foreign rulers whom they denounced as *mlechchas,* the impure ones. The rulers of Jaipur took great pride in their title 'Sawai Maharaja' (denoting one and a quarter), a title conferred on them by Emperor Aurangzeb. At a time when native rulers all over India sought to establish legitimacy through the meaningless *firmans* of the decaying Mughal Empire, the state of Mewar abhorred and looked down upon such borrowed symbols of legitimacy.

The most enduring symbolism associated with the Sisodiyas pertains to their ideology of resistance which was rooted in the concepts of love for one's land (*dhartiprem*), sense of one's duty (*swadharma*), individual honour and self-esteem (*swabhiman*). To a large extent, it was the resistance of Mewar against the Muslim conquerors for preservation of prestige and honour that not only shaped the image of a Rajput as a chivalrous suicidal warrior but also defined the paradigm of honour commonly associated with the Rajputs. The annals of Mewar are studded with powerful and inspirational symbols in the form of heroes, heroines, monuments and even the battlefields, which till date exercise a tremendous hold on the psyche of the Indians. For example, the embodiments of undaunted determination and fierce struggle for preservation of independence, Rana Swanga and Rana Pratap; of supreme sacrifice Jaimal and Patta; of loyalty, Pannadhai and Chetak (Rana Pratap's horse); of *bhakti* and rebellion, Meerabai; *virangna* like Padmini, monuments like the fort of Chittor and Kirti Stambh and the arena of war, the Haldighati. These have emerged as metaphors for values of resistance, sacrifice and pride in one's independence through which generations of Indians have derived strength and inspiration for their struggles.

II

The establishment of British rule over Mewar produced significant changes in the political situation of this premier state of Rajputana. The British approach towards the domination of this illustrious state led to curtailment of the real and sovereign powers of the maharanas while maintaining their public honour through symbols, rites and rituals within their possessions. The response of the maharanas too was characterized by ambivalence, i.e. their desire for British protection was accompanied by assiduous attempts to preserve the visibility of their supreme status in their kingdom. The period of British paramountcy was thus, marked by a subtle interplay between the virtual authority of the British and the projected authority of the maharanas .In these changed political circumstances, the symbols and rituals acquired a renewed significance for both, the British as well as the maharana.

We find that scramble for appropriation of superior monarchical symbology assumed extravagant proportions after the Rajputana states entered into treaties with English East India Company, and later on directly with the Crown. A treaty of so-called friendship, alliance and unity was concluded between Mewar and East India Company in 1818 by which the British Government engaged itself to protect the territories of Mewar and restore those which had been seized by others during the years of turmoil. The maharana agreed to act in subordinate co-operation with the British Government and acknowledge the latter's supremacy. Consequently, the maharana had to surrender his external independence and the right of negotiations. However, the internal sovereignty along with outward symbols of authority, as also their prerogative as the fountain of honour for their own subjects, was preserved. With the direct assumption of sovereignty by the Crown, after the revolt of 1857, an era of political emasculation of the native states was begun. The Crown was proclaimed as the paramount power on whom the status, rank, dignities, privileges and jurisdiction of the rulers were dependent. The Indian states, irrespective of their treaty stipulations, were now unmistakably brought under the supreme authority of the British Crown. Disregarding the terms of the treaty, which promised to adhere strictly to a policy of non-intervention in internal affairs, the royal prerogative of the Queen and her representative, the Viceroy was expanded to include right to recognize succession, assume guardianship of minor princes, confer or withdraw titles, decorations and salutes, grant passports, sanction acceptance of foreign orders etc. This led to effective intervention in the internal sovereignty of the maharanas with little or no resistance from the latter, thus enabling the British to assume control over court politics.[10]

Paradoxically, the Crown however, sought to maintain, at least theoretically, and apparently, the undisputed sovereignty of the rulers in their respective kingdoms. To that extent, they were permitted to retain their outward symbols, rituals and rites for projection and legitimization of authority. At the same time, insignia and honorifics of the British Crown were held supreme and sacrosanct, which necessitated superimposition of the superior symbology of the Crown over the monarchical emblems of the Indian ruling families.

The Rajputana princes, who could no longer derive honour through success and sacrifice in the battlefield, sought to establish their relative importance and status through symbols conferred on them by the British. From the British point of view, symbols and rituals were crucial for enforcement and dispersal of the whole imperial idea since the subjugation of

Rajputana states had been achieved 'without a single shot being fired or the exhibition of a single British soldier in the country'. Hence, their supremacy did not receive that visibility and public recognition which a conquering power acquires after armed warfare. Moreover, the vast distance between the actual seat of the paramount power, the English monarch and his subjects necessitated powerful symbols in order to build up in terms of prestige and grandeur, so that people of native states could consider the British as the paramount power. Through ritualized attempts like elaborate rites of allegiance, conferment of titles and honours, creation of an order of precedence, prescription of gun salutes for each prince etc., the people were encouraged to identify themselves with the nebulous concept of the distant British empire.

Historically too, Great Britain has acquired a distinctive status as a nation that has conceded vital spaces to ceremonial pomp and elaborate ritualistic details in their political culture. Despite transition to a democratic polity, political culture of Britain has retained the institution of kingship replete with its symbols, rites and relics. The whole monarchical idea has remained a significant element in the popular psyche of British society. The democratic way of life has not weakened the respect and bonding of the Britons for the monarch. That's why, even in their relationship with the Indian native states, their excessive emphasis on symbols, both at the level of conferment on the native ruler and retention for the Crown, is quite noticeable.

The British penchant for a superior symbolic placement was reflected even in the vocabulary that was carefully drafted so as to project the preeminence of the Crown. The native rulers were designated as 'princes' or 'durbars' who sat on *gaddis* or *masnad* and not as 'kings' who occupied the thrones. Their administrative set-up was called 'durbar' and not 'government', which was looked upon as a superior and honourable nomenclature and was to be strictly used in reference to the British Government. Any attempt to appropriate monarchical symbols like the arched crown or terms like king, kingdom, royal, throne etc. was carefully discouraged. These terms and symbols signified the authority of the British Crown and were thus their exclusive privilege. The task of governing these delicate relations between the Crown and the native princes, which involved a minute scrutiny of the royal symbolism, rested with a small group of British officials who belonged to the Foreign and Political Department of the Government of India, and later on, came to be known as Indian Political Service (IPS).

The British defended their superior ritual positioning by maintaining that Indian rulers had never enjoyed the status of sovereign kings in the real sense of the term, "They were never at any time monarchs. What we call Indian Princes had never before the coming of the British been in the position of exercising any of the prerogatives of royalty. If there was anybody entitled to these prerogatives, it was the various dynasties at Delhi... At no time was the word *Badshah* which is the Persian equivalent of king, ever applied to Indian Princes."[11] The assumption of the paramountcy was based on the theory that the rights and prerogatives of the Mughal Emperor had accrued to the British as a result of the displacement of the former. The title of Kaiser-e-Hind assumed by the Queen in 1876 immediately after the death of Bahadur Shah, the last Mughal Emperor, was a symbolic expression of the same theory. The Crown was projected as the 'apostolic or testamentary heir of the Mughal throne'.[12]

The most prominent and conspicuous determinant of the ruler's status after the Queen's proclamation was the table of 'salutes' which was drawn up in 1857 and published in 1867. As a result of the attempts by British Viceroys, beginning from Curzon, to bring the treaty states and petty principalities under one uniform category, the salute list, although arbitrary and meaningless, remained the only basis of distinction and classification among the native states. Additional grants, withdrawal and advancements subjected this 'salute table' to minor modifications from time to time. A distinction was made between dynastic salutes, which in most cases remained constant, and personal salutes, which were an addition to dynastic salutes and a particular ruler was entitled to them during his own lifetime due to his individual accomplishments or special favour of the British. The unusually higher number of gun salutes for the Viceroy and the King of England, which were 31 and 101 respectively, signified the marked inferiority of the native states in relation to the paramount power. The state of Mewar fell in the second category and was entitled to 19 gun salutes. During Maharana Fateh Singh's and Maharana Sajjan Singh's reign, these were further raised to 21 salutes.[13] The whole question of gun salutes assumed an inordinate importance among the rulers of Indian states who desired a ritual placement above their compeers and it became a prime arena of conflict and personal jealousies amongst themselves. The British succeeded in engrossing the native rulers in such petty trivialities when they should have paid attention to more serious matters of the diminishing virtual authority. A further effort to impose the British Crown's distinctive symbology on the native princes was the introduction of coat of arms devised by an expert in British heraldry in 1877 on the occasion of the proclamation of Queen Victoria as Empress of India. The 102 treaty states were provided with coat of arms complete with supporters of cows and elephants, scrolls often with English mottoes and crests that had helms but no crowns. Maharana Sajjan Singh, too at the Imperial Durbar of 1877, received the coats of arms along with British flags.[14] Ann Morrow derisively commenting on the fetish of the native rulers for imperial symbols has remarked, "Far from feeling dominated by an imperial power, they were flattered with meaningless pomp... They were honoured by gun salutes graded according to their wealth, which made them bicker like children. The lowest was a rajah with nine while a select few, a nizam and four maharajahs, had 21; still a long way from the Viceroy's 31 and the King's 101.... They were given foolish crests and coats of arms; instead of dragons, boars and fleurs-de-lis, they had monkeys,camels and elephants as supporters."[15]

The bestowal of titular designations, honorifics and

dignities formed yet another sphere where royal prerogative of the British Crown over the native princes was asserted. The Crown tried, as far as possible, to restrict the assumption of new and pompous titles by the rulers. A *Khareeta* (document recognizing the ruler's accession) from the Viceroy enumerated the specific and precise style of address and honorifics of each ruler in full and any further addition to the same had to be approved by the Government of India.[16] From 1870 onwards, the title of 'His Highness' was restricted to important rulers and their consorts. The Maharana of Udaipur as the 'Sun of the Maharajas' was entitled to the prefix 'His Highness'. Although, within the kingdom the title could be loosely used to address other members of the ruling family, the same could not be used officially outside the state for them. The Government scrupulously avoided the use of word prince for the heir apparent and the usual practice was to recognize the local *title*.[17] Accordingly, the Crown Prince in Mewar was styled as 'Maharaj Kumar' or 'Kuar'.

The grant of orders to Indian rulers from time to time was yet another means to re-assert the supremacy of the Crown. The two Indian 'Orders' were the 'Most Eminent Order of the Indian Empire' and the 'Most Exalted Order of the Star of India'. The King was patron and the Viceroy, Grand Master of both. Each order was divided into three sections; Companions, Knight Commander and Knight Grand Commander. The first class Princes were invariably granted the highest distinction of Grand Commander. A smaller distinction conferred upon the native ruler implied punishment or insult due to serious displeasure of the Viceroy or AGG.[18]

The maharana treated the conferment of such honours as a violation of their own supreme honour as the 'ornament of the 36 royal races'. When the British Government decided to confer on Maharana Shambhu Singh the order of the 'Grand Commander of the Star of India' (GCSI) in 1871,the Maharana and the nobility of Mewar expressed their disapproval of the same on the plea that the title of the illustrious Sisodiya clan has been *Hindua Sooraj* and it was considered derogatory to accept the title of Star. The Agent to the Governor General (AGG) did a great deal of convincing and was able to impress upon the maharana that such titles were given only to the equals. Ultimately, the honour was conferred in a durbar held on December 6, 1871. Similar reluctance was expressed by Maharana Sajjan Singh when he considered it against his dignity and status to accept the order of GCSI. He agreed to accept it on the condition that he should be formally invested with the insignia by the Governor General Lord Ripon himself in a durbar to be held in Chittor. In his speech Ripon justified the grant of the order by stating that this particular decoration had been worn from time to time by the British monarchs themselves as a proud distinction. Maharana Fateh Singh was made Grand Commander of both the orders. Apart from the maharana, members of the nobility were granted junior distinction of Companion of the Indian Empire (CIE).[19] Conferment of such distinctive decorations asserted the supremacy of the symbolism of the British Crown and, by implication, consolidated its entity as front-ranking and paramount political power.

The imperialist powers have universally sought to demonstrate their aura and authority through construction of magnificent and imposing monuments that served as formidable symbols and perpetual reminders of imperial authority. The construction of architectural memorabilia by the colonial masters emerged as decisive imperial statements for bolstering and projecting the authority of a distant monarch. In Mewar too, various monuments were erected during the period of British paramountcy by the maharanas, which were named after the English Monarchs and the Viceroys to symbolize their supremacy over Mewar and register their presence. In commemoration of Queen Victoria's jubilee celebrations in 1877, Maharana Fateh Singh announced the construction of a museum which was named Victoria Hall Museum and in front of the Hall a marble statue of Queen Victoria was installed which was unveiled by Prince Albert Victor, the heir apparent to the British Crown, on his visit to Udaipur, on February 8,

1890.[20] However, it needs to be emphasized that while the Maharana constructed these monuments, they continued to preserve and project their own aura by building monuments, lakes, institutions and gardens which were named after their own person.

The British not only strove to establish the supremacy of the British Crown, but they tried to erode the aura and authority of the Maharana in his kingdom by restricting certain practices which symbolized his revered position amongst his subjects. In Mewar, the most powerful oath of the maharana's subjects was *gaddikiaan* (oath in the name of the sovereign's throne) or *Maharanakiaan* (oath in the name of the sovereign's honour). Imposition of *gaddikiaan* was a practice wherein a person was stopped from doing certain unpleasant activities. Whenever two individuals had a difference of opinion or a dispute, anyone so wishing could impose durbar *kiaan* or *gaddikiaan* on the other. The latter was then constrained to act. This rite reveals the immense devotion that the Maharana was able to command from his subjects. The British abolished the practice of imposing *aan* in 1863 under the plea that it was misused by traders and wealthy classes to exploit and harass the poorer classes.[21] These attempts to deglamourise the Maharana's image met with widespread resentment. There were massive protests and general strike in the city of Udaipur against this order.

There were numerous occasions when the maharana and the Crown representatives struggled for supremacy on the ritual turf. On the occasion of the durbar to bestow the order of Grand Commander to Maharana Shambhu Singh in 1871 the AGG had asked the Maharana to make some changes in the usual arrangements of the durbar. It was suggested that the Maharana should not sit on the silver throne and also, no canopy should be raised over his seat. The AGG used to occupy a gilded chair placed lower than the maharana's seat. The maharana considered these changes as derogatory to his dignity and he informed the AGG that his chair would also be of silver and raised high to the level of the maharana's throne.

Hereafter, this spatial symbolism was adhered to in all official functions and ceremonies.[22] The maharanas, on more than one occasion, had to accept transgression of their previously held privileges in the protocol.

The most crucial intervention of the British, at the level of rituals, was the coveted role they appropriated for themselves in the *Rajyabhishek* (coronation ceremonies) of the maharana. As far as interference in the internal affairs of native states was concerned, regulation of succession formed one of the earliest areas where British sought to assert their supremacy. They were not silent observers of the process of succession but played an important role in choosing the heir to the throne both in the actual process as well as at the ritual level. As a *samskara* or ritual, it was the most important of the *raj karma* (royal rituals) since it was "not simply a public act of affirmation or confirmation, a symbolic display of royal pomp and power. It was, to the contrary, held to be 'effective' or 'constitutive' ritual by which men were transformed into Kings."[23] The *Rajyabhisek* ceremony of a paramount or independent ruler excludes external sources of legitimization, since if the person became a king through a ritual performed by others, he was dependent on others for his power. Rites administered by the brahmins and the bhils had traditionally crowned the rulers of Mewar. However, due to clear demarcation of their respective spheres, and the maharana's own supreme political status, these rituals did not reduce his status as the direct representative and appointee of the divine forces nor did it adversely affect his political supremacy. The British not only gave a theoretical confirmation to the succession of the new maharana but also sought to demonstrate their supremacy visually and ritually through participation in the installation ceremony. In the durbar, which was held to commemorate Fateh Singh's succession, the AGG Col. Bradford, the Resident Col. Walter and some other Englishmen were also present. The durbar was addressed by AGG who on this occasion advised the maharana on various political and administrative issues. The conclusion of the speech was followed by the presentation of the Governor General's *khareeta* to the maharana, which the latter placed on his head as a mark of gratitude. The *khareeta* was read to the assembled durbar who paid homage to the document by standing in its honour. The AGG then presented the maharana with a *khillat*, consisting of robes and jewels.[24] While the *khareeta* itself as a document was a symbol that confirmed the British paramountcy, the ritual drama associated with it seriously understated the maharana's independent status.

Imperial durbars emerged as the most visible symbolic device for a ritual display of the invincibility, glory and might of the British Empire not only to the ruling classes but to the wide cross-section of people ranging from powerful *jagirdars* to the ordinary peasants. The British used the word 'durbar' for these imperial assemblages to justify their stand that they were simply emulating Indian tradition by holding such congregations. As one Political Officer Thomas Cotton summed up, "We innovated nothing. The institutions, titles, customs, ceremonials were all part and parcel of what the British had inherited from the former masters of India, the Emperors of Delhi."[25] The British, thus, strove to borrow legitimacy for their political domination by nurturing the old ritual forms and redirected them to new purposes. The durbar was now an occasion when the British monarch received obeisance and gratitude of the hundreds of Indian maharajas who owed the preservation of their monarchical emblems and antiquated rights to the might of the imperial army. These imperial durbars were held on a vast and opulent scale and resembled a carefully arranged dramatic production heavily laden with well choreographed symbols. The organization of this grand spectacle sparked off a desperate race among the Indian maharajas, each one of whom wished to rank above his compeer. The rulers competed for a higher ritual placement particularly regarding precedence in the order of seating. It also, brought out clearly the immense significance attached to symbols and their ritual accompaniments, by both, the British Raj and their subordinate partners, the native rulers.

The maharanas of Udaipur, on account of their widely admired valiant saga of centuries of independence from the overlords of Delhi, had claimed precedence over all other Chiefs of India on the occasion of such imperial assemblages. The British accepted their supreme position amongst the princes of Rajputana. In 1832, when Lord William Bentinck, as Governor General of India, visited Rajasthan, he stated, "His Highness, the Maharana of Udaipur being lineally descended from one of the greatest families in the country, his rank and dignity have been highest amongst the Rajas of Hindustan and will continue to do so."[26] When Shambhu Singh, Maharana of Udaipur was invited to the Viceregal Durbar of Rajputana princes held by Lord Mayo in Ajmer in 1870, it caused serious consternation among the Mewar nobility, who were appalled at the idea of their ruler paying homage in a public durbar, which they considered incompatible with their tradition and honour. Ironically, loss of virtual power was not so much resented as the affront caused to the projected honour of the maharana. Protracted negotiations regarding the appropriate ceremonials for the Sisodiya rulers were conducted with the AGG and the Governor General but they could not obtain exemption from appearance of maharana in the open durbar. The Maharana, however, received an assurance that he would take precedence over all other Chiefs of Rajputana at the assemblage and that he would not be required to pay *nazar* (obeisance) and his reception would be marked by all the honours to which he is entitled to due to his exalted rank.

The imperial durbars for native states all over India were held on numerous occasions after timely intervals to reiterate the imperial preeminence over native states. In 1875, an assemblage of the princes was convened at Bombay to give a royal reception to H.R.H. Prince of Wales, Edward Albert. The subsequent imperial assemblages were held in 1877 to proclaim the assumption of the title of "Empress of India" or "*Kaiser-e-Hind*" by Queen Victoria; in 1903 to commemorate the accession of Edward VII as the Emperor; in 1911 to mark the visit of Emperor George V to India. The question of ritual precedence and order of seating of the Udaipur Maharana was raised on all these occasions. Maharana Sajjan Singh, after initial reservations, attended the durbar along with nine of his nobles. In 1903, Maharana Fateh Singh, known for his bold demeanour and subtle manoeuvers for resisting British interference in Mewar, raised the issue of placement in the durbar more vigorously and categorically. He left Udaipur for the pageantry at Delhi only after receiving an affirmation of highest precedence in the order of seating. However the failure of the British to keep their promise prevented the Maharana from attending the durbar on the pretext of illness.[27] In 1911, Maharana Fateh Singh again demanded the same order of precedence that placed him above all his compeers. Although the Maharana did not confront the British directly over the issue, he used some pretext or the other to avoid offering obeisance in a durbar to an external authority.

The foregoing discourse clearly establishes that the symbolic aspect of political culture is not peripheral or epiphenomenal but forms a crucial part of political processes. The symbolic devices are silent but effective communicators of different dimensions of polity-power, identity, legitimacy, hierarchy, ideology and honour. The Mewar rulers made an extensive use of symbolism as they asserted their legitimacy as sovereign rulers of Mewar. They sought to project their authority by appropriating royal emblems as also potent divine icons as their legitimizing symbols. The preoccupation with symbols that was manifest in the native states in the precolonial era literally became an obsession with the establishment of British paramountcy. Pertinently, this fetish for illustrious symbols amongst the native rulers was perhaps to cover a severe curtailment in their real authority and power. Erosion of power was sought to be concealed by the splendour and glamour of ostentatious rituals. This was, perhaps, a psychological effort through which they tried to get over their loss of power by exhibiting their power through symbols.

Interestingly, British response to appropriation of symbols was equally fastidious. These rites of allegiance evolved by the British, at times, through a re-adaptation of traditional rituals remained central to the assertion and sustenance of British paramountcy. In fact, the whole effort of replacing and replenishing the old symbology with a new and dominant one was pertinent to the creation of a distinctive imperial phenomenon. Although, they conceded a major allowance to the native sovereigns when they were allowed to flaunt their arsenal of monarchical symbolism, nevertheless, this was probably a deliberate imperial strategy to keep them engrossed in trivialities of intricate protocol and detailed ceremonies, thereby diverting them from serious matters pertaining to actual exercise of authority. The British were able to prevent solidarity among the native rulers as the rulers competed with each other for a higher ritual placement. While the British permitted the rulers to maintain a show of public dignity within their kingdom through symbols and rituals, they sought to replenish the native state's symbolism with the superior royal symbols of the British monarch. This was done to assert, emphasize and project their own paramountcy over the native states. The excessive concern over the choice and imposition of symbols was not peripheral to the process of empire building but it formed a major element in the crystallization of the imperial idea and significance and superiority of the crown among the native rulers and their subjects.Whatever may be the gap between exhibited and real authority, inherent and projected power of sovereignty, nevertheless it appears that symbols were of seminal significance in the polity that emerged during this period and also to the status and honour of both the political parties—the British as well as the maharanas.

NOTES

1. Ronald Iden, 'Ritual, Authority and Cyclic Time in Hindu Kingship', in J.R. Richards (ed.), *Kingship and Authority in South Asia*, Oxford University Press, New Delhi: p. 53.
2. David I. Koertzer, *Ritual, Politics and Power*, Yale University Press, New Haven, Connecticut: 1989, p. 25.
3. Wearing saffron robes (*kesariyabana*) is a symbol of warrior's

preparedness for the battle and at times, implying fight till death.

4. G.N. Sharma, *Glories of Mewar,* Shivalal Agrawal & Company, Agra: pp. 56-58 & 107.
5. A.C. Bannerjee, *The Rajput States and British Paramountcy,* Rajesh Publications, New Delhi: 1980, p. 43.
6. R.P. Kathuria, *Life in the Courts of Rajasthan,* S. Chand & Company Pvt. Ltd., New Delhi: 1987, pp. 149-50.
7. Charles Allen and Sharda Dwivedi, *Lives of the Indian Princes,* Eeshwar, Mumbai: 1998, p. 170.
8. Tej Kumar Mathur, *Feudal Polity in Mewar,* Publication Scheme, Jaipur: 1987, p. 217.
9. Kanhaiyalal Tank 'Mewar Mein Samantvadi Vyavastha', Unpublished M.A. dissertation, Mohanlal Sukhadia University, Udaipur. The royal insignia and protocol for every jagirdar was specified in a document called *Rah Marjad.*
10. A well-known instance of British intervention in internal affairs was the manner in which the assertive, at times, defiant and fiercely independent minded Maharana Fateh Singh (1884-1930) was forced to delegate his ruling powers to Maharaj Kumar which in fact, amounted to his virtual deposition. For details refer, D.L. Paliwal, *Mewar and the British 1857-1921 AD,* Bafna Prakashan, Jaipur: 1971 pp. 180-265, and K.M. Panikkar, *Indian States and the Government of India,* Martin Hopkinson & Co. Ltd., London: 1927, pp. 69-70.
11. Allen and Dwivedi, *Lives of Indian Princes,* p. 68.
12. Panikkar, *Indian States and the Government of India,* p. 40.
13. Ibid., p. 40; Paliwal, *Mewar and the British 1857-1921 AD,* pp. 14, 133 & 206.
14. Allen and Dwivedi, *Lives of the Indian Princes,* p. 69.
15. Ann Morrow, *The Maharajas of India,* Srishti Publishers and Distributors, New Delhi: 2006 (Fourth Impression), Introduction
16. Panikkar, *Indian States and the Government of India,* p. 72.
17. K.R.N. Swamy, *Mughals, Maharajas and the Mahatma,*Harper Collins Publishers, New Delhi: 1997. p. 75.
18. Panikkar, *Indian States and the Government of India,* p. 73.
19. The other titles which the British conferred upon the nobility and senior officials of the *durbar* were Rai and Rai Bahadur. Panikkar, *Indian States and the Government of India,* p. 75; Paliwal,

Mewar and the British 1857-1921 AD, pp. 121, 177, 168.

20. Similarly to honour the first visit of a English Prince, the Duke of Connaught to Udaipur in 1889, the Maharana constructed a dam named Connaught dam on the Dewali Lake outside Udaipur. Similarly in 1909, Minto Hall was constructed in the Kunwarpada Palace to commemorate Lord Minto's visit to Udaipur, Paliwal, *Mewar and the British 1857-1921 AD*, pp. 183-84.
21. Prakash Vyas, *Adhunik Mewar Ka Itihas*, Panchsheel Prakashan, Jaipur: pp. 297-98.
22. Paliwal, *Mewar and the British 1857-1921 AD*, p. 122.
23. Iden, 'Ritual, Authority, p. 54.
24. Paliwal, *Mewar and the British 1857-1921 AD*, pp. 181-82.
25. Allen and Dwivedi, *Lives of the Princes*, p. 170.
26. Swamy, *Mughals Maharajas*, pp. 133, 155 and 108-110.
27. It is widely believed that Maharana Fateh Singh was dissuaded from attending the *Durbar* in 1903 by the stinging verses of a poem "*Chetavanira Chungtia*" composed by Barhat Kesari Singh. The poem was presented to him first as he was preparing to leave for the Imperial Assemblage. The composition accused him of deviating from the heroic traditions of his dynasty.

12

How Federal was British Vision of Colonial India? Revisiting Concerns and Dilemmas of Princely States of Rajputana

Nidhi Sharma

The British rule in India was one of the most complicated political and diplomatic establishments in Asia. It was based on primarily two different types of administrative setups. One, the conquest which resulted in formation of British provinces, and, two, the treaties which, first, the East India Company and then, the Crown maintained with the princely states.

These treaties were maintained through different phases. Those maintained before 1813 were alliances concluded for security of British frontiers and were of an allied defensive system. Those made thereafter recognized the supremacy of British government and reduced the states to the status of protectorate. The relationship they maintained with the British was one of the most varied in nature. Although, the treaties did not provide for any intervention in the sovereignty of rulers, yet the British policy basically, from the beginning to the end, revolved round what Marquis of Wellesley firmly believed that the British must be the one paramount power in the peninsula, and that the native states could only retain the insignia of sovereignty by surrendering their political independence. The treaties prior to 1813 and after 1813 mainly differed on fundamental questions like that of succession, interference and exercise of sovereign rights. The dynastic rulers were addressed as princes, chiefs, feudatories, tributaries, protectorates etc., their territories not as kingdoms but native states or principalities.[1] The rulers, on the other hand, treated their relationship with the British on equal basis and furthermore so after 1858 when the treaties were 'handed over' to the British Crown.

Legal and constitutional complexities continued to govern this relationship till independence. The rulers were in constant search for identity, place and status. Their effort to define this relationship in terms of international law and a clear definition of paramountcy, led them to question their identity and their place in future political set up. Quite opposite to the bewildered state of the rulers, the British were very clear about their own stand. They largely upheld their position as a paramount power but differed in methods of exercising them. Writing in 1852, Sir George Campbell remarked, 'There is no uniform system and it is impossible to give any definite explanation of what things we do meddle with and what we do not.'

Concept of Paramountcy and its Operation

The relationship continued to be guided by the ever pervading concept of paramountcy. While on one hand, the Proclamation of the Queen declared on November 1, 1858 that all the Treaties and Engagements made under the authority of East India Company would be accepted and maintained by the British Crown, on the other hand, the queen assumed the title of Queen Empress of India (Kaiser-i-Hind) which was essential to claim for herself the succession to the Mughal throne. However, such a pretension was groundless as the Crown's rights over Indian states were based on the statutes which expressly laid down that treaties and obligations made by the East India Company were binding on the Crown.[2] A make-believe effect was created by the viceroy Lord Lytton through a grand durbar in 1877 C.E. forcing the chiefs to attend it and pay homage in person to establish a sovereign feudal relationship. The Delhi durbars of 1903 C.E. and 1911 C.E.

were held to continuously press upon the feudatory character of princes. The latter acknowledged their 'firm attachment and devotion to HM's person and throne and getting assurance of maintaining their rights and privileges.'[3]

R. Coupland explains the nature of relationship thus, 'Relations between British government and states were unique without a close parallel within the British empire or elsewhere, based on multitude of specific agreements The ruler on his part, accepted what came to be called the suzerainty of the British Crown and agreed to surrender all control of his relation with other states to the paramount power. The Princes retained their domestic autonomy *quamdiu se bene gesserint*, their territory did not become British soil, their subjects did not become British subjects.'[4] The British exercised their paramountcy in different ways such as the Acts of British Parliament, Direct Agreements to extend scope of original treaties or supplementary treaties or fresh activities like railways, post and telegraphs, bestowal of titles, honours, salutes, precedence, minority rule, deposition, succession/ adoption.

Nature of Relationship Between the British and the Rulers

The states were always treated as feudatories as they did not possess right of legislation, were unable to make peace or war and their political subordination was unquestioned. No international law could apply to them. The relations between the states and the paramount power were not diplomatic but political.[5] 'We have adopted in India the doctrine of extra-territoriality.....sovereignty is divisible but independence is not.'[6] As the years passed by, constitutional development of India also began to progress. Relationship between the centre and the constituent units began to be searched and explored. Various schemes were evolved to visualize cooperation between the Government of India and the princely order. H.H. Maharaja of Bikaner, Sir Ganga Singh, in response to the Lord Chancellor's request regarding the line on which the future plans of cooperation should proceed, expressed the view that the future of India and good of Indian states lay in a federation.[7] All constitutional efforts were hence directed towards a close cooperation and administration between the centre and the units which constituted India as a whole. The princes were hitherto, aware and alerted for protection of their rights.

They presented a scheme to Mr. Montagu in 1917 which visualized a basis for cooperation between Indian states and Government of British India. The Report too pointed out some kind of federation. It also occurred to its framers that some decisions made regarding Indian provinces had affected the states especially when they were not consulted. There was no machinery for collective consultation with them.

The concern on behalf of the princes came forward in form of the Chamber of Princes in 1921 when they collected, discussed problems and suggested solutions. In 1927 in a conference in Simla, the princes sought from the Viceroy the appointment of a special commission to examine existing relationship between themselves and the paramount power and to secure consultation for an effective settlement of differences.

Hence, the Butler Committee was appointed in 1927 to discuss the question of paramountcy and to define the relationship between the two parties. The princes looked forward to the findings of the Committee. Maharaja of Patiala, Bhupinder Singh wrote to the Maharaja of Jaipur on February 28, 1928, "The appointment of Indian States Commission offers to the whole order of princes an opportunity which is unlikely even to recur. We have now the chance of representing before an impartial tribunal the manner in which the existing system of conducting political relations between the state and government of India may operate to our advantage.'[8]

But contrary to all hopes, the Commission declared that paramountcy was paramount and that there could not be any definition or delineation of it. The Committee ruled out contention of the princes that the relation between the Crown and the states was founded upon any legal basis or juristic principles. Another effort was attempted at by Nehru Report which was widely criticized by the princely order. The H.H. Bikaner remarked, 'States will never accept position inferior to that of British India.'[9] He criticized its proposals regarding commonwealth of India.

Towards the Idea of Federation

As the idea of close cooperation began to float and the idea of federation emerged, the princes saw that there were two advantages to the princes by joining the federation. First, to secure internal autonomy, second, paramountcy would disappear to the extent of federal authority. However, there were two questions before them. One, how far this federation would enable them to escape tyranny of paramountcy and second, how far would this scheme take away their sovereignty and their powers of internal government?[10] It slowly dawned upon the princes that the only protection of their rights, demands and position lay in some form of bargaining for formation of a unit. Not having a say in deciding matters of common concern actually forced the princes to contemplate a federation. The princes, no doubt, had lot of dissatisfaction against the policy followed towards them. They were equally aware of their infirmity and limitations. Their sole remedial measure was the Viceroy who was also a representative of British India.

Penetration of the national movement in princely states drew them into the vortex of its current. Furthermore, as British India slowly moved towards British Commonwealth of nations, a federation appeared to be the only possible and practical scheme.

Thus, a federal constitution with strictly limited and defined powers through consent among its various units seemed best suited to the interests of the states.[11] The princes hoped that a Federation would define their relations with the Crown.

The princes nurtured several expectations from the federation especially in terms of great improvement in their constitutional position in the context of existing indefinite claims of paramountcy. They hoped that the claims of paramountcy would be curtailed and it would be treated as a matter related to dynasties of the rulers to be of direct concern of the rulers and the Crown, to be governed by the latter. "The Federation will not exercise any rights of paramountcy.'[12]

The British. too, speculated entry of the native states into the federation as a bulwark against the rising tide of democracy. Lord Reading observed, 'If the princes come into federation of all India, there will always be a steadying influence against those who agitate for complete independence of India.'[13] It also wanted to clarify its relations with the princes. The 'Princely India' dated March 23, 1928 observed, 'The Government of India is more anxious to define its relations with the states than the latter are. Often it is placed in a very ridiculous situation between duty and friendship. It is,therefore, the great desire of the government that whereas it has anything unpleasant to do with a state it is with an impersonal body and not with a prince who personally happens to be a friend of the government.'[14] B.R. Ambedkar remarked, 'Why are the states invited to enter into this federation? To put it bluntly, the motive is to use the princes to support imperial interests and to curb the rising tide of democracy in British India. It matters not that British India is under the sovereignty of the British Crown and the Indian states are under the suzerainty of the Crown.'[15]

The First Round Table Conference and the Idea of Federation

Thus, the pressure slowly mounted on both the sides to redefine and clarify their mutual relationships. In the first Round Table Conference, it was first of all debated whether the future constitution would be unitary or federal. Sir Tej Bahadur Sapru addressed the issue in favour of a federal structure. He said, 'Princes would furnish a stabilizing factor in our constitution, their adherence would enable the process of national unification to begin without delay and British India would benefit from their experience in matters of defence.'[16]

It was a call to which the princes responded quite positively. H.H. Ganga Singh in his speech on November 17, 1930 said, 'We stand without compromised on our treaty rights and all that they involve. Those treaties are with the British Crown and obviously can't be transferred to any other authority without our free agreement and assent... The Indian princes will only come into federation of their own free will and on terms which will secure the just rights of the states and the subjects.'[17]

The speech drew certain inferences. First, the concept of Indian federation was accepted by even the isolated princely order. Second, the princes treated India as one unit encompassing the princely order and the British provinces. And last, they were in favour of maintaining both the systems the monarchic and the democratic systems and wanted full protection of treaty rights.

The Conference then decided to set up a 'Federal Relations Committee' to decide the structure of a federal system of government, relations between Indian states and British India and also between provinces of British India and the centre. Among the nine sub committees established, the most important was Federal Structure sub Committee whose reports were considered 'as material of highest value for use in framing of a constitution of India.'[18] This Committee was headed by Lord Sankey and the scheme was popularly known as the Sankey Scheme.

Initial response of the rulers of Rajputana was encouraging. H.H. Jaipur in a Memorandum dated July 27, 1931 wrote, 'I am.....at this juncture, fully prepared to enter the federation on the lines adumbrated at the Round Table Conference provided adequate safeguards are forthcoming regarding our own position and no interference in the internal affairs of the state and representation on the federal legislature which I consider necessary, is guaranteed to the states.'[19] Similarly, H.H. Bikaner, too, declared boldly that the federation was no longer a danger to the states in anyway.[20] However, The scheme did not meet approval.

The Second Round Table Conference

Circumstances changed rapidly thereafter which posed the question in an entirely different context. The government was to be changed in England. Labour Party was replaced by First National Government in August 1931. Through Gandhi-Irwin Pact, the Congress geared up to join the round table conference which was bound to bring conceptual changes in the form and structure of the proposed federation. A major shift also took place in the princely order. A division of opinion erupted. Ruler of Dholpur envisaged an All-India Federation of States. On August 9, 1931, rulers of Patiala, Dholpur met rulers of Panna and Jhalawar at Bombay and evolved 'Dholpur – Patiala scheme which envisaged a federation of two units-provinces of British India and Confederation of all states. While the Bikaner-Bhopal group wanted to join the federation directly and individually, the other group wanted to join as a confederation. The former scheme did not evoke much enthusiasm or interest from the British Indian delegation.

Throughout the Conference, the princes stressed on safeguards and rights as their condition to join the federation. Finance minister of Jaipur Pt. Amar Nath Atal presents a very pessimistic picture of the entire exercise. According to him, there were various major stumbling blocks.[21] Apart from the question of seat settlement, which could cause a wide dissatisfaction, there were difficulties in distribution of allotted seats by the States. To end the deadlock in the princes' camp on question of apportionment of seats among them in the federal legislature, meeting of the princes and ministers was called in Delhi on March 11, 1932. It included Alwar, Bikaner, Dholpur rulers and Sir Manubhai Mehta from Rajasthan. The Pact here evolved came to be known as Delhi Pact. Though the Pact remained largely ineffective, yet it was significant in the light that the princes for the first time put forward their demands—fundamentals—as they call them, in a clear and consistent manner.

Dholpur still insisted on joining the federation collectively which was strongly resisted by Bikaner. In a strictly confidential

Minutes dated April 23, 1932, he referred to the decision earlier made in the meeting of the rulers held on March 27, 1932, where a great majority of rulers had refused to consider any other details of federation unless and until equal individual representation was first decided upon.[22] The Second Round Table Conference yielded no results. As the preparation for the Third Conference geared up, the rulers of Rajasthan came out with their personal observations.

H.H. Bikaner Shri Ganga Singh observed that the rulers were attempting to smash the federation by imposing impossible conditions and so on. He reminded them that no state would be forced against its free will to enter the federation and that they should wait till the whole picture was clear.[23] In fact, allocation of number of seats was the major contention among the rulers. On October 8, 1932, a meeting was held in Udaipur which defined the mandate to the joint representatives of states of Jaipur, Jodhpur and Udaipur at the Round Table Conference. All these states advocated the principle of plural representation, i.e., large and more important states should be given more seats.[24] Bikaner felt that this concept was bound to fail. Udaipur was more anxious to secure a larger number of seats owing to its claim being the foremost. Captain Shuldham, state secretary to Maharaja of Jaipur, wrote to Amar Nath Atal on November 4, 1932 that if the question pops up in the Round Table Conference about allocation of more than two seats to Udaipur, the latter should agree for allocation of three seats to Udaipur in Upper House, provided three seats are allocated to Jaipur in the Lower House.[25]

The Third Round Table Conference

Bikaner, Bundi Kotah, Kishengarh asked Manubhai Mehta to represent them. The States continuously bargained for their allocation of seats in both the Houses. Sir Sukhdev, prime minister of Udaipur, on behalf of the princes' wanted a on reservation of thirty three and a half percent and a larger upper chamber for representation of much smaller states. However, there was a large difference of opinion among the rulers themselves regarding the allocation of seats interse. The states also resisted the concept of supervision in purely state matters and accepted only in federal interests. The said powers of supervision were to be manifested in the Crown through the Governor General. The delegation in a meeting on November 30, 1932 also made it clear that the most essential safeguard in the federation ought to be the guarantee of permanent connection between India and the Crown. It pointed out that the future federal government will not have any say in the form of government prevalent in the states and method of selection of representatives of the states in federal legislature.

The note of this Conference was depressive and lacked enthusiasm. Manubhai Mehta, the prime minister of Bikaner state summed up the attitude of rulers thus, 'The princes agreed to enter the federation with two provisions—first, wanted to know the status of their position in the federation constitution along with question of paramountcy; second, the safeguards to be provided to them.' He remarked,[26] 'As soon as the picture was completed, the princes would make up their mind to join the federation and that complete picture was promised to them in form of a White Paper which would be placed in their hands by March 1933.'After much deliberations, the following general scheme of the federation evolved at the Third Round Table Conference. A federation of eight provinces was to be formed with Indian states joining in later, voluntarily. The central federal parliament was to consist of two houses, Upper with 200 members with a representation of 80 members by the states and Lower with 300 members, Indian states contributing a 100 members to it.[27]

Soon the details were worked out and the princes stood disillusioned. In March 1933, The decisions taken in the conference were published in the form of a White Paper.[28] The Paper expressed that a constitutional relationship between the states and British India, if not defined, would endanger unity of India; the special position of Indian states was fully recognized; voluntary accession of the states was agreed upon; Crown's obligation to accept the accession was refuted; and the principle that accession of sufficient number of seats was to be a precondition precedent to a federation was accepted.

Conclusively, the princes did not favour the proposal positively which was verified by a semi official letter dated October 3, 1938[29] from the Resident in Mewar, Lt. Col. W.A.M. Garstin which gives an account of the meeting of representatives from Udaipur, Jaipur and Jodhpur.

The Act of 1935 and the Federation Scheme

The Bill which received royal assent on August 4, 1935 became Government of India Act 1935. Among its 14 parts, the second one dealt with Federation of India. The Act came into force on April 1, 1937 except Part II which dealt with the All India Federation.

After the Bill was introduced in the parliament, a committee of ministers was constituted under Sir Akbar Hydari which held that in certain significant respects, the Bill departed from the agreed position arrived at during the meetings of the states' representatives with His Majesty's government, the Instrument was not in form of a bilateral agreement between the states and the Crown, and there was no declaration or covenant on part of His Majesty preserving inviolate the treaties and agreements concluded with the states.[30]

The states employed eminent lawyers and constitutionalists for advice, formally and informally. A general conference of princes met in Bombay in July 1936 and prepared a 50 page questionnaire dealing with all the aspects of the federation to help the princes in preparing their respective memoranda in regard to the limitation they would like to propose on items of the Federal Legislature list.

In October 1936, an informal Conference was called to discuss the Act as a whole where two committees were formed-one, princes' committee and two, Ministers' committee with 25 members each.[31] Eminent members who joined this Committee from Rajputana were H.H. Ganga Singh, Manu Bhai Mehta (Bikaner), Kanwar Sain (Jodhpur), Pt. Amar Nath Atal (Jaipur) and Pt. Dharm Narain (Udaipur).

The British government then geared up to speed up the matter. Sir A.C. Lothian was appointed as additional secretary in the political department for a smooth sailing of the affairs. F.V. Wylie and Courtney Latimer were appointed as special representatives of the Viceroy to go around the states to explain the scheme and secure their adhesion. Sir A.C. Lothian was appointed as additional secretary in the political department for a smooth sailing of the affairs. Former was assigned with the task of convincing the states of Rajputana. Time limit to assign the Instrument of Accession was fixed six months from January 1939.[32]

Various bigger states then appointed committees to deal with the subject of federation. While Jaipur engaged Sir Sapru for advice, Jodhpur sought the services of Mr. Wadham.[33] But soon the time limit to enter the federation ended and it was concluded that the majority of rulers were not prepared to join the proposed federation. The ruler of Dholpur, Maharaj Rana Bahadur Udaibhan wrote a letter to the Political Agent Eastern Rajputana states dated October 1, 1937 and questioned the safeguards provided in the Act and lamented the disunity among the rulers.[34] Kota Maharao Umed Singh sent to Mr. J.H. Thompson, Political Agent, Eastern Rajputana States Camp, Jaipur, a revised draft of Instrument of Accession. He also expressed his displeasure at the protection afforded for the rights of the state and dignity of the rulers.[35] and expressed his inability to join the federation.[36] The Dewan of Jhalawar also expressed his concern over lack of information on several aspects of the federation in a letter to Political Agent, Eastern Rajputana States.

It was the ruler of Bikaner H.H. Ganga Singh who appeared most discontented about the proposal. It is also surprising in the wake of information that he was a popular enthusiast about this entire scheme in the first Round Table Conference.[37] Several issues perturbed him like protection of treaty and other rights, sovereignty and integrity of the units including adequate safeguards against subversive movements and hostile actions against states from British India and the

Instrument of Accession. He felt that adequate protection was not given and that the federal list was enlarged. In his letter to the Viceroy dated July 17, 1939, Wyllie, the government's representative to convince the states about federation, remarked that nowhere he had faced such determined opposition to the federal idea as that put up by H.H. Bikaner.

Jaisalmer complained about not receiving a full seat in the federal legislature. Udaipur's Muhasib Ala, Pt. Dharm Narain, put forward a large number of unacceptable limitations.

Jaipur durbar secured services of the eminent lawyer, Sir Tej Bahadur Sapru, for advice. The state favoured exclusion of certain subjects like the one related to currency, coinage and legal tender as they were likely to infringe the autonomy and sovereignty of the ruler. Sapru's main aim was to ask for maximum autonomy for the state. The Viceroy, in turn, clearly indicated the government's inability of granting further relaxation in terms of Instrument of Accession.[38] Jodhpur had constituted a committee under the chief minister's order to consider the revised Draft of Instrument of Accession.[39]

It was only the Alwar state which decided to accede to the federation. In a letter dated August 18, 1939 to H.H. Jaipur, he wrote, 'With regard to sovereignty and internal autonomy, we rulers naturally loth to part with them. If as a result of our joining federation we loose a part of our sovereignty, that loss will be more than made up by our gaining a share in the sovereignty over a much wider area which comprises the federated territory.[40]

Clearly, some major issues remained unresolved. The rulers had not contemplated this kind of federation. They demanded a set-up of a fully responsible government at the centre. Their major emphasis was on protection of treaty rights which the federation scheme under the Act failed to meet.

Events took a rapid turn thereafter. The Second World War witnessed major changes in India and Britain. The latter was bound to display some gestures towards the former both due to internal and international pressure. In the Cripps Mission's Report, no clarity was provided to the rulers for their future status except that the British government was unlikely to transfer paramountcy. Those who would adhere to the union, would automatically lose treaty obligations with the Crown. These developments came as an eye opener to the princes. A Resolution of April 1945, of the Study Circle of Chamber of Princes understood that since British India may become a dominion even without the adherence of the states the need for accommodating the claims of the states no longer existed.

When the Cabinet Mission arrived, the ruler of Dungarpur, along with others, represented itself as a smaller state and was interviewed in April 1946. Prime Minister Attlee's Declaration of 20th February gave the rulers an edge to set in the fence as the government refused to hand over their powers and obligations under paramountcy to any government of British India and not to bring paramountcy, as a system, to a conclusion earlier than the date of the final transfer of power. There soon emerged Bikaner-Bhopal differences, the former decided to participate in the Constituent Assembly. H.H. Bikaner felt that that if the Maharaja's group (Bikaner, Jaipur, jodhpur, Patiala and Gwalior) joined the Constituent Assembly a new regime would be strengthened.[41] The British emphasized that they would not recognize any state as a separate international entity.[42] Thus, the possibilities of independent identities was thrashed, which was clear to the group not just by the principle but by the practicality of the situation which had developed thereby. It was decided that with the lapse of paramountcy the Chamber of Princes would cease to exist.

The States' Department created thereafter roped in almost all the states through the Instrument of Accession and Standstill Agreement. Patel had earlier urged the Indian states to join the union by ceding three areas of sovereignty, which, in fact, they had not exercised under British paramountcy-defense, foreign affairs and communication.

Thus, the whole discomfort which erupted from the need to define relationships, draw lines, underline constitutional limits and clarify the nature of subordination or sovereignty came to an end post independence. Merger was round the corner, still the princes hoped that the Indian constitution would be of a federal form where they postulated the existence of autonomous units.[43]

The issues remain unaddressed. Rights and prerogatives never claimed by the Company and never conceded by the Indian rulers were exercised on the general claims of succession to the Mughal pretensions. How did the Company and then the Crown claimed paramountcy, why the rulers never gained a clear assurance of their treaty rights, why and how did the British manage to run the system as per their convenience and why did the Congress and the League adopt a stand which they did? These remained the unanswered questions.

NOTES

1. Nihal Singh, *The King's Indian Allies: The Rajas and Their India,* S. Low Marston & Company, London: 1916, pp. 152, 156.
2. Panikkar, K.M., *The Indian States and the Government of India,* Kaushal Prakashan, Delhi: 1985, pp. 101-02.
3. Speech at the durbar at Delhi (1911) reproduced in the Annual Report on the Administration of Kotah State for Samwat Year 1968 (1st October to 30th September) Kota Printing Press, pp. 5-6.
4. Coupland, R., *The Indian Problem*, Oxford University Press, New Delhi: 1944, p. 13,
5. Tupper, Charles Lewis, *Our Indian Protectorate*, Longmans Green & Company, London: 1893, p. 6.
6. Ibid., p. 13.
7. Mehkma Khas Jaipur 1932, Major Head-General, Minor Head-43- Federation/ File no. 84/ subject- Third Round Table Conference- visit of Rai Bahadur Pt. Amar Nath Atal to London to attend- Jaipur District Archives, Jaipur.
8. General 43-current/ Federation and matters concerned therewith/File no. 891-Indian States Commission (Butler Committee)/Resolution passed by the Commission of ruling princes and chiefs for suggesting the outlines in connection with replies to the questionnaire issued by the-/ Jaipur District archives, Jaipur.
9. *Times of India* dated 17.9.1928 vide File no. 3/1928. Legislation in Indian states, Cuttings related to F and P department/ Rajasthan State Archives, Bikaner.

10. B.R. Ambedkar, *Federation v/s Freedom*, Gokhale institute of Politics and Economics, Kale Memorial Lecture, Pune: 1939.
11. General-43-Current/ Federation and matters concerned therewith/ File no. 899ii) Indian States Enquiry Commission (Financial) Resolution passed by committee of ruling princes and chiefs for suggesting outlines in connection with replies to the questionnaire issued by Jaipur District archives, Jaipur.
12. Ibid.
13. R. Palme Dutt, *The Problem of India*, International Publishers, New York: 1943, pp. 108-09.
14. The Princely India dated 23.3.1928/ Head- News cuttings/ sub head-1928-32/ File no. 2/1928/ sub-Indian States Enquiry Commission, Butler Committee. Speeches and views on the Commission, Rajasthan States Archives, Bikaner.
15. Ambedkar, *Federation v/s Freedom*, p. 137.
16. Coupland, *The Indian Problem*, p. 114.
17. First Round Table Conference Proceedings, Government of India Press, Simla (1931) available in Abu Collection, Central Library, University of Rajasthan, Jaipur: pp. 32, 39.
18. Indian Round Table Conferences (12 November 1930-19 January 1931) Government of India Press, Simla (1931) Abu Collection, University of Rajasthan, Jaipur.
19. Major Head- General/Minor Head-1- Administration/ File no. 297/Subject Round Table Conference/ Jaipur District Archives, Jaipur.
20. Mehkma Khas Jaipur/1931/ Major Head-General/ Minor Head-43/ File no. 7(ii) Subject- Draft Reply of Bikaner durbar to Instrument of Accession and Items of the Federal Legislature/ Jaipur District Archives, Jaipur.
21. Mehkma Khas, Jaipur (1932)/ Major Head- General/ Minor Head-43/ Federation/ File no.84/ subject: Third Round Table Conference at London/ Visit of Rai Bahadur Pt. Amar Nath Atal to London, /Jaipur District Archives, Jaipur.
22. Kocher, K.L. (Selections) *Riyasati: Rajputana se Jantantrik Rajasthan*, Rajasthan Swarna Jayanti Samaroh Samiti, Jaipur: 2002, p. 25.
23. General-43- Current/ Federal and matters concerned therewith/ File No. 91(vi) Memorandum on general scheme of federation evolved at Round Table Conference/Jaipur District Archives, Jaipur.

24. Mehkma Khas Branch 1932/ Major Head- General/ Minor head-43/ Federation and matters concerned therewith/ File no 72(i) Subject-Federal Parliament allocation of seats in- of the representation of Indian States, Jaipur District Archives, Jaipur.
25. Ibid.
26. Mehkma Khas- Jaipur/1932. Major Head-General/Minor Head-43- Federation/File no. 84, Subject—Third Round Table Conference at London, visit of Rai Bahadur Pt. Amar Nath Atal to London to attend, Jaipur District Archives, Jaipur.
27. Ibid.
28. Thompson, J.P., *India: The White Paper*, MacMillan and Co., London: 1933, p. 18.
29. Mehkma Khas branch 1932/Major Head-General/Minor head-43-Federation and matters connected therewith/File no. 72 (ii) subject- Federal Parliament/Allocation of seats in the representation of Indian states, Jaipur District Archives, Jaipur.
30. Views of the Indian States' correspondence relating to a meeting of states' rulers held at Bombay to discuss Governmnet of India bill and a provisional draft of Instrument of Accession, Government of India Press, Delhi: 1935, p. 3.
31. Bhagat, K.P., *A Decade of Indo British Relations 1937-1947*, Popular Book Depot, Bombay: 1959, p. 50.
32. A.C. Lothian, *Kingdoms of Yesterday*, John Murray, London: 1951, pp. 147-48.
33. Major Head- General/Minor head-43-Federation and matters connected therewith. File no. 68, Subject-Federal Committee, formation of-/Jaipur District Archives, Jaipur and Draft Report of the Federal Committee (appointed by Jodhpur government) to consider the revised Instrument of Accession and connected papers, Jodhpur government Press (1939)/ Rajasthan state Archives Bikaner library, Bikaner.
34. Major Head –General/Minor head—43-federation and Matters connected therewith, File no. 91 (III) Subject—Federal and Round Table Conference, Notes of Ruling Princes and Chiefs-Jaipur District Archives, Jaipur.
35. Basta no. 9/86/ Revision of Instrument of Accession/ Kota District Archives, Kota.
36. Mehkma Khas English Office, file no. 3/3C/Vol. 1, federation-views of the ruling princes and chiefs, Kota District Archives, Kota.

37. Strictly Private and Confidential letter from Ganga Singh, H.H. Bikaner dated 29th August 1939/ Basta no. 9/ Revision of Instrument of Accession/ Mehkma Khas/file no. 3/86/ Kota District Archives, Kota.
38. Major Head- General/ Minor head-43- Federation and matters connected therewith Instrument of Accession of the Indian States to the Jaipur durbar's proposed amendments to the- File no. 4(II), Jaipur District archives, Jaipur.
39. Draft Report of the Federal Commission (appointed by the Jodhpur government) to consider the revised Instrument of Accession and connected papers, Jodhpur Government Press (1939)/ Rajasthan State Archives Bikaner Library, Bikaner.
40. Major Head-general, Minor head-43- Federation and matters connected therewith- File no. 91(iii), subject- Federation and Round Table Conferences. Notes of Ruling Princes- Jaipur District Archives. Jaipur.
41. Karni Singh, *The Relations of the House of Bikaner with the Central Powers (1465-1949)*, Munshiram Manoharlal Publishers Pvt. Ltd. New Delhi: 1973, p. 304.
42. Adrian Sever, (ed.), *Documents and Speeches on the Indian Princely States*, 2 Vols., B.R. Publishing Corporation, Delhi: 1985, Document no. 169, p. 638.
43. File no. C/97/ Jodhpur Administration/ Independence of India/ Rajasthan State Archives, Bikaner.

13

Rebaris as Peripheral Nomads: Politics of Social Marginalization and Appropriation in Rajasthan

Sarita Sarsar

The society in the Indian subcontinent is very dynamic presenting varied patterns. When politically, sociologically, anthropologically and even historically studied, it churns out various schemes worthy of exploring. The layered character of the social landscape, dominates every nook and corner of the country and invariably also makes its study equally layered. Sadly, the predominance of high and low distinctions, along with notional top-down filtration theory in relativity with pollution and purity concept, has managed to colour the social understanding of one and all. Such minimal representation syndrome also dominates numerous scholarly endeavours, particularly where Indian horizons are concerned. While the topmost stratas have managed to grab well deserving attention, the other elementally essential stratas have been passed on to shadowy unjustified corners.

This selective prejudice in social study also proliferates in Rajasthan. Rajasthani society is made up of numerous groupings but only few of them dominate the research projects. Rajasthan presents a classic case, of some communities like charan, mahajans, jats, sunars, etc. clearly showing upward social mobility, while many others like chamars, bhangis, meghwals, rebaris, etc. still run from pillar to post without any apparent change in their social standing. From time immemorial the latter groupings have been 'others' or 'peripheral marginals', unfit for any general or specific study. It is not surprising that even the official histories of numerous principalities of Rajasthan or Rajputana have either completely remained silent or have mentioned the lowest pedestal of society only in passing. It is against this very background, an ethnographic study of one of the often ignored group i.e. the rebaris or raikas has been attempted. Medieval Rajasthan presents a terminal point for the evolution of various ways of inclusions and exclusions of raikas within the mainstream social world. Study of raikas as marginal pastorals overrules more familial positioning of raikas as "Politically and socially resourceful". On these grounds my paper aims to visualize the cooperative yet differentiating space in which raikas were placed from medieval centuries onwards.

Raika or rebari community, as pastoral herders, largely populate the region of north-western Rajasthan especially Marwar (Jodhpur) and Jangaldesh (Bikaner), the two areas of present study. Historically, raikas or rebaris not only represented the largest group of livestock herders but also were crucial in the political space with their employment as caretakers of royal camel-corps or troops, owing to their long association with the ship of the desert, but also as royal letter carriers or messengers, owing to their mobile character. Both these roles warranted distribution of gifts to them and also resulted in their inclusion in various archival records. The state also extracted heavy taxes like grazing tax, travel tax, trading cess, thereby multiplying its revenues extensively.

True to our knowledge, their engagements with the settled world, especially the agriculturists, by offering services of herders and sellers of cattle dung used as manures, resulted in a prevailing sense of collective association with the physical environment, allowing them to participate in various obligations pertaining to the preservation as well as understanding of nature. It is for this very reason the raikas see themselves as custodians of not only the livestock but also the eco-system. However, despite these certain engagements, their otherwise overall level of acceptance by the settled population remains absent. Thus, while their significantly important role was recognized by political echelons, who offered them rewards and positions, the inhibitions on the part of the settled folk, accounted for their low social placement making them a marginal community. Truly, the rebaris practice transhumance, which only sometimes allows direct connection with the settled population. Also equally true, before independence, the latitude shown by the Rajput states towards certain raikas, did not designate the fate of the entire group. However, living outside the pale of mainstream settlement areas, and maintaining a low profile, does not deserve the ill treatment meted out to them. This calls for a close study.

Social and political placement of rebaris or raikas who are largely distinguished by their pastoral notions have been argued. The exclusionist marginalization of raikas, despite their ever-wanted requirement in the social world, has created patterns whereby the dominant understanding of both the groups as well as historians has dismissed them as outsiders. An understanding of evolutionary processes resulting in these differentiations in political acceptance, absolute social segregation, or unacceptability, will also engage with various survival and adjustment tactics adopted by the raikas, to evolve their community attributes of herders by developing associations with nature and also to undo some of the traditional understanding in relation to them, so as to re-fashion their social traits.

These tactics ranged from learning different mechanism of cattle herding especially by shifting from maintaining big animals i.e. camels to small animals i.e. sheep, protecting bio-diversity of nature and also learning from it, different ways to cure ailments suffered by animals and the community members alike; changing and adopting names and titles which do not draw the ire or derogatory remarks of the settled population; creation of community panchayats which not only manage decorum in the community settlements but also challenge the wrong done to them by other communities; highlighting of mythological past relating to their origin and finally developing associations with popular folk deities namely Pabuji and Ramdevji were mechanisms employed by the raikas.

The profile of this huge community calls for a close scrutiny, but owing to its marginalized placement in the social fabric, it has failed to catch the attention of scholars especially from India. Clearly, non-documentation of the raikas as a historically important group, generally stems from general prejudice of overlooking the subaltern howsoever, important their tasks may be. Anthropologically some crucial additions have been made in international scholarly endeavours but appreciable historical noting is still an issue. The hiatus between the realistic placement of the raikas through historical times and their political, social and economic associations have grounded the otherwise migrating group.

Some works that have thrown open to the common eye, the world of the raikas are classic in their approach, as they either study the group in isolation, thereby highlighting the ways in which they mitigate the challenges posed by the adverse environmental conditions of the arid topography of Rajasthan, or else they study the group with a collective approach of evolving a general overview of layered social space and thereby relegating these and many 'others' to the margins of historical reconstruction, while standing forth if not in a planned manner, as champions of an elite notional syndrome. The objectification of rebaris in both these approaches clearly overlooks the processes of exclusions and appropriations, in which not only the cyclical activities of nature plays a hand, but also the historically transmitted attitude of the raikas themselves, the Rajput states or post independence Rajasthan governments, or different social segments, which have managed to traverse through time, space and rule. A hybrid approach is the need of the hour and my paper aims to explicate the personal, political, social, cultural, economic and environmental positioning of the rebari community on these very lines. Correspondingly, step by step orientations will be made on the lines of ethnological and epistemological origins of raikas, shifting purview of royal households and modern Rajasthani government, minimal acceptance and majority exclusionist attitude of settled population, traditional environmental knowledge and its transmission through time. The attempted inclusion and seclusion faced by the raikas through time will be effectively proven through this procedural approach. Contemporary accounts along with the archival records of the Rajputana state (which have been majorly ignored by contemporary writers) form the crux of the analytical documentation of this chapter. The subjective domain of raikas will be studied on these very lines in the operating field domain of early modern and contemporary Rajasthan.

Extant work on this theme is wanting, both quantitatively as well as qualitatively. Some of the works that have helped in structuring of my arguments include.

Vinay Kumar Srivastava, in his interesting work has traced the processes of social and religious conducts of raikas.[1] He has explored the mechanisms employed by the rebaris as pastoral nomads to gain a footing inside the settled geography of Rajasthan. At the religious level while the association with folk deities like Ramdevji was essential, over a period of time renunciation also emerged as a powerful technique to move away from social oppression, an aspect that has been deftly dealt in the work.

Ilse Kohler Rollefson, in an interesting piece takes us through the journey of occupational shifts within the rebari caste.[2] He highlights the roles of rebaris as tenders of royal camel tolas, as well as messengers, in the pre-British times. But a substantial change took place after the disbandment of royal camel tolas, as rebaris had to revert back to their traditional occupations as camel herders, along with being milk suppliers.

Sigrid Westphal-Hellbusch, focuses attention on aspects of changing ethnic names and their adaption by certain communities namely, jat, rebari, bharvad and charan of north-western Rajasthan.[3] These communities in order to bypass the negative connotations attached to their names and especially developed by other communities to ill-treat them, either directly ended up changing their titles or else used certain sanskritized words along with their ancestral names.

The raika Bio-cultural Protocol report brought out by the raika community of the Sadri region in the district of Pali, Rajasthan, also furnishes exclusive details about the traditional knowledge system of raikas and throws open to the eyes of the commoners the mechanisms through which they along with their livestock have managed to survive many troublesome times, especially related to natural calamities.[4] The report portrays the raikas as custodians of eco-system and is actually like an open appeal to the general public and the Rajasthani government to recognize their traditional rights.

Neeladari Bhattacharya, through his well-researched work on growing agrarian empire during the colonial times, helps us to study the implications of agrarian expansion on the traditional patterns of livelihood and sustenance in and around the area of undivided Punjab.[5] The way the local pastoral communities are displaced owing to reduction in historical breeding and grazing lands is a crucial analysis for this paper.

Suraj Bhan Bhardwaj's work brings out the nuances of the systematized pesantization of meos and their later engagement in the Mughal state building process.[6] The process of Islamization of some of the factions of the meos is another interesting aspect of the study. With the case study of meos as a background one can also draw certain comparisons towards the shifts in the professional attributes of the raikas, as they were forced out of their grazing lands, because of agrarian expansion.

Tanuja Kothiyal's work provides new insights into the mobility and identity in Rajasthan, by drawing from a rich body of archival and hagiographical accounts.[7] The chapter especially on the Itinerants of the Thar: Mobility and

Circulation, is crucial for engaging with the pastoral world.

Works by Arun Agrawal, N.S. Jodha, P.S. Kavoori, Paul Robbins, helps in charting the course of pastoral economy in Rajasthan.[8] The way the pastoral groupings help in shaping the environment and visa- versa and how over time their activities came to be regulated through the evolving character of property rights especially common properties or scared oran (pasture) land helps us to engage with the dynamics of the pastoral world.

Rebaris when studied from imperial records were also pursuing a sedentary lifestyle. Were the changing land use patterns instrumental for continuous inclusion of certain nomadic communities within the settled economy? How far the usages of names like raikas and dewasis by rebaris central to this pragmatic effort to gain social ascendance? When did these names gain initial coinage and were these new names successful in helping them to dissociate one's community from names that have acquired negative cultural images or are vulnerable to ridicule? These and many other questions can help us to understand whether there was any substantial change in the social status of the rebaris at the ground level or was it a superficial phenomenon.

Western Rajasthan: Physical Landscape of Study

Western Rajasthan is where as the concentration of raika pastorals abounds owing to the environmental conditions of the area. Western Rajasthan more popularly known as Marwar or *Maruthali* or *Marudesh* i.e. land of death, though it is also made up of Bikaner and Jaisalmer, falls on the edge of the Thar, the Great Indian Desert.[9] It is a zone of unpredictable monsoon, especially because of lying in the rain-shadow turf of the Aravalli Mountain range.

The scarce vegetation foliage is made up of *khejri* (flowering tree in the pea family), *bordi* (a plant palatable to most livestock reasonably nutritions and has medicinal uses) and *ker* (a lefless tree or shrub found in dry areas) and evidently most of the land is dominated by pastures or commons more commonly called as *gochers* (they are pastures formally recognized through provisions in the Rajasthan Panchayat Rules of 1955, where tree cutting is restricted under the authority of the gram panchayat).[10] They also comprise of sacred pastures or forestlands called *orans*. Orans are characterized by strong regulations against tree cutting. Grass may be grazed in the areas but generally not to be cut and removed, while browsing animals are allowed to eat from lower branches. It is, therefore, the act of cutting and removing by humans that is restricted rather than the use of any particular resource. Enforcement of land compliance to rules in an oran is a complex matter. Many accounts emphasize the threat of divine retribution, and cautionary tales of divine punishment by blinding and paralysis are common.[11] These pastures are dominated by perennial grasses *sevan* and *dhaman*,[12] and despite the usage of different terminologies for the pastures, in totality they form a rich component of the land-use potential of the region.

On account of large pastures, the western Marwar region appears to be abounding with flourishing pastoral economy. Fallow dry land farming and herding dominate the villages of the region and the presence of livestock in households reflects the role of the region as the traditional animal-breeding centre of northern India.[13] Evidently as noted by Regnald Heber, areas like Phalodi, Pokhran, Malani and Sankara abound with large grazing pastures, housing scattered settlements of pastoral herders like rebaris/raikas, who reared cattle, buffaloes, camels, sheep and other pastoral animals.[14] *Marwar* Pargana *ri vigat* provides vivid references to raika settlements as well as grazing taxes collected from them. *Rebariyon ri baas* or *Rebariyon ri dhani* i.e. settlement of rebaris finds a mention in the Pargana records of Jodhpur and Sajot.[15] A number of grazing taxes like *ghasmari* (cattle grazing tax on grass), *pancharai* (animals feeding on leaves), *singhoti* (grazing tax on sheep and goats) and others collected from peasants and pastoralists alike, have been mentioned by Tanuja Kothiyal, through her extensive study of Nainsi's *Vigat*.[16]

Map: Migration Routes of Pastoralists

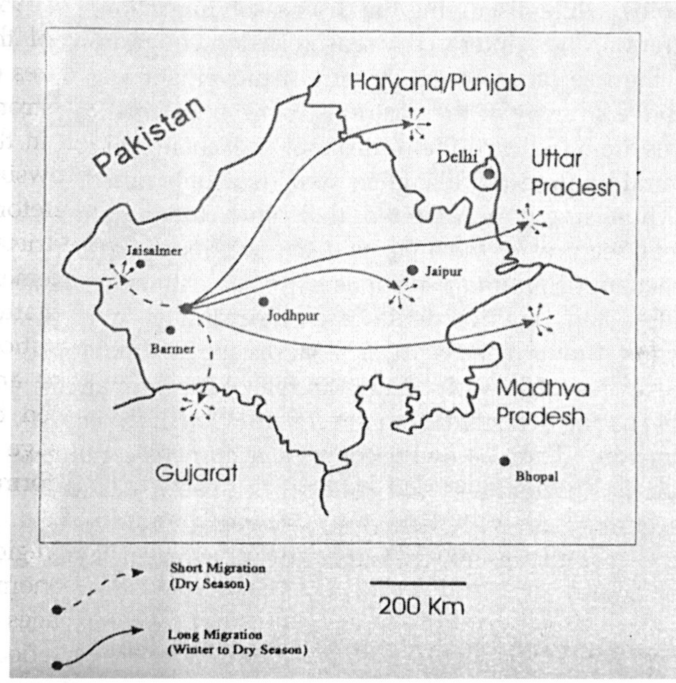

Source: Paul Robbins, Nomadization in Rajasthan, India: Migration, Institutions and Economy.

Though, *Vigat* provides evidences of settlements constructed by rebaris, their livelihood activities required long and small spans of transhumance. It is noticeable that geographical conditions like soil makeup, rainfall patterns, and arrangement of village commons play significant roles in deciding the migratory routes of the nomads.[17] The routes used by the pastoralists like raikas, have traditionally evolved in accordance to their knowledge of the monsoon and understanding of seasons. P.S. Kavoori has highlighted three routes of pastoral migration. First, the north-eastern, which relies on movement from Marwar to Uttar Pradesh, and Haryana. Second, the south-eastern, which directs the herds from Jalor, Sirohi, Nagaur, Pali and Ajmer to central India. Finally, the southern pattern, in which pastorals from

Jaisalmer, Jodhpur, Barmer and Jalor migrate to Gujarat.[18] Paul Robbins, while discussing the dry season migration, i.e. short migration, and winter to dry season i.e. long migration, argues that the rise of perennial system of movement was a major adaptive strategy of the pastorals.[19] These seasonal migration routes are budding trade routes too, as exchange in cattle and pastoral by-products like ghee, wool is widely noted.

Thus, it can be asserted that, such topographical and vegetal features of the area, as discussed above have a direct impact upon human responses to adjustments. Human culture and environments are inseparably intertwined. Mayank Kumar regards physical landscape as a tool for social constructions, by emphasizing the role of the 'human agency' as the 'nodal' determinant in the construction of the ecology of the region.[20] Thus, as will become clear humans continuously shape the environment and are also vice-versa shaped by the environment around them and accordingly create unique patterns of thoughts, language, dress, worship styles and livelihoods.[21]

Ethnological and Epistemological Origins of Raikas

The profile of the community is full of attributes that tell their own specific story. While analyzing the shifts in the nomenclature one comes across a variety of mix ups which reveal that history is continuously made and unmade and every passing day can open up channels of justifying the unjust and also glaze over identities which are hitherto not accepted by all. Rajasthan, central to the study is a classic case whereby all social classes have in one way or the other, attempted to trace genealogies through mythological associations and attachments with one or the other popular divine figure. Apparently, this mechanism of divine descendence or nearby association is virtually employed by all communities howsoever, their social placement. Rebari or raika community is also not divorced from this mythological self-proclamation. But evidently as will be made clear later, this very attempt is not easily accepted by technically those who mastered the genealogical histories especially while narrating them for folk circulation or for official writing. The boisterous attempts on the part of the rebaris have only ended up further chocking them up, as their eulogizing of nascent past has become a handy tool for those who wish to sketch out a projection full of inhumane justification. Thus glorification does not always befit all, especially those who have forever remained outside the pale of mainstream settled systems.

Historical evolutionary exploration indicates that the raikas owe their creation and ascendance on the earth to the blessings of Lord Shiva and Parvati. The story according to Mardhumshumari[22] runs thus, after Lord Shiva's creation of Nandi and its caretaker Nandiya. Parvati also insisting that her clay figure resembling a camel should be given life and accordingly a caretaker for it should also be created. Owing to continuous pestering, the clay camel was given life and Lord Shiva also created a tender. However, a twist in the tale comes when the official census depreciates the worth of raika's origins by highlighting the elements of their formation and survival. Raika as a figure got shape through dirt from Shiva's skin and therefore Shiva himself named him 'Chamad'.[23] One day raika had taken the camel out for grazing and on his way back to Kailash, he lost his way and sought protection in a roadside cremation ground. On the insistence of Parvati, Shiva lead a search for the raika and saw him sleeping in an area outside the common settlement ground and therefore called him 'Rahabari' to wake him up and even referred him as bhut as it was learnt that to quench his thirst the raika drank milk from a clay utensil initially containing the remains of a burnt body. The simplistic reasoning behind these three names stands only till mythological associations are evoked, as they were not able to earn a significant place for the raikas in the social pedestal. Infact, with time all these three terms developed specific meaning according to the attitude of the settled population. Since time immemorial raikas were engaged in pastoral activities while tending cattle especially camels, and continuously were on the move and maintained limited connections with the sedentary population, and therefore the terms bhut and chamad to settled masses indicated unclean working, as they remained too much engulfed in rearing and tending activities. Also the term rahabari decimated and corrupted down to rebari, to attain connotations of somebody who does not maintain household within the confines of the villages but instead live in close proximity of the jungles or forests.[24]

Thus understandably, these very shifts in the meanings of their different nomenclatures not only clouded their past but also hampered their future advancement. The only saving grace in the Mardhumshumari story is the highlighting of the association between a raika named Hadmal and Pabuji Rathore, a popular folk deity of Rajasthan, who is avidly followed by the raikas presently and worshipped as the God of camels.[25] In the story Hadmal is shown as an individual who at the request of Pabuji launched a quest in search for camels in the region named Lanka or Lankthali of Sindh. Owing to Hadmal's success Pabuji forever remained grateful to him, as this helped Pabuji in fulfilling the promise made to his brother's daughter who wanted white colored animals i.e. camels of distant land as a dowry gift. The conclusive remarks of the Mardhumshumari story showcases certain favour to the raikas community at large by placing the onus of introducing camels in Marwar, upon one of their popular ancestors i.e. Hadmal.

However, this leeway is not shown in other reconstructions of a rebari's daily chores and lifestyle. Some of the references like rebaris maintain unclean lifestyle, hardly take bath,[26] engage in stealing animals[27] and standing crops from the fields of settled populations,[28] and does take pride in even badly sung songs.[29] Thus, one can say that to some extent the official understanding of rebaris as a caste was clearly a continuation of broader frames in which the settled population[28] understood them. In fact nowhere in the account any reference has been made to a widely prevalent professional job of Rebaris as royal camel tenders and royal messengers. The account is virtually silent on this front and it is from certain official documents that one happens to come across these very engagements of the raikas. Thus, conclusively it can be said that the official position also accepted the raikas within the fold only professionally while socially they continued to remain outside the pale of the dominant fabric. Vinay Kumar Srivastava, in fact states that official census of India after 1932, do not even carry slightest of information about raikas and have thus further designated them as invisible marginals.[30]

Socially the raikas were never a unitary social group. Complexity defines and dominates every parameter of their existence. Both the terms raikas and rebaris are used interchangeably by others as well as even in this article. This arises from the fact that in Rajasthan, the community men had shown restraint towards the use of the term rebari as it revealed their low status. Thus the politics of community name lends another element of segregation from the rest of the Rajasthani folks. Sifts in the names, is the tool employed by many communities to outgrow their low social standing, and according to Shrivastava this is an attempt to "dissociate one's community from names that have acquired a negative cultural image or are vulnerable to ridicule".[31] In Marwar region, the community uses the term 'dewasi', meaning 'one in whom the God dwells', and is used profoundly.[32] It can be ascertained that probably the use of the terms apart from rebari became fashionable amongst those who started working as carers of royal camels and there after became a common usage name for community assertion. However, whether this transition has brought about any useful change in the status of the raikas is a questionable assertion.

Shifting Purview of Royal Households and Modern Rajasthani Government

Explorations through archival records (as has been mentioned previously too), indicate that despite being socially marginalized the raika held political and economic importance for the Rajput households and their pastoral products in the form of wool along with grazing taxes, and migration taxes furnished a major share in state revenue. Also owing to their constant transhumance patterns they acted as goods carriers, and even as royal messengers.[33] Archival account namely *Hukumat ri bahi* points that certain raika families served the royal lineages as camel breeders.[34] In the area of Bikaner the raikas entered the system of political associations after the state was established in 15th century and the Jangaldesh, as the state was formally known, employed migrant raika families to manage the imperial camel-herds (tolas). Westphal Hellbusch says that culturally the raikas were renowned as 'camel riding messengers'.[35] *Sanad Parwana Bahi* of Jodhpur, contains numerous references to raikas employability as letters and political instructions carriers.[36] The engagement of local tribal turned peasant bands into postal services is an aspect also highlighted in context of meos by Suraj Bhan Bhardwaj, in his seminal work relating to changing identity of meos as *Khidmatiyyas* under the Mughals.[37] The role of meos as 'Dak Meors' in the dak chowkis (postal stations), also helps us to understand the role of raikas as letter carriers, on account of their widely traversed knowledge of routes, survival capabilities in hostile weather and terrain.[38] The fact that raikas similar to Dak Meors were viable employable options on travelled surfaces helped their deeds to be handsomely rewarded with gifts and titles. They were correspondingly allowed to graze their livestock in the pastures and forests, officially owned by the Rajput royal households.[39] Many folklores especially popular was the character of Hadmal Raika, also point towards this very trustworthy and chivalrous role of the raikas but apparently these folklores have found a powerful source of circulation only amongst the raika households and have failed to move beyond the community. Also, it is apparent that even though the state employed the services of raikas but when a call needed to be made upon their social mobility, in corresponding return for the services rendered, even the state more or less acted the same as the other co-habiters of the raikas. The state also used mechanism of submissive designations and representations of these pastoral folks. Mardhumshumari as indicated earlier, heaps lousy comments over the day to day conduct of the raikas and rather than writing a worthy account ends up highlighting the shoddy side of the otherwise indispensable components of the royal servicemen.

The official practice of recruiting the services of raikas for varied royal activities namely for the two mentioned above, continued well beyond 1920's and ended when Maharaja Ganga Singh of Bikaner objected to some of the suspicious activities on the part of the raikas.[40] Apart from this 20th century episode of disbandment, one notices that another shift in the fortunes of the raikas came in post independence India, where owing to dissolution of princely states, they had to move under the control of the new Indian government. The period embarked another major transition in the political, social and economic status of the raikas. Not only did some of the raikas families loose out their source of income, but many others were disallowed their traditional grazing rights in the pastures, commons and forest areas since it is the state that has official claims over the natural resources.[41] It turns out that after independence the Indian government in line with its role of upkeep for the common good of all and not select few has seriously objected to any kind of encroachment over the pastures and forests, howsoever rightful medium it had been for many others. The state land distribution policies have negatively affected the pastoral access to the land.[42] Consequently, the impending fear of 'landless pastoralism' has become a fact of life for the rebari population.[43] Moreover, the selling of village common (oran) rights to private beneficiaries, precipitated loss of pastoral control over the ecosystem capital (land, water sources and vegetation).[44] Arun Agrawal, engages with the politics around the use of *oran* and asserts that the benefits from the village commons is mostly harvested by the higher castes as though the fodder requirement of their cattle is fulfilled by the private residues from cultivated fields but the raikas are extensively dependent on the oran (as most of them are landless, are always on the move and their cattle stocks need village commons only when they return from their migration cycle). But their use of *oran* as grazing land is closely monitored by the higher castes who also dominate the village panchayats.[45]

Since prior permission for indulging in grazing activities was required and getting the permission was always a difficult task, one notices that many raikas have given up upon their traditional livestock keeping activities and are grooming up for a more settled life. Whether settled life brought any rich dividends is still very much questionable, as despite settling down the practice of maintaining exclusionism has continued. Also majority of the raikas families have managed to steeler through co-terminus practices of living i.e. sedentary pastoralism or agro-pastoralism.

Minimal Acceptance and Majority Exclusionist Attitude of Settled Population

As mechanisms to enter into the fold of settled population despite maintaining a secluded outlook, the raikas have always employed certain social, political, cultural diagnostic tactics which necessitates their presence even if on the margins. The rebaris due to their livestock tending activities, had always been able to take good care of the cattle herds and therefore some folk songs indicate that for these very reasons the services of the raikas were always required by the other communities as during their busy schedules the caring and grazing of their personal livestock, could be easily taken care of, as is apparent from the line of the following folk song, wherein village folks are always on lookout of people who would take care of their cattle wealth— *Aayo aayo chomasa, kun re charasi revadeiya, koi kun ri charasi mahari gai.*[46] Also on many occasions the raikas also helped in manuring the fields of the agriculturists by either leaving their livestock on the fields or else by selling off the dung, which could be used as manure. There are many references of confinement of pastoral small ruminants (sheep and goats) within small areas of the cropland over night, so that faeces and urine could be collected.[47] For long distance mobility too the settled population always relied upon the camel carts driven by the raikas. Animal products like milk and wool, have always been of great demand in the market.[48] The traditional ailment curing knowledge of the Raikas has also come in handy while interacting with the settled population. N.S. Jodha, asserts that due to their intimate association with camels, the raikas have accumulated a large body of indigenous knowledge related to camel management and breeding and especially disease treatment, and therefore they were addressed as 'native camel doctors'.[49] It is also apparent from certain archival records that these very engagements of the rebaris also helped them to enter into the settled economy too.

During annual migrations, they continuously maintained their animal stock, and on certain occasions also settled down for few months in areas, which were full of grazing lands. Study of Pokhran segment of *Marwar* Pargana *ri Vigat*, also throws open the account of growing grazing lands, which were initially flourishing villages, but owing to increasing dryness, were deserted and thereafter served as pastures. In one of the references, one village named Baghwe remained deserted from a long time and consequently pastoral communities, relying upon water drawn from a well, settled down in the area i.e. *Kal- dukal tala jape (water is taken from well) tare govli kahd-char log (pastorals), drav (livestock) chaare (grazing) tin ri charaaye aaye base.*[50] The following phrase also, exemplified the mixed pastoral and sedentary associations, *Gaon Devdo- 10 Rs) unnbaab ra, 14 Rs) rewara ne laagta v.s. 1869 ra baras me rebari kitra ek mar gaya haume ghar 3 teena re 10 Rs)*[51] i.e. "the community of rebaris living in village Devra of Pargana Siwana of Marwar, was paying 14 rupees as grazing tax (uunbaab), but due to deaths of few members the community, there was considerable decline in the ratio of Rebari population and therefore the tax was reduced to 10 rupees".

The above references of certain mixing between raikas and the settled population was however not always peaceful and evidently due to certain possible feuds Maharaja Ganga Singh in the years after 1920, also displaced the raikas from many grazing pockets of Bikaner. Evidently it was pointed out that raikas in order to settle scores with certain agriculturists in the villages they resided deliberately left their livestock to graze on the fields containing standing crop and thereby ended up destroying the crop. This became a major cause of tussle and further pushed them to the margins.[52]

Further, the process of expansion and intensification of agriculture at the cost of the pastoral activities has in fact hampered the process of co-habitation. During both pre-colonial and colonial setups, as the grazing lands were curtailed, the area under agriculture was increased. Though it is true from some cases that pastoralists like raikas were forced into agro-pastoralism, on account of changes in the pastoral economy as a consequence of agrarian expansion.[53] The induction of the raikas into agricultural activities was not as promising as was the case of jats and meos. As pointed out by Suraj Bhan Bhardwaj, the process of peasantization of meos in Mewat proved very beneficial, as some of them rose to very powerful positions during the process of state formation under Mughal.[54] Though, the time frame of study of both the cases are different but common to them are process of discontinuation of traditional activities (banditry in the case of meos) and introduction to settled peasant life. While, the enterprising communities of jats and meos managed to change their social standing, the raikas on the contrary faced relocation and resettlement[55] on account of about 30-50 percent increases in arable land in both colonial as well as post-independent India.[56] Neeladari Bhattacharya in his interesting study on the rise of 'canal colonies' in undivided Punjab, articulates that diverse traditional customs and livelihood related to land use were reshaped to create a new agrarian world.[57] Exemplifying the argument he discusses about the decrease in camel breeding by raikas around the Kumbhalgarh sanctuary (due to protection of traditional pastures) and Indira Gandhi Canal (on account of transformation into farmlands).

Evidently, the raikas also faced displacement on account of reduced demand of pastoralist cattle produce in dairy business in the post-independent India, as farmer owned fodder eating dairy cattle is considered better and healthier option than the open land foraging cattle of raikas.[58] Extension of agriculture has also narrowed their traditional transhumance routes resulting on many occasion conflicts with the settled masses that see them as burdens.[59] Long range migration has become more difficult due to enclosure of forest common lands and relegation of many community lands to the legal status of 'revenue waste land'.[60] Due to reduction in grazing lands it is seen that migration beyond Rajasthan is increasing, a fact studied by P.S. Kavoori, who discusses 'pull factors', i.e. opening of grazing opportunities on the stubble of newly irrigated fields in neighboring states especially Haryana.[61]

Thus it can be justifiably argued that certain occasions of associations did prove crucial to the economy of the settled world but was not equally good for raikas. In fact nowhere these engagements allowed the rebaris to enjoy any shift in their social status. To some extent their counting amongst the scheduled tribe groups in contemporary times, without even being able to claim any justified share in the reservation policies, clearly shows that the changing times, and even the changing governments have not been able to secure them positions of worth, as the notional attitude of differentiation still largely dominates the larger population. It is because of these very reasons that beyond the political and social level of acceptability, it is the traditional knowledge base of the Raikas that has stood forth as the major factor behind the continuous survival and evolution of the raikas as a community.

Traditional Environmental Knowledge and Its Transmission Through Time

As pastorals, the raikas have always been able to overcome some of the challenges that have been posed by nature, particularly in the semi arid zones of Rajasthan. Their continuous mobility and seeking of shelter in the forested areas may have drawn the ire of all the other settled communities, but for the raikas per say this has proved to be a boon. Associations with the animals and vegetations of forests, made them evolve traits through which they could easily not only secure themselves from any attack or diseases in forested areas but also in the long run themselves emerged as the custodians of the forests. Tactics of survival learnt in forest residing periods has also allowed them to evolve food security mechanisms in times of drought. Also since for them livestock and the animals are the centre of their very existence, they as a community hardly engage in animal killing or sacrifice and are largely renowned for their vegetarian ways.

The consistent engagements with nature have created a channel of exclusive knowledge through which the raikas have evolved means of engaging in selective breeding of sturdy livestock, who can easily withstand the dry Rajasthan environment.[62] The animal genetic diversity these livestock embody enables the raikas to respond to the changes in the natural environment. Some of the popular livestock varieties namely, nari cattle, kankrej cattle, boti sheep, bhagli sheep, sirohi goat, marwari goat, and dromedary camels are the stocks that have been specifically developed by the raikas and these animals are sturdy and healthy enough to survive natural calamities, as by keeping the changing environmental patterns in mind these stocks have been created through cross- breeding. Also since most of the decisions central to these livestock evolving tactics are taken through proper community panchayats, one can clearly say that the systems of control focuses on a proper sync with nature.[63] Distinguished environmental understanding of the raikas placed them highly on the platform of the knowledge system, owing to proximity with day-to-day mediums to cure both common and uncommon diseases affecting the larger human and animal population, thereby bringing them closer to the settled life. Ethno-veterinary knowledge amassed and evolved through centuries of experience of animal tending has also resulted in the evolution of extensive local treatment systems among these pastoral herders. This knowledge decimating down to all without gender differentiation comes in handy when the animals are struck with diseases or illness.

Unfortunately, the intricate community-embedded mechanisms for managing animal genetic resources and evolved ethno-veterinary knowledge of the raikas, have a low visibility to outsiders. Accordingly, the rhetoric emanating from formal institutions dealing with the livestock sector decries livestock breeders as backward.[64] In contrast I having studied, that the traditional patterns of raikas' survival tactics, totally agree with Rollfsen's premise, that states should support dryland communities through better infrastructure, services, animal health care, marketing opportunities and other interventions which would make a significant contribution to both poverty elevation and food security on one hand as well as to the conservation and sustainable management of animal genetic resources.[65]

It is on these very lines we notice that a strategic attempt was made by the raika community around the Sadri area in Pali district of Rajasthan in June 2009, to make their bio-cultural importance noted to the larger public and the government alike. With the support of the Lokhit Pashu Palak Sansthana and the League for Pastoral Peoples and Endogenous Livestock Development, the raika community through six days community panchayat, reached certain decisions, in order to reclaim their stake in the grazing rights and forests custodianship and reproduced the very same in the form of a published protocol report. The very same bio-cultural protocol report, has been utilized to reach an understanding of the personal perspective of the raikas, while shifting their occupational base, from early modern to contemporary times and how they have tried to reignite their crucial associations with nature. The protocol report furnishes the following crucial details.

With the dissolving of royal presidencies and the merging of these territories within the mainstream Indian governmental domain, the royal tolas were disbanded, leading to the curtailment of only few mechanisms employed by the raikas to maintain their standard of livelihood and standards of social circulation. Also even when the royal camel herds came under the upkeep of the raikas, their means to maintain them further diminished with decreasing pastures and reduced access to forested grazing lands. The traditional knowledge base and the role of the raikas as the custodians of biodiversity have gone for a toss or has been badly impacted. Some of the policies framed in the 21st century namely, "the biological diversity act of 2002 and the biodiversity rules of 2004; the scheduled tribes and other traditional forest dwellers act 2006; the national policy for farmers, have indeed jotted down mechanisms through which biodiversity and its protectors can be protected but have failed to attain much long term impact. The traditional livelihood of these indigenous nomadic pastoralists is based upon their access to forests, guchar (village communal grazing land) and oran (sacred groves attached to temples) and the shrinkage of rights to rely upon them has stood forth not only in cutting upon the specific provisions enjoyed by the community but also has inadvertently impacted the biological systems of self-replenishments. The exclusion of these communities from forested lands is changing the ecosystem and leading to degraded ecology. Control over livestock grazing has culminated in abated growth of forest foliage leading to sudden fires resulting in disequilibrium. The discontinuation of their traditional role as custodians and protectors of forests and forests animals has resulted in unchecked and even unreported incidences of illegal poaching, illegal logging etc. If the process of removal goes unabated, sooner or later, indeed the desert lands will spread to many newer frontiers but the keepers to secure the ecology of this very essential system will be nowhere to be seen.

Religious Affiliations of Raikas

While traditional environment knowledge of the raikas allowed them to develop good ties with the ecosystem, culturally symbolic religious engagements especially relating to their participation in the folk cult of popular deities Pabu and Ramdev pir, allowed them to evolve their spiritual self. The fact that raikas are vegetarian and consider their livestock crucial for survival, worshipping of Ramdev and Pabuji also is closely related to cattle protecting powers of these deities. As indicated previously the Pabuji had close linkages with the raika named Hadmal and together they introduced camels in Marwar. The association between raikas and Ramdevji can be traced to latter's' lifetime itself as is indicated in the following reference and this has become the major reason for his veneration—*Utho Raika bira tod pilano, gad pugal bhal jaae.*[66] Here a man of the raika community is portrayed as the close ally of Ramdev, who had appointed him to carry out certain tasks. Since the cattle herd is the main scope of incorporation, the association with Ramdevji was expected. Many references from Ramdev's bani's clearly indicate that Ramdevji, was a cattle protector and he was against their indiscriminate killing.

These deities who are also equally venerated by the agriculturists caste and many other lowly placed communities of Rajasthan, have emerged has channels if not full- proof, through which the raikas could have association levels with the settlers. The annual fairs conducted at the shrine of these two deities at Kolu in Jodhpur and Ramdevra in Jaisalmer, are from historical times sites for cattle fairs too. The stock sold in these fairs are generally provided by the raikas and while providing revenue to the state, the fairs also generate opportunity for the communities of agriculturists to get hold of the best bullocks for their daily field work. Also certain communities procure sheep, goats, and cows, to fulfill the need of their daily milk consumption. However, it is sad that despite these superior though familiar associations, the unsettled world of the raikas could never catch the appreciating eye of contemporary co-habitors. Their wandering nature has culminated in reduction of their strategic importance to the larger political and social classes and has relegated them outside settled space.

From the above discussions, it can be concluded that time and governments have changed in Rajasthan, but the logistics of managing social space has the remained same. The dominant communities continue to enjoy all benefits while 'others' have been further pushed to the margins of oblivion. The migratory pastoralists of Rajasthan are conceived as marginal people that are bound by traditions and unwilling to change and this perception is shared by much of the rural, urban and the official population. Pastoralists seem to most people to be an outdated, outmoded remnants of specialized adaptations of risky environment. Such views conflate the demise of pastoralism. Each pastoral group represents a single small community and more often than not forms an isolated whole, being a homogenous more or less self-sufficient unit retaining some distinctive qualities.[67] The raikas, in particular have the reputation of being the most "socially-backward", caste. Analogous to their marginalization from the mainstream of social and political processes, pastoralists also seem to suffer a marginalization within the scholarly imagination. Age-old inhibitions are slow to die down and in the long run also implicate the way the coming generations too accept things. Raikas as a community face a two-pronged challenge. Despite leading a semi-settled life their inclusion within the dominant fold is far from reality, and also owing to limited sedentary lifestyles, the young ones from the community are moving away from the customary traditions of herding and are drawn towards life in urban centres. The taboo of belonging to marginal strata still plagues their social, economic growth.

However, one can easily discern that raikas as a community despite several super-imposed political restrictions, social segregations and financial issues has managed to carve a niche for itself. Truly, the raikas have been outnumbered by those who wish their overall extinction and fail to recognize their bio-cultural significance. But the spirited self of the community at large has allowed them to survive all odds, be it social, political and environmental. As the anecdote goes, "Facing of hardships and challenges can make a man come out as a strong individual", we also find that the raikas have also been able to outgrow their unjust social placement. Their reluctance to give up the old ways, their tenacity in sticking to time honoured customs, and their refusal to abandon old patterns of animal production, which also has up to now conserved what is left of Rajasthan's indigenous animal genetic resources, has allowed them to rise above all odds. In view of Rajasthan's frequent droughts and rapidly depleting ground water supplies, pastoralism probably represents by far the most sustainable land-use option. It is also interesting to observe that a binary ecosystem embracing both pastoralism and agriculture may at times permeate groups and even families.[68] However, in case of rebaris the engagement with agriculture is a temporary process largely catering to fulfill the requirement of households when, selective seasons of settlement are active. On the whole, raikas are more renowned for their control over cattle and sale of sheep, goats and camel and becomes central mechanism of employability. The raikas also keep their herds in the fields of agriculturists and provide dung on the field, which is used as manure. These two are the rarest means through which connections are worked between traditional nomads and settlers.

NOTES

1. Vinay Kumar Srivastava, *Religious Renunciation of Pastoral People*, Oxford University Press, Delhi: 1997.
2. Ilse Kohler Rollefson, "From royal camel tenders to dairymen: Occupational changes within Raikas", in *Desert, Drought and Development*, eds. Rakesh Hooja and Rajendra Joshi, Rawat Publications, Jaipur: 1999, pp. 305-15.
3. Sigrid Westphal-Hellbusch, "Changes in the Meaning of the Ethnic Names as Exemplified by the Jat, Rabari, Bharvad and Charan in Northwestern India", in *Pastoralists and Nomads in South Asia*, eds. Lawrence Sadia Leshnik and Gunther-Dietz Sontheimer, Germany: 1975, pp. 117-38.
4. *Raikas Bio-cultural Protocol Report*, Lokhit Pashu Palak Sansthan, Sadri; District Pali, Rajasthan. 8-13 June, 2009.
5. Neeladari Bhattacharya, *The Great Agrarian Conquest—The Colonial Reshaping of Rural World*, Permanent Black, Ranikhet: 2018.

6. Suraj Bhan Bhardwaj, *Contestations and Accommodations: Mewat and Meos in Mughal India*, Oxford University Press, Delhi: 2016.
7. Tanuja Kothiyal, *Nomadic Narratives—A History of Mobility and Identity in the Great Indian Desert*. Cambridge University Press, Delhi, 2016, pp. 121-59.
8. Arun Agrawal, "Shepherds and their Leaders: Among the Riakas of India: A Principal-Agent Perspective", *Journal of Theoretical Politics*, Vol. 9(1), 1997, pp. 235-63; N.S. Jodha, *Life on the Edge: Sustaining Agriculture and Community Resources in Fragile Environments*, Oxford University Press, Delhi: 2000; and Paul Robbins, "Authority and Environment: Institutional Landscapes in Rajasthan, India", *Annals of the Association of American Geographers*, Vol. 88, 1998, pp. 410-35.
9. James Tod, *Annals and Antiquities of Rajasthan*, Vol. 2, Rupa & Co., Delhi: 1997.
10. Robbins, "Authority and Environment: Institutional", p. 419.
11. Ibid.
12. Ibid., p. 414.
13. Ibid., pp. 414-15.
14. R. Heber, *Narrative of a Journey through the Upper Provinces of India from Calcutta to Bombay (1821-25)*, Vol. 2, William Clowes and Sons, London: 1944, p. 34.
15. Muhanta Nainsi, *Marwar* Pargana *ri Vigat*, Vol. 1, Rajasthan Oriental Research Institute, Jodhpur: 1986, pp. 227, 405.
16. Kothiyal, *Nomadic Narratives*, p. 136.
17. G.R. Gowane, "Migration Pattern of Desi Sheep of Gujarat", *Journal of Livestock Biodiversity*, Vol. 8, 2018, pp. 16-19.
18. Kothiyal, *Nomadic Narratives*, pp. 42-43.
19. Paul Robbins, "Nomadization in Rajasthan, India: Migration, Institutions, and Economy", *Human Ecology*, Vol. 26, 1998, pp. 87-112.
20. Mayank Kumar, *Monsoon Ecologies: Irrigation, Agriculture and Settlement Patterns in Rajasthan during the Pre-Colonial Period*, Manohar, Delhi: 2013.
21. Paul Robbins, "Eroding Cultures and Environments: What a Rapidly Changing Earth Means for the Richness of Human Experience", *Georgetown Journal of International Affairs*, Vol. 16, 2015, pp. 133-34.
22. *Report Mardhumshumari Raj Marwar, 1891 Census Report of*

Marwar, Shri Jagdishsingh Gehlot Shodh Sansthan, Jodhpur: 1997, pp. 567- 579.

23. Ibid., p. 568.
24. Ibid., p. 570.
25. Ibid., p. 569.
26. Ibid., p. 571.
27. Ibid., p. 572.
28. Ibid., p. 573.
29. Ibid., p. 577.
30. Srivastava, *Religious Renunciation….*, p. 7. He further opines that presently no departments, government or otherwise have any record of total number of raikas, either in Rajasthan or wholly in India.
31. Ibid., p. 12.
32. Westphal-Hellbusch, "Changes in the Meaning ...", p. 119.
33. Rollefson, "From royal camel tenders to dairymen...", pp. 305-15.
34. Satish Chandra, Raghubir Sinh, and G.D. Sharma (eds.), *Marwar Under Jaswant Singh (1658-1678): Jodhpur Hukumat Ri Bahi*, Manohar Publications, Delhi: 1976.
35. Westphal Hellbusch, "Changes in the Meaning ...", pp. 124-28.
36. *Sanad Parwana Bahi*, No. 11, VS1828/1771CE and No. 12, VS1829/1772CE, Rajasthan State Archives, Bikaner.
37. Bhardwaj, *Contestations and Accommodations*, pp. 124-34.
38. Ibid.
39. Raika Bio-cultural Protocol Report, pp. 1-24.
40. Shrivastava, *Religious Renunciation….*, p. 14
41. Mayank Kumar, "Claims on Natural Resources: Exploring the Role of Political Power in Pre-Colonial Rajasthan, India," *Conservation and Society*, Vol. 3, 2005, pp. 134-49.
42. Richard P. Cincotta and Ganesh Pangare, "Population Growth, Agricultural Change and Natural Resource Transition: Pastoralism amidst the Agricultural Economy of Gujarat", *A collection of papers from Gujarat and Rajasthan*, pp. 17-35. (Available on Google pdf's).
43. Ibid., pp. 17-35.
44. Ibid.
45. Arun Agrawal, "I don't need it, but you can't have it: Politics on

the Commons", *A collection of papers from Gujarat and Rajasthan*, pp. 36-55. (Available on Google pdf's).

46. Krishna Mohan, "Rajasthan ke pashu sambandhit gram geet", *Shodh Patrika*, Vol. 4, 1951, pp. 178-86.
47. Cincotta, "Population Growth, Agricultural Change...", pp. 17-35.
48. Kothiyal, *Nomadic Narratives...*", pp. 137-44.
49. Jodha, *Life on the Edge: Sustaining Agriculture....*
50. Muhanta Nainsi, *Marwar* Pargana *ri Vigat*, Vol. 2, Rajasthan Oriental Research Institute, Jodhpur: 1986, p. 342.
51. Chain Vansur, *Marwar* Pargana *ri Farsat-post 18th century*, Rajasthani Shodh Sansthan, Jodhpur: 2005, p. 59.
52. Shrivastava, *Religious renunciation...*, p. 14.
53. Cincotta, "Population Growth, Agricultural Change...", pp. 17-35.
54. Bhardwaj, *Contestations and Accommodations*, pp. 93- 134.
55. Ibid., pp. 17-35.
56. Jodha, *Life on the edge...*
57. Bhattacharya, *The Great Agrarian Conquest*.
58. Cincotta, "Population Growth, Agricultural Change...", pp. 17-35.
59. Gowane, "Migration pattern of desi sheep of Gujarat", pp. 16-19.
60. Robbins, "Eroding Cultures and Environments.
61. Rollefson, "Pastoralism in Western India; P.S. Kavoori, *Pastoralism in Expansion: The Tranhuming Herders of Western Rajasthan*, Oxford Uuniversity Press, 1999.
62. Raikas Bio-cultural Protocol Report, p. 4.
63. Arun Aggarwal, "Shepherds and their Leaders: Among the Riakas of India: A Principal-Agent Perspective", *Journal of Theoretical Politics*, Vol. 9, 1997, pp. 235-63.
64. Richard Armonia and Sussane Gura, *Experiences in Farmer's Biodiversity Management: Report on the International Workshop on Animal and Plant Genetic Resources in Agriculture*, Germany: 2001, p. 52.
65. Iise Kohler Rollefson, *Building an International Legal Framework on Animal Gentic Resources*, Germany: 2005, p. 4.
66. Harzi Bhatti, *Ramdevji ro Badhawo*, Granthak No. 139, Anup Sanskrit Library, Bikaner.

67. M.L. Murthy, "Prehistoric Background to Pastoralism in the Southern Deccan in the Light of Oral Traditions and Cults of Some Pastoral Communities", in *Essays on Religion, Literature and Law*, (eds.) Gunther Dietz Sontheimer, Aditya Malik et al, Manohar, Delhi: 2004.
68. Ibid, p. 159.

14

Native Constructs and the Colonial Gaze: Social Identities of the Bishnois

Neekee Chaturvedi

In the wake of recent awareness of environmental challenges, the bishnois of Rajasthan are often described as the first eco-warriors of the world. Their eco-friendly tenets were devised more than five hundred years ago but are celebrated today by the global community. Not long ago were they described as "unusually quarrelsome and given to use bad language."[1] The Lieutenant Governor blamed the bishnois for loss of face. "Though recruiting was thrown open to the bishnois, very few came forward and I am afraid those who were enrolled a soon deserted. My face was blackened by this failure, but I trust it is not too late for the bishnois to redeem their good name."[2] It is reflected in the official records that their environmental concerns were not enough to endear them to the ruling elites. Quite often they had to take cudgels against them and their practices were much misunderstood.

This chapter seeks to examine the accounts about the bishnois focusing largely on the colonial enterprise and analyzing them with the perspective contained in the community's popular literature. Some of this analysis also seeks to understand the process of formation of social identity of the bishnois and how the pre-modern state's and colonial perspectives contributed to it. The literature of bishnois survived through oral transmission in regional dialect, a form retained when they were compiled in written form. Even a cursory perusal clarifies that the ecological commitment of the bishnois has its origins in local needs and topographic context of the Thar Desert. It originated much earlier than the present environmental crisis and must have posed challenges for expanding imperial powers in the region fifteenth century onwards. Nevertheless, the practices of sustainable livelihood gained popularity with common people and the bishnoi sect thrived as a folk religion and folk community. Their sacrifices, solidarity, and sustained community ethos find an unbridled mention in their own accounts unlike state-supported histories. Conventionally, the historians working on pre-modern Rajasthan explored official documentation, chronicles, records, normative texts, coins, inscriptions etc. The efforts to engage with oral and folk narratives have been few and far between. The meta-narratives evolving from such an approach form part of Rajput-centric historiography in which many events, episodes and cultural practices significant in the oral narratives of marginal communities like the bishnois remained insignifcant. A careful examination of some facets mentioned in the narratives of bishnois, originating in an oral tradition, is essential to understand the collective identity manifested by the community. Zaidi observes, "Religious history in pre-modern South Asia is quite complex. We need to go not only beyond Hinduism and Islam, but also beyond the well-known Sufi orders and bhakti sects."[3] Bishnois manifest the creation of a unique religious paradigm based on conservation of water and vegetation but their own understanding and the perception of colonial enterprise preserved, shaped, and shifted their social identities.

While the community tries to uphold its values and action in glory, the colonial accounts by the British seem to struggle with their unique existence. The imperial gaze of the British passed through the lens of their understanding of Indian society comprising of Hindus and Muslims and communities like bishnois and their practices were made to pass through one prism or the other to fit into some category of classification. The census reports and gazetteers give us an outsider perspective of the colonial power.

It is important to understand the origin and socio-economic-political contexts of both the popular literature created by bishnois and ethnographies produced by the British Raj. By looking at both the accounts with a special focus on the colonial anthropology, we are trying to inquire, how the bishnoi identity develops and gets crystallized as a separate caste and how the blurred boundaries of caste become inflexible and distinct; how popular literature creates a perception of the community for itself and the society it thrived in; and how 'the gaze of the west' impacts 'the framings of the east'.[4] Cohn, Dirk and Fuller have successfully questioned the census-based view of caste, that rested on seeing the system as one of separate castes to be counted and classified[5] and Peabody laments the neglect of indigenous sources and native agency in knowledge creation[6] while Samarendra posits that 'the birth of caste is directly linked with the census operations in colonial India'.[7] An analysis of colonial census operations in India provides key information of the colonial gaze because the British considered caste and religion as sociological keys to understand Indian people. Cohn perceives the importance of the colonial census data in two ways—one, in effects on consciousness of caste, and second in being a major source in shaping the scholarship on caste.[8] This paper is also an attempt to underscore stages of knowledge-making and the transformative impact of accounts with insider and outsider perspectives on social reality and to present bishnoi identities in process when they were being created, reinforced, and modified.

Origins: Ecology over Divinity?

Religious sects like the bishnois have played an important role in the formation of regional culture but the region has impacted the development and nature of cults. 'Every human collectivity has a sense of place, a subjective connection to its natural and man-made environment, with its physical features, institutional and social patterns, historical traditions and cultural landscapes'.[9] Ecologically sustainable world view is an integral part of the origin and existence of the bishnois with a due regard for the local context of desert conditions. The bishnoi community came into existence as a result of commitment to sustainable environmental practices. Bishnoi emerged as a community where the guiding world view can be termed 'faith-based ecology'. The word religion is not applicable to their world view as ecology is their *dharma*—an obligatory sense of duty that binds all the members. Faith in the context of bishnois is a set of 29 principles, ecology being their central theme. Thus, the most dominant identity that comes to fore in the present scholarly discourse is ecological.

The ecological identity of the bishnois is while not unrepresentative but as a sole projection is an offshoot of more recent environmental concerns and shifts in understanding of community in development studies. As anthropologists begin to pay greater attention to the historical experiences of 'people without history'[10], it has become increasingly obvious that if local communities in the past had used resources without destroying them, they had done so even as they remained in contact with other peoples which was not always 'a golden harmonious past.' In the case of bishnois, the origin of the community is based on managing conflicts and scarcity through an uncompromising conservation ethics. They have shown exemplary courage in confronting the highest echelons of power whenever they tried to disrupt their uncompromising dedication to nature. Heeralal Maheshwari[11] expressed that the cultural foundations of bishnois differs from other religious communities as they have transformed religious beliefs and ideological traditions into real life practice. The vision of bishnois as a small, integrated community using locally-evolved norms and rules to manage resources sustainably and equitably is a powerful conservation narrative. However, the contemporary understanding of the term environmental consciousness in the context of global warming and degradation is recent historical development. Concern for subsistence and sustenance is different from present environmental crisis.[12]

Some leading environmental historians[13] have argued

that jatis are natural adaptations to local environments while many other historians[14] question such assumptions of environmental and social stability, seeing jatis as more fluid cultural constructions with their composition changing with migrations, intermarriages, shifting socio-economic roles and state policies.[15] Although the traditions connected with religious figures like Jambhoji in the fourteenth and fifteenth centuries in Rajasthan can be located in the broad context of the *bhakti* (devotional) movements, they cannot be fully understood without delving into their individual complexity and originality. For instance Ramdev and Mallinath have been classified as *lok-devata* (folk deities), whereas Jambhoji and Jasnathji enjoy the ranks of *sant* and *siddha*. The reasons are fairly clear as 'both are known to be the founders of specific religious traditions or sects (*sampradaya, panth*) which have subsisted to this day as well-defined and structured movements, with their lineages of gurus and disciples, their sacred scriptures, and their shrines.'[16]

For the bishnois, however, Jambhoji is much more than a *sant* or an 'ecologist' which is revealed in the idea of divinity expressed in their hagiographical literature. He is an *avatar* of the formless Vishnu. For the bishnois, historical knowledge is handed down as narratives which construct the social memory as a guide to the present. For any social grouping to have a collective identity there has to be a shared interpretation of events and experiences.[17] The hagiographical literature of the bishnois serves this purpose by lending authenticity to the community's accepted beliefs about the origins and emphasizing vivid turning points and symbolic moments that consolidate the self-image and aspiration of the group. 'Social memory is not stable as information; it is stable, rather at the level of shared meanings and remembered images.'[18] Memory is crucial to social integration. Jacque le Goffe opines that memory is an essential element of collective identity of a community.[19] In the oral stage the narrative is formulated to specifically bring people together but in subsequent scribal stages the text becomes a nostalgic repository of local and institutional legend through which the saints gain local resonance.[20]

Legend says that at the edge of the desert, in such climatic adversity, the warriors of Rajasthan decided to adorn their empires with outlandish palaces. To erect, they had to feed the lime kilns and fell trees by the thousands. As a result, terrible drought began to ravage the region. At the heart of the disaster, a humble peasant took a stand whose name was Jambheshwar. He realized that the popular perception of drought being punishment of the gods is a fallacy. It is the result of ill-treating and abusing the kindness of nature. With some men and women of good sense, he founded a community that allows the survival of all through the implementation of twenty nine simple principles. The bishnois and their adherence to twenty nine principles is sacrosanct and every bishnoi, even now, pledges allegiance to them. They go back to the very origin and are associated with the founder himself. Guru Jambheshwar is the guiding light of the ecological foundations of the bishnoi community. Thus, we realize that ecological identity of the bishnois is imbued with divinity and cannot be correctly understood independent of it.

Bishnoi, Vishnoi, Prahladpanthi: Nomenclature

Jambhoji was born to his parents after a long period of childlessness as a result of a boon from a sadhu. He is said to have performed many miracles in childhood. For many years he did not utter a word and a priest was called. The priest was shown a miracle by Jambhoji, who uttered his first couplet of a long series of *sabads* (sayings). Significantly his first words are recorded as 'Recognize the Guru!' Recognizing his divine nature, his devotees accepted him as a form of Krishna and as the promised tenth incarnation of Vishnu. There are two chief theories regarding the roots of the name of the community. There is also a slight confusion whether to render it as vishnoi or bishnoi. The perplexity is slight only because of the little significance given to it but the haze covering it is rather opaque. The puzzle is also connected to explanation for its origin. Bishnois are regarded as devotees of Vishnu, Jambhoji, their founder being his incarnation. They were called Vishnu where he is called *Nikalank avatar., jug chhaute dasvo visen santa karan sambhal'*—'During the fourth Age the tenth Vishnu has come for the benefit of the pious'[21]. The Punjab Census, 1881 expresses their plausible connection to Vishnu but states, 'They themselves derive it from 29 (bis-nau) articles of faith inculcated by the founder.' but 'they can be confused with Vaishnav which the British have at times erroneously entered as baishnav or bishnoi.'[22]

There is another name recorded for the community—Prahladvanshis. The myth recounted for this name is that when Prahlad rescued people from the cruelties of Hiranyakashyap, by inciting God Vishnu's intervention at the behest of his spiritual exertion, he requested Vishnu to ensure liberation of others also. As a result Vishnu is said to have reincarnated as Jambhoji whose teachings would lead to salvation. Those who became his disciples came to be known as disciples of the devotee Prahlad.[23] The festival of holi connected closely to the legend of Prahlad is celebrated differently by the bishnois. "They observe *holi* in a different way from other Hindus. After sunset on that day they fast till the next forenoon, when, after hearing the account of how Prahlad was tortured by his infidel father Hiranyakshyap for believing in the god Vishnu, until he was delivered by the god himself in his incarnation of the Lion-man. And mourning over Prahlad's sufferings, they light a sacrificial fire and partake of consecrated water, after distributing jaggery in commemoration of Prahlad's delivery from the fire into which he was thrown, they break their fast."[24] The day is not a celebration but an occasion of solemn observance. Dominique-Sila Khan has tried to trace a connection of bishnois with ismaili shia muslims by invoking the fifteenth century Pir, Tajuddin was also known as Prahlad. Jambhoji is also recorded to have said that he was above all distinctions of sects and castes.[25]

The description of the bishnoi community, its tenets and practices by Wilson recorded in the Sirsa Settlement Report, became the standard description which has been often repeated in later documents, in entirety or in parts. Marwar Census, 1891 quotes it to say that an extract from the Punjab Census Report, 1881 will fully explain the tenets and practices of the bishnois. The Panjab Census Report states, 'The Bishnois are really a religious sect and not a tribal religion.'[26] This report records the bishnois as 'Minor Hindu Castes' in the section titled 'Marwar Castes, Tribes, Races.' All the gazetters, census reports, documentation of castes, even collection of speeches or travelogues by the British administrators use the term bishnoi with no reference to vishnoi even when a connection to the deity Vishnu or the sect vaishnava is being explained. It is possible that 'bishnoi' became standardized in official parlance as Heeralal Maheshwari prefers to use the term 'vishnoi' His argument is that the verse says bishnoi is one who follows *unatees* (Marwari for 29) tenets, the term is not *bis-nau* (Marwari for 20 and 9).[27] The absence of *bees-nau* for 29 for Maheshwari nulls the connection of the term bishnoi with 29 principles. Also, it is completely possible that vishnoi became bishnoi due to a linguistic vagary of spoken dialect. However, using the term *unatees* and not *bis nau* is not a clinching argument as the two are synonyms. There is no clear mention in the vernacular literature of the bishnois to indicate the connection of the naming of the community to Vishnu, although at many places devotion to Vishnu, and Jambhoji as reincarnation of Vishnu has been clearly established. The association with Vishnu is just as ubiquitous as the core 29 tenets in the popular literature, both competing pretty stiffly with each other. Maheshwari feels that tracing the origin of the name bishnoi from 29 tenets is merely a figment of imagination of the British gazetters, which may be a little harsh but points to the possibility that a popular perception might have gotten standardized without the community's agency. Some later poets like Vilhoji and Surjanji describe *visnoi* as ones who have taken refuge in *Visan* (Vishnu in marwari dialect)

Surjandas visañan ke saranai, soi saro visnoi[28]

(Those who have taken refuge in Vishnu, they become

Vishnoi)

Guṇatīs dharma kī āṅkdī hridaya dhạriyo joye
Jāmbhojī kirpā kari nām Bishnoī hoye[29]

(One who embraces the twenty nine ethics by heart becomes a bishnoi by the blessings of Jambhoji)

Anyway, the 29 rules and teachings are the foundation of the eco-religion of the bishnois. They are displayed at temples and recited regularly. Not only have they been integrated into daily life practices but have also led the bishnois to take concrete action to ensure adherence. These measures include positive steps to conserve flora and fauna, construct and preserve water bodies while negative measures include persistent, strong protests against poachers and hunters. Thus, a peek into the history of their conservation practices and activism, preserved in their popular literature, brings to fore bishnoi environmentalism as a lived reality.

Narratives of Bishnois

The sermons of the founder, Jambhoji, are compiled as *Sabad* (*Jambhsāgar*) and many poets of the community have compiled *sākhīs*. Most of these compositions are in *marubhāṣā*, some in *pingal* and *khaḍī bolī* as well. Heeralal Maheshwari writes that the use of Arabic and Persian words attract attention and the language is reflective of the colloquial folk idioms of the contemporary society.[30] According to James Wilson, 'The sayings (*sabd*) of Jambhji to the number 120 were written down by his disciples, and have been handed down in a book (*pothi*) written in the nagari characters and in a dialect similar to bagri, seemingly a marwari dialect."[31] Each *sabad* consists of a series of *dohas* or couplets. A poem consisting of eight couplets and entitled *Untees Niyam* (Twenty Nine Rules) is also ascribed to the founder which contains principle tenets of the sect. The bishnoi literature also comprises various devotional compositions in the form of ballads, *sakhis*, and *vanis* in the Rajasthani language. They are signed by various authors with either Hindu or Muslim names, all considered disciples of Jambhoji. 'A critical analysis of these texts shows that they should be considered works of oral literature and that the *chhaps* (authorship) are not a guarantee of authorship. The first manuscript transcribing the poems is said to have been the work of the bishnoi guru, Parmanandji, around 1761, thus relatively late…'[32] These accounts contain the valorous struggles and sacrifices and collective action of the community for the cause of environment.

Creating Community Ethos

After the demise of Jambhoji, there were some nefarious efforts to monopolize the temples when the *jamāt* or *panchayat* of the bishnois interfered and averted needless conflict. A contemporary poet Raichand Suthar writes to request the *jamat* to have compassion and take the matter in its hands—*Thay ī jamāt raham karo, joti na khancho āpṇī.*[33] The panchayat also zealously propgated *shuddhi-prathā* through which the persons who had given up on bishnoi faith were taken back into the fold. Much of this was under the able leadership of Vilhoji, disciple of Jambhoji. He took many steps to encourage the spread of the faith which included organizing public fairs, getting royal edicts that facilitated bishnois and composing vernacular literature to depict the ecological teachings.

His disciple Kesoji formulated many pragmatic plans for the development of the community. He is attributed with devising an administrative design for taking care of *sathris* through the *guru-shishya* tradition. He appointed five sadhus and their branches called *aeil* which still exist. He also formulated a semi-judicial system to check activities contrary to the bishnoi value system. The deviant behaviour was to be reported in the fairs or panchayats (termed *helo uṭhāṇā*) and a judgement was passed by the same (termed *helo deṇa*). The panchayats maintained their records as *likhat*. One such record from Rudakli, Jodhpur gives details of *helo* for killing of a rooster.[34] The judicial powers are no longer exercised but were practiced until after India became independent.

Jammā and *Jāgaraṇ* are held regularly to create spiritual solidarity. *Jammā,* which means to collect together, is a gathering in which *sākhis* related to Jambhoji are sung and their interpretation is discussed. *Jāgaraṇ* is a similar gathering in which worship of Hari is added. The recital of nine *sākhis,* called *jamme ki Sākhiyañ,* precede all else in both gatherings. Other *sākhis* can be sung while *harjas* (compositions in praise of Hari) are sung in *Jāgaraṇ*. At midnight, for *ārti,* a lamp is lighted and the hymn composed by Padam Bhagat is sung. This hymn indicates a work oriented householder life after marriage of Krishna and Rukmini, by the mother-in-law of Krishna which underscores the importance of an active worldly life. This is usually followed by *ākhyāyans* of Jambhoji. In the morning, the singers are given some rewards and money after the *hawan*. Presently, only *Jāgaraṇ* is held and the difference between the two has blurred. Periodic gatherings have always been a norm to foster the collective solidarity of bishnois of a region.

Hailing the Martyrs[35]

Bishnois always took action against those who harmed nature from very early times and celebrated martyrs. More than five hundred years ago, it could hardly be visualized that a community could rise to protect trees or wild deer by risking their lives. Jambhoji's humanitarian and pragmatic philosophy earned him a large band of dedicated followers. The bishnois soon grew in numbers and strength. Stories of their relentless dedication to the preservation of animals and trees began early and were widely circulated through vernacular compositions. Many *sākhis* mention incidents of life-sacrifice for trees.

Vilhoji's *Karmā aur Gorā ki Sākhi* narrates that in 1604 AD, two bishnoi women from Ramsari village, Karma and Gora, are believed to have sacrificed their lives in an effort to prevent the felling of khejri, at the behest of the local feudal lord. . *Tilvāsāni ki Sākhi* narrates an episode around 1670 AD when Thakur Gopaldas Bhati of Khejadla village sent an emissary, Kirpa to cut a *khejri* tree in Tilvasani village of Jodhpur. The bishnoi leader politely requested him to refrain from cutting the tree. The agents paid no heed and lifted their axes. Seeing this horror, Kheenwani, a woman from the bishnoi community hugged the tree. She was cut by the cruel axe of the violent perpetrators. Kesoji's *Bucho ji Echara ki Sākhi* recounts that in the second half of the 17th century medta feudatory Thakur Narasinghdas of Rajod got trees of *khejri* cut before Holi from a village of Nagaur, Polas. When the Bishnois came to know of this, the community passed a resolution to get the offenders punished with the words "*Sir dhan aawe sir saate, sir saate sanman/Sir saate labhe surag, jo sir dino jaye//*" This popular couplet recounts their desire to uphold the tenets at the cost of getting beheaded. Rajod Thakur refused to comply with their request. Bucha Ram took the responsibility for the protection of ecological ethics by sacrificing his life. Word spread in the neighbouring areas too and a huge crowd gathered. Such persistent opposition angered the feudal lord and Bucha Ram was beheaded by his men. Bishnoi poet Gokulji in *Khejarli ki Sākhi* presented an eyewitness account of the famous khejarli massacre. The *sākhi* begins with Jodhpur ruler Ajit Singh and ends with the sacrifice by 363 ordinary bishnoi men and women of extraordinary courage and conviction led by Amrita Devi. The episode is outstanding and heart rendering due to the magnitude of sacrifice for trees and struggle and victory against imperial prowess.

Sometimes the historicity of these events is questioned as the only evidence is folk memory and popular literature. Interestingly, names, gotras and villages of all martyrs of the khejarli massacre are recorded in detail at the site and circulated in bishnoi periodicals.

Coping with State Mechanism: Resistance and Patronage

The faith of bishnois was never a state religion nor received royal patronage but many rulers showed reverence to the strict adherence to ecological tenets by the bishnois. *Sabadvani* narrates the intention of Rao Satal of Jodhpur to abolish land revenues completely for the bishnois but Jambhoji insisted on paying one-fifth of the produce. Many rulers offered relaxation in land revenues and other taxes to the bishnois. In a *sākhi* by Kesoji (*Katha Medte ki)* it is indicated that the bishnois regarded themselves as *'Akar'*—the one who is not taxed. Vilhoji expressed a sympathetic attitude of Rawal Jaitsi in his *Katha Jaiselmer Ki.* The bishnois also resisted the state machinery if they were unduly burdened with taxation. Kesoji narrates the sacrifice of Ramuji Khod when an arbitrary tax was imposed in the *Chaitra Melā,* a regularly held fair, at Kaparheda village in Jodhpur in 1642 . (*Haṭwāḍe Halchal Huwo*)

Sabad and *sākhis* are replete with such examples but evidence can be culled from official documents as well. Many kings issued orders that bishnois shall be taxed as per tradition and shall be exempted from *begār,* the labour compelled by state. Jodhpur ruler Maharaja Vijaysingh (1763), Mansingh (1802), Bheem Singh (1816) issued *parwana*s to this effect. Similar orders were issued for bishnois of Pur by Udaipur ruler Maharana Bheem Singh (1866) and Jawan singh (1877) to 'to respect the Bishnois as per tradition and tax them according to the convention'.[36]

Not just taxation and state duties but the state power showed sympathy for the environmental concerns of the bishnois. Bikaner ruler Anoop Singh's *parwana* (1694), in the records of Mukam, issued order to prohibit felling of green trees. Jodhpur ruler Mansingh (1820) issued orders to prohibit cutting of khejri trees while Takhtsingh ji (1844) issued a *parwana* to ban hunting in bishnoi villages.[37] On suspicion of killing of animals, the animal were taken away from their owners as per a *parwana* of Mehkama Council Rajshree Bikaner.[38] The state of Bikaner had issued orders that no butcher would pass through a bishnoi village carrying an animal.[39]

Mayank Kumar posits quite convincingly that "The number of followers increased manifold in the arid region of Bikaner and Jodhpur. This sect became so influential that the rulers of these states were forced to respect their sermons."[40]

Gaze of the Colonial Power: A Strange Creed

There has been a lot of discussion around the British depiction of India. The British ruled over India for a long time and had to interact with various groups and communities of this diverse country. The records in the form of census reports, administrative documents, gazetteers needed neat and clear-cut categorizations that were not always entirely possible. We see a struggle in the British records to categorize the bishnoi community as either Hindu or Muslim. Some scholars call them a liminal community. In fact, the vernacular literature expresses the liminality by refusing to identify as either or criticizing practitioners of both. In the very beginning, British left them as a minor agricultural caste but soon their customs were analyzed in reference to Hindu and Muslim traditions. The bishnoi community relied largely on collective solidarity and took cudgels with the imperial powers even before the British came. The local rulers developed a functional relationship with the bishnois, who resisted the formal state powers, but agreed to pay revenue and demanded concessions in view of their eco-friendly lifestyle. With the British, the struggle was harder, as it was difficult to make them understand the community-specific and region-specific ethos, yet we see a collective persistence of the bishnois having their way sometimes.

This perspective offers the potential for understanding of the Other in relation to the Occidental self, which is 'necessarily a political construct, forged in public discourse, located in history, and carved in debate'.[41] While visiting a village Sadalpur, Malcolm Lyall Darling writes, 'The most interesting thing about this village was not its banks but its religion. It is inhabited by a strange sect called Bishnoi.'[42] He wrote a couple of books on his travels of Punjab to understand the customs and people of the villages. The trope of the *'Stranger Contra'* or the 'antithetical stranger' may not be a demonized cultural Other here but certainly a misunderstood one. The strangeness had not only to do with ecological commitment of the bishnois but it arose from the unease of fitting them into a neat category with non-permeable boundaries that the census operations aspired for. Bishnois in their origin were a conglomerate of many castes coming together as a community and seemed to follow both Hindu and Islamic customs. They largely seemed to be within the fold of Hinduism but there were characteristics that differed from it quite distinctly. They had retained the caste name from which they originally came but identified themselves only as bishnois when asked. The colonial anthropology with a mission to classify seemed to spur the construction of identity boundaries.

It is recorded that 'Bishnois are different from other Hindus' as 'the case of the Bishnois of Haryana who are chiefly reunited from two very different castes is still more striking.'[43] The officer finds it difficult to fit the Bishnois into a specific category 'Thus, the figure of my tables of tribes and caste include groups formed upon several very distinct types…or of believers in a [*strange creed]* like the Bishnois.'[44] There was a big debate whether the bishnois were really a religion or a caste. It is explicitly mentioned at one place, 'The Bishnois are really a religious sect and not a true caste.'[45] The distinctive feature of the religion was identified that, 'They worship Jambhaji, whom they regard as an incarnation of Vishnu.'[46] This did not seem to solve the problem and mostly it was listed as a Hindu sect but it was not a caste yet the caste names had been retained. It remained strange that caste names were never used for caste identification. It was even stranger that there was no idol worship, dead were to be buried, and no *pheras* (circumambulations around the pole), were taken like Hindu marriages. The identity as both a caste and religion defied neat categories and betrayed confusion due to multiple overlaps.

The overlap or 'mixture of two distinct traditions' is what made the bishnois unique in the eyes of the Briritsh and not so much their ecological concerns for which they are hailed today. 'There is not perhaps very much in the teaching of Jhambaji (sic.) to distinguish him from the orthodox pattern of Hindu saints, and in some points of his doctrine, more especially with regard to the preservation of life, is only an intensification of the ordinary Vaishnava tenets.'[47] Though in 1896 in *The Tribes and Castes of the North-Western Provinces and Oudh,*[48] they are entered as worshippers of Vishnu. 'Usually, as at the last census, classed as a sub-tribe of banias, but really a distinct religious sect.' Though, Panjab Census and the general perception depicts them largely as jats originally but they were a conglomerate and banias formed a sizeable component in some areas. Isharat Jahan[49] also notes the connection "Abul Fazl (1590) refers to 48 sub-castes of the Banias. W. Geleynseen de Jongh (1623-40, posted in India) reported that the Banias were divided into four major sects...more important and respected, namely, Sarrawacka (*Sravaka*), Sammaract (*Samrat), jogi,* and the fourth Bissino (*Bishnoi*)." This was the time when banias had become considerably powerful. Kabir, a medieval poet, had used bania as a metaphor for God who can trade without a balance, *"Sai mera Bania sahaj kare vyapar"*.

"Like Kabir, Jambhoji was also regarded as a reformer by the British records to resolve some of the confusion and reconcile to some of the changes observed in their customs and practices. "...in the omission of the pheras at the marriage, the cutting-off of the choti or scalp-lock, the special ceremony of initiates, and the disregard for the Brahmanical priesthood, we find indications of the same spirit as that which move the other Hindu reformers of the period."[50]

There were certain customs of the bishnoi that caught the attention of the British anthropologists as distinguishing features vis-à-vis Hindu religion as understood by them. The primary observations[51] were that "Brahmins are not revered" as they have their own priests called *sadhs*, 'When the initiation takes place, the *choti* is cut off.' which was quite a significant difference for them, expressed very clearly that they 'do not leave a scalp-lock [*like the Hindus*]' And the difference in a 'standardised physical Hindu appearance' that these British officials had in mind was violated further as 'they allow the beard to grow, only shaving the chin on father's death.'

The British were trying to understand and portray Hinduism as somewhat monolithic, homogeneous religion and seem to be analysing bishnois through a lens of standardized Hinduism. This awareness was based mostly on sanskrit scriptures or elite, urban practices. Therefore, rural or remote variants were considered inconsistent with 'ordinary Hinduism'. Even the practice of greeting by invoking name of a Hindu deity Vishnu appeared a digression from Hindu way of life. "They bathe and pray three times a day, in the morning, afternoon, and the evening, saying *Bishno! Bishno!* Instead of ordinary Hindu *Ram! Ram!*"[52] In the beginning, the bishnois may have been Hindus, non-Hindus or not mainstream Hindus. Some scholars consider them 'liminal'[53] communities who identified exclusively neither as Hindus or Muslim yet their analysis in reference to one or the other, created a basis for perceived formulation of Hinduism in general and influenced identity formation of the bishnois in particular.

Their frequent bathing, emphasis on cleanliness, and ceremonial purity also drew attention of the census officials sometimes to depict affinity with Hindu customs. Malcolm Lyall Darling received an explanation from a bishnoi in Sadalpur village, "Every 'eater of grain', that is everyone over five, must bathe in the morning before tasting food."[54] He further observed that the cleanliness of bishnoi villages is "proverbial" and the village lanes are as clean as the households. Ibbetson quotes a popular saying that explains the proverbial emphasis on purity by the bishnois. He writes that if there is a line of ten camels and the food for a bishnoi is placed on the first camel, he will not eat the food if someone touches even the tenth camel. Such descriptions regarding the bishnois were compiled by James Wilson in the Sirsa Settlement Report which was part of the Punjab Census and it was reproduced in many reports that followed it. 'They will eat from the hands of none but their own clansmen.'[57] Their compassion towards flora and fauna is sometimes compared with Jain tenets also.

Nevill comments in *The Bijnor Gazetteer* that, 'Bishnois differ little from strict Hindus, being particular in matter of ceremonial purification and having a strong aversion to taking life as the Jains.'[58] Although in the early literature of the bishnois, attributed to Jambhoji, many sects find mention except the Jains. Some of the later poets criticized some Jain practices. Some scholars have tried to find origin of bishnoi sect in Jainism[59] but in view of this passing reference by the British and omission in vernacular works, the theory seems far-fetched.

One more feature that was found unique was their disregard for astrology in selecting an auspicious day for a marriage ceremony. According to their saying, 'Everyday is as good as Sankrant, everyday is as good as Amavas. The Ganges flows every day, and he, whose preceptor has taught him the most truth will get the most truth by bathing in it.'[60]

Apart from the differences from Hindus, certain Muslim practices of the bishnois have also been recorded. Ibbetson recounts, 'In their marriage ceremonies, they mingle Mohammadan with Hindu forms, verses of Quran being read as well as passages of Sastras, and the *phera* and circumambulation of the sacred fire being apparently omitted. The intermixture is said to be due to the injunction of one of the kings of Dehli to the founder of the sect.'[61] Marwar census, 1891 cites Punjab census while stating that "In their rites and ceremonies, they partake both Hindu and Mussalman religion.'[62] Erskine attempts an explantion in *Rajputana Gazeteers* 'The Muhammadans were in power in Nagaur at this time, not approving of Jambha starting a new religion, told him to incorporate some of their tenets in it.' These additions included burial after death, after taking the name of Vishnu, the words Allah Bismillah to be repeated, no *pheras* in the marriage, and during the marriage ceremony the priest reading from Hindi books should also read from Muhammadan ones. It appears like an effort to incorporate all the practices that did not fit into the perception of Hindu practices. It also tried to include the differences in appearance and grooming by including two more 'instructions' from the ruler to shave off the head completely, getting rid of the Hindu scalp-lock and to not separate the hair of beard.[63]

The incorporation of Islamic traditions was manifest with regional variations. Ibettson added a footnote 'The Bishnois of Bijnaur ...repect the Quran and incline generally towards

Islam though now less so than formerly.'[64] The premise for this inclination is graphically narrated in *The Tribes and Castes of the North Western Province and Oudh,* 'The bishnois of Bijnor appear to differ from those of the Panjab in using Musalman form of salutation, salam alaikum, and the title of Shaikhji. They account for this by saying that they murdered a Muhammadan Qazi who prevented them from burning a widow and were glad to compound the offence by pretending to adopt Islam.'[65] *The Bijnor Gazetteer* furnishes specific details of this 'Hindu sect'. 'This sect is said to have been founded by one Jhambaji, otherwise known by the Muhammedan appellation of Sheikh Makhduna Jahania Jahangasht. Till recently, his followers used to adopt Musalman names and customs, but those have been renounced, and the Bishnois differ little from strict Hindus…'[66]

According to Heeralal Maheshwari, bishnoi literature is largely set in Hindu milieu but addresses Muslims also. First *sabad* questions listeners that being Hindu why are they not chanting the name of Hari[67], while *sabad 14* appeals to the Muslims that only the honest can come close to Allah[68]. Many *sabads* directly appeal to the Muslims to show compassion to animal life.[69] Maheshwari feels that Islamic practices are not found in bishnoi literature and that the British got confused by the spirit of tolerance and some Muslim followers.[70] He writes that shaving the scalp lock was only a mark of identification and the burial of dead is practiced by many Hindu communities. Nevertheless, bishnois had syncretic practices and a composition that drew from different traditions.

Development into a Caste

A little before the British launched a grand statistical and anthropological enterprise and paid attention to classifying castes and religions of India, Tod was making his own compilation of customs of Rajputana. In *Annals and Antiquities of Rajasthan,* Tod made a reference to 'Bishnoi Brahmans' of desert and Sind as burying their dead on thresholds. "Bishnoi is the most common sect of Brahaman in desert and Sind…they are a law unto themselves…they cultivate, and tend cattle…"[71] Hutton cites Rose and clarifies that though the Bishnois are "spoken of as Bishnoi Brahmans by Tod, they are, in fact, derived from various castes, particularly, (according to Rose, *Tribes and Castes,* Vol. II, S.V. Bishnoi) from jats and khatris.[72] Even vernacular literature mentions drawing followers from different communities. *Sabad 14* (couplets 3-4)[73], mentions jats explicitly while other poets mention kshatriya, vaishya, charan, kayasth, brahmins and Muslim followers.[74]

Jat, Bhat Jogi Sanyas, Bambhan sudar kare gur aas
Khan peer parachya surtan, Rajav vansa mahajan jan
(Surjanji, Katha Autar ki)[75]

Thus, bishnois were a sect that had a separate identity although the members originally belonged to different castes and their original professions and caste traits did not get obliterated completely.

Charan Kayath Parchya Jaan
Unch Neech sahjaat bakhan (Gokalji Sakhi)[76]

By the British, they are generally seen and recorded as a Hindu sect and at times registered as a Minor Agricultural Caste as in Marwar Census, 1891. In Panjab and Haryana, they are said to have comprised mainly from jats, tarkhans, and khatis. In Marwar, the followers were largely identified as jats while in Central Provinces of Bijnor, Moradabad etc. they were mostly banias, the merchant class although they were still a conglomerate of various caste groups. "Mahant Atmaram, known as Maharaj or mahat, the present leader of Moradabad Bishnois…names nine endogamous sub-divisions of them."[77] The gradual additions to the professions of bishnois in the census indicates that they emerged as agro-pastoral groups, mainly cultivators practicing animal husbandry, and with time also became or incorporated landowners, money lenders and merchants.[78] In Moradabad, many of the Bishnoi traders are said to have amassed considerable wealth.[79]

The set of prayers and partaking holy water under the supervision of a bishnoi priest comprised of the ritual of initiation called *pahal* recorded as very similar to the Sikhs. It also points to the fact that anybody having faith in the 29 tenets could join the community. Gradually, it appears that in practice the conversions stopped. The Census of 1901 0f Rajputana reports "The important community of Bishnois, originally a religious sect, who are chiefly found in the Western Division are said to no longer admit converts, and to have become a distinct caste..."[80] The British realize that Bishnois have developed as a caste or begin to classify it as such. "... they have all written their caste as Bishnoi and in Marwar and Bikaner, their chief home, they are certainly regarded as a separate caste."[81] *Rajputana Gazetteer*, The Mewar Residency corroborates the emerging of Bishnois as a separate caste, certainly for the purposes of the census reports. "They are not a distinct tribe, but are made up of jats, khatris, rajputs, and banias, but they always try to sink their tribe in their religion, and give their caste as bishnois merely. They retain the language, dress and other characteristics of the Bagris."[82] This passage particularly brings out the multiple layers of identities/sub-identities of region, caste, community, sect, language, costume etc. could exist in the society but proved difficult for categorization and comprehension by the British. Therefore, the phenomenon required an explanation sought in the process of Hinduization of the bishnois. "The Bishnois of Central Provinces are gradually becoming an ordinary Hindu caste, a fate which has several times befallen the adherents of reformers."[83] In these regions, it was also observed that bishnois have adopted certain Hindu practices and given up some core bishnoi ones. The Moradabad branch of the bishnois used to throw the corpses in Ganges.[84] According to the description of *Tribes and Castes of the Central Provinces of India*, "The dead are never burnt, but their bodies are weighted with sand bags and thrown into a stream." The ritual of cremation is the core of Hindu funeral ceremony not adopted by the bishnois in the modification ensuing regional adaptation. It appears that it was completely passed up that it is possible to have plurality, where worshipping another deity does not take away from being a bishnoi or the giving up of the custom of burial is mentioned in the district of Hoshangabad, situated on the banks of River Narmada. The corpse is not burnt among the bishnois and some other desert communities to save firewood, a purpose met equally well by relegating the corpse to a flowing river. Nevertheless, it appears that gradually the bishnoi community while preserving its own traditions got identified with Hinduism, not infrequently as a distinct caste. Their conglomerate composition notwithstanding, the exclusive caste identity of the bishnois crystallized in the British records so much that they were seen as a neatly separated group even from jats, who were numerically largest among the bishnois of Marwar. This was reflected in the analysis of sex ratio in the 1901 Census of Rajputana. 'There is, however, a still more marked difference between the Bishnois, originally a religious sect of Jats, who have by far the highest ratio of females, and the Jats who are at the bottom of the large agricultural tribes.'[85]

Environmental Concerns and the Colonial State

The underlying context of the relatively higher sex ratio of females leads to certain general perceptions about the bishnois. 'The strict attention which the Bishnois pay to cleanliness and the great care they take of all living animals may be some of the causes of the greater proportion of women among them...'[86] There are numerous references to the scattering of birdfeed, not killing any living creature, and they do utmost to prevent others from doing so. Consequently, their villages are generally swarming with antelopes, black bucks, peacocks and other animals.[87] The love for animals also led to a ban on hunting in bishnoi areas.[88] "They forbid their Musalman neighbours to kill them and try to dissuade European sportsmen from interfering with them."[89] From the British point of view, they refuse to accompany a hunting expediton and were of no use to a sporting company. Their insistence on preventing hunting down of animals led to an official circular issued to ban hunting in the listed bishnoi villages in Hissar and Ferozepur districts. The Deputy Commisioner, Ferozepur, issue an order on 8th march 1899 with reference to a previous letter from Chief Secretary to Government Punjab, dated 3rd February, 1896. It cites "affrays with the villagers" and Punjab Government's orders contained in their circular no. 1-115 dated 3rd February 1898 and clearly prohibited the shooting of black buck within the lands cultivated or uncultivated belonging to the bishnoi villages.

The obstacle to hunting was a minor obstacle that the British administration could cope with. The other issues like unwillingness towards military recruitment did not sit well nor was the demand for concessions in revenue assessments something the colonial power was willing to relent. Dweyer exhorted the bishnois, in a speech at Ambala Darbar, 1917, to join the army. He showed disappointment with their disinterest and lamented that the limited number who joined have also left the army.[90] On the basis of their love and compassion for animals, the bishnois requested James Wilson to assess their land at lower rates as they allow antelopes to damage their crops. It was a customary concession that the rulers of Marwar ceded in the preceding era. But Wilson "pitted their piety against their guile and told them that, if he consented to the remission begged for, it would lessen the merit of their action of protecting animals" is how he was hailed in an account *Sirsa and Sirsa Folk.*[91] It is more convincing to construe the unwillingness to give up on a revenue concession and nip any such demands in the bud as Punjab Census, 1881 states, "..but I told them this would lessen the merit (*pun*) of their action in protecting the animals, and they must be treated just as the surrounding villages were." The conniving use of the indigenous term *pun* corroborates the premise for this whole exercise to create a better understanding of indigenous customs to facilitate administration, not aiming for good governance but for best serving imperial interests.

There was some misunderstanding about the adherence to the tenet of animal compassion that actually emanated from an error of translation. Many British writers mention that bishnois deviate from their own tenets and use bullocks "without scruples" in agricultural work This was not an injunction upon the bishnois but Wilson had incorrectly translated one of the tenets as 'Do not plough with bullocks'[92] whereas the bishnois were instructed not to castrate the bulls. The 1901 Census mentions 'the misunderstanding due to mistranslation of Mr. Wilson'[93]. Avoiding castration was a practice they continued to adhere to. "No one now, except the small Bishnoi sect, objects to castration." pointed out Darling in his travelogue.[94]

'They also seem to be unusually quarrelsome in words and given to use bad language'[95] "Quarrelsome in words" indicates harsh language which must have been reported by other natives, difficult for the British to work out such linguistics nuance, It perpetuated a stereotype because bishnois are not pacifists. They resist and do not desist in preventing others to harm trees and animals.

Jat sago kari jeenman baisola, tini ro bhadiki vigavo
Thool sagai swang lad kiriya lajiya hu val jovo (Redoji, Sakhi)[96]

Although some vernacular couplets, like the one above, also expressed that jats were short-tempered and never used the honorific *jee* when addressing. Heeralal Maheshwari comments that the trait of using harsh language applied to a lot of agricultural communities of the time.

Their activism is much misunderstood. 'They are, however of an overbearing and quarrelsome disposition, and somewhat addicted to litigation, which often tells the form of false criminal charges.'[97] Strangely the words of bishnois and their evidence were given more credence by the locals, Erskine records with characteristic disdain for the natives, "They are as lax in the matter of truth as any tribe or a caste in the district" and with these word, he disparages the whole populace in one sweep.[98] Truth is one of the twenty nine core tenets of the bishnois. "A liar can never attain respect of others. It is insult to the gift of speech. There was a time when even the courts used to accept the testimony of Bishnois as hard evidence."[99] In a *sabad*, Jambhoji instructs that there is no gain in anything accomplished through falsehood and core 29 tenets instruct to discard falsehood along with theft, gossip and argumentation.

Chori, ninda, jhooth varajiyo
Vaad na karano koi[100]

The sustainable livelihood and the hard work it entails were accepted to be economically beneficial too. 'The bishnois are thrifty, frugal and industrious; agriculture is by no means their only resource, and they are ever ready to turn every chance of profit to advantages. The consequence is that they are in more comfortable circumstances than any other peasantry in the district.'[101] Though this would rather be a simplification superficially this description of the relative status of the community has endured in western Rajasthan.

Conclusions

Indigenous literature of the bishnois provides an understanding of origins, orientation, experiences, development of a world view from the perspective of the community while the British reports or Raj ethnographies amalgamate in this, observations of the British and perceptions of the general populace. It is now an accepted theory that the British tried to impose a western paradigm in the caste census, which for communities like bishnois, failed in creating a fixed expected category. In fact, the case of bishnois shows that the fluidity of the composition and self- represented identity was arrested in course of time and the statistical exercises must have played some role. The British not only manifested an orientalist approach in general by relegating the entire social organization, and chiefly caste system as the other but also created another standard framework based largely on the brahminical varna system, and Islam as its anti-thesis and created a situation of 'double othering' for communities like the bishnois, who did not fit well into either paradigm. At the same time, there was a concerted effort to ignore the multiple identities that some bishnois must have carried rather they were used to establish them as customs of either Hinduism or Islam. It is understood through the vernacular compositions that disciples came from different traditions, the spiritual leader addressed different communities and some customs emanated from regional necessities, environmental orientation rather than from one religion or the other.

Both the accounts have many similarities as far as a description of practices is concerned but the attitude towards them is not always the same. Where medieval rulers, regional powers, supported their philosophy and customs, the British ruled as colonial powers, with an isolated stance and providing not much of the traditional concessions to the bishnois. It should not be wide off the mark to suggest that the ban on hunting must have come as the bishnois are unrelenting and the British must have feared that they might take the law in their hands.

There are many historical episodes like Jambhoji's meeting with Sikandar Lodi that do not find mention in mainstream history and remain limited to bishnoi literature. Thus, these sources must be revisited for corroboration and unraveling of historical facts too. There must be other factors at work in formation of social identity that can be unearthed in the light of present analysis. A comparative study while critiquing the accounts creates a better understanding of social history of the evolution of bishnois into a caste identity and helps understand the process of formation of socio-religious identities and its political context. These pages of history can bring to light the changing values, definitions and identities which are a result of many forces at work. While it is now well accepted that creation of colonial knowledge created a grid that separated communities yet a nuanced analysis with indigenous narratives of the bishnois and marking changes in various census reports helps in understanding the standardization that the bishnois achieved and over time did away with elasticity and porous boundaries.

NOTES

1. *Punjab District Gazetteers* Vol. II-A. *Hissar District and Loharu State,* Civil and Military Gazette Press, Lahore: 1904, p. 112; See

also p. 77 for similar perception.

2. Michael O'Dwyer, *War Speeches of Sir Michael O'Dwyer*, Government Press Punjab, Lahore: 1918, p. 41.
3. Sunita Zaidi, 'Oral Tradition and Little Culture: Jasnathis in Historical Perspective' in Surinder Singh and Ishwar Dayal Gaur, eds., *Popular Literature and Pre-Modern Societies in South Asia*, Dorling Kindersley, Delhi: 2008, p. 175 (162-77).
4. These terms are borrowed from Shanta Nair-Venugopal analysis of Orientalist Enterprise over Malay Society in Shanta Nair-Venugopal, (ed.), *The Gaze of the West and Framings of the East*, Palgrave MacMillan, Hampshire: 2012.
5. Bernard S. Cohn, *An Anthropologist among the Historians and Other Essays*, Oxford University Press, Delhi: 1987; Nicholas B. Dirk, *Castes of Mind: Colonialism and the Making of Modern India*, Princeton University Press, Princeton: 2001; C.J. Fuller, 'Colonial Anthropology and the Decline of the Raj: Caste, Religion and Political Change in India in the Early Twentieth Century', *Journal of Royal Asiatic Society*, Vol. 26, Issue 3, July 2016, pp. 463-86.
6. Norbert Peabody, "Cents, Sense, Census: Human Inventories in Late Pre-colonial and Early Colonial India", *Comparative Studies in Society and History*, Vol. 43, No. 4, 2001, p. 843 (819–50).
7. Padmanabh Samarendra, 'Census in Colonial India and the Birth of Caste', *Economic and Political Weekly*, Vol. XLVI, Issue 33, August 13, 2001, p. 51 (51-58).
8. Bernard S. Cohn, 'The Census, Social Structure and Objectification in South Asia', in Cohn, *An Anthropologist among the Historians and Other Essays*, Oxford University Press, New Delhi: [1987] 1990, pp. 241-42 (224-54).
9. Karine Schomer et al (eds.), *The Idea of Rajasthan*, Manohar, Delhi: 2001, p. x.
10. Eric Wolf, *Europe and the People Without History*, University of California, Berkley: 1982.
11. Heeralal Maheshwari, *Jambhoji, Bishnoi Sampradaya aur Sahitya*, Vol. 1, B.R. Publications, Calcutta: 1970, p. 17.
12. Ann Grodzins Gold and Bhoja Ram Gujar, *In the Times of Trees and Sorrows: Nature, Power, and Memory in Rajasthan*, Oxford University Press, New Delhi: 2002, passim.
13. Madhav Gadgil and Ramchandra Guha, *This Fissured Land: An Ecological History of India*, Oxford University Press, Delhi: 1992.
14. Susan Bayly, *Caste, Society and Politics in India from the Eighteenth*

Century to the Modern Age, Cambridge University Press, Cambridge: 1999; Sumit Guha, *Environment and Ethnicity in India, 1200-1991,* Cambridge University Press, Cambridge: 1999.

15. Michael H. Fisher, *An Environmental History of India: From Earliest Times to the Twenty-First Century,* Cambridge University Press, Cambridge: 2018, pp. 70-71.
16. Dominique-Sila Khan, *Conversions and Shifting Identities,* Manohar, New Delhi: 2003, p. 19.
17. John Tosh, *The Pursuit of History – Aims, Methods and New Directions in the Study of History,* Routledge, New York: 2015, p. 2.
18. Ibid., p. 255
19. Jacques Le Goff, *History and Memory,* Translated by Rendall and Claman, Columbia University Press, New York: 1992, p. 98.
20. David Frankfurter, 'Hagiography and the late reconstructions of local religions in late Egypt memories, invention and landscapes', *Church Hsitory and Religious Culture,* Vol. 86, No. 1/14, 2006, p. 18 (13-37).
21. K.L. Bishnoi, *Bishnoi Dharm Sanskar,* Dhok Dhora Prakashan, Gangashahar: 1992, p. 2.
22. H.A. Rose, *A Glossary of the Tribes and Castes of the Punjab and North-West Frontier Province, Based on the Census Report for the Punjab, 1883 By Late Sir Denzil Ibbetson and Census Report for the Punjab, 1892 by Hon. Mr. MacLagan,* Civil and Military Gazette Press, Lahore: 1911, p. 111.
23. Ibid.
24. Ibid., p. 113.
25. Khan, *Conversions and Shifting Identities,* p. 188-89.
26. Hardayal Singh, *The Castes of Marwar being Census Report of 1891,* Books Treasure, Jodhpur: 1990, p. 47.
27. Maheshwari, *Jambhoji, Bishnoi Sampradaya,* p. 437.
28. Ibid.
29. Also a saying extremely popular with all followers.
30. Heeralal Maheshwari, *Jambhoji ki Sabadvani (Mool aur Teeka),* (The Sabad of Jambhoji – Original and Commentary), B.R. Publications, Calcutta: 1976, p. 10.
31. Rose, *A Glossary of the Tribe,* p. 111.
32. Khan, *Conversions and Shifting Identities,* p. 199.
33. Maheshwari, *Jambhoji, Bishnoi Sampradaya,* p. 442.

34. Ibid., p. 458.
35. This section draws largely from an earlier article—Neekee Chaturvedi, 'Dharmic Activism and Ecological Worldview of the Bishnois', in Sangeeta Sharma, Urvashi Sharma and G.S. Gupta (eds.), *Conversations on Conservation: Narratives from Rajasthan,* Centre for Rajasthan Studies, University of Rajasthan, Jaipur: 2019, pp. 90-119.
36. Maheshwari, *Jambhoji, Bishnoi Sampradaya,* p. 457.
37. Krishnananda Acharya, *Shri Guru Jambheshwar Dwara Uchcharit Jambhavani – Jambhsagar* (The Words uttered by the teacher Jambheshwar – Ocean of Jambh), Akhil Bharatiya Bishnoi Mahasabha, Mukam: 2012, 24th *Prakaran.*
38. 1872, place of accession Mukam.
39. *Parwana Bikaner Adalat ka, AD 1850,* Accessed from Thapan Bandhu, Mukam referred by Maheshwari, *Jambhoji, Bishnoi Sampradaya,* p. 133.
40. Mayank Kumar, 'The Ancien Regime and Conservation of Environs', in Sangeeta Sharma, Urvashi Sharma and G.S. Gupta (eds.), *Conversations on Conservation – Narratives from Rajasthan,* Centre for Rajasthan Studies, University of Rajasthan, Jaipur: 2019, pp. 19-27, 24.
41. Ashis Nandy, *The Intimate Enemy: Loss of Recovery and Self under Colonialism,* Oxford University Press, Delhi: 1983 cited in a review article by Appadurai, Arjuna, 'Is Homo Hierarchicua?', *American Ethnologist,* Vol. 13, No. 4, 1986, p. 749 (745-61).
42. Malcolm Lyall Darling, *Wisdom and Waste in the Punjab Village,* Oxford University Press, London: 1934, p. 150.
43. Rose, *A Glossary of the Tribes,* p. 112.
44. Sir Denzil Ibbetson, *Panjab Castes, Being a Reprint of the Chapter on "Race, Castes and Tribes of Panjab"in the Report on the Census of Panjab published in 1883 by Sir Denzil Ibbetson,* Superintendent Printing Press, Lahore: 1916, p. 13.
45. Ibid., p. 263.
46. Ibid., p. 242.
47. Ibid., p. 114.
48. W. Crooke, *The Tribes and Castes of the North-Western Provinces and Oudh,* Vol. II, Office of the Superintendent of Government Printing India, Calcutta: 1896, p. 120.
49. Ishrat Alam, 'Extracting Social History from Documents of

Medieval India', in Ishrat Alam, and Syed Ijaz Husain (eds.), *The Varied Facets of History*, Primus, Delhi: 2011, p. 62 (59-70).

50. Ibbetson, *Panjab Castes*, p. 114.
51. Ibid., p. 113.
52. Crooke, *The Tribes and Castes*, p. 123.
53. Pankaj Jain, *Dharma and Ecology of Hindu Communities: Sustenance and Sustainability*, Ashgate, Surrey: 2011, p. 55.
54. Darling, *Wisdom and Waste in the*, pp. 150-51.
55. Ibbetson, *Panjab Castes*, p. 123.
56. James Wilson, *Final Report on the Revision of Settlement of the Sirsa District of the Punjab*, Calcutta Central Press Company Ltd., Calcutta: 1884.
56. Crooke, *The Tribes and Castes*, p. 127.
58. H.R. Nevill, *Bijnora: A Gazetteer, District Gazetteers of the United Province of Agra and Oudh*, Vol. XIV, Superintendent, Government Press, United Province, Allahabad: 1908, p. 95.
59. Herman Brockmann and Renato Pichler, *Paving the Way for Peace: Living Philosophies of Bishnois and Jains*, D.K. Publishers, New Delhi: 2004.
60. R.V. Russell, (Assisted by Rai Bahadur Hiralal), *The Tribes and Castes of the Central Provinces of India*, Vol. II, MacMillan & Co. Ltd., London: 1916, p. 342.
61. Ibbetson, *Panjab Castes*, p. 123.
62. Singh, *The Castes of Marwar*, p. 47.
63. K.D. Erskine, *Rajputana Gazetteers, The Western Rajputana States Residency and the Bikaner Agency*, Vol. III A, The Pioneer Press, Allahabad: 1909, pp. 90-91.
64. Ibbetson, *Panjab Castes*, p. 123.
65. Crooke, *The Tribes and Castes*, p. 127.
66. Nevill, *Bijnora*, p. 95.
67. Maheshwari, *Jambhoji ki Sabadvani*, p. 14.
68. *Hindu ho ke Hari kyun na japyo.*
69. Maheshwari, *Jambhoji ki Sabadvani*, p. 17.
70. *Alla rasit Iman.*
71. Maheshwari, *Jambhoji ki Sabadvani*, pp. 17-20, *Sabad* 7, 8, 9, 10 & 11.
72. Maheshwari, *Jambhoji, Bishnoi Sampradaya*, pp. 442-43.
73. Colonel James Tod, *Annals and Antiquities of Rajasthan*, Vol. III,

Oxford University Press, London: 1920, p. 1297.

74. J. Hutton, *Caste in India: Its Nature, Functions and Origins*, Cambridge University Press, Cambridge: 6, p. 278.
75. Maheshwari, *Jambhoji ki Sabadvani*, pp. 32-33.
76. *Jatan hute paat karilo,ai kisan chirat parwano.*
77. Maheshwari, *Jambhoji, Bishnoi Sampradaya*, p. 462.
78. Ibid.
79. Ibid., p. 98.
80. Crooke, *The Tribes and Castes*. The castes mentioned by the leader are Jat, Bishnoi, Banya Bishnoi, Brahman Bishnoi, Ahir Bishnoi, Sunar Bishnoi, Nai Bishnoi, Chauhan Bishnoi, Bayha Bishnoi.
81. Nevill, *Bijnora*, p. 266.
82. H.R. Nevill, *Moradabad: A Gazetteer, Being Volume XVI of the District Gazetteers of the United Province of Agra and Oudh*, Superintendent Government Press, United Province: 1911, p. 74.
83. Captain A.D. Bannerman, *Census of India, 1901*, Vol. 25 (Rajputana), Naval Kishore Press, Lucknow: 1902, p. 48.
84. Bannerman, *Census of India, 1901*, p. 144.
85. Erskine, *Rajputana Gazetteers*, p. 77.
86. Russell, *The Tribes and Castes*, p. 343.
87. Crooke, *The Tribes and Castes*, p. 127.
88. Bannerman, *Census of India*, 1901, pp. 74-75.
89. Ibid., p.75.
90. Rose, *A Glossary of the Tribes*, p. 112; Erskine, *Rajputana Gazetteers*, p. 15.
91. Erskine, *Rajputana Gazetteers*, p. 15.
92. Rose, *A Glossary of the Tribes*, p. 112.
93. O'Dwyer, *War Speeches*, p. 41.
94. Thomas S. Smith, 'Sirsa and Sirsa Folk', *The Calcutta Review*, Vol. XCIV, 1892, p. 63.
95. Ibbetson, *Panjab Castes*, pp. 112-13.
96. Bannerman, *Census of India, 1901*, p. 144.
97. Darling, *Wisdom and Waste*, p. 158.
98. Ibbetson, *Panjab Castes*, p. 112.
99. Maheshwari, *Jambhoji, Bishnoi Sampradaya*, p. 192.
100. Erskine, *Rajputana Gazetteers*, p. 77.
101. Ibid.

102. Neekee Chaturvedi, *Cultural Tourism and Bishnois of Rajasthan*, Rajasthani Granthagar, Jodhpur: 2018, p. 26.
103. Maheshwari, *Jambhoji ki Sabadvani*, p. 253.
104. Erskine, *Rajputana Gazetteers*, p. 77.

15

Ideologies and the Thoughts of Anthropologists on Tribes in Indian Historical and Political Anthropology in the Early Twentieth Century

Netrapal Singh

Anthropologists played an important role in the formation of tribal identities in twentieth century colonial India. The interpretations relating to aboriginal identity, absorption of tribal elements into caste, Hindu and non-Hindu identity of tribes came from different schools of thoughts in historical anthropology which emerged in the late nineteenth and early twentieth centuries. Ideologically oriented academic debates in historical anthropology had been focused on various shades of tribal identity and reached its decisive phase in 1940s. The anthropologists who made significant contributions in the field of tribal anthropology and sociology may be classified into two important categories on the basis upon their affiliation with political ideology and the positions taken by them on tribal policy. According to political ideology they were known as colonialist, Hindu nationalist, and marxist anthropologists. There were some who were known for their independent views and it was difficult to fix them in a watertight ideology classification. Ideological orientation of the anthropologists influenced their approach in advocating the framing of tribal policy. From the point of view of approaches such anthropologists were known as protectionists, assimilationists and integrationists. The

Colonialists adopted protectionist and the Hindu nationalist anthropologists advocated assimilationist positions on tribal policy in India. Anthropologists who took an entirely different position from the Colonialists and the Hindu nationalists were classified as integrationist anthropologists.

This chapter is focused on the anthropologists' thoughts and ideas related primarily to tribal or aboriginal identity instead of policy formation. The debate of identity formation of tribes among anthropologists was focused on two important questions. The first question was related to their historicity. Were the tribes in India aboriginals? And the second question was focused on their religious identity. Whether the tribes were Hindus or Non-Hindus? These questions have been inquired on the basis upon intellectual contributions made by prominent anthropologists such as J.H. Hutton, W.V. Grigson, Verrier Elwin, N.K. Bose, G.S. Ghurye, M.N. Srinivas, B.R. Ambedkar and D.D. Kosambi. The investigation includes methodological and ideological aspects of these anthropologists to understand their thoughts and theories about the origins, evolutions and historical transformations of the Indian social Institutions. In ideological orientated classification Hutton, Grigson, and Elwin are known as colonialist anthropologists; Bose, Ghurye, and Srinivas as Hindu nationalist anthropologists; and Kosambi as Marxist anthropologist. Ambedkar is known for his own independent views having some Marxist influence in his anthropological writings. Therefore both Kosambi and Ambedkar have been included in a separate category for the similarity of their ideas and thoughts on the interpretation of Indian society. So many great anthropologists are well known for their important works on tribal communities particularly in the early twentieth century India. Hutton, Grigson and Elwin; Bose, Ghurye and Srinivas; Ambedkar and Kosambi have been included in this chapter for their seminal intellectual contributions in widening and transforming the understanding of people about tribal communities and their contributions in the making of Indian society. The thoughts and theories of these intellectuals and anthropologists had widely influenced the intelligentsia and academia for understanding various issues and aspects of the Indian tribal world. However, these intellectuals actively participated in the process of identity formation and policy formation for the upliftment and welfare of tribal or aboriginal communities in various official and academic capacities. They played into the roles of administrators, missionaries, social activists and policy makers but their inclusion in this study is based primarily on their contributions as professional academic anthropologists who have been taught in Indian academic institutions.

Some important recent studies on the meo tribe of eastern Rajasthan[1] and the bhil tribes found in southern Rajasthan, western Madhya Pradesh and eastern Gujarat[2] explore the transformation and survival of tribal identities and polities since the medieval period to the early colonial period in eighteenth century.

I

The foundation of Hutton's philosophical and theoretical formations about Indian social institutions is based on his field tours and experience with the Naga tribes. His theory of primitiveness was established in his monographs *The Sema Naga* and *The Angamis*. He considered the sema nagas as the most primitive tribe in India untouched by the influences of modern civilizations. Hence he examined the term 'animism' suffered with serious limitations to represent the religion of tribes in India, therefore invented a new term "tribal religion" *The Sema Naga*. In the early census operations and reports the religion of the semas was termed as animism. Hutton questioned Edward Tylor's definition of animism as a "belief in spiritual beings". In his view, Tylor's definition of animism was too simplistic that covered most of the human beings as animists under its ambit. In place of Tylor's notion of animism, he accepted James Frazer's thoughts on transformation of religious beliefs of the tribes expressed in *The Golden Bough*. According to Frazer, "When definite deities with specific names and function are recognized, the Animist has become a Polytheist and the term Animism is no longer strictly applicable."[3] Then Hutton further argued, "If this be so, the Sema is in the process of ceasing, if he has not already ceased, to be an 'Animist.'[4]

Hutton distinguished 'Tribal Religion' from 'Animism' on the basis of the primitive notions of taboo, *mana,* and soul-matter. These were the fundamental elements of tribal religion explained by Hutton in his *Caste In India* published in 1946. Initially, in *The Sema Naga* the conception of soul and magic were noticed as two primary elements of Nagas' religion. Soul was accepted as "shadow" in metaphysical sense that was 'not confined to human or even animates beings.' He observed that there were different views on the final departure of the soul from its former inhabitation in naga beliefs. He interpreted the importance of magic in religious ceremonies practised by the semas as propitiatory rather than magical. He observed that 'among the semas magical ceremonies originally were intended to control the operations of Nature, and the ceremony was performed partly in the belief that to omit it would be displeasing to the spirits and partly with the direct object of pleasing them by offerings.'[5] In addition to this, the feasts organized at the time of religious ceremonies or some other occasions were used as means of raising social status or distinction among the semas.

The scope of Hutton's anthropological inquiry was not limited only to the northeastern naga tribes. A glimpse of true sub-continental level scope of anthropological inquiry was revealed in his *Caste in India*. He had described about various tribes and castes of different regions of India, including the tribes of central India and Chota Nagpur, drawing a picture of their racial elements and primitiveness. In his view, 'the subcontinent of India had been linked to a deep net into which various races and peoples of Asia had been drifted and been caught.'[6] He stated that the earliest human inhabitants of Indian peninsula were negritos. They had survived in the purest form in the Andaman Islands. Traces of their blood were found in Cochin forest in southern India, the Rajmahal Hills of Bihar, and naga villages on the northeast frontier between Assam and Burma. They constituted the earliest tribal population in eastern and southern India. Proto-Australoids were the next comers 'who allied to primitive races spread over the Indian archipelago and were very widely spread all over India, particularly among the lower castes and humbler classes of society.'Later elements were probably of Mediterranean and Iranian origin, Armenoid, Eurasiatic contributed to Indian population.

In Hutton's inquiry each racial element made its specific contribution to social formations in India particularly to the tribal religion and the institution of caste. It became the basis of socio-religious identities of various categories in India. The theory of soul-matter, *mana*, head-hunting and totemism as the elements of tribal religion were his fundamental contributions in understanding the importance of tribal identity or primitive identity in the formation of Hinduism and the caste system in India. The tribes who continued to live in the forests and hills had never been part of the Hindu caste system and in that sense their social position has never been defined in relation to Hindu society. According to Hutton, from the earliest times the primitive tribes who remained unassimilated were never downgraded to the rank of low castes.

Hutton adopted the "principle of conflicts" rather than "principle of ethics and idealism" in his proposition of the formation of social institutions. In his view, according to the principle of conflicts, 'the institutions of human society were generally the result of conflicting principles in which self-seeking and economic considerations played almost as great a part as superstition, while sublimation came in at a later stage when the results were appreciated as being far from ideal.' In his view, the theories of the origin of caste interpreted by brahminical scholars and others, lay stress on the phenomena rather than cause of the caste system. The formation of the institution of caste was the outcome of the interaction between the primitive conceptions of totemism, *mana,* and soul-stuff: the tribal system of pre-Dravidian and the occupational class of system of the Dravidian, on the one hand, and the Indo-Aryan Varna system, on the other.

Hutton introduced the theory of *mana* that he observed first among the nagas in the naga hills in 1923-24 and later among various other communities from lower to upper sections of Indian society in different regions of India including the central provinces. The theory of *mana* was based on two hypotheses. The first was the vivid belief in *mana* among the nagas and the magical effects of food on the consumer for creating taboos because certain foods were peculiar to certain exogamous clans. The second was the belief that the food of strangers was itself dangerous for certain exogamous clans. Hutton explained the relationship between the two hypotheses and stated that: "Both depend for their force on the belief in *mana* and in the resulting taboo on food or other contacts, which may be infected with the dangerous soul-matter of strangers; this soul matter is particularly perilous if such strangers are new and, what is same thing, mysterious arts and therefore magical powers."[7] The occupational taboo in which tribal village was observed as an independent political and occupational unit was sufficed by commensal taboo. It was observed that beliefs in life-matter, or soul-stuff, were closely associated with beliefs in *mana* and with the practice of magic. Such ideas were common over the whole area of southeast Asia and Australia from India to New Zealand, and possibly the ideas of *mana* and taboo were distributed to Indonesia and Pacific from the Indian peninsula in Hutton's opinion. But the uniqueness of the caste as a social institution in India emerged, Hutton stresses, due to largely the social and political impact of the Rigvedic Aryan invaders with their definitely graded social classes that was responsible for introducing the principle of social precedence into a society already divided into groups isolated by taboos.

Hutton became an admirer of the tribal anthropology, developed a circle of friendship with some of his contemporary British administrators, and encouraged them to study the tribal communities in India to produce ethnographic knowledge for the purpose of benevolent British administration. Anthropologist-administrator W.V. Grigson was one such among them who made significant contributions to the understanding of cultural identity and socio-economic problems of tribal communities in central India.He advocated framing a tribal policy according to the tradition and customs of the aboriginals.

As an administrator Grigson realized the importance of anthropology for studying tribal institutions and culture for a benevolent and just administration. Some of the nationalist politicians criticized the British anthropologists for their advocacy for the isolation and protection of tribal or aboriginal identity and culture from the influence of Hindus and also from the Christian missionaries. Grigson replied to them that as an academic discipline 'anthropology had a very practical value to all charges with the administration of other races if it could discover the thoughts and need of those races.'[8] He emphasized that in the absence of appropriate anthropological knowledge and subsequent information many adverse conditions and problems emerged against the aboriginal tribes in central India. More specifically such problems were related to the implementation of the policies of land revenue, police department and judicial administration in the cases of the maria tracts of Bastar and on a larger scale on the bhils, the gonds and the korkus in Bombay Presidency and the central provinces particularly in the post 1919 period. Such policies and subsequent outcomes encouraged Grigson to explore the field of anthropology to investigate the problems of aboriginal tribes in Bastar, and subsequently in Hyderabad State.

Grigson realized that anthropological research was a means of administrative success and a mechanism of understanding social, economic, political and cultural problems, and psychology of the aboriginal tribes. In his ethnological monograph *The Maria Gonds of Bastar* (1938), he emphasized the importance of regular involvement and engagement of an administrator on those whom he had to administer. He adopted the method of participation for his study to understand the life of the maria gonds. In his view the divorce of administration from anthropology was the cause of policy failure and misreading of the aspirations and feelings of aboriginal tribes.

In one of his important papers "The Aboriginal in the Future India"[9] Grigson highlighted the importance of anthropology and outlined its course of development as an academic discipline to fulfill the administrative objectives and destroy political biases about various communities, particularly the aboriginal tribes, in post-colonial India. He emphasized the economic and political side of the problem of the aboriginals rather than cultural in examining the safeguards provided for the aboriginals in British India in the constitution of 1935. Grigson synthesized cultural elements of the aboriginals with economic and political. In his view, understanding of culture leads to understanding economic and political matters of aboriginal tribes. He set the principle in which economic and political autonomy of aboriginal tribes precedes cultural autonomy. To achieve this objective Grigson suggested, "Teach him to hold his head high in economic and political matters, and he will of his own accord re-assert his cultural autonomy."[10] *The Maria Gonds of Bastar* was his most important work to understanding the cultural aspects of aboriginal marias. In this monograph, he followed his own style of anthropological inquiry that include his tours, interactions, observations, information supplied by his assistant officials and its cross examination with reliable observers, and mixing it with already existing ethnographic and ethnological literature and the anthropometric measurements taken from the field. It became an interesting study from the point of view of methodological inquiry different from the Huttonian and the Elwinian methods of anthropological research.

Grigson on the basis of the ethnographic material collected from various sources established the theory of the mother-earth as the centre point of the religious philosophy of the marias of Bastar. According to this theory, the whole life of the maria was primarily directed towards raising of food from the earth, either by cultivation, gathering the fruits from forests, fishing, hunting or trapping. Agriculture determined sites of villages and regulated matrimonial relationships between husband and wife in the maria community. 'The feasts and festivals of Marias were designed to ensure the benevolence of the earth, the ancestors and the clan-god. The human population to him was the crop of men that the Bhum or Earth raised for the clan, or for the Ruling Chief.'[11] The notions of the cult of *bhum* (the earth), the clan-god, and the 'village mother' were the primary elements of religious ideology of the marias. There were two perspectives to explain the fundamental relation between the earth, the clan-god, and the village mother in Marias' philosophy. Firstly, the village mother was tempting to regard her as the personification of the female and the clan-god as that of the male element in the reproductive powers of the earth or *bhum* in a hill and bison-horn village. Secondly, the clan-god was the earth in its dealings with the clan, and the mother the earth in its dealings with the village. Grigson further stated, "The Earth, then, as clan-god, is the god of nourishment and reproduction, and of life itself; the Marias are his children, fed by him. For them to raise their sustenance he divided up the land among the clans, and the clan-area among the villages, and in each clan and village he appointed priests or headmen who alone might communicate with him, and to whose first ancestor he revealed the clan and village boundaries, which knowledge has been handed down from father to son. The Maria leaves his penda slope for another after two or three years because the god is suffering from having too much nourishment extracted from that slope, but he will return to it when the god has recovered from his exhaustion. Children are but one of the god's crops."[12] Thus, the religious philosophy of the hill marias and bison-horn marias was based on natural phenomena. In their religious ideology, the universe was *bhum,* the sky being *pogho-bhum,* and the earth *adi-bhum.* To them the sun was a koitor, the moon his woman, and the stars were their children.

Grigson found that the process of Hinduization had

generated different castes out of the primitive race of gonds under new names such as raj-gond, raj-korku, raja-muria, naik gond, and pit-bhattra. Contrary to the Hinduization of aboriginal tribes, he also witnessed the process of tribalization among some groups of gonds returning back to their aboriginal cultural and linguistic roots in particular, and to the whole confederations of tribes in general. The parjas were the best example of the re-tribalization beyond the Jeypore border in Bastar state that included seven different tribes speaking munda, dravidian, and aryan dialects despite differing widely in customs and degree of advancement. The formation of a religious philosophy and the fusion of cultures among the gonds were the outcomes of intermixing of their different racial elements such as the pre-dravidian the dravidian and the brachycephalic. In his assessment a pre-dravidian element was modified by a dravidian and mixed with alpine element. But Grigson concluded that all three racial types of gonds were the 'aboriginals' of India.

Verrier Elwin was an anthropologist who earned respect and a very high position in British anthropology. The understanding of tribals of India remains incomplete without Elwin. The prestigious Oxford University Press recognizes Elwin's contribution on tribal culture accepting that any discussion on anthropological writing in India necessarily foregrounds Verrier Elwin's work. Truly, "Verrier Elwin's approach to the study of tribal culture in India was coloured neither by orientalism nor paternalism, the then dominant approaches to the cultural study of the 'other'. Elwin's involvement was spurred by genuine concern and empathy.'[13] At the time when Elwin entered the field of anthropological research, 'The 'tribal' was essentially a political premise and the colonial government had managed to seal it off from the twentieth-century intellectual thinking about Indian society. It was natural, therefore, the tribals were already a forgotten issue in Indian politics and society. It was Elwin's historic burden to re-examine the category, turn it upside down, and gain sympathy, if not respectability, for the tribes. He carried out this seemingly impossible task with unparalleled dedication."[14] His dedication to scientific inquiry of the tribal culture yielded in *The Baiga* published in 1939. In Hutton's view 'it was a full account of the Baiga that came after a hundred years of wait in anthropology, but Elwin had paid the debt fully as any single author could who had to work on a tribe after its tribal life and organization had largely gone.'[15]

Elwin described his methodology used in *The Baiga,* which was almost similar to the methodology adopted by Hutton and Grigson in their primary works. He distanced himself from an official and a missionary on account of their limitations in anthropological inquiry. Thus he was free from the burden of an official who might seem too alarming, and a missionary who might seem too respectable. Although, he was simply regarded as an amicable and eccentric person who was interested in everybody and everything, and to whom people could say anything that came into their heads. Such a position was immensely important from the point of a researcher in an anthropological inquiry.

Elwin had nineteen books to his credit on tribal culture and many had gained a near-classic status. But in *The Baiga* and *The Aboriginals* (1943), Elwin dealt with the question of aboriginal identity of the Indian tribes, their problems and policy for upliftment and welfare. They were important for sparking a debate on cultural and religious identity of tribes and the policy of protection raising it to the highest level. Elwin's ideas and thoughts related to the aboriginal identity received praise and criticism from the scholars, anthropologists and policy makers. His views on the policy of protection of the baigas particularly provoked the Hindu nationalist anthropologists to counter his propositions proposed in *The Baiga*. In *The Baiga* Elwin discussed the cult of bewar, magic, the diagnosis and cure of disease, the knowledge of the legendry past, the art of recreation, and the art of love as the baiga's own unique cultural elements. Subsequently, racial affinities with early history, tribal language and anthropometric elements were discussed in his famous and controversial pamphlet *The*

Aboriginals. Elwin said that *The Baiga* was the outcome of his deep admiration and affection for the baiga in the hope that it would also stimulate similar feelings among those who were not familiar with their culture and customs. According to him it was this hope that led him to propose the policy of "National Park" for the protection of baigas.

Elwin proposed that the baigas were the original owners of the country. These 'original owners' were known for practicing the *bewar*. He stated that 'the *Bewar*-an ancient method of shifting cultivation was the religion of the Baiga In the Baiga country the bewar was the foundation of the economic and social life of the Baiga tribe. It was their own possession of life made them different from all others. More important than the passion the bewar was a right and duty laid on them from the beginning of the world by the God. Mother the earth (Dharti Mata) was respected as Anna Dai, the goddess of crop. Using the plough for plowing the land was equated with tearing the breast of Mother the earth. It was like committing a great sin and inviting a curse on them.'[16] The British government created the Baiga Chak-a demarcated area for the settlement of the baigas to practice *bewar* within it under the Malguzari system of land revenue settlement in Mandla. Elwin made a distinction between the Baiga Chak and the National Park. 'The National Park was a place where the baiga was supposed to be carrying on their ancient tribal life. But the Chak was a Reformatory under strict supervision and increasing official pressure, where the Baigas were slowly weaned from their primitive habits.'[17]

In *The Aboriginals,* Elwin discussed racial affinities and anthropometric characters for proving aboriginality of tribes in a historical sense. He stated that at the time of writing this pamphlet, language and racial coefficient were not safe tests for racial identity of tribes in anthropology. He adopted Von Eickstedt's racial classification of Indian tribes on the basis of historical periodization. Hence, Elwin was not satisfied with the classification of the aboriginal tribes on the basis of language and racial elements. He adopted cultural approach for studying the aboriginal problems because the social, economic and political problems of the aboriginal tribes, in his opinion, originated due to cultural differences rather than linguistic and racial difference.

Elwin introduced his own scheme of the classification of aboriginal tribes on the basis of cultural developments. He classified them into four main cultural classes with separate administrative treatment. The first class of aboriginals used to live in remote hill areas and retained their primitiveness and original traditions; and the second class inhabited in equally remote areas and were equally attached to their solitude and ancient traditions but with a change in many small and subtle ways. Elwin observed that the first two classes constituted a small number of aboriginals of real primitive living in the hills. Their religion was characteristic and alive; their tribal organization was unimpaired; their mythology vitalized the healthy organism of tribal life. The third class of the aboriginals, the most numerous, came in contact with the influence of external contact, primarily Hindu infiltration, and began losing their hold on tribal culture, religion and social organization. The process of Hinduization was responsible for all these losses. The fourth class of aboriginals consisted of the old tribal aristocracy represented by the bhil and naga chieftains, the gond rajas, the korku noblemen, wealthy santals and uraons and the highly cultural mundas. According to Elwin they retained the old tribal names and their clan and totem rules and observed elements of tribal religion, though they had generally adopted the full Hindu faith and lived in modern and even European style. The fourth class of aboriginals had thus won the battle of cultural-contact.

Elwin preferred to enable the tribesmen of the first two classes to advance directly into the fourth without having to suffer the despair and degradation of the third. Actually, for him, it was the real problem of the aboriginal tribes in India. To resolve their problems, he advised adoption of the principle of love and reverence as the basis of the formation of tribal; policy for tribal upliftment and development. The aboriginal tribes had the first right on the resources of the country because, Elwin stated, "The aboriginals are the real swadeshi product of India, in whose presence everyone is foreign. They are the ancient people with moral claims and rights thousands of years old. They were the first: they should come first in our regard."[18] Thus Elwin advised framing of tribal policy on the basis of distinct aboriginal identity of the tribes, as they were the earliest or the first inhabitants of India.

Elwin produced another seminal work on the religious identity of the aboriginal savara or soaras tribe in central India in *The Religion of an Indian Tribe* published in 1955. Although he had began his investigations about the religion of the soaras since 1944. In his view, the term savara was synonymous to the words 'aboriginal', 'bhumijan' or 'adibasi' that included within its domain the kols, kurkus, bhils, santals, bhuiyas, mundas, hos, bhmij, and juangs.

Elwin suggested that the soaras were an important and widely scattered tribe who were broken up into different groups from the earliest period. The savaras from the earliest times to the middle ages were the dominant race of aboriginals having the qualities of bravery in organized war and independence in social and political affairs. It was believed that the aboriginal tribes were lacking in organized religious structure and functionaries. But Elwin fulfilled this gap of knowledge revealing a full view of savara's organized religious structure and religious functionaries both men and women with religious process of performing rituals and ceremonies. It was equally important that they had included women as religious functionaries in their religious organization. Elwin clearly indicated that Buddhism and animism or tribal religion were closely associated with each other. Buddhism as a religious philosophy and as a way of life was the advanced stage of the tribal religion and tribal life. Buddhist institutions and tribal institutions were similar in nature. Therefore, the savanas transformed their lives according to the principles of Buddhism. It was Elwin's greatest contribution that completely transformed the identity of the tribes from 'criminal' to 'aboriginal' with the historical legacy of Buddhism—a religion based upon the principles of humanity and rationality.

II

The Hindu nationalist school of thought in anthropology looked into tribal identity from revivalist Hindu perspective in the first half of the nineteenth century. The biggest critique of the colonial anthropologists and the British anthropology came from the Hindu nationalist anthropologists. The strongest voices and prominent critiques were N.K. Bose, G.S. Ghurye and M.N. Srinivas.

N.K. Bose's original interest was in cultural anthropology especially in the material culture. His professional career as a field anthropologist began as early as 1924-25, when he was a student of master's degree in anthropology at the University of Calcutta. In 1929, he brought out *Cultural Anthropology*, presenting a developing world view of anthropology and culture. His first independent field research was among the Juang tribes of Orissa. His brief spell of field research developed his basic insights to explore the methods of absorption of tribes into the fold of Hinduism. He was of the view that there could be no set ways for actual fieldwork. The nature of the task should guide the researcher to adopt suitable tools of investigation or the fashion depending on the problem of inquiry. He wrote in an article (1950) that there could be no general method with which to solve all possible problems. He consistently stressed upon the importance of careful and meticulous observation in a field research. In an introduction to *Peasant Life in India* (1961) Bose stated that a deep acquaintance with the facts of life was the best introduction to any form of social science.

Association of Bose with Gandhi and his active participation in the nationalist movement influenced his ideas in interpreting the structure of Hindu society. He imagined constructing Indian society on the gandhian principles. Gandhism and the ideals of Hindu nationalism were the guiding forces of his theory of the Hindu method of tribal absorption. In the background of the nationalist movement, he proposed the theory of 'Hindu Method of Tribal Absorption'. The idea of absorption was first introduced in 1941 in a paper presented by Bose before the Indian Science Congress (Anthropology Section) held at Benaras and later published with the same title in the journal *Science and Culture*. It was a brief account of the relationship between tribes and civilization in Indian history, and might be considered as a kind of broader theoretical framework of his work. Bose proposed to apply the principles and ideology of Hindu nationalism in the reconstruction of Hindu society to bring all social divisions in India under the umbrella of Hinduism. In his view, 'the whole Hindu society was one but the differences among its social classes had to be sorted out to combine as a nation unified in political aspiration as well as in in national action. A proper and exhaustive survey on these lines would reveal the true nature of the foundations of underlying Hindu society, and this would naturally help us a great deal in our task of future social reconstruction.'[19] Thus he was setting up a nationalist agenda in Indian academic pursuit to destroy all smaller and separate independent socio-cultural, religious and political identities for merging them in a larger Hindu identity according to the gandhian explanation of Hindu society based upon the system of varna and caste. Bose also believed that one of the prominent contributions of the freedom struggle was that it narrowed down the society's diversity.

He worked among the juangs, a tribe of Chhotanagpur, and drew his theory on the basis of observations made among them. He said, 'The significant fact is this, that the Juangs had started worshiping a Hindu goddess, although it was done in their own way. The bath in the morning, the offering of sun-dried rice, the term *satya, devta, dharma,* all proves how strongly Juangs' religious ceremonies have been influenced by those of neighbouring brahminical people.'[20] From a materialistic point of view, Bose considered Hindu mode of production more advanced than the tribal mode of production in India.

In the Hindu productive organization, the Juangs enjoyed a virtual monopoly in basket making in the state of Pal Lahara, because of the fact, that no other Hindu caste was willing to engage in the profession of basket making for fear of losing its social status. He considered this economic affiliation to Hindu society as a fact of superiority of Hindu culture and absorption of Juangs into Hinduism. He also stated that similar process of Hinduization was found among the santals and mundas in Chhotanagpur. This conclusion was not based on his own investigation among them rather he drew it on the basis of anthropologist Sarat Chandra Roy's monographs *Oraon Religion and Customs* and *The Mundas and their Country*.

Bose justified his field observations related to his theory of tribal absorption on the basis of Hindu scriptures especially the codes of Manu. His theory of tribal absorption was based on three fundamental methods: 1. In the scheme of four varnas of Hindus, the tribes were placed in the fourth *varna*, or as the shudra. 2. Once they became part of Hindu society they were guaranteed a monopoly in a particular occupation at the time of absorbing a new tribe or while creating a new *jati* by differentiation of occupation to each caste within a particular region. 3. In specific conditions, the same *jati* was allowed to practice a different trade if the prescribed hereditary occupation was found no longer economically satisfactory. Thus Bose interpreted the foundation of the caste system within the principles of economic determinism. In his interpretation the economic and social legislators of ancient India built up a social organization on the basis of hereditary monopolistic guilds as the base of the caste system. The success of such monopolistic guild organization yielded two important results in Indian history: the absorption of tribes within the fold of productive organization of the Hindus; and they did not revolt when they were relegated to a lowly position within Hindu society. The success of the tribal absorption in Hinduism depended upon the strategy in which 'the Hindus hardly left any economic freedom to *jatis* but they left in tact the original social and religious culture of the tribes in so far as that was possible. Their policy was not to eradicate the old beliefs and practices where they were not inconsistent with Brahminical moral ideas.'[21] This policy was the basis of distinction between the Hindu method of tribal absorption and the methods adopted by the Christian and Islamic people in Bose's observation. It is important to notice that in Bose's theory of the Hindu method of tribal absorption it was economic absorption rather than cultural absorption. Thus Bose proposed economic interpretation of tribal absorption into Hinduism distinguished from Srinivas's theory of cultural interpretation. In Srinivas's cultural interpretation these were the tribes who imitated Hindu cultural symbols, practices and customs to raise their social status and position but in Bose's model these were the Hindus who imposed their economic organization on the tribes. But in both the cases the tribes were considered inferior and assigned a lower position in the Hindu social and economic order.

Bose expanded his views on the tribal absorption, relationship between tribe and Hindu civilization, the formation of Hindu society and the historical dynamisms of its transformation in his study *The Structure of Hindu Society* (1949). Bose's methodology in this study represents a mix of methodologies of an ethnographer, indologist and a historian. Similarly it may be divided into three parts. The first part deals with the domain of ethnology in which he discussed the primary data and material collected by him and others through fieldwork mainly among the juangs, savaras, santals and mundas. The second part deals with Indology where an account of theory and practice of Hindu social life set in some of the principal Hindu classical texts. The third part deals with social history of Hindu society and the elements of change in Hindu social structure.

Bose talked about two modes of social organization, namely the 'brahminical' and the 'tribal' and their coexistence in Indian history. In his observation, the former was superior in technological advancement, larger in scale and complex in nature in comparison to the latter. Technical superiority attracted the tribal communities towards Hindu culture rather than the superior political power of the brahminical civilization. Interestingly, the influence of aryan or brahminical civilization was greater among the mundas and oraons than the juangs or savaras though the former were superior to the latter in technology. It was common knowledge imparted by anthropology that the tribals learned the skills of agriculture from the caste Hindus.

The most orthodox arguments and interpretations related to religious identity of tribes came from Hindu nationalist anthropologist-sociologist G.S. Ghurye. He prolonged the debate of cultural and religious identity of tribes in the first half of the twentieth century to another level opposing the legacy of colonial anthropology. Ghurye, as a professional academician and scholar was the synthesis of an indologist, a social anthropologist and a historian. Receiving his initial training as a sanskritist, Ghurye began to work on a synthesis of indological and sociological-anthropological approaches. He realized the importance of combining the sociological-anthropological approach with historical-textual approach and applied it in his research. Ghurye developed a firm and strong belief in historical and empirical facts and the value of fieldwork from his apprenticeship at the Cambridge University.

The ideology of Hindu nationalism and brahminism had a great influence on Ghurye's writings and views. The influence of Hindu nationalism in his works came from his ideological background. Sociologists A.R. Momin observed that 'the ideology of narrow and exclusivist nationalism advocated by the Brahmin elite, represented by Vishnushastri Chiplunkar in Maharashtra, had a formative influence on Ghurye. His early background in the classics and his life-long preoccupation with textual and scriptural sources led him to adopt the Brahminical model of Indian society, which is too idealistic and over-arching away from the empirical reality.'[22] Ghurye's writings as a nationalist thinker and academician might be examined from the perspective of Hindu ideology.

Ghurye's *The Aborigines-So-called- And Their Future* (1943) was written in Hindu nationalistic framework. In some scholarly opinion, it was Ghurye's biggest contribution to social anthropology after his *Caste and Race in India* (1932). In *The Aborigines* Ghurye was seen as the biggest critique of colonial anthropology championing the revivalist Hindu nationalist anthropology. He observed that colonial anthropology mooted the idea in which the Indian tribes were treated as the aborigines or the original inhabitants of India since the 1891 Census. They were the people who used to practice animistic religion distinct from Hinduism, Islam and Christianity. Ghurye criticized the census administrators and officials starting from Baines to Hutton and the anthropologically minded administrators like Grigson and especially Elwin for their propositions of aborigines and animism. Ghurye in his *The Aborigines* focused on the tribes of central India for the treatment of their identity and problems.

Ghurye proposed the theory of a 'Backward Hindu' in *The Aborigines* against the theory of the 'Aborigines' proposed by the colonialist anthropologists. He rejected Elwin's proposition of the 'Aboriginals.' He argued that 'many of the so-called aboriginal tribes have come to the present habitat from somewhere else in India. They cannot, therefore be considered to be autochthones or the original owner of the soil of their present tracts.'[23] In his opinion linguistically the speakers of the dravidian (the paharias, the oraons, the gonds, and the konds) and the kherwari (the santals, the mundas, and the korkus) languages in central India immigrated to India through the Punjab and Sind like the rigvedic aryan-speakers of Indo-Aryans tongue. Racially, the negritos were the earliest inhabitants of India followed by the proto-australoids (dravidian). After them the austro-asiatic (kherwari) came from northeast and then the Indo-Aryans migrated to India. Such conclusions led him to reject the theory of tribes as the aboriginal people of India.

Ghurye was completely opposed to accept tribes as the aborigines to determine their claim for special treatment and safeguards in the constitutional policy introduced in the Government of India Act, 1935. In his view the constitutional rights and safeguards for the representation of tribes or aborigines in legislature, welfare and upliftment were the means of disintegration of national unity. He argued that 'the policy of special treatment and safeguards was likely to meet with the stoutest opposition and create a feeling of hostility towards them. The claims of representation of different strata of the Indian society on the grounds of their antiquity were a frightfully difficult task and their implementation would only liberate the forces of disunity.'[24] Thus Ghurye denied the existence of separate identity of tribes and the need for a separate policy for tribal representation because they were the backward Hindus in his opinion.

Ghurye classified the tribes into three categories on the basis of their cultural relationship with the Hindus First, were the sections of tribes that properly integrated in the Hindu society. Second, a large section loosely assimilated into Hinduism.Third was the section of the hills and forest tribes which were untouched by Hinduism. It was almost similar to Elwin's classification of tribes in his investigation. Ghurye argued that 'the Aborigines were imperfectly the integrated classes of Hindu society. He said that for the sake of convenience they might be designated the tribal classes of the Hindu society. It was a social fact that they had retained much more of the tribal creeds and organization than many of the castes of Hindu society. Despite that they were Hindus but backward.'[25] Ghurye's explanation of the theory of tribes as backward Hindus was empirically weak because his arguments were tediously repetitive, polemical and defensive. The title of the book was also polemical. He had repeated the arguments of the British census officials and anthropologists.

Ghurye produced many of the first generation sociologists and anthropologists in India who made significant contributions to the discipline of anthropology.

Sociologist M.N. Srinivas was a distinguished student of Ghurye. He was born in a brahmin family in Mysore in southern India and came to the University of Bombay for higher studies. Srinivas completed his MA and PhD degrees in sociology under the guidance of Ghurye from the University of Bombay.

In the early 1940s Srinivas came under the influence of the nationalist movement and gandhian thoughts in Bombay. In a memoir Srinivas stated that 'he was interested in studying Gandhi for his doctoral research but Ghurye forced him to pursue ethnographic fieldwork based on "Socio-Ethnic Study" of the Coorgs in Southern India on a fellowship applying the diffusionist approach.'[26] Srinivas on the basis of ethnographic fieldwork interpreted the concept of functional unity by explaining the interaction in ritual context of different castes of coorg, mainly brahmins (priests), kaniyas (astrologers and magicians), bannas and panikas (low castes). While Srinivas was doing his research under Ghurye, Ghurye was seriously working on his *The Aborigines So-called and Their Future* (1943) to counter the Elwinian propositions made in his *The Baiga* (1939) and *The Loss of Nerve* (1941).

Srinivas introduced a method of macro-sociological generalizations based upon micro-anthropological insights in the field of anthropological investigation in his work on the Coorgs. His work among the Coorgs led the foundation of his formulation of the notion of brahminization to highlight the imitation of lifeways and ritual practices of brahmins by the lower-caste Hindus. It was used as an explanatory device to interpret social changes observed in the ritual practices and lifeways of the lower castes through intensive and careful field study. It was similar, rather enlarge version with different label, to N.K. Bose's concept of the 'Hindu Method of Tribal Absorption' proposed in 1941 as a process of social change among the tribal communities.

Later, Srinivas introduced the notion of sanskritization instead of brahminization because his own field data and those of many others indicated limitations of using only brahminic model as a frame of reference for the conceptualization of social changes in Indian society. Interpreting the intricacies and limitation of his brahminic model, Srinivas said, I now realize that both in my book on Coorg religion and my "Note on Sanskritization and Westernization", I emphasized unduly the Brahminical model of Sanskritization and ignored the other models-Kshatriya, Vaishya and Shudra. Even the Brahminical model was derived from the Kannada, Tamil and Telugu Brahmins, and not from Brahmin castes in other regions.'[27] Srinivas introduced the notion of sanskritization as a substitute to the concept of brahminization in his *Social Change in Modern India* in 1966. He widened the meaning of sanskritization to explain the processes of social change in a more subtle way. In his definition, 'Sanskritization is the process by which a "low" Hindu caste, or tribal or other group, changes its customs, ritual, ideology and way of life in the direction of high, and frequently, "twice-born" caste. Generally such changes are followed by a claim to a higher position in the caste hierarchy than that traditionally conceded to the claimant caste by the local community. The claim is usually made over a period of time, in fact, a generation or two, before the "arrival" is conceded.'[28] Hence, the change in social position of a low caste or a tribe in 'Sanskritization is generally accompanied by, and often results in, upward mobility for the caste in question; but mobility may occur without Sanskritization and *vice versa.* However, the mobility associated with Sanskritization results only in *positional change* in the system and does not lead to any *structural change.*'[29] In addition to the notion of sanskritization Srinivas also proposed the notion of westernization. Nonetheless, sanskritization brought changes within the framework of Indian tradition whereas westernization was a change resulting from the contact of British socio-economic and cultural innovations.

III

Two great scholars Dr. B.R. Ambedkar and D.D. Kosambi were neither colonialist nor 'Hindu nationalist' in their approaches to anthropological investigations and interpretations of Indian society. The contributions of both the scholars in the field of social and political anthropology were not given due recognition and importance. There were many similarities between them from the point of view of their educational, biographical, religious and ideological backgrounds. Ambedkar and Kosambi both got opportunities to study in the American Universities of Columbia and Harvard. Academic careers of both the scholars had taken shapes in two important cities of Maharashtra namely Bombay and Poona and they were trained professionally in the disciplines of economics and mathematics. But they had made their vital intellectual contributions in the fields of sociology, anthropology and history. Ideologically they were nationalists but not the 'Hindu nationalists', and the greatest critiques of both British imperialism and the Hindu caste system. Buddhism had a very deep influence on their religious philosophy and marxism as a political ideology influenced their political thoughts and even their intellectual contributions. In public life their followers out of respect used to call Ambedkar and Kosambi as 'Babasaheb' and 'Baba'.

Ambedkar originally was interested in Economics and Law and started his academic career as an economist. His contributions in the fields of economics and law are widely known in intelligentsia and academia but he also made significant contributions in historical and social anthropology. From the point of view of identity formation he as a social anthropologist, authored *Castes in India: Their Mechanism, Genesis and Development* (1916), *Who Were the Shudras: How They Came to be the Fourth Varna in Indo-Aryan Society* (1946) and its sequel *The Untouchables: Who Were They and Why They Became Untouchables* (1948) were the significant intellectual contributions to social and historical anthropology. He produced *The Shudras and The Untouchables* published nearly after three decades of his first thought provoking paper on *Castes in India,* in which he discussed the identity of tribes and their relationship with the formation of Hindu society. In these anthropological works he contributed his original ideas, thoughts and theories, and examined theories related to the identities of various communities of India proposed either by the colonial anthropologists or the Hindu nationalist anthropologists.

Ambedkar, as an anthropologist, used indological and ethnological material for the interpretation of the formation of identities of various social groups including the tribes, the untouchables and the shudras. In his own style and method of scientific inquiry he had left marxist imprints in interpreting Indian society in his historical-anthropological investigations. He as an historian relooked the historical material used by historians for the re-construction of India's historical past. He especially applied the tools of imagination and intuition with the instrument of hypothesis and causation theory especially in a situation where the link of historical facts was missing. Ambedkar explained his methodological framework in his book *The Untouchable* (1948) in which he defined the role of a historian. In his view, 'The historian's duty is to separate the truth from the false, the certain from the uncertain, and the doubtful from that which cannot be accepted.'[30] But what was the role of a historian when he had to encounter a situation of missing link of historical facts between important events in historical inquiry. Ambedkar suggested that in such a case 'it was permissible for him to use his imagination and intuition to bridge the gaps left in the chain of facts by links yet not discovered to propound a working hypothesis.'[31] Therefore, in his opinion, the trained imagination was the essence and the hypothesis as the soul of fruitful scientific inquiry or historical investigation.

Ambedkar read the paper on *Castes in India* at the anthropology seminar organized by Professor A. A. Goldenweiser of Columbia University in 1916 in which he interpreted castes from anthropological point of view. In this Ambedkar proposed two important theories of *Castes in India*: the theory of fusion of tribal elements into Hindu society and, the theory of imitation for origin of castes. He rejected the racial and occupational theories of the origin of castes proposed by the colonial ethnographers and anthropologists in the late nineteenth century. He called the theories of Ibbetson, Nesfield, Senart and Risley 'a disguised form of the *Petitio Principii* of formal logic.'[32] As a true nationalist thinker, he criticized them for their racial attitude and argued that 'European students of castes had unduly emphasized the role of colour in the caste system. Themselves impregnated by the colour prejudices, they very readily imagined it to be the chief factor in the caste problem.'[33] Ambedkar to counter their view observed that 'the population of Indian was a mixture of Aryans, Dravidians, Mongolians and Scythians. But in a historical process through constant contact and mutual intercourse they evolved a common culture that superseded their distinctive cultures. Thus, various races of India occupying definite territories had more or less fused into one another and possessed cultural unity which was the only criterion of a homogeneous population.'[34] Ambedkar in his book *Annihilation of Castes* published in 1936, further explained, 'The caste system cannot be said to have grown as a means of preventing the admixture of races or as a means of maintaining the purity of blood. As a matter of fact caste system came into being long after the different races of India had coming in the blood and culture. To hold that distinctions of castes are really distinctions of races and to treat different castes as though they were so many different races is a gross perversion of facts.'[35] In support of his theory of the mixing of races for the origin of castes, he compared the brahmin and the chamar of the Punjab as well as the brahmin and the pariah of Madras, and a racial distinction between the brahmin of the Punjab and the brahmin of Madras; and observed that there was no racial difference between them in both the cases. He concluded that the caste system is a social division of the people of the same race.

Ambedkar in his study observed that tribal elements were fused into Hindu society. A fundamental difference may be noticed between the fusion of tribal elements and the absorption of tribes into Hindu society. The fusion is a natural process but the absorption is artificial when two or more communities interact with each other in a historical process of evolution of social and religious identities. The Hindu nationalists anthropologists stressed on absorption rather than fusion to prove the superiority of Hindu society. Contrary to the notion of absorption and Hinduization of tribes Ambedkar observed the process of fusion and tribalization of Hindus as follows: 'No society of today presents more survivals of primitive times than does the Indian society. Its religion is essentially primitive and its tribal code, in spite of the advance of time and civilization, operates in all its pristine vigour even today. One of these primitive survivals…is the *custom of exogamy*. The prevalence of exogamy in the primitive worlds is a fact too well known to need an explanation. With the growth of history, however, exogamy has lost its efficacy, and excepting the nearest blood-kins, there is usually no social bar restricting the field of marriage. But regarding the people of India the law of exogamy is a positive injunction even today. Indian society still savours of the clan system, even, though there are no clans; and this can easily be seen from the law of matrimony which centres round the principle of exogamy, for it is not that *Sapindas* (blood-kins) cannot marry, but a marriage between *Sagotras* (of the same class) is regarded a sacrilege.'[36] Further he argued, 'The various *gotras* of India are and have been exogamous: so are the other groups with totemic organization. It is no exaggeration to say that with the people of India exogamy is a creed and none dare infringe it, so much so that, in spite of the endogamy of the castes within them, exogamy is strictly observed and that there are rigorous penalties that for violating exogamy than there are for violating endogamy.'[37] In Ambedkar's view, endogamy was foreign to the people of India that was superimposed on exogamy. Superimposition of endogamy on exogamy resulted in the creation of castes.

Examining the origin of caste, Ambedkar advanced the notion of imitation of the origin and mechanism of caste system in India in which he established the relationship between exogamy and endogamy. He accepted endogamy as the only characteristic of the origin of caste. The origin of caste meant the origin of the mechanism for endogamy in his view. From the point of view of the formation of a society, he stated, 'Individuals make up society is trivial; society is always composed of classes. It may be an exaggeration to assert the theory of class-conflict, but the existence of definite classes in a society is a fact. Their basis may differ. They may be economic, intellectual, or social, but an individual in a society is always a member of a class. This is a universal fact and early Hindu society could not have been an exception to this rule... *A caste is an enclosed class.*'[38] He observed that 'the Hindu society was composed of classes and the earliest known were the (1) Brahmins, or the priestly class; (2) the Kshatriya, or the military class; (3) the Vaishyas, or the merchant class and (4) the Shudras, or the artisan and menial class. Particular attention has to be paid to the fact that this was essentially a class system, in which individuals, when qualified, could change their class, and therefore classes did change their personnel. At some time in history, of the Hindus, the priestly class socially detached itself from the rest of the body of people and through a close-door policy became a caste itself. The other classes being subject to the law of social division of labour underwent differentiation, some into large, others into very minute groups. The Vaishya and the Shudra classes were the original inchoate plasm, which formed the sources of the numerous castes of today.'[39] He further explained, 'Endogamy or the close-door system, was fashion in Hindu society, and as it had originated from the Brahmin caste it was whole-heartedly imitated by all non-Brahmin sub-divisions or classes, who, in turn, became endogamous castes. It is "the infection of imitation" that caught all these sub-divisions on their onward march of differentiation and has turned them into castes.'[40] Ambedkar concluded that the whole process of the origin of castes in India was a process of imitation of the higher by the lower. Almost half a century later in 1966, it was proclaimed as the process of sanskritization by sociologist M. N. Srinivas.

Ambedkar advanced his thesis of the fusion of tribal

element from *Castes in India* (1916) to *The Untouchables* (1948) He rejected the argument advanced by the colonial census officials and ethnographers that the real unit of the Hindu social system and the basis of the fabric of Hindu society was the sub-caste founded on the rule of endogamy. Contrary to this argument, Ambedkar stated: 'Nothing can be a mistake greater than this. The unit of Hindu society is not the sub-caste but the family founded on the rule of exogamy. In this sense Hindu family is fundamentally a tribal organization not a social organization as the sub-caste is. The Hindu family is primarily guided in the matter of marriage by consideration of K*ul* and *Gotra* and only secondarily by consideration of caste and sub-caste. *Kul* and *Gotra* are Hindu equivalents of the totem of the 'Primitive' Society. This shows that the Hindu society is still in its organization with the family as its base observing the rule of exogamy based on *Kul* and *Gotra*. Castes and sub-castes are social organizations, which are superimposed over the tribal organization, and the rule of endogamy enjoyed by them does not do away with the rule of exogamy enjoyed by tribal organization of *Kul* and *Gotra*.'[41] It may be concluded that the foundation of Hindu society was exogamous tribal organization of *Kul* and *Gotra* endogamous caste. The Hindu nationalist anthropologists, hence, were superimposing caste on tribe either by the notion of absorption or assimilation.

In support of his thesis on the basis of his anthropological investigation, Ambedkar found the existence of same *gotras* between the marathas and the untouchable mahars of Maharashtra and the chamars and the jats of the Punjab belonging to the same race. Ambedkar also observed that the four names aryans, dravidians, dasas and nagas discovered from India's past were not different races rather they were different names of the same race. The aryans were not a single homogeneous group. There were the Rig Vedic Aryans and the Atharv Vedic Aryans who had different cultures. The Dasas, the nagas and the dravidians were the same people. The nagas who were different from the aboriginals or the nagas of northeast, were the non-aryans. The nagas and the aryans represented two different cultures and thoughts rather than two different races.

Besides the question of the fusion of tribal elements into Hindu society for the origin of castes, the question of the social position of the aboriginal tribes in the Hindu social order was equally significant. The Hindu nationalist anthropologists had explained the place and position of the tribes, except few tribal chieftains, in the fourth varna of the Hindu social order in the early half of twentieth century during the movement of transfer of political power from the British to the Hindus. Their explanation has been incomplete and lacked in answering the question as to why few aboriginal tribes were positioned as kshatriyas and majority were degraded to the status of the shudras. Dr. Ambedkar searched the answer from a different perspective in a set of two questions, which is clear from the title of the book *Who Were the Shudras*. The first question is related to the origin of identity and the second is to the mechanism of identity formation of the shudras against the existing body of literature. Ambedkar already rejecting the theory of aryan race and invasion in his investigation and arrived at the conclusions that: '1. The *Shudras* were one of the Aryan communities of the solar race. 2. There was a time when the Aryan society recognized only three *Varnas*, namely, *Brahmins, Kshatriyas* and *Vaishyas*. 3. The *Shudras* did not form a separate *Varna*. They ranked as part of the *Kshatriya Varna* in the Indo-Aryan society. 4. There was continued feud between the *Shudra* kings and the *Brahmins* in which the *Brahmins* were subjected to many tyrannies and indignities. 5. As a result of the hatred towards the *Shudras* generated by their tyrannies and oppressions, the *Brahmins* refused to perform the *Upanayana* of the Shudras. 6. Owing to the denial of the *Upanayana*, the *Shudras* who were Kshatriyas became socially degraded, fell below the rank of the *Vaishyas* and thus came to from the fourth *Varna*.'[42] Thus Ambedkar observed that it was the contempt of the brahminical ideology by the kshatriyas or tribes of ruling clans in Indian civilization that dubbed them as the shudras in the fourth varna.

Ambedkar also examined the question of the origin and identity of both tribes as well as of untouchables in his book *The Untouchables* that was a sequel to *The Shudras.* In a preface to *The Untouchables* he wrote that besides the shudras, the Hindu civilization had also produced three social classes: the criminal tribes, the aboriginal tribes and the untouchables whose existence had not received the attention it deserve in Hindu scholarship and anthropology. He examined their history and proved that there was a deep social and cultural relationship between the aboriginal tribes and the untouchables in his inquiry of the institution of untouchability in India. Ambedkar's thesis of the origin of untouchability comprised the following propositions: '1. There is no racial difference between the Hindus and the Untouchables; 2. The distinction between the Hindus and the Untouchables in its original form, before the advent of Untouchability, is the distinction between Tribesmen and the Broken Men from alien Tribes. It is the Broken Men who subsequently came to be treated as Untouchables; 3. Just as Untouchability has no racial basis so also has it no occupational basis; 4. There are two roots from which Untouchability has sprung: (a) Contempt and hatred of the Broken Men as of Buddhists by the Brahmins: (b) Continuation of beef-eating by the Broken Men after it had been given up by others....'[43] He emphasized on distinguishing the untouchable from the impure as they were distinct from each other. There had been a relationship between Buddhism and untouchability in his theory of broken men in Hindu civilization. The broken men as alien tribes were Buddhists, hence, the hatred for them by the Brahmins and the beef eating by them were the primary reason of the origin of the untouchables from the tribes in Indian civilization. Ambedkar rejected the racial theory of untouchability because in his observations it was contradictory to the results of anthropometry and found a trivial support from the known facts about the ethnology of India.

Both Ambedkar and Kosambi had historical and ideological relationship with each other in the field of anthropological history and historical anthropology. They were almost common in their theoretical propositions related to the anthropological interpretations of Indian society. An advanced and wider explanation of Ambedkar's important propositions particularly related to the fusion of tribal elements, the broken men and their relationship with Buddhism might be seen in Kosambi's historical investigations in the light of archaeological evidences.

Kosambi inherited the legacy of intellectual tradition from his father who was a Buddhist, a marxist and a reformist nationalist. Eminent marxist historian Irfan Habib observed that the seeding of marxism in Kosambi's intellectual pursuit began in late 1930s. In Habib's observation, 'Kosambi's *The Introduction to the Study of Indian Civilization* (1956) climaxed a number of successive papers and reviews that he had begun writing in 1938-39.'[44] Kosambi's major findings since the late 1930s might also be discovered in two of his major contributions *Myth and Reality* (1962) and *Culture and Civilization of Ancient India in Historical Outline* (1965). Kosambi in *The Introduction to the Study of Indian Civilization* adopted a completely different kind of methodological approach that revolutionized the Indian historiography. In a preface he wrote that that 'this book does not pretend to be a history of India. It is merely a modern approach to the study of Indian history.' He defined his methodology as a critique to the colonial historiography and argued: 'The light-hearted sneer India has had some episodes, but no history is used to justify lack of study, grasp, and intelligence on the part of foreign writers about India's past. The considerations that follow will prove that it is precisely the episodes -lists of dynasties and kings, tales of war and battle spiced with anecdote, which fill school texts -that are missing from Indian records. Here, for the first time, we have to reconstruct a history without episodes, which means that it cannot be the same type of history as in the European tradition.'[45] Kosambi used the marxist framework of historical materialism in his work for explaining historical anthropology. This is evident from this statement: 'History is defined as the presentation, in chronological order, of successive developments in the means and relations of production.'[46] He made a great emphasis on honest fieldwork with rational attitude in conducting historical anthropological inquiry. In his view, 'such field work has to be performed with critical insight, taking nothing for granted, or on faith, but without the attitude of superiority, sentimental reformism, or spurious leadership which prevents most of us from learning anything except from bad textbooks.'[47] For application of such valuable insights in scientific study, his work became the finest example of methodological technique in conducting historical investigation in a combination of ethnography and archaeology. Marxist scholar Prabhat Patnaik observed that Kosambi's notion of acculturation did not provide classical marxist interpretation of cultural history of India as it 'falls outside usual Marxist analysis'[48] because Kosambi believed that 'Marxism was far from economic determinism, therefore any intelligent determinism must discuss conditions rather than causes'[49] for the interpretation of cultural history. Kosambi's *The Introduction to the Study of Indian Civilization* is a classical example of this approach.

Kosambi's works are a testimony of systematic and comprehensive critique of the revivalist Hindu nationalist historians as well as to the anthropologists in historical anthropology that glorified the caste system and the absorption of tribes into castes. In interpreting India's historical past, Kosambi gave importance to ethnographic material over indological material. But revivalist Hindu nationalist historians and anthropologists preferred indological material in their interpretation. He combined his archaeological method with ethnographic material because it was essential to understand Indian history and culture. In *The Introduction* Kosambi observed that: 'It is not the primitive tribes of other countries that are of primary interest here, nor primitive Indian survivals in marginal territory such as the Khasias, Nagas, Oraons, Bhils, Todas, Kadars. The social clusters that survive even in the heart of fully developed areas, say in and around cities, with others which mark all strata of a caste society as having developed at some older date from the absorption of tribal groups, constitute priceless evidence for the interpretation of some ancient record or archaeological find.' In Kosambi's methodology it was not only the ethnographic and archaeological materials, although 'the different methods whereby the tribal elements were formed into a society or absorbed into pre-existing society were prime ethnic material for any real historian.'[50] Scholars and historians have accepted that it was Kosambi's methodological brilliance that developed an extraordinary relationship between archaeology and ethnography in Indian historiography for the interpretation of historical developments in India with the help of the patterns and methods of fusion of tribes into caste.

On the basis of ethnographic material Kosambi explained his thesis of the tribalization of Hindus instead of Hinduization of tribes in Indian civilization. According to Kosambi, 'The entire course of Indian history shows tribal elements being fused into a general society. This phenomenon, which lies at the very foundation of the most striking Indian social feature, namely caste, is also the great basic fact of ancient Indian history.'[51] Kosambi stated that the process of fusion of tribal elements into brahminism was mutual and a peculiar characteristic of India. 'This has generally been completely neglected by those who take Sanskrit liturgical books as the basis of their study, creating a fictitious line of pseudo-historical descent from antiquity to modern times on the basis of such written works alone. In this "reasoning," it is ignored that the greater part of the population pays little attention to what the upper classes and their Brahmin priests take as the 'pure' observances.'[52] Kosambi's thesis of fusion of tribal elements into caste or Hindu society was opposite to both the notions and explanation of revivalist Hindu nationalist historians and anthropologists who limited the existence of tribal elements at the lower level of Hindu society. But in Kosambi's interpretation, the fusion of tribes was found from top to bottom of Hindu society in a reverse process of acculturation of Hindu rituals and customs.

Kosambi noted that pre-class society was organized into tribes. The tribes were subdivided into exogamous units clans or *gotras*. Thus a tribe was a composition of *gotras,* a basic unit of Indian society. Kosambi did not observe the racial element between the Aryans and the non-Aryans. He also traced the assimilation of tribal *gotras* among the Aryan Brahmins. In early history 'The first brahmins were a result of interaction between the Aryan priesthood, and the ritually superior priesthood of the Indus culture. There are innumerable *gotras* in seven main divisions of the brahmins, each of which must marry outside its own gotra, which thus corresponds to the Latin gens.'[53] There were also the non-Aryan Brahmins in the pre-Aryan period who were known by their mother's name. In Kosambi's view, only the non-Aryans were the principal vedic city-dwellers. The brahmin clannames retain a clear impress of tribal names, from the earliest stages down into historical times. In a modern city like Poona, Kosambi traced the extension of tribal *gotras* from a nomadic Pardhi tribe to the marathas and brahmins. 'The Pardhis have six exogamous clans or septs whose names have become surnames of feudal Maratha families: Bhonsale, Powar, Cavhan, Jadhav, Sinde, Kale. The last is actually a Citpavan brahmin surname; the penultimate once denoted son of a slave-girl (without acknowledged father) till it was ennobled by rising to the kingdom of Gwalior.'[54] Surprisingly, these *gotra* names were acquired during the period of Maratha dominance in western India. Kosambi gave specific examples of the inheritance of tribal *gotras* from archaeology to support his thesis. The brahmin *gotra* Bhrigu was derived from Sigru, which is mentioned in a Kushana inscription at Mathura and means a 'drumstick tree'. Kosambi concluded that the totemic nature of such a tribal name was not in doubt. However, the survival of the name Bhrigu designates one of the main brahmin *gotra* and comes from classical sanskrit text from early history to the present times. Yet in sanskrit classical text the name Bhrigu appears to be the enemy of the Aryan king Sudas and Kosambi stated that this was obviously then a tribe.

Significantly Kosambi examined the attitudes and psychological manifestations of dominant upper caste Hindus in Indian politics on the basis of two fundamental elements: a) the presence of foreign element; and b) the influences of the primitive tribal element in Hinduism. Both the factors had equal presence and influence on Hindu society. But the former was accepted and the latter was rejected for obvious reasons of status, position and power in the nationalist movement. Kosambi observed that 'the presence of foreign element among the dominant Indian classes and on India's urban life was generally admitted by upper caste Hindus but revivalist Hindu nationalists influenced by patriotism depreciated the role of foreign invaders in modern Indian history. Hence, the indelible mark of primitive origin of Indian religious institutions which infuriated most Indians of the middle class who felt their country ridiculed or their own dignity insulted.'[55] Exactly this was the political ideological position represented by the revivalist Hindu nationalist anthropologists and historians ignoring the influence and presence of tribal element in their theoretical propositions. Kosambi also pointed out that it were not only the Indians who consciously choose to ignore this influence of tribal culture but most observers miss 'the reciprocal influence of tribesmen on the Indian peasant and even on the upper classes.'Against such anti-tribal attitude of the upper caste Hindus, Kosambi stated that: 'Primitive cultures are neither ridiculous nor undignified till debased by contact with vicious by-products of the feudal or bourgeois mode. India's development was in its own way more 'civilized' than in the other countries. The older cults and forms were not demolished by force but assimilated.'[56] In the process of cultural continuum, Kosambi attempted to highlight positive attributes of tribal elements assimilated into Hindu society.

The process of assimilation of tribal elements into Hindu society was remarkable and incredible. In the hierarchy of Hindu gods, the tribal element was present from top to bottom. Kosambi observed it as follows: 'The mechanism of assimilation is particularly interesting. Not only Krishna, but the Buddha himself and some totemic deities including the primeval Fish, Tortoise and Boar were made into incarnations of Vishnu-Narayana. The monkey faced Hanuman... with an independent cult of his own, becomes the faithful companion-servant of Rama, another incarnation of Vishnu. Vishnu-Narayana uses the great earth-bearing Cobra as his canopied bed to sleep upon the waters; at the same time the same cobra is Siva's garland and a weapon of Ganesha. The elephant-headed Ganesha is son to Siva, or rather of Siva's wife. Siva's bull Nandi was worshipped in the south Indian neolithic age without any human or divine master; he appears independently on innumerable seals of the Indus culture... This conglomeration goes on forever, while all the tales put together form a senseless, inconsistent, chaotic mass. The importance of the process, however, must not be underestimated. The worship of these newly absorbed primitive deities was part of the mechanism of acculturation, a clear give-and-take.'[57] According to Kosambi's inquiry and interpretation of ethnological and archaeological facts, cultural history of Hindus proves that the process of tribalization of Hindus through fusion and the Hinduization of tribes through assimilation or absorption had been in progress mutually side by side in Indian civilization.

The investigation of Hindu philosophy based on brahmanical scriptures is essential to understand the Hindu process of the assimilation of tribes. Literary historical sources of brahminic tradition helped to understand the patterns and methods of assimilation. Kosambi observed that in Hindu philosophy the brahmin scriptures made kingship essential for maintaining the social order. In the brahminical social order, 'the ascendency of a tribal chief was secured, with the backing of few nobles freed from tribal law to become a ruler of his former tribe, acquiring an upper caste status, usually kshatriya, with the *gotra* of the Brahmin priest while rest of the ordinary tribesmen merged into a new peasantry with a lower caste status. Sometimes the Brahmin went to discover an upper caste lineage for the tribal chief in the epics or the *Puranas,* and occasionally even got him married into the tribe, normally to create new tribal Brahmins. The whole exercise was not aimless as all this amounted to keeping down a newly created set of vaisyas and sudras by Brahmin precept and Kshatriya arms.'[58] About the sixth century A.D. in central India, occasionally, the rulers of mixed descendants might have ruled the tribe.

In Kosambi's investigation the mechanism of acculturation also highlights that the tribes were assimilated into developing peasantry society without any explicit use of violence and simultaneously it achieved the isolation of the tribe. It splintered the tribe into two distinct classes. Thus the isolation and splintering were two distinct and significant results of the process of acculturation. Each of them could have been a potentially violent process but the significance of the fact was that acculturation obviated the use of violence and should not be underestimated. Similarly, Kosambi investigated the long-term loss done by the process of acculturation to India's intellectual and cultural life. Despite overcoming the isolation of the tribe, the process of acculturation could never fully overcome the isolation of the village society as a whole. But its other important results were as follows: 'it inhibited the scope of commodity production with cultural exchange; it promoted superstition; it led to the proliferation of a mass of senseless ritual; it discouraged codification and recording; it subscribed to the concept of a "logic" divorced from all reality; it thwarted scientific advance; and it privileged "hierarchy" over "equity" which was the original meaning of Ashoka's *dhamma*.'[59] In Kosambi's view, the Buddhist monastic order functioned along the lines of a tribal (sabha) council; the Buddhist precepts were meant for a class society far beyond the tribe, caste, or cult.

IV

Recent studies on the meos of Mewat in eastern Rajasthan by Shail Mayaram *Against History, Against State* and by Suraj Bhan Bhardwaj *Contestations and Accommodations* are important additions to the understanding of the transformation and contestation of tribal identity since Delhi Sultanate till Mughal Empire to British rule. Both the works are also important from the point of view of approaches to the study of a community and the selection and exploration of historical and cultural sources to develop and construct an image and understanding about a community in a particular time and space. Mayaram has applied a post-modernist and subaltern approach in *Against History, Against State* while Bhradwaj has adopted a marxist approach mixing it with Dumontian model of Indian society. The case of meos as a tribe is also more interesting as they were Islamized rather than Hinduized in the historical process of transformation by their socio-cultural identity. In conventional ethnography the transformation of tribes in India has been prone towards Hinduization instead of Islamization. Two different images and identities of the meos have been constructed in both the works.

Mayaram's study of the meos is a critique of state forms of textual discourses of ethnography and history. In her observation, 'Narratives of the state and its others, which have been called history or ethnography, are also aspects of the product of stateness. The professional discipline of history has been overwhelmingly oriented towards monarchy, thereby ignoring the institutions of people who did not archive statehood. History isolates the study of the past from the present, masking the concerns of the state or of the historian. The ethnographer has often tended to sever the present form of history, exoticising or demonizing subjects.'[60] Hence, Mayaram relies upon the oral records of the "folk" and the "lore" of the meos in which 'the state imaginary of Meos is juxtaposed with the meo imaginary of the state.' She contested the construction of the identity of Meos in the written historical archival sources of Indo-Persian chronicles. In these sources, she observed, 'the meos became the elements of disorder while kingship epitomized order in medieval historical representation. They were held responsible for a continuous war that ruptured the peace that had to be constantly reestablished by the state. They were described as threatening Delhi so that its gates had to be closed against them. This was only one example of the construction of the mythology of the sultanate as a weak state. It was echoed in the construction of Mughal and British sovereignty. The assertion ignored the nature of Meo existence and their marginalization in terms of land and power.' She argued that it was not only the Indo-Persian written records that represented the state construction of meo identity, it was post-colonial academic scholarship too that tended to draw considerably upon the state's perception of meo resistance.

Mayaram argued that the meos were constituted subjects by different states, imperial (used in her work to refer to the sultanate and Mughal Empire), colonial, and princely. Opposite to the official memory available as the histories associated with these state formations, she tries to bring the margin into representation through an analysis of narratives of oppositional practices grounded in the cultural facts of folklore in oral traditions of the meos. On the basis of these narratives, in *Against History, Against State*, Mayaram constructed and reconstructed the identity and social being, and also order in the past through broken histories of the meos who have inhabited for at least previous seven centuries in the region called Mewat. She argues that the meos were socially organized on the basis of *pal* (lineages) which traditionally enjoyed the status of autonomous self-governing communities, and that their *pal chaudharis* acted like sovereign kings in taking decisions related to their *pal* communities. She further argues that the meo *pal* polity was hostile to the monopolistic sovereignty and favoured decentralization of power, and that the *pal* retained this pristine character of theirs without undergoing any change over a long period of time. Engaging in raid and plunder and resisting the powerful Mughal and Rajput states were integral part of the *pal* polity. The very nature of their polity implicitly rendered them incapable of state formation.

Suraj Bhan Bhardwaj in *Contestations and Accommodations* counters Mayaram's constructions and conclusions. His arguments and narratives have been constructed on the basis of archival historical material produced by the state administrative machinery and institutions as a historian's crafts and tools in a conventional style and method of history writing to construct the histories of the meos. Opposite to Mayaram's thesis, he observed that 'during medieval period, the Meos underwent unprecedented social, economic, and cultural changes in the wake of their peasantization as well as islamization. The adoption of agriculture as their means of sustenance led their cultural and social transformation from a tribal to a settled agricultural community. He saw the transformation of tribal identity into a caste identity within the framework of Hindu model of tribal absorption proposed by the British and the Hindu nationalist ethnographers. He emphatically pointed out that like the caste Hindus, they also received *gotra* identities and emerged as the dominant community in Mewat.'[61] Thus, he further argues, Mayaram's thesis on the changeless, autonomous *pal* polity is ahistorical because no records of the Mughal period, Rajasthani or Persian, prove her argument, and the material used by her are largely the folk tradition of the late nineteenth century. He emphasized that the inhabitation of meos was between Delhi and Agra that became the capital of Mughals in succession therefore the possibilities to maintain the pristine character of *pal* polity remained far more less.

Bhardwaj also counters Mayaram's thesis that the meos perpetually and uncompromisingly were against the state, whether Mughal or Rajput, that ultimately resulted into their marginalization in the historical process. He argues that 'Historically no peasant community, however defiant and rebellious, could survive on resistance against the state alone; in times of peace, it could find ways and means of negotiating with the state and expressing its grievances to get concessions and relief.'[62] In his historical inquiry of Rajasthani documents

(Indo-Persian chronicles, village and pargana -level revenue records, and reports preserved at Rajasthan State Archives, Bikaner) he found that the meos presented a large number of petitions before the Mughal emperors and their *diwans* (chief ministers) from time to time, against the highhandedness of the Amber officials and the non-customary taxes imposed by them. In his study on the meos and their relationship with the Delhi sultans and early Mughal rulers, he says that the Indo-Persian chronicles are helpful in understanding the nature of state formation under the sultans and Mughals and the relationship of Khanzada chiefs of Mewat with the Delhi Sultanate and Mughal state, and other regional potentates.

In *Contestations and Accommodations* the author has applied the theory of Rajputization of the meos in transforming their tribal identity into a caste identity by linking their relationship with the adoption of Hindu *gotras* and their origin with the Jadon-Rajputs on the basis of the Jagga records. More importantly Bhardwaj has explored the historical circumstances of the migration of the meos from the Aravali hills to the plains and their peasantization with anthropological interpretations of the transformation from a tribe to a peasant caste. He attributed three important factors responsible for the peasantization of the meos: 'first, the rigorous military campaigns by the sultans of Delhi to curb their 'lawless' activities; second, the growth of meo population in the Aravali hills; and third, the conversion of forest land into agricultural land.'[63] In addition to these factors, the formation of the states of Khanzadas, who were Jadon Rajputs before their conversion to Islam, was another significant factor that helped in socio-economic transformation of meo population in the region of Mewat.

The case of bhils as tribes in southern Rajasthan and the adjoining areas of eastern Gujarat and western Madhya Pradesh is important from the point of view of transformation and survival of tribal identity and polity in addition to the meos of Mewat in eastern Rajasthan. Sumit Guha in *Environment and Ethnicity* highlights that in central highlands some tribal politics, especially Jawar (*koli*) and Ramnagar (*Bhil*) in medieval India were the finest examples of autonomous state formation and competitive survivals and participation in mainstream political economy of empires. These polities unfold over 500 years as forest chiefs fought and negotiated with the Sultanate of Gujarat, the Portuguese Estado, the Mughal Empire, the Maratha states and finally the British Empire.[64] The relationship between centralized state i.e. maratha and bhil polities in seventeenth and eighteenth centuries, it seems that bhil polities always were not at lower hand with maratha state in western India. Maratha state shared the sovereignty with bhil polities in Dangs.

Against the conventional model of rajputization of state formation, Ajay Skaria in *Hybrid Histories*, a study on the bhils, observes a completely distinct process of state formation—a model of 'bhil raj' or the process of bhilisation in pre-colonial and colonial western India. His arguments are based on appropriate historical material. He finds that 'Rajput Chiefs were quite willing to marry into powerful bhil lineages. Claiming and participating in the wildness of being Bhil, was not something that only *Jangli jatis* like koknis did even Rajputs were fascinated by, and claimed their involvement in enactments of wildness.[65] Except this, ritually superior Dangi communities the bhils like gomits, chodharis, valvis or koknis made their claim to be part of Bhil Raj, and claimed to be bhil (kokni bhil). Skaria calls this process Bhilisation[66] which is contrary to rajputization. On the other hand, kinship ties were less significant among rajput lineages in the initial stages of power building for often the founder of a lineage would have migrated to a new territory with a small number of kinsmen. Only in the later stages of the developmental cycle of a Rajput lineage when it had succeeded in dominating the sizeable area of land, did a large body of kinsmen organize into stratified and distinct tiers.[67]

Sumit Guha in his study on central highland forest polities, covering a span of period since Delhi Sultanate to the post colonial state, has placed three interacting but distinct models of tribal state formation as well as their competency for substances. The first, follows Sinha's argument, was achievement of transition to the rajput kingdom by a regional chiefdom, but failed and lost to history. The second, the regional chieftaincy made transition to rajput kingdom but lost its links to the local forest elite and was marginalized by competition from a third. The third was a tribal clan chieftaincy that sustained itself by retaining its kinship ties with the local dominant forest tribe and avoiding pretensions to rajput status.[68]

The first half of the twentieth century was the most critical period of formation of religious and political identity of various communities in India. The religious identity was accepted as the basis of political representation in Indian legislature including education and public services. The academic exercises in anthropology were streamlined according to religious and political ideologies making religious identity as its foundation. The political developments and situation influenced the arguments, dialogues and writings of anthropologists during this period. The arguments of anthropologists were in tune with religious identities by labeling the identity of tribes as aboriginal, Hindu, Christian, Muslims and Buddhist at pan-India level. Speaking in terms of religious or political identity of anthropologists and scholars, primarily the Hindu or nationalist, and the Christian or colonial anthropologists and the Buddhist or marxist scholars were engaged in debates over religious identity of tribes in the first half of the twentieth century. However, classification of anthropologists and historians and the academic disciplines of anthropology and history on the basis of religion ideologies as Christian, Hindu and Buddhist has not been a common tradition in academic scholarship but it is not completely out of fashion. There has been a normal practice of classifying scholars and disciplines in academics on the basis of political ideologies. But religious ideologies such as Christianity, Hinduism and Buddhism too had influenced the political ideologies such as colonialism, nationalism and marxism having a close historical relationship with each other. Taking an account of such perspectives, the anthropologists have been classified into religious categories.

The idea of aboriginal and the shades of academic anthropology have been highlighted in the arguments and dialogues of anthropologists in their ethnographic, anthropological and historical studies. Christian or colonial anthropologists like Hutton, Grigson and Elwin used the platform of colonial ideology for highlighting the aboriginal identity of tribes of India. Colonial anthropologists believed that Indian tribes were aboriginals and their theory of aboriginality was based upon racial interpretation of Indian society. But Bose, Ghurye and Srinivas as revivalist Hindus or nationalist anthropologists rejected the theory of aboriginality. They interpreted the identity of the tribes within the religious framework of Hinduism and caste system proposing the models of assimilation and sanskritization for the Hinduization of tribes. Hence, finally they proved the tribes as the backward Hindus. Contrary to the Hindu nationalist anthropologists, buddhist or marxist anthropologists such as Ambedkar and Kosambi highlighted the tribalization of Hindus or fusion of tribal elements into Hindu society from the standpoint of a reformist or economic nationalism. Instead of racial and religious interpretation, they proposed cultural interpretation of Indian history and society. Recent studies by marxist and subaltern historians, ethnographers, anthropologists and political scientists have made significant contribution in understanding the tribal world of India.

The anthropologists portrayed tribal identity with different colours and shades of religious and political ideologies. The anthropological and historical writings of these anthropologists highlight the processes, patterns and methods of the formation of identities in their anthropological and historical investigations from the perspectives of race, religion and culture. Their writings invented a wide range of anthropological notions, theories, propositions, ideas, thoughts, methodologies and ideologies in broadening the understanding of the process of identity formation of various social groups and communities in the first half of the twentieth century.

NOTES

1. Shail Mayaram, *Against History, Against State: Counter Perspectives from the Margins,* Columbia University Press, Columbia: 2004; Suraj Bhan Bhardwaj, *Contestations and Accommodations: Mewat and Meos in Mughal India,* Oxford University Press, New Delhi: 2016.
2. Sumit Guha, *Environment and Ethnicity in India 1200-1991,* Cambridge University Press, Cambridge: 1999; Ajay Skaria, *Hybrid Histories: Forests, Frontiers and Wilderness in Western India,* Oxford University Press, New Delhi: 1999.
3. J.H. Hutton, *The Sema Naga,* Macmillan, London: 1921, p. 191. Hutton quoted Frazer from his *The Golden Bough* to prove his proposition of 'Tribal Religion.'
4. Ibid., p. 191.
5. Ibid., p. 213.
6. J.H. Hutton, *Caste in India: Its Nature, Function and Origins,* Cambridge University Press, Cambridge: 1946, p. 1.
7. Ibid., p. 185.
8. W.V. Grigson, *The Maria Gonds of Bastar,* Oxford University Press, London: 1938, p. xvii.
9. W.V. Grigson, 'The Aboriginal in the Future India', The *Journal of the Royal Anthropological Institute of Great Britain and Ireland,* Vol. 74, No. 1/2, 1946, pp. 33-41. This paper was reprinted in W.V. Grigson, *The Challenge of Backwardness,* Government Press, Hyderabad-Deccan: 1947.
10. Grigson, *The Challenge of Backwardness,* p. 97.
11. Grigson, *The Maria Gonds of Bastar,* p. 125.
12. Ibid., p. 197.
13. Verrier Elwin, intro. Ganesh N. Devy, *The Oxford India Elwin: Selected Writings,* Oxford University Press, New Delhi: 2009, p. xii.
14. Ibid., p. xvii.
15. Hutton in Foreword written on July 25, 1939 to Verrier Elwin, *The Baiga,* John Murray, London: 1939, p. xxi.
16. Ibid., pp. 118, 315, 515.
17. Ibid., p. 118.

18. Ibid., p. 32.
19. Andre Beteille in Introduction to B.K. Bose, trans. Andre Beteille, *The Structure of Hindu Society*, Orient Longman, New Delhi: 1975, p. 168. It was originally written by N.K. Bose in Bangla with a title *Hindu Samajer Garan* in 1949 and translated into English by his associate and former student Beteille in 1975 with an introduction.
20. Ibid., p. 169.
21. Ibid., p. 175.
22. A.R. Momin, in A.R. Momin, ed., in *The Legacy of G.S. Ghurye: A Centennial Festschrift*, Popular Prakashan, Bombay: 1996, p. vii.
23. Ibid., p. 12.
24. Ibid., p. 14.
25. Ibid., p. 21.
26. M.N. Srinivas, "Professor Ghurye and I: A Troubled Relationship" in A.R. Momin, ed., *The Legacy of G.S. Ghurye: A Centennial Festschrift*, Popular Prakashan, Bombay: 1996, p. 3.
27. Ibid., p. 7.
28. M.N. Srinivas, *Social Change in Modern India*, Orient Longman, New Delhi: 1995, p. 6, University of California Press, Berkeley, published its first edition in 1966.
29. Ibid., p. 6.
30. B.R. Ambedkar, Comp. Vasant Moon, *Dr. Babasaheb Ambedkar Writings and Speeches*, Vol. VII, Education Department, Government of Maharashtra, Bombay: 1990, p. 242
31. Ibid., p. 243.
32. B.R. Ambedkar, comp. Vasant Moon, *Dr. Babasaheb Ambedkar Writings and Speeches*, Vol. I, Education Department, Government of Maharashtra, Bombay: 1979, p. 17.
33. Ibid., p. 21.
34. Ibid., p. 8.
35. Ibid., p. 48.
36. Ibid., p. 9.
37. Ibid.
38. Ibid., p. 15.
39. Ibid., pp. 17-18.
40. Ibid., p. 18.
41. B.R. Ambedkar, *Dr. Babasaheb Ambedkar Writings and Speeches*, Vol. VII, Dr. Ambedkar Foundation, New Delhi: 1989, pp. 303-04.
42. Ibid., p. 12.

43. Ibid., p. 242.
44. Irfan Habib, "What Kosambi Has Given Us," in D.N. Jha (ed.), *Many Careers of D.D. Kosambi: Critical Essays,* Left Word, New Delhi: 2011, p. 34.
45. D.D. Kosambi, *The Introduction to the Study of Indian Civilization,* Popular Prakashan, Bombay: 1956, p. 1.
46. Ibid.
47. Kosambi in a Preface to *The Introduction to the Study of Indian Civilization.*
48. Prabhat Patnaik, "Kosambi and Frontiers of Historical Materialism," in D.N. Jha (ed.), *Many Careers of D.D. Kosambi,* p. 47.
49. Kosambi, *Introduction,* p. 10.
50. Ibid., p. 7.
51. Ibid., p. 27.
52. Ibid.
53. Ibid., p. 20.
54. Ibid., p. 102.
55. Ibid., p. 28.
56. D.D. Kosambi, *Culture and Civilization of Ancient Indian in Historical Outline,* Routledge and Kegan Paul, London: 1965, p. 23.
57. Ibid., p. 44.
58. Ibid., p. 23.
59. Ibid., p. 170.
60. Ibid., p. 171.
61. Mayaram, *Against History, Against State,* p. 11.
62. Bhardwaj, *Contestations and Accommodations,* p. 2.
63. Ibid., p. 3.
64. Bhardwaj, *Contestations and Accommodations,* pp. 96-97.
65. Guha, *Environment and Ethnicity,* p. 8.
66. Ajay Skaria, "Being jungle: the politics of wildness," *Studies in History* 14, no. 2, 1998, p. 213.
67. Skaria, *Hybrid Histories,* no. 2, 1989, p. 113.
68. Richard Fox, *Kin, Clan, Raja and Rule,* University of California Press, Berkeley: 1971, pp. 70, 75.
69. Guha, *Environment and Ethnicity,* p. 8.

List of Contributors

Abha Singh is Professor of Medieval Indian History at Indira Gandhi National Open University (IGNOU), New Delhi. Her areas of interest are political, socio-economic and religious history of medieval India. The focus of her research is Mughal India. She has done her PhD on 'Suba of Delhi Under the Mughals, 1580-1719' from Aligarh Muslim University, Aligarh. Currently she is working on 'Satnamis of Narnaul' for which she was awarded Commonwealth Fellowship. She has presented and published a number of research papers in International and National Conferences.

Jaspal Kaur Dhanju is formerly Dean Research, Dean Colleges, Professor-in-Charge Maharana Pratap Chair, Department of History, Punjabi University, Patiala. She has published two books; *Economy and Society of North Gujarat 1750-1850* (1994) and *History and Post Modernism* (2006). She has also published a number of research articles in national and international journals of repute. Her areas of interest include pre-modern and modern Punjab/India with special reference to Sikh Historiography and Women/Gender studies.

J.S. Kharakwal is currently the head of the Department of Archaeology and is also working as Director of Sahitya Sansthan, J.R.N. Rajasthan Vidyapeeth, Udaipur, Rajasthan. He spearheaded a multidisciplinary Indo-Japanese archaeological research project at Kanmer, a Harappan site in Kachchh, Gujarat along with the excavation of Chandravati, near Abu Road.

He has co-authored three books with Prof. D.P. Agrawal, *Prehistory of South Asia* (2002), *Bronze and Iron Ages of South*

Asia (2003) and *Central Himalayas* (1998), besides a few monographs and several research papers. Apart from these, there is also the *Kanmer Excavation Report*, published by Research Institute for Humanity and Nature, Kyoto, Japan. He was Fellow at the Japan Society for Promotion of Science at the International Research Centre for Japanese Studies, Kyoto and Visiting Professor at the Research Institute for Humanity and Nature.

Lalit Pandey did his PhD from Gurukul Kangri University, Haridwar in 1983 on Bureaucracy During the Period of the Maurya Dynasty. He worked at J.R.N. Rajasthan Vidyapeeth, Udaipur from 1983-2014 and retired as Professor and Director, Institute of Rajasthan Studies. He also served as Dean, Faculty of Social Science & Humanities, B.N. University, Udaipur.

He initiated Field Research at Vidyapeeth and excavated six archaeological sites in collaboration with Deccan College, Pune, New Hemisphere and Kennesaw State University, USA. He has to his credit a monograph, five edited books and several research papers.

Mayank Kumar teaches History at Satyawati College (Evening), Delhi University. Along with several articles published in reputed journals such as, *Conservation & Society* (2005), *Studies in History* (2008 & 2016), *Medieval History Journal* (2013) and *Pratiman* (2016) he has a monograph, *Monsoon Ecologies: Irrigation, Agriculture and Settlement Patterns in Rajasthan during the Pre-Colonial Period*, Manohar, Delhi, 2013 to his credit. Recently, he has co-edited: *Revisiting the History of Medieval Rajasthan: Essays for Professor Dilbagh Singh*, Primus, Delhi, 2017. He was associated with the Decision Centre for Desert City, Arizona State University as Fulbright fellow. He was a Fellow at the Nehru Memorial Museum and Library before availing the UGC Research Award.

Mayurakshi Kumar is Assistant Professor, Hansraj College, University of Delhi. He is pursuing PhD on 'Eighteenth Century Jaipur Kingdom: Politics, Society and the New Capital', from the Department of History, University of Delhi. Research Area: Social, Political, Urban History of Rajasthan. Publication: "Exploring the Court Culture and the Social Ordering of 18th Century Jaipur Kingdom through Dastur Komwar", *Itihas- Sanshodhan Journal*, 2015. He is the recipient of the Prof. Mohan Kumar Mathur Memorial Young Achievers Award, 2015 from Central Indian Historical Research Foundation, Gwalior.

Neekee Chaturvedi is presently Associate Professor, Department of History and Indian Culture and has served as Deputy Director, Centre for Museology and Conservation, University of Rajasthan, Jaipur, India. She is the recipient of the prestigious International SAARC Research Grant 2014-15. She has worked extensively on early Buddhism and is presently engaged with anthropological investigation of culture of Rajasthan. She has authored and edited several books that include *Cultural Tourism, Bishnois of Rajasthan* and *Conserving Buddhist Heritage*. Notwithstanding her active academic engagements, she finds time to dabble in theatre and has staged many plays.

Netrapal Singh teaches History at Motilal Nehru College, University of Delhi, New Delhi. He is a postgraduate in History from the Centre for Historical Studies, Jawaharlal Nehru University, New Delhi and received the Master of Philosophy from Babasaheb Ambedkar National Institute of Social Sciences, DAVV, Mhow, Indore and Doctorate from Department of History and Culture, Jamia Millia Islamia, New Delhi. He has presented papers and chaired sessions at international and national seminars and conferences in India and abroad. He has four research papers to his credit published in national and international journals and two research papers in edited volumes.

Nidhi Sharma received her education from Jaipur, Rajasthan with a meritorious record. She completed her PhD under the late Dr. Pratibha Jain in 1998. She has authored 'Transition from Feudalism to Democracy' which is an extension of her doctorate. She has contributed numerous research papers in various journals and seminars for the past 25 years. Her field of specialisation is modern Rajsthan history. At present she is working as Associate Professor in the Government Arts College, Kota, Rajasthan.

Rajender Kumar is presently working as an editor of two research journals: *Global Researcher View* and *Juni Khyat*. He was a Post Doctoral Fellow associated with Indian Council of Historical Research, New Delhi (2013-15). Trade and Commerce of the 18th Century Western Rajputana and the Military system of Marwar State have been primary areas of his research. His monograph *Military System of Marwar State* is expected soon. He has participated in more than 40 national and international seminars, conferences and workshops. He has more than 25 research papers published in reputed journals.

Rameshwar Prasad Bahuguna is Professor at the Department of History and Culture, Jamia Millia Islamia, New Delhi. His research interests include the formation of Sant-based religious communities during the 16th to 18th centuries; the role of Vaishnava communities in the process of Rajput state formation and legitimation during the 18th century. He has published many papers on these themes in various journals. He is the co-editor of *Negotiating Religion: Perspectives from Indian History*, Manohar, Delhi, 2012 and *Revisiting the History of Medieval Rajasthan: Essays for Professor Dilbagh Singh*, Primus, Delhi, 2017.

Sangeeta Sharma is Associate Professor in the Department of History and Indian Culture, University of Rajasthan, Jaipur. Her research interests have focused on Gender Studies, Arya Samaj Movement, Rajasthan Studies and Partition. Her publications include *Bhartiya Stri (Sanskritik Sandarbh)*, 1998, *Honour, Status and Polity*, 2004, *Women's Liberation: Arya Samaj Movement in India*, 2010 , *Exploring Identity, Space and Challenge of Resettlement: Narratives of Sikh Migrants in Jaipur City*, 2016, *Women's Struggles in Rajasthan, Crossing Barriers, Claiming Space*, 2018 and *Conversations on Conservation: Narratives from Rajasthan*, 2020. Besides, she has published research papers in esteemed journals and edited volumes. Presently, she is working on an ICHR research project titled 'British Women in India: Lives and Socialisation (1850–1947)'.

Sarita Sarsar is Assistant Professor at Zakir Husain College, University of Delhi. She completed her PhD from the Centre for Historical Studies, Jawaharlal Nehru University (2016).

Her area of research has been Popular Culture, Folk Deities, Social and Cultural Histories of Rajasthan. She has a few research papers to her credit: "Bhukhi Mata (Famine): Its Frequency, Nature and Impact on the Population in Medieval Rajasthan", *Itihas–Sanshodhan Journal,* 2014, and "Economic Contours of Hero's Den: Untalked Dynamics of Gogamedi Shrine in Medieval Rajasthan", Indian History Congress Proceedings, Cuttack Session, 2013.

Suraj Bhan Bhardwaj taught History at Motilal Nehru College, University of Delhi. His area of research is agrarian history of medieval Rajasthan. Along with several articles published in reputed journals like *Studies in History, Medieval History Journal, Indian Historical Review,* Dr. Bhardwaj has a few monographs, *Contestations and Accommodations: Mewat, and Mews in Mughal India* published by Oxford University Press and *State, and Peasant Society in Medieval North India: Essays on Changing Contours of Mewat*, Primus, Delhi, 2019. Recently, he has co-edited: *Revisiting the History of Medieval Rajasthan: Essays for Professor Dilbagh Singh*, Primus, Delhi, 2017.

Yaqub Ali Khan obtained his doctorate from Aligarh Muslim University. He began teaching at Vardhaman Mahavir Open University, Kota before joining as Professor, Centre of Advanced Study, Department of History, AMU. His area of research is Socio-Cultural History, Sufism, Architecture, Epigraphic Studies and Historiography. He has three books and several research articles in national and international journals to his credit. He has delivered prestigious Prof. R.P. Vyas Memorial Lecture at the Rajasthan History Congress, 2019. He was also honoured by Maulana Abul Kalam Azad Arabic and Persian Research Institute, Tonk, Rajasthan for his expertise in Persian sources.